LIVING HISTORY
WHAT LIFE WAS LIKE IN ANCIENT TIMES

LIVING HISTORY

WHAT LIFE WAS LIKE IN ANCIENT TIMES

THE STONE AGE, MESOPOTAMIA, ANCIENT EGYPT, ANCIENT GREECE,
THE ROMAN EMPIRE, THE CELTS, THE VIKINGS, THE AZTECS AND MAYA,
THE INCAS, ANCIENT JAPAN, THE CHINESE EMPIRE, ANCIENT INDIA,
THE ARCTIC WORLD, NORTH AMERICAN INDIANS

CONSULTANT EDITOR: DR JOHN HAYWOOD

ARMADILLO

CONTENTS

Introduction 6

PART ONE: GREAT EMPIRES The March of Progress...12

PART TWO: LIFE AND WORK Great Themes of Everyday Life...258

Introduction

History is about people – how they found food, built shelters, raised children, fell in love and quarrelled with their neighbours. It describes how they worshipped gods, saw mysterious visions and dreamed fantastic dreams. It records how they created wonderful arts and crafts and fantastic entertainments, and enjoyed all kinds of sports and games. It tells how – and why – they built cities, fought wars, and explored the world around them.

The First Peoples

Human history stretches over a vast timespan, from the date, around 500,000 years ago, when early people first started to live in organized groups to events that happened yesterday. It also covers an enormous area: the whole inhabited

world. It tells us how past peoples developed ways of life best suited to their local environments, and invented tools, containers, weapons, boats, wheels and many other useful devices to help them survive.

The earliest humans, who evolved in Africa, were hunters and gatherers. They lived nomadic lives, travelling to hunt wild animals or gather wild nuts, seeds and berries. Then, around 12,000 years ago, the 'farming revolution' in Mesopotamia created a new way of living, based on growing crops and raising animals. Farming remained the usual way of life in most

LIFE UNDERGROUND
Some prehistoric peoples lived in caves to protect themselves from harsh conditions. Arctic peoples used bones to support the structure.

societies until around AD1700, except in regions like the Arctic. There, the climate was too cold for crops and families survived by hunting and fishing. Farming practices varied from managing

THE FARMING REVOLUTION
Once families settled in villages, they could make the best of poor soil and conditions, as here in these Spanish vineyards.

WORKING THE LAND
Farmers used oxen and other cattle to help them plough the land. Guiding the blade of the plough through rough ground was a skilled and backbreaking job.

flood-waters in ancient Egypt to cutting terraces to grow rice in China, tending olive groves and vineyards in ancient Greece and Rome, and constructing artificial 'chinampas' (lakeside vegetable gardens) in Aztec Mexico.

Settling Down

Like farming, housing and clothing varied from place to place and time to time. In cold regions, such as northern Europe, Celtic and Viking peoples built sturdy homes of wood or stone with thick thatched roofs. In North America, families in the Great Plains region lived in portable buffalo-skin tipis.

North Americans, Celts and Vikings all made clothes of animal skins and fur. Early Indian peoples discovered how to grow and spin cotton fibres; ancient Greeks and Romans wore wool. Everywhere, clothes – mostly made by women, along with other household items – were decorated with striking local designs that often had symbolic meanings.

WORKING FROM HOME
Life in this Celtic roundhouse centred around the home. Cattle and geese were valuable, and people shared their houses with them.

Honouring the Gods

History also reveals how societies were shaped by their religious beliefs. These had an enormous impact on the way people lived – and died. Many early peoples pleased their gods by offering sacrifices – sometimes of human beings, as in ancient China, Aztec Mexico, Celtic Europe and Inca Peru. Others, like Arctic and native American communities, relied on shamans (magic healers) to help them make contact with the spirit world.

Some later faiths, such as Hinduism from India and Shinto from Japan, remained closely linked to their homeland, where they inspired temples, poetry, dances and drama. Others, including Christianity and Islam (which both originated in the Middle East) spread round the world.

HOLY KNIFE
This sacrificial knife was made by Incas in South America to kill captives for sacrifice.

Fabulous Tombs

Belief in the afterlife was common in many societies, and was one of the reasons why important people were often buried in magnificent tombs, such as the pyramids of ancient Egypt. Mesoamerican temples were tombs as well as places of sacrifice. Many ancient peoples, such as the ancient Greeks and Romans, also built impressive monuments to commemorate dead leaders or family members.

TEMPLE OF SACRIFICE
The Toltecs built the Temple of the Warriors at the city of Chichen Itza in Mexico. They believed that unless they offered human lives to the gods, the Sun would die and the world would end.

Rules and Records

Over the centuries, as world's population increased, new leaders rose to power, and made new laws to replace old community rules and tribal customs. Society became more complex as populations grew in size. Leaders claimed to protect their subjects, and help them live together peacefully and productively.

For many tribal peoples, such as the Celts and the Vikings in Europe, fighting for new land was a way of life and survival. Although some rulers were just and fair, others were cruel and greedy, relying on brutal force to stay in power. Many ancient rulers, including Egyptian pharaohs and Japanese and Maya emperors, claimed divine authority. Only the ancient Greeks in Athens experimented with a limited form of democracy, a system of government that allowed some men to vote. Women and slaves did not have the vote.

A PALACE FIT FOR A KING
Toksugung Palace was built in the 1400s in Seoul, in what is now Korea, as a villa for the king's brother. Several royal coronations have been held here.

Early historians recorded rulers' names, alongside lists of important events, such as battles, plus tax payments and traders' lists. The first picture-symbols were invented in Mesopotamia, around 3400BC. Not long after, people in China, India and Egypt were using similar ways of writing. In America, Maya and Aztec scribes prepared codexes (folding books), and Inca officials recorded information on knotted strings, called quipus. These records, together with traditional histories, myths and legends passed on by word of mouth had a powerful effect on the way in which past peoples saw their own place in the world.

TRIBAL LEADER
Chief Oscelo fought hard in the 1830s to resist the United States government's attempts to remove the Seminole people from Florida.

Market Traders

From 20,000BC, and maybe even earlier, societies were linked by trade. At first, traders bartered food or raw materials, such as Stone Age flints and shells. But as peoples' craft skills developed, so did trading centres – fairs, markets and towns – where buyers and sellers could meet. Some of the world's earliest cities, in the Indus Valley in India, for example, developed in this way.

Peoples in different civilizations became famous for specialized products – silk from China, spices from India, and gold from Inca South America. Daring merchants from India, China, southern Europe and the Middle East pioneered long-distance travel, by sea and over land, to profit from international trade. Europeans also sailed to the west, to America in 1492, and, from 1521, right round the world.

PUTTING TO SEA
The Vikings came from Scandinavia and were the most expert sailors of their day, knowing about winds, currents and tides. Their longships were speedy and could sail as far as North America in under a month.

An Unequal Society

As trade and travel increased, societies became wealthier. But this wealth was not shared equally. Some families and communities became very rich and powerful. Others became poor, and some even became slaves. Ancient Greek and Roman civilization depended on slavery. Viking slave-traders made regular raids in Russia and eastern Europe, to seize captives to sell. Warlike, ambitious leaders conquered neighbouring peoples to create vast empires, in China, ancient Rome, and South America. They also imposed taxes, to pay administrators, clerks and soldiers to govern and guard. From around 1500, European settlers arrived in North and South America, destroying local civilizations and setting up new colonies in their search for gold.

Looking Back at the Past

History is based on many sources from different civilizations, all round the world. It investigates, questions, records and constructs stories to try to describe what happened in the past. It is full of strange facts, extraordinary characters, triumphs, tragedies, delights and disasters. It can make us feel proud, or fill us with horror and shame. It lets us compare past societies with each other, and with our own times today. It can give us a sense of belonging, and help us understand who we are.

EQUIPPED TO KILL
Roman soldiers were known for their good weapons. A legionary carried a dagger, a short iron sword, a javelin and a wooden shield.

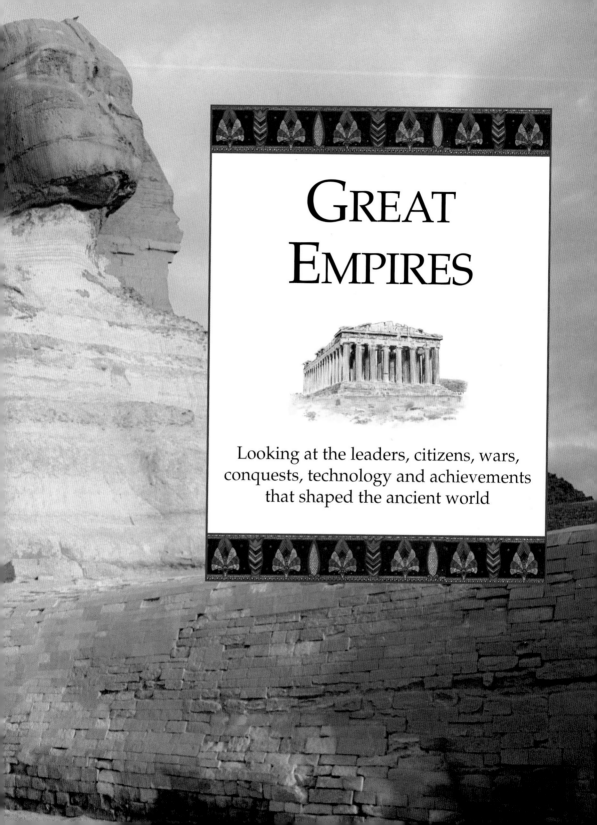

GREAT
EMPIRES

Looking at the leaders, citizens, wars,
conquests, technology and achievements
that shaped the ancient world

The March of Progress

Throughout history, stories abound that chart the rise and fall of great civilizations – their mighty battles, remarkable leaders and outstanding achievements. This section explores the ways in which the most important ancient empires came into being, and how they made their mark on the world. It charts their evolution – from the first small clans, or family groups, to the long-lasting dynasties of such peoples as the ancient Egyptians and Chinese.

MIGHTY PHARAOHS
The Egyptian empire lasted 3,000 years. Thutmose III was a pharaoh in one of its long-lived dynasties, or ruling families.

Civilizations had to organize their social life and govern themselves, which led them to develop a complex society. They were breeding grounds for new ideas. Discoveries in science and technology helped people understand their world, live a better quality of life and sometimes make war with their neighbours. In times of peace and prosperity, people developed fine crafts to enrich their lives and display their wealth and power.

Which empire lasted longer, Rome or Egypt? When did Viking pirates first attack Ireland and Britain? When was the horse brought over to North America, and how did it change the way Native Americans lived? By looking at the time lines, you can compare the important dates of civilizations, to see how they were alike or different from each other.

CONQUERING THE WAVES
The Vikings were expert shipbuilders. They used oak, ash and pine to build swift boats that helped them raid and settle in new lands. Because Viking homelands were mountainous and roads were impractical, they relied on ships as their main method of travel.

The Rise of Civilizations

The roots of the world's major societies can be traced to the first tribes and ancient civilizations. In the beginning, humans lived in small family groups called clans. They hunted wild animals, fished the rivers, lakes and seas, and gathered wild plants for food.

HUNTING FOR SURVIVAL
The first humans lived as hunter-gatherers. They moved from place to place to find supplies of animals to hunt and plants to gather for food.

Gradually, some people began to settle in one place, farming to raise animals and grow crops. Farmers grew more food than they needed to feed their own families, so they could sell their surplus to other families. With more food to go around, populations grew faster and faster. People began to live in larger

ALONG THE SILK ROAD
Trading posts like this one in India sprang up along the Silk Road, an ancient 7,000-km trade route that ran across Asia from China to Turkey. Eventually, the trading posts attracted more people, and grew into towns and city-states.

groups, and more organized societies were established.

Tribes and states developed when many people gathered in one place. Sometimes states consisted of just one city; sometimes they were made up of many towns and villages and the areas around them. Ancient Greece had hundreds of city-states – the most famous were Athens and Sparta. The ancient kingdom of Egypt consisted of an entire people or nation.

When a state grows to a vast size by conquering many different peoples and nations, it becomes an empire. The world's first empire was created in *c.*2300BC by Sargon, the ruler of the city of Akkad in Mesopotamia (present-day Iraq). Around 2,000 years ago, Rome grew from a small city-state to a large empire after conquering many areas in Europe and Africa.

NILE DEVELOPMENT
Ports along the fertile River Nile became cities and towns. These cities were eventually united to become one state: the kingdom of Egypt.

In many parts of the world, tribal groups developed from clans. For instance, the Celts were a group of tribes scattered over Europe. The area that is now the United States and Canada was home to many groups such as the Inuit, Cherokee and Hopi. In the 1500s, European countries sent expeditions to the Americas. They set out to conquer native peoples and make them part of their empires.

CAPTURING THE AZTECS
In 1521, Spanish invaders captured the Aztec city of Tenochtitlan in Central America by trickery. From across the ocean in Europe, Spain ruled the Aztec Empire.

Getting Organized

With the rise of large communities, people needed to develop rules so that jobs would get done and everyone would know how to behave. In smaller groups, it had been easy for each person to have a say. But decision-making becomes harder as more and more people become involved and leaders are needed. Learn about the ways that people organized themselves and how political leaders were chosen.

In places where the soil was especially fertile, large communities with thousands of people arose. This was too much work for one person

KEEPING RECORDS
The Assyrians of Mesopotamia were among the first people to use a writing system to keep business records. Here, one scribe writes on a clay tablet; the other, on a leather roll.

to rule alone. So governments were created, with administrators, advisors and record keepers. Mesopotamia was one of the first places where this happened, over 5,000 years ago.

Sometimes governments worked under the direction of kings who claimed they were appointed by the gods. Indeed, the pharaohs of Egypt actually believed they became gods when they died. In tribal groups, such as the Celts, leaders called chiefs held great power over their people. At first, the most wealthy and powerful people ended up being the leaders, and ordinary people had little say in what they did. Later, a system called democracy was introduced by the Athenian Greeks. This allowed members of the community to vote on important issues. Today, most Western governments are based on this system.

RESOURCEFUL RULER
The first emperor of ancient China was Qin Shi Huangdi. He united China's seven states into one kingdom in 221BC.

BUILDING A CIVIL SERVICE
In the Han dynasty in China, the emperor Gaozu began a civil service – a group of scholars who ran his political and business affairs.

Travel and Conflict

When people began to search for new land to farm, the need for travel arose. Sometimes people wanted to live in places that were already settled, so they would wage war against the inhabitants. People developed many different kinds of transport and warfare for use at land and sea through either need or greed. Early farmers discovered that large animals could help them plough and work the land, so they trained horses and oxen to do this. These animals could also carry goods great distances, and they became the first method of transport. Later, carts and chariots were developed by the Mesopotamians, who also developed sail boats about 6,000 years ago. Phoenician and Greek sailors spread their shipbuilding skills to the Mediterranean and beyond.

Many civilizations used ships and land transport to conquer new lands. Organized warfare began only after farming became established. People now had possessions, fields and livestock to defend, and they sometimes wanted to seize

CHARIOT WARFARE
The Assyrians and Hittites used chariots in battle, which made it easy for them to conquer enemies who fought on foot.

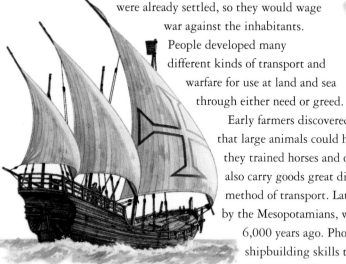

SAILING THE OPEN SEAS
The Portuguese developed a boat called the caravel, which was sturdy enough to sail on the open seas. They used caravels to explore the African coast in the 1400s.

their neighbours' property. Tribal peoples such as the Celts and the Vikings often raided each other to steal cattle. Chiefs and kings who were good war leaders could become wealthy and powerful.

Defeated peoples were rarely killed. It made more sense to make them into slaves to work for free. Or, they could be left to work on their farms and be made to pay taxes to their new rulers. Ancient empires, such as Rome, China and that of the Incas, worked on these principles.

BOLD AND BRAVE
Boudicca was the wife of the chieftain of the Iceni, a British tribe. She was a fierce warrior who battled against the invading Romans in AD60–1.

Ingenuity and Innovation

As travel and warfare developed around the world, so did science, craft and technology and new inventions and ideas spread from one country to the next. Both were strongly influenced by technology. In China, fine silk-making became an art, and papermaking and book-printing thrived. With an abundance of gold and silver to hand, the Inca became excellent metalworkers.

Some inventions completely changed the way people lived – the wheel was one of the biggest breakthroughs. Wheeled vehicles could be used to carry heavy loads over land more efficiently, and later, to move soldiers on the battlefield. The materials used were also important. Metal was tougher and more versatile than stone. The Aztec and Inca peoples of Central and southern America relied on stone and wooden tools. But they were quickly conquered by the Spanish, who used more advanced iron tools and weapons.

POTTERY MAKERS
People of the Indus Valley in India made pottery and other clay objects. This clay model shows a cart transporting heavy pots.

PORCELAIN BEAUTY
The Chinese created a fine, delicate type of pottery called porcelain. They decorated the porcelain, such as this urn, with beautiful patterns and glazes.

In the ancient world, science was seen as part of religion and philosophy. Babylonian and Egyptian scientists studied the stars and other natural events to try and understand what the gods wanted them to do. The Maya people of Central America developed a calendar so that they could pay seasonal homage to their gods with sacrifices and offerings. Ancient Greece had more scientists than any other ancient culture. Its great thinkers, such as Pythagoras and Plato, laid the groundwork for science, mathematics and philosophy for centuries to come.

Ancient civilizations are most often remembered for their great achievements. Often, these benefited only the rich and powerful minority. For ordinary people, it was the everyday inventions, such as useful tools with which to work, that made the most difference to their lives.

GOLDEN OPPORTUNITY
The Inca people of South America were expert goldsmiths. This golden funeral mask shows the skill and beauty of their art.

Tribes, Empires & Civilizations

Discover how and why some societies developed into great civilizations or mighty empires, while other cultures held on to a tribal existence. Journey through more than 50,000 years of human history to explore the forces that shaped it, and meet the leaders who created nations. Trace the rise and fall of powerful nations and the impact they had on their neighbours.

A World of Difference

TODAY, WE KNOW a lot about people who live in different countries all over the world. We see them on television and read about them in books. But for many groups of people in the past, their tribe was their world. Everyone knew everyone else within the community. The earliest groups probably had no idea of the true extent of the world and what everyday life was like outside their tribe.

Tribal people develop a particular way of doing things – of dressing, cooking and living, of traditions and crafts – based on the raw materials they have. If there is no need to change, or no ideas come from outside to inspire change, tribal societies often continue living in the same way, with the same language and traditions, for centuries.

The members of a Stone Age community go about their everyday life. Groups of families joined forces so that they could protect themselves better. They could also pool their resources and skills to hunt more successfully and improve their way of life. Several communities like this might be part of a tribal culture that shared a similar language, beliefs, traditions and way of living.

There's a world of difference in a civilized society. People no longer travel from place to place to hunt for food, as the early tribal societies did, but settle in villages, towns and cities. There are more people, with many different occupations and activities. They have more wealth and an endless catalogue of needs – for homes and other buildings, roads and transport, goods and services. Law and social organization became necessary to help things run smoothly and people

Early settlements grew up near rivers, lakes or the sea. The land had to be fertile to grow crops for food. Fish was a good alternative source of food, and water provided transport as well as irrigation for crops. These communities were the first step towards civilization.

The hanging gardens of Babylon were King Nebuchadnezzar's gift to his wife. They were to make her feel more at home in the desert, as she came from a country of green hills. One mark of a civilization is an upper class with plenty of wealth to spend. Rulers usually liked to create something by which they would be remembered for eternity, such as splendid temples and palaces.

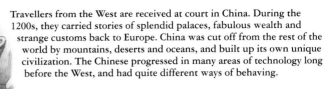

Travellers from the West are received at court in China. During the 1200s, they carried stories of splendid palaces, fabulous wealth and strange customs back to Europe. China was cut off from the rest of the world by mountains, deserts and oceans, and built up its own unique civilization. The Chinese progressed in many areas of technology long before the West, and had quite different ways of behaving.

to live together peacefully. Life in a civilized society is very complicated – this is what makes it so different from tribal life. Solving the problems of such large and complicated communities are a constant spur to human ingenuity and inventiveness. New inventions and ways of making life easier are tested out all the time and the pace of progress and change is fast.

The people of the very first civilizations, such as Mesopotamia and Egypt, had to learn how to solve these problems for themselves. No one else had ever had to face them before. Later civilizations, such as Rome, learned from the older ones as new ideas came in from the outside – from traders, travellers and soldiers. Civilizations became exciting melting pots of many different people, ideas and lifestyles.

In every civilization and culture, there are rulers, thinkers and inventors who have shaped the course of history. King Ashurbanipal (669-631BC) contributed the world's first library to civilization. He was also a ruthless empire-builder. Throughout history, there have been leaders like him, who have wanted to increase their power and conquer other lands. They forced the conquered countries to give them a share of their wealth and resources. Some empire-builders, such as Alexander the Great, allowed conquered nations to keep their national identities. Others, such as the Spanish in Mesoamerica, wiped out the native religion, language, laws and lifestyle almost completely.

The world is very different today. There are fewer subject peoples and no great empires. Countries have their own national identities, but may be made up of many different races and tribes, religions and ways of life. This book presents some of the building blocks of today's world.

The Romans marked the northern limit of their empire in Britain by building Hadrian's Wall from coast to coast. Beyond it lived the barbarians! It was hard work and very expensive for an empire to keep control of the territories it had won.

Life in the Stone Age

THE STONE AGE is the longest period of human history. It began two million years ago, when the ancestors of modern humans started to use stone tools. Gradually, using their tools and their intelligence, they learned how to adapt to different environments. Humans began to move out of Africa, where they had first evolved, and by 10,000BC they had settled on every continent except Antarctica. The Stone Age came to an end when people began to work metals on a large scale.

Stone Age people lived in groups called clans, that were made up of several families, probably closely related to each other. It was safer to live in a clan than as a single family unit, and groups of people could work as a team when hunting or gathering food. As generations passed, the clans grew into bigger, tribal communities. Close family relationships diluted through the generations, but everyone shared the same ancestor. Some communities grew bigger still and split into different tribes that moved to other areas. They kept the same language, beliefs and traditions – they were still part of the same tribal culture. In some tribal cultures, different tribes gathered at certain times of the year, for festivals or meetings. Their lifestyle remained much the same for the rest of the year, though, as hunter-gatherers or simple farmers.

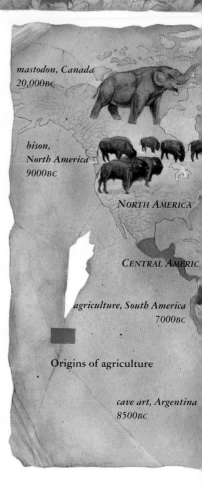

mastodon, Canada
20,000BC

bison,
North America
9000BC

NORTH AMERICA

CENTRAL AMERIC

agriculture, South America
7000BC

Origins of agriculture

cave art, Argentina
8500BC

TIMELINE 50,000BC–3,500BC

Stone Age tools

The huge periods over which human prehistory took place mean that, even with scientific dating, timings can only be approximate.

50,000BC Humans settle in Australia.

38,000BC Modern humans are living at Cro-Magnon in France.

24,000BC Small sculptures of women (Venus figurines) are made in Europe.

einkorn wheat

15,000BC Stone Age cave paintings and carvings of bone and antler are made in Europe.

10,500BC Pottery is made in Japan.

10,500BC People are living in South America.

10,000BC The last glacial period (Ice Age) ends. The climate becomes warmer.

10,000BC Grindstones for making flour are used in Egypt and Nubia in Africa.

squash and maize

9000BC Einkorn wheat is harvested in Syria.

8500BC Sheep and goats are domesticated in Mesopotamia.

8500BC Vegetables are grown in Peru.

8000BC Grains are harvested in the Near East.

50,000BC   15,000BC   9000BC   8000BC

migrating reindeer, Russia
15,000BC

EUROPE

clay figurine,
Czech Republic
24,000BC

ASIA

cave art, France
15,000BC

pottery, Japan
10,500BC

settlement,
Turkey
6,500BC

rock art,
Sahara
6000BC

Peking Man, China
460,0000BC

Homo erectus *skull*,
Java, 120,000BC

AFRICA

Homo habilis *skull*, Kenya
2.5 million years ago

SOUTH AMERICA

N

cave art, Namibia
8000BC

AUSTRALIA

THE STONE AGE WORLD
This map shows places of
importance during the Stone Age.

indigenous peoples,
Australia
50,000BC

8000BC Jericho grows in size to become the first town.

7000BC The sea separates America and Asia.

6300BC Potatoes are cultivated in Peru.

6300BC Dugout canoes are used in the Netherlands.

6000BC Farming begins in the Sahara.

*dugout canoe
being paddled*

5300BC Farming
and pottery
begin in central
Europe.

5000BC Rice farming
is carried out in China.

4500BC Rice farming
begins in India.

4500BC Farming begins in
northwest Europe.

4400BC Horses are domesticated in Asia.

sheep

4100BC Rice
and sorghum
are cultivated
in Africa.

4000BC Bronze
casting begins in
the Near East.

4000BC Increase in
flint-mining in
northern Europe.

3500BC The plough and wheel are
invented in the Near East.

5300BC

4100BC

3500BC

Mesopotamia's First Empires

MESOPOTAMIA IS THE NAME of an ancient region where some of the world's first cities and empires grew up. Mesopotamia means 'the land between the rivers' – for the country lay between the Tigris and the Euphrates, two mighty rivers that flowed from the highlands of Turkey in the north down to the Gulf. Today, most of it lies in modern Iraq.

The first farmers settled in the low, rolling hills of the north about 9,000 years ago. Here, there was enough rainfall to grow crops and provide pasture for animals. The land in north Mesopotamia became known as Assyria.

The first cities developed about 3,500 years later, mostly in the fertile plains of the south. This area had rivers and marshes which provided water to irrigate crops and reeds to build houses and boats. Fish, dates and other food were easy to find. At first the south was called Sumer. Later it was known as Babylonia.

SUMERIAN WORSHIPPERS
Statues of a man and woman from Sumer are shown in an act of worship. The Sumerians were some of the earliest people to live in the south of Mesopotamia. They lived in small, independent cities. At the centre of each city was a temple built as the home for the local god. These two Sumerians had statues made of themselves and put in a temple, so that the god could bless them.

THE WORK OF GIANTS
Most of what we know about the ancient civilizations of Mesopotamia has come from excavations by archaeologists over the last 150 years. In 1845, the British archaeologist Henry Layard unearthed the remains of a once-magnificent palace in the ancient Assyrian city of Nimrud. He found walls decorated with scenes of battles and hunting, and a statue of a human-headed, winged lion so huge that local people were astonished and thought it had been made by giants.

TIMELINE 7000BC–2100BC

Humans have lived in northern Iraq since the Old Stone Age, when hunter-gatherers lived in caves and rock shelters and made stone tools. Mesopotamian civilization began when people began to settle in villages. They learned how to grow crops and keep animals. Later, city-states grew up, and people developed writing. They became good at building, working metal and making fine jewellery.

painted pottery

7000BC The first villages are established. Edible plants and animals are domesticated, and farming develops. Pottery is made and mud-bricks used for building.

6000BC Use of copper. First mural paintings, temples and seals. Irrigation is used in agriculture to bring water to the fields. Decorated pottery, clay and alabaster figurines. Wide use of brick.

clay figurine

4000BC Larger houses and temples are built. Terracotta sickles and pestles are developed.

3500BC Growth of towns. Development of the potter's wheel, the plough, the first cylinder seals and writing. Bronze, silver and gold worked. Sculptures are made. Trading systems develop.

writing tablet

3000BC Sumerian civilization begins. City-states and writing develop.

7000BC 4000BC 2700BC

TEMPLES OF THE GODS

The ziggurat of Nanna, the Moon god, rises above the dusty plains of modern Iraq. It was once part of the massive temple complex in the city of Ur. Ziggurats showed how clever the Mesopotamians were at building. They were designed as a link between heaven and earth.

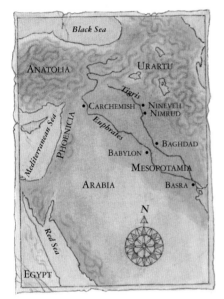

WRITING TABLET

A clay tablet shows an example of some of the earliest writing in the world. The symbols were pressed into a damp clay tablet using a reed pen. The Sumerians originally used writing to keep accounts of goods bought and sold including grain and cattle. Later on, kings used clay tablets as a record of their victories and building activities. Scribes wrote letters, poems and stories about heroes.

POWERFUL NEIGHBOURS

By about 2000BC the Assyrians were trading with Anatolia in the north-west of Mesopotamia. The Assyrians later conquered Phoenician cities in the west and fought Urartu in the north.

Sumerian chariot

2700BC Early Dynastic period. Kings and city administrations rule.

2600BC Royal Standard of Ur made, probably as the sounding box of a lyre.

2500BC Royal Graves of Ur made. Queen Pu-abi and other wealthy individuals buried in tombs with soldiers, musicians and court ladies.

2440BC Inter-state warfare. Kings of Lagash go to war with Umma.

2334BC Sargon of Agade becomes king. He creates the world's first empire, which is maintained by his grandson Naram-sin.

Pu-abi

2200BC The Agade Empire comes to an end. The Gutians, a mountain people, move into Mesopotamia

ziggurat of Ur-nammu

2141BC Gudea takes the throne of Lagash. Ambitious temple-building programme at Girsu.

2112BC Ur-nammu of Ur tries to re-create the Agade Empire. He builds the famous ziggurat of Ur.

2500BC   2200BC   2100BC

City-states of Mesopotamia

MANY OF THE GREAT EMPIRES in Mesopotamia grew up around small city-states. Each state consisted of a city and the surrounding countryside, and had its own ruler and god. Uruk, in the south, was the first state to become important, in 2,700BC. Its leader was called Gilgamesh and many legends grew up around him.

Around 2300BC, a leader called Sargon conquered all the cities of Mesopotamia and several in neighbouring lands. In doing so, he created the world's first empire. After his dynasty died out in about 2150BC, the kings of Ur, a city further south, tried to re-create Sargon's empire, but with limited success. Ur fell to the Elamites, invaders from a region in the east. About 100 years later, a nomadic people called the Amorites settled in Mesopotamia. They took over the old Sumerian cities, including Babylon, and several of their chiefs became kings.

Meanwhile, in the north, the Assyrian Empire had grown from its beginnings in the city-state of Ashur. It developed slowly over 2,000 years and reached a glorious peak around 645BC. The Empire crumbled when the Babylonians conquered their key cities in 612BC. Babylonia became the most powerful empire in the known world until it was conquered by the Persian king, Cyrus, in 539BC.

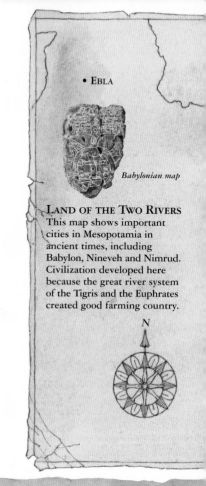

• EBLA

Babylonian map

LAND OF THE TWO RIVERS
This map shows important cities in Mesopotamia in ancient times, including Babylon, Nineveh and Nimrud. Civilization developed here because the great river system of the Tigris and the Euphrates created good farming country.

N

TIMELINE 2100BC–1000BC

2004BC Ibbi-Sin, last king of Ur, is captured by Elamites and taken to Susa.

2000BC Fall of the Sumerian Empire. Amorites interrupt trade routes. Ur attacked by Elamites and falls. Assyria becomes independent and establishes trading network in Anatolia.

1900BC Amorite chiefs take over some cities as rulers.

1792BC Hammurabi, an Amorite ruler, becomes King of Babylon.

Hammurabi

1787BC King Hammurabi conquers the major southern city of Isin.

1763BC Hammurabi conquers the city of Larsa.

1761BC Hammurabi conquers Mari and Eshnunna and may have conquered the city of Ashur.

1740BC Expansion of the Hittite kingdom in Anatolia, based on the city of Hattusas.

scorpion man

1595BC The Hittite king, Mursulis, conquers North Syria. Marching further south, he destroys Babylon but does not take over the city.

1570BC The Kassites, a foreign dynasty, begin a 400-year rule of peace and prosperity. King Kurigalzu builds a new capital city, naming it after himself. Babylon becomes a world power on an equal level with the kingdom of Egypt.

2100BC   1790BC   1600BC   1500BC

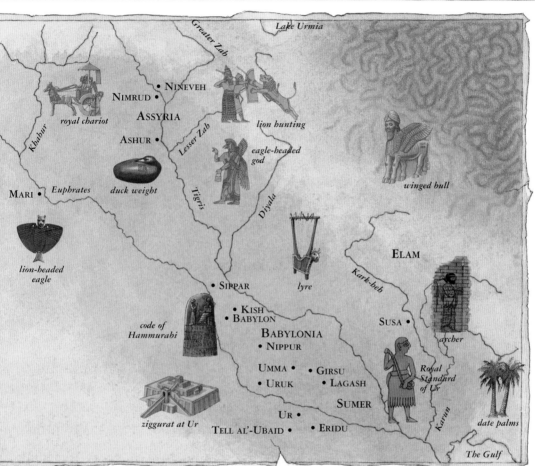

Lake Urmia

Greater Zab

NINEVEH

NIMRUD

ASSYRIA

royal chariot

lion hunting

ASHUR

Lesser Zab

eagle-headed god

Khabur

duck weight

Tigris

Diyala

winged bull

MARI

Euphrates

lion-headed eagle

ELAM

Kark-heh

SIPPAR

lyre

KISH
BABYLON

SUSA

archer

code of Hammurabi

BABYLONIA
NIPPUR

UMMA

GIRSU

Royal Standard of Ur

URUK

LAGASH

SUMER

Karun

UR

ziggurat at Ur

TELL AL'-UBAID

ERIDU

date palms

The Gulf

1500BC Mitanni, a new state, develops to the north of Mesopotamia. The people speak Hurrian and fight in two-wheeled horse-drawn chariots. They conquer land from the Mediterranean to the Zagros Mountains, including Assyria.

1365BC Ashur-uballit becomes King of Assyria and gains Assyria's independence from Mitanni.

1150BC The Elamites conquer Babylon, ending Kassite rule.

1124BC Nebuchadnezzar I, a later king of Babylon, successfully attacks Elam, bringing back large amounts of booty, including the statue of Marduk, the Babylonian god the Elamites had captured some years earlier.

1115BC Tiglath-pileser I becomes king. He expands Assyrian territory and captures Babylon and other southern cities. First written account of the royal hunt in Mesopotamia. Egyptian king sends him a crocodile as a present.

copper peg

1076BC Death of Tiglath-pileser I.

1050BC Ashurnasirpal I becomes king.

1000BC Assyria is attacked by many enemies, including the nomadic Aramaeans, who move into Mesopotamia and take over large areas. Their language, Aramaic, and its alphabetic script gradually replace Akkadian and cuneiform.

Humbaba the giant

1130BC

1100BC

1000BC

Mesopotamian Leaders

THE NAMES OF Mesopotamian kings are known because their victories and other achievements were recorded on clay tablets and palace wall decorations. The kings wanted to be sure that the gods knew that they had ruled well, and that their names would be remembered for ever. The names of ordinary soldiers and temple builders, the craftsmen who created the beautiful painted wall reliefs and the authors of the sagas and histories were not written down. Some astrologers, army commanders and state officials are known by name because they wrote letters to the king.

SARGON OF AGADE (2334–2279BC)

King Sargon created the world's first empire by conquering all the cities of Sumer, Mari and Ebla. He founded the city of Agade, no trace of which has yet been found. A legend tells that when Sargon was a baby, his mother put him in a reed basket and set him afloat on a river. The man who found him trained him to be a gardener. When Sargon grew up, it was believed that he had been favoured by the goddess Ishtar, and he became cup-bearer to the king of Kish (a city north of Babylon).

EANNATUM OF LAGASH (C. 2440BC)

Eannatum was king of Lagash, a city in southern Sumer. He was a great warrior and temple-builder. His victory over the nearby state of Umma was recorded on the Vulture Stela, a limestone carving that showed vultures pecking at the bodies of dead soldiers.

ENHEDUANNA(C. 2250BC)

The daughter of King Sargon of Agade is one of the few women in Mesopotamian history whose name is known. She held the important post of high priestess to the Moon-god at Ur. Her hymn to the god made her the first known woman author.

TIMELINE 1000BC–500BC

911BC Adad-nirari becomes king. Assyria recovers some of her lost possessions and defeats the Aramaeans and Babylon.

879BC Ashurnasirpal II holds a banquet to celebrate the opening of his new palace at Nimrud.

858BC Shalmaneser III, son of Ashurnasirpal II, spends most of his 34-year reign at war, campaigning in Syria, Phoenicia, Urartu and the Zagros Mountains.

stela of Ashurnasirpal II

c. 845BC Palace of Balawat built.

744BC Tiglath-pileser III brings more territory under direct Assyrian control. Deportation of conquered peoples begins.

721BC Sargon II decorates his palace at Khorsabad with carved reliefs showing his battle victories.

black obelisk of Shalmaneser III

705BC Sennacherib becomes king of Assyria.

701BC Sennacherib attacks Hezekiah in Jerusalem.

694BC Ashur-nadin-shumi rules Babylon on behalf of his father Sennacherib. He is captured by the Elamites and taken to Susa. In revenge, Sennacherib burns Babylon to the ground.

Balawat Gates

1000BC   850BC   710BC   690BC

ASHURBANIPAL OF ASSYRIA (669–631BC)

A great warrior king, Ashurbanipal reigned at the peak of the Assyrian Empire. He fought successfully against the Elamites, Babylonians and Arabs, and even made Egypt part of his empire for a time. But his greatest gift to civilization was the vast library in his palaces at Nineveh. Here, over 25,000 clay tablets were collected, including letters, legends and astronomical, mathematical and medical works.

NEBUCHADNEZZAR II (604–562BC)

As crown prince, Nebuchadnezzar fought at the side of his father, the king of Babylon, and brought the Assyrian Empire to an end. Under his own rule, the Babylonians conquered neighbouring countries, such as Palestine, and became one of the world powers of the time. Nebuchadnezzar built great fortifying walls around the city of Babylon and a magnificent ziggurat. He features in the Bible, as the king who captured Jerusalem and sent the people of Judah into captivity.

HAMMURABI (1792–1750BC)

King Hammurabi of Babylon collected 282 laws concerning family, town and business life and had them recorded on a black stela, a large stone. Other rulers had made laws, but his is the largest collection to survive. The picture shows Shamash, god of justice, giving Hammurabi the symbols of kingship. Towards the end of his reign, he went to war and created an empire, but it did not last long after his death.

681BC Sennacherib killed by his eldest son. His youngest son Esarhaddon becomes king.

671BC Esarhaddon invades Egypt and captures the Egyptian capital of Memphis.

668BC Ashurbanipal becomes king of Assyria. His brother Shamash-shum-ukin becomes king of Babylon.

Tiglath-pileser III

664BC Ashurbanipal invades Egypt and destroys the southern city of Thebes.

663 or 653BC Ashurbanipal begins a series of wars with Elam.

652BC Rebellion of Shamash-shum-ukin. Ashurbanipal invades Babylonia.

648BC Ashurbanipal lays siege to Babylon, which suffers starvation.

631BC Death of Ashurbanipal. Assyrian Empire begins to collapse.

Nimrud

612BC Babylonians attack and burn the Assyrian cities of Nimrud and Nineveh.

605BC Assyrians defeated by the Babylonians at the battle of Carchemish.

Ashurbanipal on horseback

604BC Nebuchadnezzar II becomes King of Babylon, and Babylon becomes a world power.

562BC Nebuchadnezzar II dies.

539BC Cyrus of Persia takes Babylon.

663BC   620BC   500BC

Egyptian Civilization

HORUS' EYE
This symbol can be seen on many Egyptian artefacts. It is the eye of the god Horus.

EGYPT IS A COUNTRY at the crossroads of Africa, Europe and Asia. If you could step back in time 5,000 years, you would discover an amazing civilization – the kingdom of the ancient Egyptians.

Most of Egypt is made up of baking hot, sandy deserts. These are crossed by the river Nile as it snakes its way north to the Mediterranean Sea. Every year, floods cover the banks of the Nile with mud. Plants grow well in this rich soil, and 8,000 years ago farmers were planting crops here. Wealth from farming led to trade and to the building of towns. By 3100BC a great kingdom had grown up in Egypt, ruled by royal families.

Ancient Egypt existed for over 3,000 years. Pyramids, temples and artefacts survive from this period to show us what life was like in the land of the pharaohs.

AMAZING DISCOVERIES
In 1922, the English archaeologist Howard Carter made an amazing discovery. He found the tomb of the young pharaoh Tutankhamun. No single find in Egypt has ever provided as much evidence as the discovery of this well-preserved tomb.

LIFE BY THE NILE
Tomb paintings show us how people lived in ancient Egypt. Here people water and harvest their crops, using water from the river Nile.

TIMELINE 6000BC–2100BC

The kingdom of ancient Egypt existed for over 3,000 years. The most successful periods of Egyptian power are known as the Old Kingdom, the Middle Kingdom and the New Kingdom.

wheat

sheep

boat with sail

c.6000BC
Early people settle in the fertile Nile valley. They grow wheat and barley.

c.5020–4500BC
Craftsmen make clay figures and fine pottery vessels. They also carve objects from ivory.

c.4800BC
Farmers keep sheep, cattle and other animals.

c.4000BC
Sails are used on Egyptian ships for the first time.

| 6000BC | 5500BC | 5000BC | 4500BC | 4000BC |

Rosetta (el-Rashid)
Alexandria
Nile delta
Giza
Saqqara
LOWER EGYPT Dahshur Memphis
Maidum
Sinai

Beni-Hasan
Akhetaten (el-Amarna)

UPPER EGYPT

Abydos
Valley of the Kings
Karnak
Thebes (Luxor)

Kharga Oasis

Aswan
Philae

▲ Pyramid
◉ Valley of the Kings
♀ Ancient Site

Abu Simbel

THE KINGDOM OF EGYPT

This map of Egypt today shows where there were important cities and sites in ancient times. The ancient Egyptians lived mostly along the banks of the river Nile and in the green, fertile lands of the delta. Through the ages, the Egyptians built many imposing temples in honour of their gods and mysterious tombs to house their dead. Most of these temples and tombs were built close to the major cities of Memphis and Thebes.

SURVIVORS OF THE DESERT

The face of the great pharaoh Ramesses II stares out at us. Huge statues of Ramesses were part of a temple cut from the rock face at Abu Simbel in 1269BC. During the 1960s the statues had to be raised because a new dam at Aswan turned this part of the Nile into a lake. Temples, tombs and statues such as those at Abu Simbel have survived for thousands of years in the dry desert heat. More recently, many monuments have started to disintegrate because of the polluted air around modern cities such as Luxor.

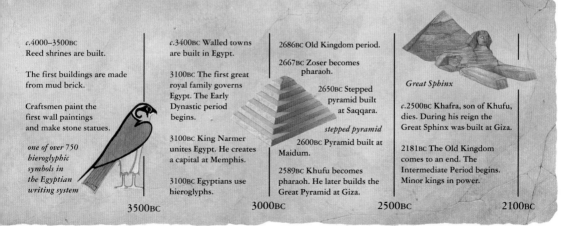

c.4000–3500BC
Reed shrines are built.

The first buildings are made from mud brick.

Craftsmen paint the first wall paintings and make stone statues.

one of over 750 hieroglyphic symbols in the Egyptian writing system

c.3400BC Walled towns are built in Egypt.

3100BC The first great royal family governs Egypt. The Early Dynastic period begins.

3100BC King Narmer unites Egypt. He creates a capital at Memphis.

3100BC Egyptians use hieroglyphs.

2686BC Old Kingdom period.

2667BC Zoser becomes pharaoh.

2650BC Stepped pyramid built at Saqqara.

stepped pyramid

2600BC Pyramid built at Maidum.

2589BC Khufu becomes pharaoh. He later builds the Great Pyramid at Giza.

Great Sphinx

c.2500BC Khafra, son of Khufu, dies. During his reign the Great Sphinx was built at Giza.

2181BC The Old Kingdom comes to an end. The Intermediate Period begins. Minor kings in power.

3500BC   3000BC   2500BC   2100BC

The Kingdom on the Nile

THE STORY OF ANCIENT EGYPT began about 8,000 years ago when farmers started to plant crops and raise animals in the Nile Valley. By about 3400BC the Egyptians were building walled towns. Soon after that the northern part of the country (Lower Egypt) was united with the lands upstream (Upper Egypt) to form one country under a single king. The capital of this new kingdom was established at Memphis.

The first great period of Egyptian civilization is called the Old Kingdom. It lasted from 2686BC to 2181BC. This was when the pharaohs built great pyramids, the massive tombs that still stand in the desert today.

During the Middle Kingdom (2050–1786BC), the capital was moved south, to the city of Thebes. The Egyptians gained control of Nubia and extended the area of land being farmed. Despite this period of success, the rule of the royal families of ancient Egypt was sometimes interrupted by disorder. In 1663BC, control of the country fell into foreign hands. The Hyksos, a group of Asian settlers, ruled Egypt for almost 100 years.

In 1567BC the Hyksos were overthrown by the princes of Thebes. The Thebans established the New Kingdom. This was the highest point of Egyptian civilization. Traders and soldiers travelled into Africa, Asia and the lands of the Mediterranean. However, by 525BC, the might of the Egyptians was coming to an end and Egypt became part of the Persian Empire. In 332BC rule passed to the Greeks. Finally, in 30BC, conquest was complete as Egypt fell under the control of the Roman Empire.

AFRICA

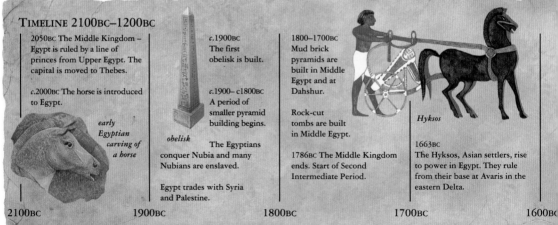

TIMELINE 2100BC–1200BC

2050BC The Middle Kingdom – Egypt is ruled by a line of princes from Upper Egypt. The capital is moved to Thebes.

c.2000BC The horse is introduced to Egypt.

early Egyptian carving of a horse

obelisk

c.1900BC
The first obelisk is built.

c.1900– c1800BC
A period of smaller pyramid building begins.

The Egyptians conquer Nubia and many Nubians are enslaved.

Egypt trades with Syria and Palestine.

1800–1700BC
Mud brick pyramids are built in Middle Egypt and at Dahshur.

Rock-cut tombs are built in Middle Egypt.

1786BC The Middle Kingdom ends. Start of Second Intermediate Period.

Hyksos

1663BC
The Hyksos, Asian settlers, rise to power in Egypt. They rule from their base at Avaris in the eastern Delta.

2100BC   1900BC   1800BC   1700BC   1600BC

EUROPE

Mycenaean Empire

Hittite Empire

Kadesh battle site

MINOAN CRETE

Mediterranean Sea

Byblos

LEVANT

Megiddo

SYRIA

Jerusalem

Avaris

PALESTINE

LOWER EGYPT

Memphis Sinai

MESOPOTAMIA

ASIA

NORTH

EGYPT

River Nile

Western Desert

Thebes

UPPER
EGYPT

NUBIA

Red Sea

ARABIA

MAP OF THE NEAR EAST

In 1279BC, at the height of
the New Kingdom,
Egypt was a leading
power in the Near East.
The country was very
prosperous and rich, trading with
Minoan Crete, Syria, the Levant and
Nubia. Nevertheless, it faced threats from
enemies such as the Hittites.

Akhenaten

c1567BC The Hyksos are
defeated by Egyptians from the
southern city of Thebes.

1550BC The New Kingdom
is founded. Royal
tombs are built in the
Valley of the Kings.

1525BC Amenhotep
becomes pharaoh.

1500BC A village is
founded at Deir el-
Medina, near the
Valley of the Kings.

1498BC Queen Hatshepsut
rules as co-regent with the
child king Thutmose III.

1483BC Hatshepsut dies.

1478BC The rebellious
prince of Kadesh is
defeated by
Thutmose III at the
Battle of Megiddo
in the Near East.
*the cartouche of
Tutankhamun*

Thutmose III

1379BC
Akhenaten
introduces
worship of the
Sun god, Aten, as
the only religion.
A new capital is
established at el-Amarna.

c1334BC Smenkhkare,
Akhenaten's successor, moves
the capital back to Memphis.

1325BC Tutankhamun is
buried in the Valley of
the Kings.

1291BC Seti I comes to power.
He builds the Hypostyle Hall
at Karnak.

1279BC
Ramesses
II becomes
pharaoh.

Ramesses II

1274BC Ramesses II fights
the Hittites at the battle
of Kadesh.

1500BC   1400BC   1300BC   1200BC

Famous Pharaohs

FOR THOUSANDS OF YEARS ancient Egypt was ruled by royal families. We know much about the pharaohs (kings) and queens from these great dynasties because of their magnificent tombs and the public monuments raised in their honour.

Egypt's first ruler was King Narmer, who united the country in about 3100BC. Later pharaohs such as Zoser and Khufu are remembered for the great pyramids they had built as their tombs.

Pharaohs usually succeeded to the throne through royal birth. However, in some cases military commanders such as Horemheb came to power. Although Egypt's rulers were traditionally men, a few powerful women were made pharaoh. The most famous of these is the Greek queen Cleopatra, who ruled Egypt in 51BC.

KHAFRA
(reigned 2558–2532BC)
Khafra is the son of the pharaoh Khufu. He is remembered for his splendid tomb, the Second Pyramid at Giza and the Great Sphinx that guards it.

AMENHOTEP I
(reigned 1525–1504BC)
The pharaoh Amenhotep led the Egyptian army to battle in Nubia. He also founded a village for workmen at Deir el-Medina.

HATSHEPSUT
(reigned 1498–1483BC)
Hatshepsut was the half-sister and wife of Thutmose II. When her husband died, she was appointed to rule Egypt until her young stepson Thutmose III was old enough. However Queen Hatshepsut was ambitious and had herself crowned pharaoh. Hatshepsut is famous for her trading expeditions to the land of Punt. The walls of her temple at Deir el-Bahri show these exotic trips.

TIMELINE 1200BC–AD1960

1198BC Mediterranean Sea peoples attack Egypt.

1182BC Ramesses III, the last great warrior pharaoh, comes to power. He defeats the Mediterranean Sea peoples in battle.

1151BC The last great pharaoh, Ramesses III, dies.

Ramesses III

c.1070BC The New Kingdom ends. Start of Third Intermediate Period.

900–700BC Brief periods of calm between conquest by invading armies.

671BC Assyrians conquer Egypt as far as Memphis.

Darius I

525BC Beginning of the Late Dynastic Period. Egypt becomes part of the Persian Empire.

332BC Egypt is invaded by Alexander the Great and is ruled by Greek kings. Alexandria is built.

305BC Ptolemy I, a commander in Alexander the Great's army, takes power after his death.

Alexander the Great

51BC Cleopatra VII, Ptolemy's XII's daughter, reigns in Egypt.

Cleopatra VII

30BC Egypt becomes part of the Roman Empire under the emperor Augustus.

1200BC   900BC   600BC   300BC   AD0

TUTANKHAMUN
(reigned 1334–1325BC)
This pharaoh came to the throne when he was only nine years old. He died at the age of 18. Tutankhamun is remembered for his tomb in the Valley of the Kings, which was packed with amazing treasure.

THUTMOSE III
(reigned 1479–1425BC)
Thutmose III is remembered as a brave warrior king. He launched many military campaigns against the Syrians in the Near East. Records from the time tell of Thutmose marching fearlessly into battle at the head of his army, unconcerned about his own safety. He won a famous victory at Megiddo and then later at Kadesh. Thutmose III was buried in the Valley of the Kings.

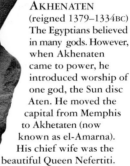

AKHENATEN
(reigned 1379–1334BC)
The Egyptians believed in many gods. However, when Akhenaten came to power, he introduced worship of one god, the Sun disc Aten. He moved the capital from Memphis to Akhetaten (now known as el-Amarna). His chief wife was the beautiful Queen Nefertiti.

RAMESSES II
(reigned 1279–1212BC)
One of the most famous pharaohs of all, Ramesses II, was the son of Seti I. He built many fine temples and defeated the Hittites at the Battle of Kadesh in 1274BC. The chief queen of Ramesses was Nefertari. Carvings of this graceful queen can be seen on Ramesses II's temple at Abu Simbel. Ramesses lived a long life and died at the age of 92. He was buried in the Valley of the Kings.

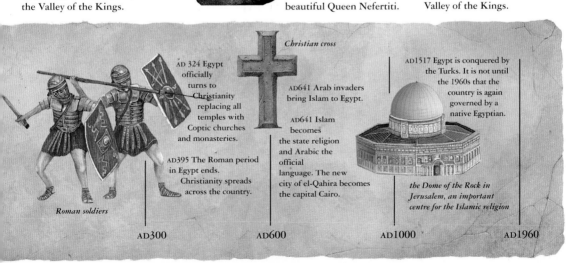

Christian cross

AD 324 Egypt officially turns to Christianity replacing all temples with Coptic churches and monasteries.

AD641 Arab invaders bring Islam to Egypt.

AD1517 Egypt is conquered by the Turks. It is not until the 1960s that the country is again governed by a native Egyptian.

AD395 The Roman period in Egypt ends. Christianity spreads across the country.

AD641 Islam becomes the state religion and Arabic the official language. The new city of el-Qahira becomes the capital Cairo.

the Dome of the Rock in Jerusalem, an important centre for the Islamic religion

Roman soldiers

AD300   AD600   AD1000   AD1960

India's Glorious Heritage

THE INDIAN SUBCONTINENT IS HOME to one of the world's most varied civilizations because many different groups of people have travelled over the Himalayan mountains and settled there. From the arrival of Aryan tribes about 3,000 years ago until the invasion of the Mughals in the 1500s, each new wave of people brought fresh ideas and ways of life. As a result, India's religious and artistic life became very rich and mixed.

Two major world religions – Hinduism and Buddhism – developed in India, and for hundreds of years, India was also at the heart of Muslim life in Asia. These three religions shaped the course of India's history, and led to the building of magnificent monuments, many of which still stand.

With its Hindu and Buddhist temples and sculptures, and the sumptuous palaces of the Muslim rulers, India is full of amazing treasures from the past.

DAWN OF INDIAN CIVILIZATION
Ancient stone buildings, such as the Great Bath at Mohenjo-Daro in the Indus Valley, tell archaeologists a great deal about the dawn of civilization in India. Fewer buildings of later times have been excavated, partly because later houses were made of mud, thatch and wood, none of which has survived.

BEAUTY IN STONE
A beautiful carving of a Yakshi (tree spirit) from Bharhut in central India. It is made of red sandstone and dates from 100BC. This Buddhist sculpture has a distinctive Indian style that you can see in sculptures from much later periods. Buddhism was the first religion in India to inspire people to build monuments and make sculptures.

TIMELINE 6000BC–AD400

From early times until the coming of the British in 1757, India was divided into many kingdoms. It was never a single state. The regions of Ancient India were linked by a common culture, rather than by politics, religion or language.

*c.*6000BC Neolithic settlements in Baluchistan.

*c.*2800–2600BC Beginnings of settlements in the Indus Valley region.

statue of priest king from Indus valley

rice cultivation

*c.*2300–1700BC The great cities of the Indus Valley (Mohenjo-Daro and Harappa), the Punjab (Kalibangan) and Gujarat (Lothal) flourished.

*c.*1700BC Sudden and mysterious decline of the Indus Valley civilization.

*c.*1500–1200BC Immigration of Vedic Aryans into north-western India.

*c.*1200–600BC The Vedic texts are composed.

*c.*800BC Use of iron for weapons and the spread of Aryan culture into the Gangetic plains (the area near the River Ganges).

*c.*500–300BC Rice cultivation and the introduction of iron agricultural tools in the eastern Gangetic plains lead to the formation of more complex societies, cities and states.

fragment of pot with brahmi inscription

| 6000BC | 2500BC | 1200BC | 500BC |

TEMPLE OF THE SUN

A huge carved stone wheel forms a panel on the wall of the Sun Temple at Konarak on India's east coast. This part of the temple is carved in the shape of a gigantic twelve-wheeled chariot, drawn by seven stone horses. It dates from the 1200s, when medieval Hindu kings built magnificent temples to their gods.

GRAND ENTRANCE

The Alamgiri Gate is one of three magnificent entrances built by the Mughal emperor Aurangzeb to the Shahadra fort at Lahore (in modern-day Pakistan). The fort doubled as a luxurious palace.

LIFE STORY

A limestone frieze dating from AD100 shows a good deed carried out by the spiritual leader, Buddha. The frieze comes from Amaravati, in south-eastern India, which was an important Buddhist site from 300BC. Stories of the Buddha's past lives, called jatakas, were popular in ancient India.

A COUNTRY OF MOUNTAINS AND PLAINS

India is bounded to the north by the Himalayan mountains. The central Deccan plateau is framed by mountain ranges known as the Eastern and Western Ghats. The first settlements grew up near rivers on the fertile plains in the north.

c.500–400BC Inscribed fragments of pots from Sri Lanka discovered.

c.478–400BC Life of the Buddha. He is born a prince but leaves his family and lives in poverty.

coin of Alexander the Great

327–325BC Alexander the Great arrives in north-western India.

320BC The rise of the Magadhan Empire under the Maurya family, founded by King Chandragupta I.

268–233BC King Ashoka, the grandson of Chandragupta I, issues the first royal edicts on pillars and rocks throughout the subcontinent.

c. 50BC–AD100 Intensive trade connections with the Roman Empire.

AD50–AD200 Kushanas and Shakas (tribes from Central Asia) set up kingdoms and adopt Indian religions. Indian dynasty of Satavahanas arises in southern India.

Ashokan pillar

c. AD150 Kushana and Shaka kings in the north and west adopt Sanskrit as the courtly language.

c. AD200–400 *Ramayana*, *Mahabharata* and the *Bhagavad-Gita* Hindu epic poems are composed in their final form.

AD400 Nearly all courts are using Sanskrit.

gateway to Buddhist stupa

300BC   AD100   AD400

The Land of Ancient India

INDIA IS ISOLATED FROM THE main continent of Asia by the world's highest mountains, the Himalayas. The mountains made it difficult for people to invade. The easiest overland route, taken by the earliest settlers from Asia, is from the north-west (present-day Afghanistan) through the Karakoram mountains. However, it was still a difficult journey. Once people had arrived in India, they tended to stay.

The first people settled in the bare mountain foothills, and survived by keeping herds of animals such as sheep and goats. People gradually moved south of the Himalayas, to areas where mighty rivers run through huge, fertile plains. Here, the climate enabled them to grow various crops.

India's climate is dominated by the monsoon, a wind that brings alternating seasons of hot, dry weather and heavy rain and flooding. In the drier west and north, wheat was the main crop from very early times, while higher rainfall in the east and south was ideal for growing rice. Rice cultivation was so successful in the plains around the Ganges river that many people settled there. This led to the growth of cities from around 300BC. Later, cities developed along rivers farther south.

From the 1st century AD, people no longer needed to make the overland journey into India. They came by ship from as far away as the Mediterranean Sea to ports on the west coast, in search of trade.

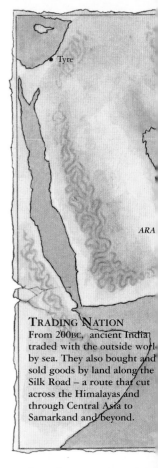

TRADING NATION
From 200BC, ancient India traded with the outside world by sea. They also bought and sold goods by land along the Silk Road – a route that cut across the Himalayas and through Central Asia to Samarkand and beyond.

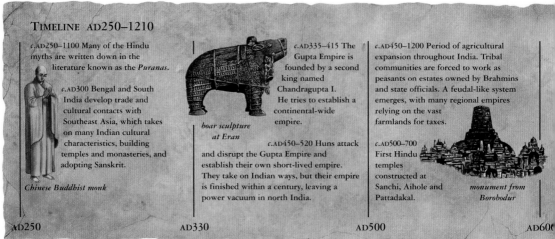

TIMELINE AD250–1210

*c.*AD250–1100 Many of the Hindu myths are written down in the literature known as the *Puranas*.

*c.*AD300 Bengal and South India develop trade and cultural contacts with Southeast Asia, which takes on many Indian cultural characteristics, building temples and monasteries, and adopting Sanskrit.

Chinese Buddhist monk

boar sculpture at Eran

*c.*AD335–415 The Gupta Empire is founded by a second king named Chandragupta I. He tries to establish a continental-wide empire.

*c.*AD450–520 Huns attack and disrupt the Gupta Empire and establish their own short-lived empire. They take on Indian ways, but their empire is finished within a century, leaving a power vacuum in north India.

*c.*AD450–1200 Period of agricultural expansion throughout India. Tribal communities are forced to work as peasants on estates owned by Brahmins and state officials. A feudal-like system emerges, with many regional empires relying on the vast farmlands for taxes.

*c.*AD500–700 First Hindu temples constructed at Sanchi, Aihole and Pattadakal.

monument from Borobodur

AD250　　　　　　　　AD330　　　　　　　　AD500　　　　　　　　AD600

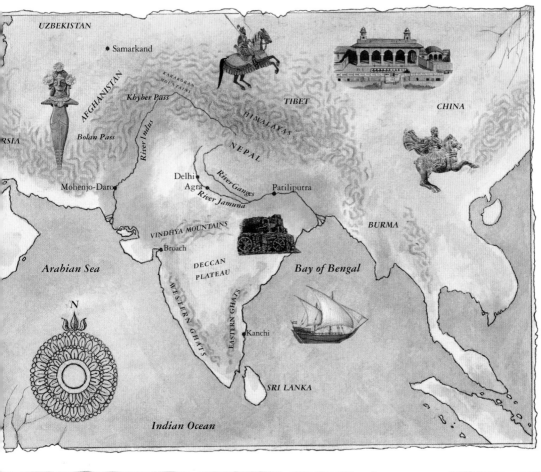

UZBEKISTAN

• Samarkand

AFGHANISTAN

KARAKORAM MOUNTAINS

Khyber Pass

TIBET

CHINA

Bolan Pass

River Indus

HIMALAYAS

PERSIA

NEPAL

Mohenjo-Daro

Delhi

Agra

River Ganges

River Jamuna

Patiliputra

BURMA

VINDHYA MOUNTAINS

• Broach

DECCAN PLATEAU

Bay of Bengal

Arabian Sea

WESTERN GHATS

EASTERN GHATS

N

Kanchi

SRI LANKA

Indian Ocean

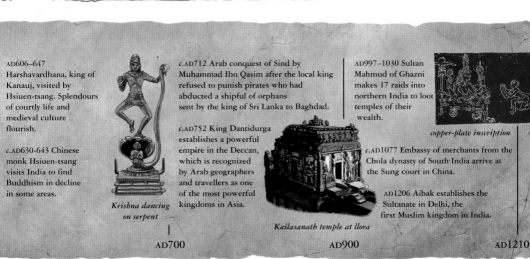

AD606–647
Harshavardhana, king of
Kanauj, visited by
Hsiuen-tsang. Splendours
of courtly life and
medieval culture
flourish.

c.AD630-643 Chinese
monk Hsiuen-tsang
visits India to find
Buddhism in decline
in some areas.

*Krishna dancing
on serpent*

c.AD712 Arab conquest of Sind by
Muhammad Ibn Qasim after the local king
refused to punish pirates who had
abducted a shipful of orphans
sent by the king of Sri Lanka to Baghdad.

c.AD752 King Dantidurga
establishes a powerful
empire in the Deccan,
which is recognized
by Arab geographers
and travellers as one
of the most powerful
kingdoms in Asia.

Kailasanath temple at Ilora

AD997–1030 Sultan
Mahmud of Ghazni
makes 17 raids into
northern India to loot
temples of their
wealth.

copper-plate inscription

c.AD1077 Embassy of merchants from the
Chola dynasty of South India arrive at
the Sung court in China.

AD1206 Aibak establishes the
Sultanate in Delhi, the
first Muslim kingdom in India.

AD700

AD900

AD1210

India's History Makers

MANY OF THE REMARKABLE FIGURES of Indian history who shaped the country's destiny were great leaders. Ashoka was a powerful ruler 2,500 years ago who encouraged the spread of Buddhism. Many centuries later, Babur, a warlord from Samarkand in Central Asia, founded the Mughal Empire in India in the early 1500s. His grandson, Akbar, was a gifted politician and soldier who ruled for 49 years. The Mughal period was a time of huge development in the arts. Some Mughal rulers built magnificent cities, and many of their fine monuments and royal tombs can still be seen today.

From the time of the ancient civilization of the Aryans in the Indus Valley, religious teachers and scholars were respected. This may be because poverty and suffering have always been problems in India, which led people to think about why life was so difficult, and to seek ways of coping. Two of the most famous religious leaders are Gautama Buddha, who established the Buddhist way of life, and Guru Nanak, who founded the Sikh religion.

AN INFLUENTIAL LEADER
A statue of Gautama Buddha seated on a lotus flower. He founded Buddhism, which shaped life in India for thousands of years. Buddhism eventually died out in India, but it spread through many other parts of Asia. This created a link between India and many different eastern peoples and cultures.

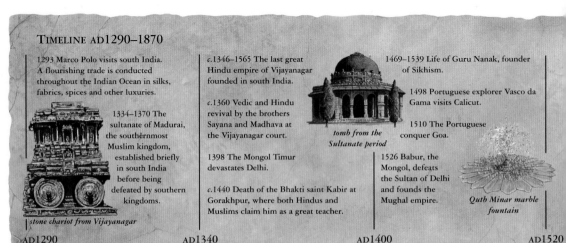

TIMELINE AD1290–1870

1293 Marco Polo visits south India. A flourishing trade is conducted throughout the Indian Ocean in silks, fabrics, spices and other luxuries.

1334–1370 The sultanate of Madurai, the southernmost Muslim kingdom, established briefly in south India before being defeated by southern kingdoms.

stone chariot from Vijayanagar

c.1346–1565 The last great Hindu empire of Vijayanagar founded in south India.

c.1360 Vedic and Hindu revival by the brothers Sayana and Madhava at the Vijayanagar court.

1398 The Mongol Timur devastates Delhi.

c.1440 Death of the Bhakti saint Kabir at Gorakhpur, where both Hindus and Muslims claim him as a great teacher.

tomb from the Sultanate period

1469–1539 Life of Guru Nanak, founder of Sikhism.

1498 Portuguese explorer Vasco da Gama visits Calicut.

1510 The Portuguese conquer Goa.

1526 Babur, the Mongol, defeats the Sultan of Delhi and founds the Mughal empire.

Qutb Minar marble fountain

AD1290   AD1340   AD1400   AD1520

ASHOKA'S PILLAR
An edict (order) of Ashoka, the ruler of India's first empire, is inscribed on this pillar. He published his edicts on pillars and rockfaces throughout the land. Ashoka was a Buddhist. He claimed to have improved the lives of humans and animals, and had helped to spread justice.

ROYAL HANDWRITING
This signature of Emperor Harsha (AD606–647) is carved in copper. Harsha was a patron (supporter) of arts and literature, and during his reign, the richness and elegance of the court reached new heights.

A SAINTLY LIFE
A statuette of Karaikal Ammaiyar, a woman who lived in southern India around AD600. She was so devoted to the god Shiva that she left her home and family, and gave her life entirely to him. She fasted as a symbol of her faith and became incredibly thin. Karaikal Ammaiyar is revered as a saint even today in southern India.

ART LOVER
Shah Jahan was one of the greatest statesmen of the Mughal Empire. He extended Mughal power south into the Deccan plateau and north into Afghanistan. However, he did not fulfil the Mughal dream of capturing the trading city of Samarkand, the 'blue pearl of the Orient', in Central Asia. Shah Jahan was a great patron of architecture.

1556–1605 Reign of Akbar, the most enlightened Mughal emperor.

1739 Nadir Shah sacks Delhi and carries off the Peacock Throne.

Mongol horseman

palace at Phata Pursi

1757 Nawab of Bengal defeated by the British at Plassey.

1758 The Mughal rulers in Bengal give the British East India Company the right to collect land taxes.

1857–8 The British government imposes direct rule and the East India Company is dissolved.

1870 Construction of Red Sea telegraph brings direct link with Britain.

farman (order) of Mughal emperor to East India Company

AD1750   AD1850   AD1870

The Chinese Empire

IMAGINE YOU COULD travel back in time 5,000 years and visit the lands of the Far East. In northern China you would come across smoky settlements of small thatched huts. You might see villagers fishing in rivers, sowing millet or baking pottery. From these small beginnings, China developed into an amazing civilization. Its towns grew into huge cities, with palaces and temples. Many Chinese became great writers, thinkers, artists, builders and inventors. China was first united under the rule of a single emperor in 221BC, and continued to be ruled by emperors until 1912.

China today is a modern country. Its ancient past has to be pieced together by archaeologists and historians. They dig up ancient tombs and settlements, and study textiles, ancient books and pottery. Their job is made easier because historical records were kept. These provide much information about the long history of Chinese civilization.

REST IN PEACE
A demon is trodden into defeat by a guardian spirit. Statues like this were commonly put in tombs to protect the dead against evil spirits.

ALL THE EMPEROR'S MEN
A vast model army marches again. It was dug up by archaeologists in 1974, and is now on display near Xian. The lifesize figures are made of terracotta (baked clay). They were buried in 210BC near the tomb of Qin Shi Huangdi, the first emperor of all China. He believed that they would protect him from evil spirits after he died.

TIMELINE 7000BC–110BC

Prehistoric remains of human ancestors dating back to 600,000BC have been found in China's Shaanxi province. The beginnings of Chinese civilization may be seen in the farming villages of the late Stone Age (8000BC–2500BC). As organized states grew up, the Chinese became skilled at warfare, working metals and making elaborate pottery and fine silk.

Banpo hut

c.7000BC Bands of hunters and fishers roam freely around the river valleys of China. They use simple stone tools and weapons.

c.3200BC Farming villages such as Banpo produce pottery in kilns. This way of life is called the Yangshao culture.

c.2100BC The start of a legendary 500-year period of rule, known as the Xia dynasty.

c.2000BC Black pottery is made by the people of the so-called Longshan culture.

Shang bronze vessel

c.1600BC Beginning of the Shang dynasty. Bronze worked and silk produced. The first picture-writing is used (on bones for telling fortunes).

Zhou spearheads

1122BC Zhou ruler Wu defeats Shang emperor. Wu becomes emperor of the Western Zhou dynasty.

7000BC   2100BC   1600BC   780BC

A HEAVENLY HALL

The Hall of Prayer for Good Harvests (*shown right*) is part of Tiantan, the Temple of Heavenly Peace in Beijing. It was originally built in 1420, but had to be rebuilt in the 1890s after it was destroyed by lightning. Buildings like these tell us about traditional technology and design, as well as about Chinese religious beliefs.

THE HAN EMPIRE (206BC–AD220)

China grew rapidly during the Han dynasty. By AD2 it had expanded to take in North Korea, the south-east coast, the south-west as far as Vietnam and large areas of Central Asia. Northern borders were defended by the Great Wall, which was extended during Han rule.

THE JADE PRINCE

In 1968, Chinese archaeologists excavated the tomb of Prince Liu Sheng. His remains were encased in a jade suit when he died in about 100BC. Over 2,400 pieces of this precious stone were joined with gold wire. It was believed that jade would preserve the body.

Zhou soldier 771BC Capital city moves from Anyang to Luoyang. Beginning of Eastern Zhou dynasty. c.604BC Birth of the legendary Laozi, founder of Daoism. 551BC Teacher and philosopher Kong Fuzi (Confucius) born.	513BC Iron-working develops. 453BC Break-up of central rule. Small states fight each other for 200 years. Work begins on Grand Canal and Great Wall. 221BC China unites as a centralized empire under Zheng (Qin Shi Huangdi). Great Wall is extended. 213BC Qin Shi Huangdi burns all books that are not 'practical'. *Chinese writing*	210BC Death of Qin Shi Huangdi. Terracotta army guards his tomb, near Chang'an (modern Xian). 206BC Qin dynasty overthrown. Beginnings of Han dynasty as Xiang Yu and Liu Bang fight for control of the Han kingdom. 202BC The Western Han dynasty formally begins. It is led by the former official Liu Bang, who becomes emperor Gaozu. 200BC Chang'an becomes the capital of the Chinese Empire.	 *terracotta warrior and horse* 112BC Trade with the peoples of Western Asia and Europe begins to flourish along the Silk Road.
550BC	210BC	140BC	110BC

The Centre of Civilization

CHINA IS A VAST COUNTRY, about the size of Europe. Its fertile plains and river valleys are ringed by many deserts, mountains and oceans. The ancient Chinese named their land Zhongguo, the Middle Kingdom, and believed that it was at the centre of the civilized world. Most Chinese belong to a people called the Han, but the country is also inhabited by 50 or more different peoples, some of whom have played an important part in Chinese history. These groups include the Hui, Zhuang, Dai, Yao, Miao, Tibetans, Manchus and Mongols.

The very first Chinese civilizations grew up around the Huang He (Yellow River), where the fertile soil supported farming villages and then towns and cities. These became the centres of rival kingdoms. Between 1700BC and 256BC Chinese rule spread southwards to the Chang Jiang (Yangzi River), the great river of Central China. All of eastern China was united within a single empire for the first time during Qin rule (221–206BC).

The rulers of the Han dynasty (206BC–AD220) then expanded the Empire southwards as far as Vietnam. The Chinese Empire was now even larger than the Roman Empire, dominating Central and South-east Asia. The Mongols, from lands to the north of China, ruled the Empire from 1279 to 1368. They were succeeded by the Ming dynasty, which was in turn overthown by the Manchu in 1644. In later centuries, China became inward-looking and unable to resist interference from Europe. The Empire finally collapsed, with China declaring itself a republic in 1912.

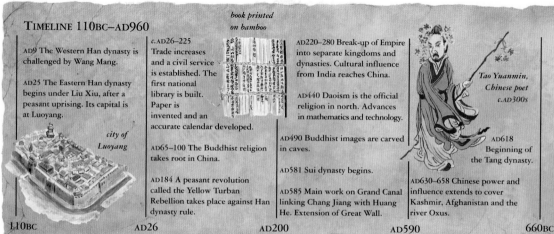

TIMELINE 110BC–AD960

book printed on bamboo

AD9 The Western Han dynasty is challenged by Wang Mang.

AD25 The Eastern Han dynasty begins under Liu Xiu, after a peasant uprising. Its capital is at Luoyang.

city of Luoyang

c.AD26–225 Trade increases and a civil service is established. The first national library is built. Paper is invented and an accurate calendar developed.

AD65–100 The Buddhist religion takes root in China.

AD184 A peasant revolution called the Yellow Turban Rebellion takes place against Han dynasty rule.

AD220–280 Break-up of Empire into separate kingdoms and dynasties. Cultural influence from India reaches China.

AD440 Daoism is the official religion in north. Advances in mathematics and technology.

AD490 Buddhist images are carved in caves.

AD581 Sui dynasty begins.

AD585 Main work on Grand Canal linking Chang Jiang with Huang He. Extension of Great Wall.

Tao Yuanmin, Chinese poet c.AD300s

AD618 Beginning of the Tang dynasty.

AD630–658 Chinese power and influence extends to cover Kashmir, Afghanistan and the river Oxus.

110BC   AD26   AD200   AD590   660BC

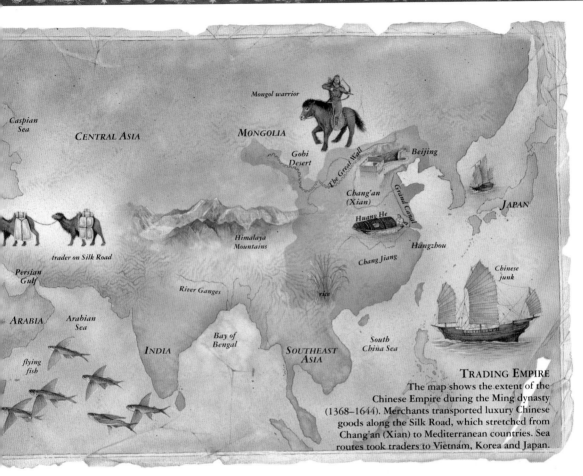

Caspian
Sea

CENTRAL ASIA

MONGOLIA

Mongol warrior

Gobi
Desert

The Great Wall

Beijing

Chang'an
(Xian)

Grand Canal

Huang He

JAPAN

trader on Silk Road

Persian
Gulf

Himalaya
Mountains

Hangzhou

Chang Jiang

*Chinese
junk*

ARABIA

Arabian
Sea

River Ganges

rice

South
China Sea

INDIA

Bay of
Bengal

SOUTHEAST
ASIA

*flying
fish*

TRADING EMPIRE

The map shows the extent of the
Chinese Empire during the Ming dynasty
(1368–1644). Merchants transported luxury Chinese
goods along the Silk Road, which stretched from
Chang'an (Xian) to Mediterranean countries. Sea
routes took traders to Vietnam, Korea and Japan.

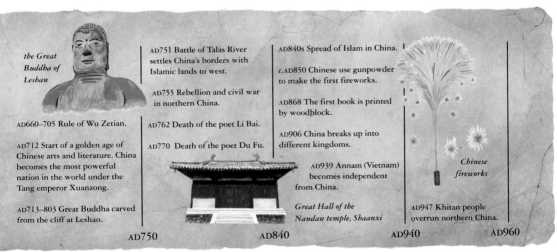

*the Great
Buddha of
Leshan*

AD751 Battle of Talas River
settles China's borders with
Islamic lands to west.

AD755 Rebellion and civil war
in northern China.

AD660–705 Rule of Wu Zetian.

AD762 Death of the poet Li Bai.

AD712 Start of a golden age of
Chinese arts and literature. China
becomes the most powerful
nation in the world under the
Tang emperor Xuanzong.

AD770 Death of the poet Du Fu.

AD713–803 Great Buddha carved
from the cliff at Leshan.

AD840s Spread of Islam in China.

c.AD850 Chinese use gunpowder
to make the first fireworks.

AD868 The first book is printed
by woodblock.

AD906 China breaks up into
different kingdoms.

AD939 Annam (Vietnam)
becomes independent
from China.

*Great Hall of the
Nandan temple, Shaanxi*

*Chinese
fireworks*

AD947 Khitan people
overrun northern China.

AD750

AD840

AD940

AD960

People of the Chinese Empire

GREAT EMPIRES ARE made by ordinary people as much as by their rulers. The Chinese Empire could not have been built without the millions of peasants who planted crops, built defensive walls and dug canals. The names of these people are largely forgotten, except for those who led uprisings and revolts against their rulers. The inventors, thinkers, artists, poets and writers of imperial China are better known. They had a great effect on the society they lived in, and left behind ideas, works of art and inventions that still influence people today.

The royal court was made up of thousands of officials, artists, craftsmen and servants. Some had great political power. China's rulers came from many different backgrounds and peoples.

Many emperors were ruthless former warlords who were hungry for power. Others are remembered as scholars or artists. Some women also achieved great political influence, openly or from behind the scenes.

LAOZI (born *c.*604BC)
The legendary Laozi is said to have been a scholar who worked as a court librarian. It is thought that he wrote the book known as the *Daodejing*. He believed people should live in harmony with nature, and his ideas later formed the basis of Daoism.

KONG FUZI (551–479BC)
Kong Fuzi is better known in the West by the Latin version of his name, Confucius. He was a public official who became an influential teacher and thinker. His views on family life, society and the treatment of others greatly influenced later generations.

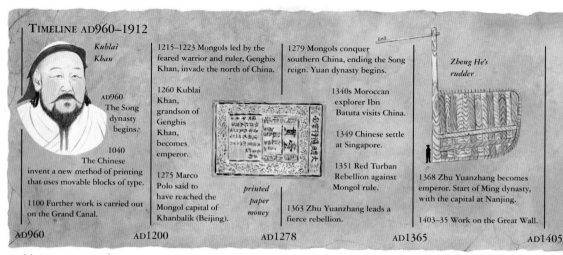

TIMELINE AD960–1912

Kublai Khan

AD960 The Song dynasty begins.

1040 The Chinese invent a new method of printing that uses movable blocks of type.

1100 Further work is carried out on the Grand Canal.

1215–1223 Mongols led by the feared warrior and ruler, Genghis Khan, invade the north of China.

1260 Kublai Khan, grandson of Genghis Khan, becomes emperor.

1275 Marco Polo said to have reached the Mongol capital of Khanbalik (Beijing).

printed paper money

1279 Mongols conquer southern China, ending the Song reign. Yuan dynasty begins.

1340s Moroccan explorer Ibn Batuta visits China.

1349 Chinese settle at Singapore.

1351 Red Turban Rebellion against Mongol rule.

1363 Zhu Yuanzhang leads a fierce rebellion.

Zheng He's rudder

1368 Zhu Yuanzhang becomes emperor. Start of Ming dynasty, with the capital at Nanjing.

1403–35 Work on the Great Wall.

AD960   AD1200   AD1278   AD1365   AD1405

QIN SHI HUANGDI (256–210BC)

Scholars plead for their lives before the first emperor. Zheng came to the throne of a state called Qin at the age of nine. He went on to rule all China and was given his full title, meaning First Emperor of Qin. His brutal methods included burying his opponents alive.

EMPRESS WU ZETIAN
(AD624–705)

The emperor Tang Gaozong enraged officials when he replaced his legal wife with Wu, his concubine (secondary wife). After the emperor suffered a stroke in AD660, Wu took control of the country. In AD690 she became the only woman in history to declare herself empress of China.

HAN GAOZU (256–195BC)

In the Qin dynasty (221–206BC) Liu Bang was a minor public official in charge of a relay station for royal messengers. He watched as the centralized Qin Empire fell apart. In 206BC he declared himself ruler of the Han kingdom. In 202BC he defeated his opponent, Xiang Yu, and founded the Han dynasty. As emperor Gaozu, he tried to unite China without using Qin's harsh methods.

KUBLAI KHAN (AD1214–1294)

The explorer Marco Polo was said to have visited emperor Kublai Khan at Khanbalik (Beijing). Kublai Khan was a Mongol who conquered northern, and later southern, China.

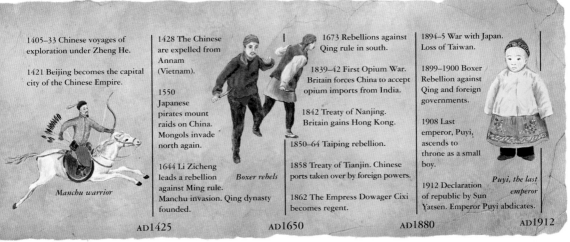

1405–33 Chinese voyages of exploration under Zheng He.

1421 Beijing becomes the capital city of the Chinese Empire.

Manchu warrior

1428 The Chinese are expelled from Annam (Vietnam).

1550 Japanese pirates mount raids on China. Mongols invade north again.

1644 Li Zicheng leads a rebellion against Ming rule. Manchu invasion. Qing dynasty founded.

Boxer rebels

1673 Rebellions against Qing rule in south.

1839–42 First Opium War. Britain forces China to accept opium imports from India.

1842 Treaty of Nanjing. Britain gains Hong Kong.

1850–64 Taiping rebellion.

1858 Treaty of Tianjin. Chinese ports taken over by foreign powers.

1862 The Empress Dowager Cixi becomes regent.

1894–5 War with Japan. Loss of Taiwan.

1899–1900 Boxer Rebellion against Qing and foreign governments.

1908 Last emperor, Puyi, ascends to throne as a small boy.

1912 Declaration of republic by Sun Yatsen. Emperor Puyi abdicates.

Puyi, the last emperor

AD1425   AD1650   AD1880   AD1912

A Golden Age in Greece

O N THE SHORES of the eastern Mediterranean, 3,000 years ago, one of the most enduring and influential civilizations of the Western world emerged. Ancient Greece was made up of a number of self-supporting city states, each of which developed a strong, individual identity. They developed from an agricultural society that wrote in simple pictograms into a sophisticated culture. Centuries on, the Greek legacy survives in parts of modern society. The origins of democracy, mathematics, medicine and philosophy can be traced back to this time in history. Even some of our modern words are made up from ancient Greek. 'Telephone' comes from the ancient Greek words 'tele' meaning far and 'phonos' meaning sound.

A FEAT OF PERFECTION
The Parthenon is regarded as the supreme achievement of Greek architecture. It was the most important building in Athens, where it still sits on top of the Acropolis. The temple took 15 years to build and was dedicated to Athena, guardian goddess of Athens. Around 22,000 tonnes of marble, transported from over 15km away, were used in its construction.

TIMELINE 40,000BC–1100BC

The first people lived in Greece about 40,000 years ago. They lived in a tribal, hunter-gatherer society. Settlements and the beginning of farming did not occur until 6,000BC. The first great Greek civilization, and also the first in Europe, flourished on the island of Crete around 2000BC. This was the mighty Minoan civilization whose decline heralded in the glorious age of the Mycenaeans. After this a period known as the Dark Ages began. It was followed

a drinking vessel (rhyton) in the shape of a bull's head from Knossos

by the golden age of Classical Greece which lasted from about 500BC to 336BC.

c.6000BC The first settlers arrive on the island of Crete and the Greek mainland.

c.2900–1000BC The Bronze Age in Greece. People discover how to mix copper and tin to make bronze.

disc from Crete with unique pictographic script

c.2000BC Minoan civilization flourishes on Crete. The Minoans use a script called Linear A, which has not yet been deciphered.

c.1600BC The Mycenaeans dominate mainland Greece.

statuette of worshipping woman from Mycenae

40,000BC   6000BC   2000BC   1450

CENTRE STONE

The omphalos was a carved stone kept at the shrine at Delphi. The ancient Greeks thought that this holy sanctuary was the centre of the world. The omphalos stone was placed there to mark the centre. It was said to have been put there by Zeus, ruler of the gods. It may have also served as an altar on which sacrifices were made.

THE PAST REVEALED

Archaeological evidence in the shape of pottery such as this vase help us to piece together the history of Greece. This vase is typical of the superior craftsmanship for which the Greeks were admired. It was common for vases to be decorated with pictures showing historical events. In this one, we see a scene from the siege of Troy in which the king is being murdered. The siege was an important event in Greek folklore. These decorative vases were used as containers for liquids such as oil, water and wine. The export of such pottery contributed an enormous amount of wealth to the Greeks.

THE ANCIENT GREEK WORLD

The map above shows the main ports and cities through which the Greeks traded. The ancient Greek world centred on the Aegean Sea, but the Greeks were adventurous seafarers. Trade took them from the Aegean Sea to the Atlantic Ocean and the shores of the Black Sea, where they formed many settlements. These colonies helped Greece to spread its influence beyond the mainland and its offshore islands.

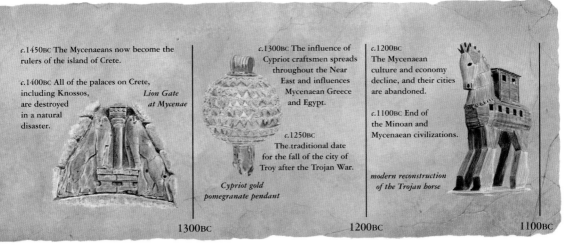

c.1450BC The Mycenaeans now become the rulers of the island of Crete.

c.1400BC All of the palaces on Crete, including Knossos, are destroyed in a natural disaster.

Lion Gate at Mycenae

c.1300BC The influence of Cypriot craftsmen spreads throughout the Near East and influences Mycenaean Greece and Egypt.

c.1250BC The traditional date for the fall of the city of Troy after the Trojan War.

Cypriot gold pomegranate pendant

c.1200BC The Mycenaean culture and economy decline, and their cities are abandoned.

c.1100BC End of the Minoan and Mycenaean civilizations.

modern reconstruction of the Trojan horse

1300BC   1200BC   1100BC

Greek Civilizations

THE HISTORY OF ANCIENT GREECE spans 20 centuries. It starts with the Minoan civilization on the island of Crete, which reached its height between 1900 and 1450BC. This culture was also the first to develop in Europe. The Minoans were a lively and artistic people who built palaces and towns and were also great seafarers. Their achievements greatly influenced the Mycenaeans, who built their own civilization on the Greek mainland from around 1600BC. Both the Minoan and Mycenaean cultures collapsed, probably under the impact of natural disasters and warfare, and were followed by centuries of poverty.

Revival was under way by 750BC, and the Greek world reached its economic peak during the 5th century BC. This period is known as the Classical Age, when Athens was at the height of its power and prosperity. During this century, Athens led the Greeks into many victorious battles against Persia. However, Athens itself later suffered an economic decline because of a series of wars fought against its rival, Sparta. Then, in the 4th century BC, Greece was conquered by Macedonia. The Macedonian ruler, Alexander the Great, spread Greek culture throughout his empire. Finally, between 168 and 146BC Macedonia and Greece were absorbed into the Roman Empire, and Greek civilization became part of the heritage that Rome passed on to the rest of Europe.

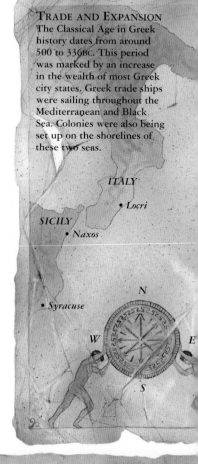

TRADE AND EXPANSION
The Classical Age in Greek history dates from around 500 to 336BC. This period was marked by an increase in the wealth of most Greek city states. Greek trade ships were sailing throughout the Mediterranean and Black Sea. Colonies were also being set up on the shorelines of these two seas.

ITALY

• Locri

SICILY
• Naxos

• Syracuse

N

W   E

S

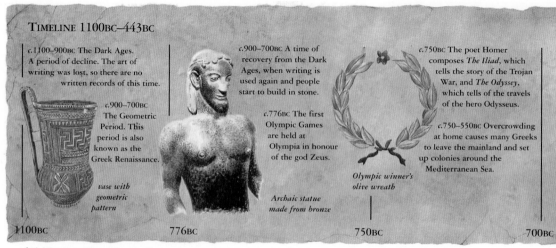

TIMELINE 1100BC–443BC

*c.*1100–900BC The Dark Ages. A period of decline. The art of writing was lost, so there are no written records of this time.

*c.*900–700BC The Geometric Period. This period is also known as the Greek Renaissance.

vase with geometric pattern

Archaic statue made from bronze

*c.*900–700BC A time of recovery from the Dark Ages, when writing is used again and people start to build in stone.

*c.*776BC The first Olympic Games are held at Olympia in honour of the god Zeus.

Olympic winner's olive wreath

*c.*750BC The poet Homer composes *The Iliad*, which tells the story of the Trojan War, and *The Odyssey*, which tells of the travels of the hero Odysseus.

*c.*750–550BC Overcrowding at home causes many Greeks to leave the mainland and set up colonies around the Mediterranean Sea.

1100BC   776BC   750BC   700BC

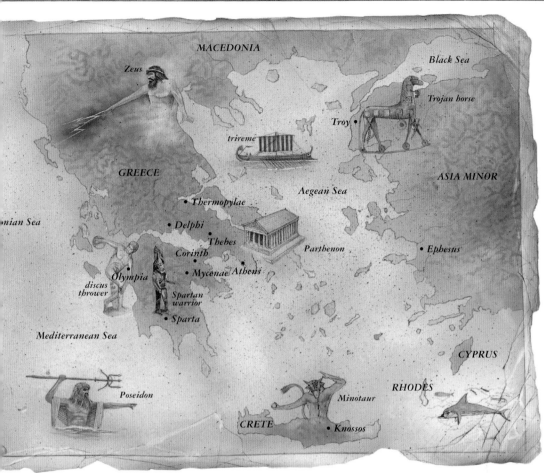

MACEDONIA

Zeus

Black Sea

Trojan horse

Troy

trireme

GREECE

Aegean Sea

ASIA MINOR

• Thermopylae

nian Sea

• Delphi

• Thebes

Parthenon

• Ephesus

Corinth

Olympia

• Mycenae Athens

discus
thrower

Spartan
warrior

• Sparta

Mediterranean Sea

CYPRUS

Poseidon

RHODES

Minotaur

CRETE

• Knossos

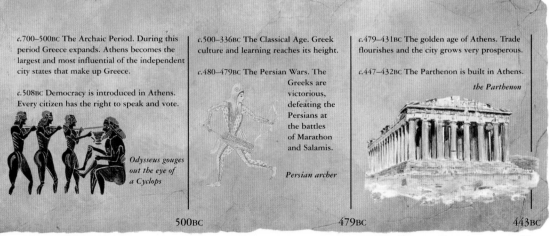

c.700–500BC The Archaic Period. During this period Greece expands. Athens becomes the largest and most influential of the independent city states that make up Greece.

c.508BC Democracy is introduced in Athens. Every citizen has the right to speak and vote.

Odysseus gouges out the eye of a Cyclops

c.500–336BC The Classical Age. Greek culture and learning reaches its height.

c.480–479BC The Persian Wars. The Greeks are victorious, defeating the Persians at the battles of Marathon and Salamis.

Persian archer

c.479–431BC The golden age of Athens. Trade flourishes and the city grows very prosperous.

c.447–432BC The Parthenon is built in Athens.

the Parthenon

500BC

479BC

443BC

Heroes of Greek Society

THE GREEKS TREASURED THEIR rich store of myths and legends about the gods, but they also took a keen interest in human history. They valued fame and glory far more than riches. Their ultimate aim in life was to make a name for themselves that would live on long after death. Statues were put up in prominent places to honour Greeks who had won fame in different ways – as generals on the battlefield, as poets, teachers, philosophers, mathematicians, orators or sportsmen. These heroes represented the human qualities the Greeks most admired – physical courage, endurance and strength, and the intelligence to create, invent, explain and persuade.

HOMER (c700BC)
The blind poet Homer (above) was honoured for writing two epic tales. The first is *The Iliad,* a story about the siege of Troy. The other is *The Odyssey* which follows the adventures of Odysseus in his travels after the battle of Troy. Scholars now believe that the tales may have been written by two poets or even groups of several poets.

SAPPHO (c600BC)
The poet Sappho was born on the island of Lesbos. She wrote nine books of poetry, but only one complete poem survives. Beauty and love were the subjects of her poetry. Her work inspired other artists of the time and influenced many writers and poets in later centuries.

SOPHOCLES (496–406BC)
Only seven of Sophocles' plays have survived. He is thought to have written 123 altogether. Besides being a playwright, Sophocles was also a respected general and politician. His name means 'famed for wisdom'.

TIMELINE 443BC–146BC

443–429BC The great statesman, Pericles, dominates politics in Athens.

431–404BC The Peloponnesian Wars take place between Athens and its great rival, Sparta. The Spartans defeat the Athenians.

399BC The Athenian philosopher, Socrates is condemned to death because his views prove unpopular.

marble bust of the philosopher, Socrates

371BC Sparta is defeated by Thebes. Thebes becomes the leading power in Greece.

362BC Sparta and Athens combine forces to defeat the Thebans at the battle of Mantinea.

338BC The Greeks are defeated by the Macedonians at the battle of Chaeronea. Philip II of Macedonia becomes ruler of Greece.

iron corselet, which is thought to have belonged to Philip II of Macedonia

336BC Philip II of Macedonia dies and is succeeded by his son, Alexander the Great. Alexander builds a huge empire, stretching from Greece as far east as India.

bronze statuette of Alexander the Great

443BC   371BC   336BC   334BC

PERICLES (495–429BC)

A popular figure and brilliant public speaker, Pericles was elected as a general 20 times. While in office, he built up a powerful navy and organized the building of strong defences, beautiful temples and fine monuments. He also gave ordinary citizens more say in government. Pericles' career ended after he led Athens into a disastrous war against Sparta. He was ostracized (expelled) as punishment for his misjudgement.

ALEXANDER THE GREAT (356–323BC)

Alexander was the son of Philip II of Macedonia. His life was spent in conquest of new territory, and his empire stretched across the Middle East, Persia and Afghanistan as far as the river Indus. His empire was swiftly divided when he died after suspected poisoning.

SOCRATES (469–399BC)

A renowned teacher and philosopher, Socrates encouraged people to think about how to live a good life. The Athenians sentenced him to die by drinking hemlock (a poison). Plato, Socrates' most brilliant pupil and himself a great philosopher, recorded his teacher's last days.

ARCHIMEDES (287–211BC)

The mathematician, scientist, astronomer and inventor, Archimedes came from Syracuse. When his city was besieged by the Romans, he designed a huge lens that focused sunlight on the Roman ships and set them on fire. He also devised a screw for raising water out of the ground and studied the concepts of floating and balance.

334BC Alexander the Great invades Persia to include it in his empire.

333BC The Persian army, led by King Darius, is defeated by Alexander the Great at the battle of Issus.

331BC Alexander the Great becomes king of Persia after defeating the Persians at the battle of Gaugamela.

King Darius of Persia

Romulus and Remus, legendary founders of Rome

323BC Alexander the Great dies, and his successors fight over the throne.

275BC Greek colonies are taken over by the Romans.

168BC Rome defeats the Macedonian rulers of Greece.

147–146BC The Achaean War. The Romans take control of Greece and Macedonia.

Roman soldier in full armour

323BC   168BC   146BC

Rome: From City to Empire

THE CITY OF ROME today is a bustling place, full of traffic and crowds. But if you could travel back in time to around 800BC, you would find only a few small villages on peaceful, wooded hillsides along the banks of the river Tiber. According to legend, Rome was founded here in 753BC. In the centuries that followed, the Romans came to dominate Italy and the Mediterranean. They farmed and traded and fought for new lands. Rome grew to become the centre of a vast empire that stretched across Europe into Africa and Asia. The Empire lasted for centuries and brought a sophisticated way of life to vast numbers of people. Many Roman buildings and artefacts still survive to show us what life was like in the Roman Empire.

ROMAN ITALY
As the city of Rome prospered, the Romans gradually conquered neighbouring tribes. By 250BC they controlled most of Italy. This map shows some of the important towns and cities of that time.

ANCIENT AND MODERN
In Rome today, people live alongside the temples, marketplaces and public buildings of the past. This is the Colosseum, a huge arena called an amphitheatre. It was used for staging games and fights, and first opened to the public in AD80.

TIMELINE 750BC–300BC

Rome's rise to power was sudden and spectacular. Its eventful history includes bloody battles, eccentric emperors, amazing inventions and remarkable feats of engineering. The Roman Empire prospered for almost 500 years, and still influences the way we live today.

Romulus, the first king of Rome

*c.*753BC The city of Rome is founded by Romulus, according to legend.

673–641BC Tullus Hostilius, Rome's third king, expands the city's territory by conquering a neighbouring settlement. Rome's population doubles as a result.

641–616BC Pons Sublicius, the first bridge across the river Tiber, is constructed. The harbour town of Ostia is founded at the mouth of the Tiber.

600BC The Latin language is first written in a script that is still used today.

inscription in Latin, carved in stone

750BC   753BC   600BC   550BC

CLUES TO THE PAST

The coin on this necklace dates from the reign of the Emperor Domitian, AD81–96. Gold does not rot like wood and other materials, so jewellery like this can give us clues about Roman craft methods, changing fashions, trade and even warfare.

SECRETS BENEATH THE SEA

Divers have discovered Roman shipwrecks deep under the waters of the Mediterranean Sea. Many have their cargo still intact. These jars were being transported over 2,000 years ago. By examining shipwrecks, archaeologists can learn how Roman boats were built, what they carried and where they traded.

ARCHAEOLOGISTS AT WORK

These archaeologists are excavating sections of wall plaster from the site of a Roman house in Britain. Many remains of Roman buildings and artefacts, as well as books and documents, have survived from that time. These all help us build up a picture of what life was like in the Roman Empire.

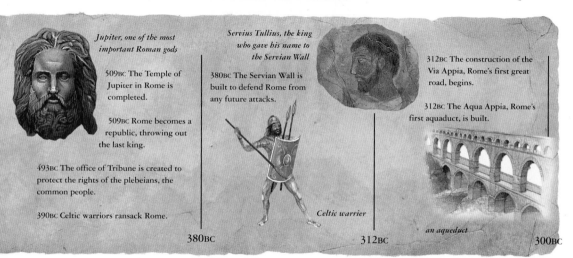

Jupiter, one of the most important Roman gods

509BC The Temple of Jupiter in Rome is completed.

509BC Rome becomes a republic, throwing out the last king.

493BC The office of Tribune is created to protect the rights of the plebeians, the common people.

390BC Celtic warriors ransack Rome.

Servius Tullius, the king who gave his name to the Servian Wall

380BC The Servian Wall is built to defend Rome from any future attacks.

312BC The construction of the Via Appia, Rome's first great road, begins.

312BC The Aqua Appia, Rome's first aquaduct, is built.

Celtic warrior

an aqueduct

380BC

312BC

300BC

The Vast Roman Empire

BY THE YEAR AD117, the Roman Empire was at its height. It was possible to travel 4,000km from east to west and still hear the trumpets of the Roman legions. As a Roman soldier you might have had to shiver in the snowy winters of northern Britain, or sweat and toil in the heat of the Egyptian desert.

The peoples of the Empire were very different. There were Greeks, Egyptians, Syrians, Jews, Africans, Germans and Celts. Many of them belonged to civilizations that were already ancient when Rome was still a group of villages. Many revolted against Roman rule, but uprisings were quickly put down. Gradually, conquered peoples came to accept being part of the Empire. From AD212 onwards, any free person living under Roman rule had the right to claim "I am a Roman citizen". Slaves, however, had very few rights.

In AD284, after a series of violent civil wars, this vast empire was divided into several parts. Despite being reunited by the Emperor Constantine in AD324, the Empire was doomed. A hundred years later, the western part was invaded by fierce warriors from the north, with disastrous consequences. Although the Western Empire came to an end in AD476, the eastern part continued until 1453. The Latin language survived, used by the Roman Catholic Church and by scientists and scholars in Europe. It is still learned today, and is the basis of languages such as Italian, Spanish, French and Romanian.

TIMELINE 300BC–1 BC

264BC First record of a gladiatorial contest.

264–241BC The first of three wars between Rome and Carthage, which came to be known as the Punic Wars.

250BC Rome controls most of Italy.

a gladiator

one of Hannibal's war elephants

240BC The first Roman dramas are performed on stage.

218–201BC Second war between Rome and Carthage. Hannibal, a Carthaginian general, crosses the Alps by elephant.

c.211BC The first Roman silver coin, *denarius*, is minted at Rome.

206BC Rome conquers Iberia (present-day Spain).

200BC The Romans are using concrete in buildings.

196BC Rome defeats the Macedonian rulers of Greece. Triumphal arches are built in Rome.

a triumphal arch, built to celebrate a victory

300BC   240BC   206BC   196B[C]

GERMANY

Caspian Sea

Black Sea

Po

ITALY

Tiber

CORSICA

Rome

SARDINIA

Mediterranean Sea

Carthage

SICILY

Mediterranean Sea

GREECE

TURKEY

SYRIA

CYPRUS

CRETE

EGYPT

Nile

Red Sea

NORTH AFRICA

The extent of the Roman Empire in AD117

A HUGE EMPIRE

The Roman Empire reached its greatest size in AD117. This map shows its extent, stretching thousands of kilometres to the east, west, north and south. Present-day names are used on the map to help compare the Empire to Europe and the Middle East today.

Roman soldiers armed for battle

149–146BC Third and final war between Rome and Carthage in which Carthage is destroyed.

146BC Greece and North Africa come under Roman rule.

73BC Spartacus leads a slave revolt in southern Italy.

58–50BC Roman armies, led by Julius Caesar, conquer Gaul after a series of wars.

55BC Pompey's Theatre, the first stone-built theatre in Rome, is completed.

slaves in chains

55–54BC Roman attacks on Britain begin.

44BC Julius Caesar is murdered in the Senate.

a Roman open-air theatre

31BC Battle of Actium – Octavian defeats Cleopatra of Egypt and Mark Antony, bringing an end to civil war.

29BC Egypt becomes part of the Roman Empire.

27BC Octavian becomes Rome's first emperor and is given the title Augustus.

60BC

40BC

1BC

History Makers of Rome

THE PEOPLE who made Roman history came from many different backgrounds. The names of the famous survive on monuments and in books. There were consuls and emperors, successful generals and powerful politicians, great writers and historians. However, it was thousands of ordinary people who really kept the Roman Empire going – merchants, soldiers of the legions, tax collectors, servants, farmers, potters, and others like them.

Many of the most famous names of that time were not Romans at all. There was the Carthaginian general, Hannibal, Rome's deadliest enemy. There were also Celtic chieftains and queens, such as Vercingetorix, Caractacus and Boudicca.

ROMULUS AND REMUS
According to legend, Romulus was the founder and first king of Rome. The legend tells how he and his twin brother Remus were abandoned as babies. They were saved by a she-wolf, who looked after them until they were found by a shepherd.

AUGUSTUS (63BC–AD14)
Augustus, born Octavian, was the great-nephew and adopted son of Julius Caesar. After Caesar's death, he took control of the army. He became ruler of the Roman world after defeating Mark Antony at the Battle of Actium in 31BC. In 27BC, he became Rome's first emperor and was given the title Augustus.

CICERO (106–43BC)
Cicero is remembered as Rome's greatest orator, or speaker. Many of his letters and speeches still survive. He was a writer, poet, politican, lawyer and philosopher. He was elected consul of Rome in 63BC, but he had many enemies and was murdered in 43BC.

TIMELINE AD1–AD476

AD43 The Roman conquest of Britain begins.

AD50 Rome is the largest city in the world – population about 1 million. Roman traders reach Bengal and India.

AD60 Queen Boudicca leads an uprising in Britain.

AD64 The Great Fire of Rome.

AD75 Rome sets up trade links across the Sahara.

Vesuvius begins to erupt

AD79 The volcano Vesuvius erupts, burying Pompeii and Herculaneum.

AD117 The Roman Empire is at its largest.

AD118–128 The Pantheon in Rome is built.

AD122 Work begins on Hadrian's Wall, a defensive barrier across northern Britain.

AD165–167 Plague spreads through the Empire.

c.AD200 Road system covers all parts of the Empire.

AD212 All free people in the Empire are granted citizenship.

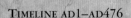

Boudicca, queen of the Iceni in Britain

AD1   AD75   AD150

the Pantheon in Rome   AD250

HADRIAN (AD76–138)

Hadrian became emperor in AD117 and spent many years travelling around the Empire. He had many splendid buildings constructed, as well as a defensive barrier across northern Britain, now known as Hadrian's Wall.

NERO (AD37–68) AND AGRIPPINA

In AD54 Nero became emperor after the death of his adoptive father Claudius. A cruel ruler, he was blamed for a great fire that destroyed much of Rome in AD64. Agrippina, his mother, was a powerful influence on him. She was suspected of poisoning two of her three husbands, and was eventually killed on her son's orders.

CLEOPATRA (68–30BC)

An Egyptian queen of Greek descent, Cleopatra had a son by Julius Caesar. She then fell in love with Mark Antony, a close follower of Caesar. They joined forces against Rome, but after a crushing defeat at Actium in 31BC, they both committed suicide. Egypt then became part of the Roman Empire.

JULIUS CAESAR (100–44BC)

Caesar was a talented and popular general and politician. He led Roman armies in an eight-year campaign to conquer Gaul (present-day France) in 50BC. In 49BC, he used his victorious troops to seize power and declare himself dictator for life. Five years later he was stabbed to death in the Senate by fellow politicians.

the cross, a symbol of Christianity

AD270 A new defensive wall is built around Rome by the Emperor Aurelian.

AD284 New laws and taxes. Divisions in the Empire appear.

AD313 Christianity is made legal.

AD324 The Emperor Constantine reunites the Empire and founds Constantinople (present-day Istanbul, in Turkey).

AD330 Constantinople becomes Constantine's new capital in the east.

AD395 The Roman Empire is divided into two parts – Eastern and Western.

the Emperor Constantine, depicted on a Roman coin

AD410 The city of Rome is raided and ransacked by Visigoth armies from Germany.

Vandal warrior

AD455 Vandal armies from Germany ransack Rome.

AD476 Fall of the Western Empire – the Eastern Empire survives until 1453.

AD330　　　　　　　AD400　　　　　　　AD476

The Coming of the Vikings

THE YEAR IS AD795. Imagine you are an Irish monk, gathering herbs to make medicines. Walking along the river bank you hear the sound of creaking oars and curses in a strange language. Through the reeds you see a long wooden ship slipping upstream. It has a prow carved like a dragon. Inside it are fierce-looking men – battle-scarred warriors, armed with swords and axes.

Incidents like this happened time after time around the coasts of Europe in the years that followed. In the West, these invaders were called Northmen, Norsemen or Danes. In the East, they were known as Rus or Varangians. They have gone down in history as Vikings. This name comes from a word in the Old Norse language meaning sea raiding. Who were they? The Vikings were Scandinavians from the lands known today as Denmark, Norway and Sweden. Archaeologists have found their farms and houses, the goods they traded, the treasure they stole and their fine wooden ships.

BATTLE ART
The Vikings were skilled artists, as well as fierce warriors. This Danish battle axe is made of iron inlaid with silver. It has been decorated with beautiful swirling patterns.

INTO THE PAST
Archaeologists have excavated Viking towns and found ships, weapons and hoards of treasure. This excavation is in York, in northern England.

SEAFARERS
The outline of the Viking ship, with its high prow and square sail, became widely feared. This carving is from the Swedish island of Gotland.

TIMELINE AD750-875

The Vikings were descended from German tribes who moved northwards into Scandinavia. They were restless, energetic people. By the AD780s, they were raiding other lands. Soon they were exploring, settling and trading far from home, from North America to Baghdad. By 1100 the Vikings had become Christian and their lands had become more like the other countries in western Europe.

Viking sword

AD750 Trade opens up between northern Europe and the East. Trading routes are established.

c.AD750 Small trading and manufacturing towns flourish, such as Ribe in Denmark, Paviken on Gotland and Helgo in Sweden.

treasure hoard

AD789 Vikings raid southern England.

AD793 Vikings raid Lindisfarne, an island off the north-east coast of England.

massacre at Lindisfarne

AD795 Vikings raid Scotland and Ireland.

AD750   AD775   AD800

THE VIKING HOMELANDS

The Vikings came from Scandinavia. This map shows some of the most important Viking sites. Most of these were in present-day Denmark, southern Sweden and along Norway's coastal fjords.

INVASION FLEET

The Vikings invaded England in AD866. They went on to defeat and murder Edmund, King of the East Angles. Much of our knowledge of the Vikings comes from accounts written by their enemies. Many of these, such as this one about the life of St Edmund, were written later.

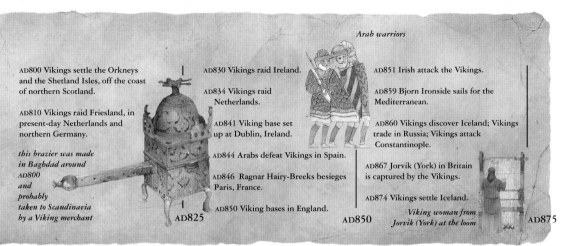

AD800 Vikings settle the Orkneys and the Shetland Isles, off the coast of northern Scotland.

AD810 Vikings raid Friesland, in present-day Netherlands and northern Germany.

this brazier was made in Baghdad around AD800 and probably taken to Scandinavia by a Viking merchant

AD825

AD830 Vikings raid Ireland.

AD834 Vikings raid Netherlands.

AD841 Viking base set up at Dublin, Ireland.

AD844 Arabs defeat Vikings in Spain.

AD846 Ragnar Hairy-Breeks besieges Paris, France.

AD850 Viking bases in England.

Arab warriors

AD850

AD851 Irish attack the Vikings.

AD859 Bjorn Ironside sails for the Mediterranean.

AD860 Vikings discover Iceland; Vikings trade in Russia; Vikings attack Constantinople.

AD867 Jorvik (York) in Britain is captured by the Vikings.

AD874 Vikings settle Iceland.

Viking woman from Jorvik (York) at the loom

AD875

The Viking World

THE VIKINGS took to the sea in search of wealth, fortune and better land for farming. At that time, Denmark was mostly rough heath or woodland. The other Viking homelands of Norway and Sweden were harsh landscapes, with mountains and dense forests, which were difficult to farm.

From the AD780s onwards, bands of Vikings launched savage attacks on England, Scotland, Ireland and Wales. They later settled large areas of the British Isles, including the Orkneys, Shetlands and the Isle of Man. Viking raiders also attacked settlements along the coasts and rivers of Germany, the Netherlands and France. The area they settled in France became known as Normandy, meaning land of the Northmen.

Viking warriors sailed as far as Spain, where they clashed with the Arabs who then ruled it. They also travelled west across the Atlantic Ocean, settling in Iceland, Greenland and even North America.

Viking traders founded states in the Ukraine and Russia and sailed down the rivers of eastern Europe. They hired themselves out as the emperor's bodyguards in the city they called Miklagard – also known as Constantinople (modern Istanbul).

By the 1100s, the descendants of the Vikings lived in powerful Christian kingdoms. The wild days of piracy were over.

N

L'Anse aux Meadows

CANADA

NEWFOUNDLAND (VINLAND)

TIMELINE AD875–1000

carved prow

Viking longship

proclamation of Althing

AD878 In England, Alfred (whom the Victorians called The Great) of Wessex defeats the Vikings.

AD885 Viking army attacks Paris.

AD886 Danelaw treaty in England.

AD900 Harald Finehair becomes first king of a united Norway.

AD910 Anglo-Saxon king, Edward the Elder, recaptures large areas of England from the Danes.

AD911 French give Normandy to the Vikings under King Rollo (Hrolf).

AD930 One of many meetings of the Iceland Althing. The settlement of Iceland is largely completed.

AD937 At the Battle of Brunanburh, Athelstan of Wessex defeats an alliance of Danes, Scots and Welsh.

AD940 Edmund of Wessex makes peace with Olaf of Jorvik.

AD875

AD900

AD925

AD950

GREENLAND

Greenland Sea

Norwegian Sea

NORWAY

SWEDEN

Thingvellir
ICELAND

Brattahlid

HEBRIDES

North Atlantic Ocean

SCOTLAND

Kaupang

Birka

Lindisfarne
priory is
burned

DENMARK
Ribe

Dublin
WALES

York
(Jorvik)

Hedeby

IRELAND

ENGLAND

FRANCE

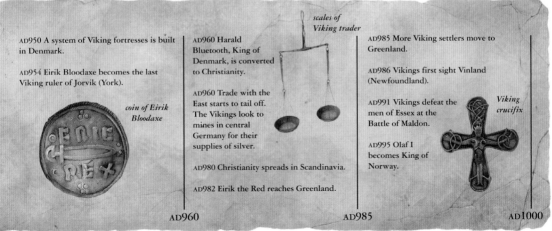

scales of
Viking trader

AD950 A system of Viking fortresses is built in Denmark.

AD954 Eirik Bloodaxe becomes the last Viking ruler of Jorvik (York).

coin of Eirik Bloodaxe

AD960 Harald Bluetooth, King of Denmark, is converted to Christianity.

AD960 Trade with the East starts to tail off. The Vikings look to mines in central Germany for their supplies of silver.

AD980 Christianity spreads in Scandinavia.

AD982 Eirik the Red reaches Greenland.

AD985 More Viking settlers move to Greenland.

AD986 Vikings first sight Vinland (Newfoundland).

AD991 Vikings defeat the men of Essex at the Battle of Maldon.

AD995 Olaf I becomes King of Norway.

Viking crucifix

AD960

AD985

AD1000

Viking Heroes

Bravery and a spirit of adventure were greatly admired by the Vikings. The names and nicknames of their heroes — explorers, ruthless pirates and brave warriors — have gone down in history. Two of the most famous were Ragnar Hairy-Breeks, who terrorized the city of Paris in AD846, and a red-bearded Norwegian, called Eirik the Red, who named and settled Greenland in AD985.

The Vikings we know most about were powerful kings. Harald Hardradi (meaning stern in counsel) saw his brother, King Olaf of Norway, killed in battle. He then fled to Russia and went on to join the emperor's bodyguard in Constantinople. After quarrelling with the Empress Zoë, he returned to Russia before becoming ruler of Norway.

BLOODAXE
This coin is from Eirik Bloodaxe's reign. He was the son of Norway's first king and ruled Jorvik (York).

Viking women could be just as tough and stubborn as their men. They were well respected, too. Archaeologists found two women buried in a splendid ship at Oseberg in Norway. One was a queen, the other her servant. They were buried with beautiful treasures.

MEMORIAL IN STONE
This memorial was raised at Jelling in Denmark by King Harald Bluetooth. An inscription on it says that King Harald 'won all of Denmark and Norway and made all the Danes Christians'.

FROM WARRIOR TO SAINT
Olaf Tryggvasön was Harald Finehair's grandson. He seized the throne of Norway in AD995. King Olaf became a Christian and was made a saint after his death in AD1000.

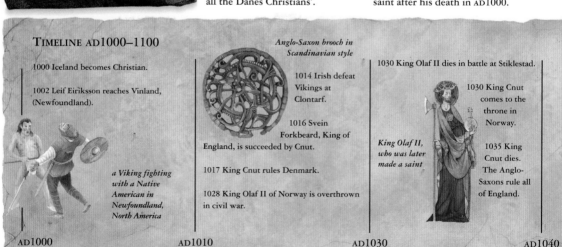

TIMELINE AD1000–1100

1000 Iceland becomes Christian.

1002 Leif Eiríksson reaches Vinland, (Newfoundland).

a Viking fighting with a Native American in Newfoundland, North America

Anglo-Saxon brooch in Scandinavian style

1014 Irish defeat Vikings at Clontarf.

1016 Svein Forkbeard, King of England, is succeeded by Cnut.

1017 King Cnut rules Denmark.

1028 King Olaf II of Norway is overthrown in civil war.

1030 King Olaf II dies in battle at Stiklestad.

1030 King Cnut comes to the throne in Norway.

King Olaf II, who was later made a saint

1035 King Cnut dies. The Anglo-Saxons rule all of England.

AD1000   AD1010   AD1030   AD1040

LEIF THE LUCKY

Leif the Lucky was Eirik the Red's son. He sailed even further west than his famous father. In about AD1000 he reached Canada, sailing to a land he named Vinland. This was probably Newfoundland. Other Vikings, including Leif's brother Thorwald, tried to settle these North American lands, but with little success.

THE WISE RULER

Cnut was the son of Svein Forkbeard, King of Denmark. He led extremely savage raids on England, becoming its king in 1016. He proved to be a kinder and wiser king than he had been a warrior. By 1018 he was King of Denmark and by 1030 he had become King of Norway as well. He died at Shaftesbury, England in 1035.

THE NORMANS

Hrolf, or Rollo, was a Viking chief. In AD911 he and his followers were granted part of northern France by the French king. The region became known as Normandy, and the Normans went on to conquer Britain and parts of Italy.

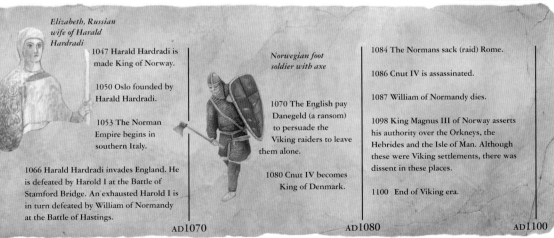

Elizabeth, Russian wife of Harald Hardradi

1047 Harald Hardradi is made King of Norway.

1050 Oslo founded by Harald Hardradi.

1053 The Norman Empire begins in southern Italy.

1066 Harald Hardradi invades England. He is defeated by Harold I at the Battle of Stamford Bridge. An exhausted Harold I is in turn defeated by William of Normandy at the Battle of Hastings.

Norwegian foot soldier with axe

1070 The English pay Danegeld (a ransom) to persuade the Viking raiders to leave them alone.

1080 Cnut IV becomes King of Denmark.

1084 The Normans sack (raid) Rome.

1086 Cnut IV is assassinated.

1087 William of Normandy dies.

1098 King Magnus III of Norway asserts his authority over the Orkneys, the Hebrides and the Isle of Man. Although these were Viking settlements, there was dissent in these places.

1100 End of Viking era.

AD1070   AD1080   AD1100

Mesoamerican Civilizations

THE AZTECS LIVED IN MESOAMERICA – the region where North and South America meet. It includes the countries of Mexico, Guatemala, Honduras, El Salvador and Belize. During the past 3,000 years, Mesoamerica has been home to many great civilizations, including the Olmecs, the Maya, the Toltecs and the Aztecs. The Aztecs were the last of these to arrive, coming from the north in around AD1200. In about 1420 they began to conquer a mighty empire. But in 1521 they were themselves conquered by Spanish soldiers, who came to America in search of gold. Over the next hundred years, the rest of Mesoamerica also fell to the Spaniards.

Even so, the descendants of these cultures still live in the area today. Many ancient Mesoamerican words, customs and beliefs survive, as do beautiful hand-painted books, mysterious ruins and amazing treasures.

OLMEC POWER
This giant stone head was carved by the Olmecs, the earliest of many great civilizations that flourished in Mesoamerica. Like the Maya and Aztecs, the Olmecs were skilled stone workers and built great cities.

UNCOVERING THE PAST
This temple is in Belize. Remains of such great buildings give archaeologists important clues about the people who built them.

TIMELINE 5000BC–AD800

Various civilizations were powerful in Mesoamerica at different times. The Maya were most successful between AD600–900. The Aztecs were at the height of their power from AD1428–AD1520.

Olmec figure

5000BC The Maya settle along the Pacific and Caribbean coasts of Mesoamerica.

2000BC People begin to farm in Belize, Guatemala and south-east Mexico.

2000BC The beginning of the period known as the Preclassic era.

1200BC Olmec people are powerful in Mesoamerica. They remain an important power until 400BC.

1000BC Maya craftworkers begin to copy Olmec pottery and jade carvings.

900BC Maya farmers design and use irrigation systems.

600BC The Zapotec civilization begins to flourish at Monte Alban.

Maya codex

300BC The Maya population starts to grow rapidly. Cities are built.

292BC The first-known Maya writing is produced.

150BC–AD500 The people living in the city of Teotihuacan grow powerful.

AD250 The beginning of the greatest period of Maya power, known as the Classic Maya era. This lasts until AD900.

mask from Teotihuacan

5000BC   2000BC   300BC   AD500

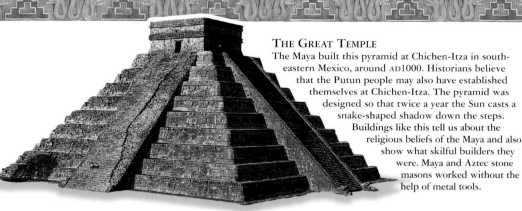

THE GREAT TEMPLE

The Maya built this pyramid at Chichen-Itza in south-eastern Mexico, around AD1000. Historians believe that the Putun people may also have established themselves at Chichen-Itza. The pyramid was designed so that twice a year the Sun casts a snake-shaped shadow down the steps. Buildings like this tell us about the religious beliefs of the Maya and also show what skilful builders they were. Maya and Aztec stone masons worked without the help of metal tools.

THE FACE OF A GOD

This mask represents the god Tezcatlipoca. It is made of pieces of semi-precious stone fixed to a real human skull. Masks like this were worn during religious ceremonies, or displayed in temples as offerings to the gods.

MESSAGES IN CODE

These are Aztec picture-symbols for days, written in a folding book called a codex. Mesoamerican civilizations kept records of important people, places and events in picture-writing.

Home of the Mesoamerican civilizations

MESOAMERICA IN THE WORLD

For centuries, Mesoamerica was home to many different civilizations, but there were links between them, especially in farming, technology and religious beliefs. Until around AD1500, these Mesoamerican civilizations had very little contact with the rest of the world.

AD550 This is the time of the Maya's greatest artistic achievements. Fine temples and palaces in cities such as Kabah, Copan, Palenque, Uxmal and Tikal are built. These great regional city-states are ruled by lords who claim to be descended from the gods. This period of Maya success continues until AD900.

temple at Tikal

AD615 The great Maya leader Lord Pacal rules in the city of Palenque.

AD650 The city of Teotihuacan begins to decline. It is looted and burned by unknown invaders around AD700.

AD684 Lord Pacal's rule ends. He is buried in a tomb within the Temple of the Inscriptions in Palenque.

jade death mask of Lord Pacal

Bonampak mural

AD790 Splendid Maya wall-paintings are created in the royal palace in the city of Bonampak.

AD600   AD700   AD800

The Rise and Fall of Empires

MESOAMERICA IS A LAND of contrasts. There are high, jagged mountains, harsh deserts and swampy lakes. In the north, volcanoes rumble. In the south, dense, steamy forests have constant rain for half the year. These features made travelling around difficult, and also restricted contact between the regions.

Mesoamerica was never ruled as a single, united country. For centuries it was divided into separate states, each based on a city that ruled the surrounding countryside. Different groups of people and their cities became rich and strong in turn, before their civilizations weakened and faded away.

Historians divide the Mesoamerican past into three main periods. In Preclassic times (2000BC–AD250), the Olmecs were most powerful. The Classic era (AD250–900) saw the rise of the Maya and the people living in the city of Teotihuacan. During the Postclassic era (AD900–1500), the Toltecs, followed by the Aztecs, controlled the strongest states.

Each civilization had its own language, laws, traditions and skills, but there were also many links between the separate states. They all built big cities and organized long-distance trade. They all practised human sacrifice and worshipped the same family of gods. And, unlike all other ancient American people, they all measured time using their own holy calendar of 260 days.

Sierra Madre Occidental

MEXICO

N

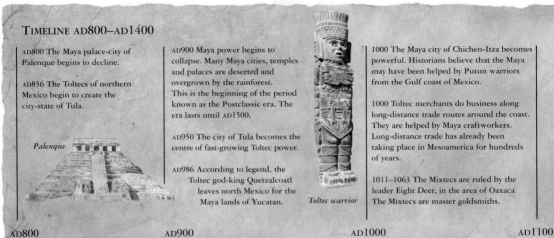

TIMELINE AD800–AD1400

AD800 The Maya palace-city of Palenque begins to decline.

AD856 The Toltecs of northern Mexico begin to create the city-state of Tula.

Palenque

AD900 Maya power begins to collapse. Many Maya cities, temples and palaces are deserted and overgrown by the rainforest. This is the beginning of the period known as the Postclassic era. The era lasts until AD1500.

AD950 The city of Tula becomes the centre of fast-growing Toltec power.

AD986 According to legend, the Toltec god-king Quetzalcoatl leaves north Mexico for the Maya lands of Yucatan.

Toltec warrior

1000 The Maya city of Chichen-Itza becomes powerful. Historians believe that the Maya may have been helped by Putun warriors from the Gulf coast of Mexico.

1000 Toltec merchants do business along long-distance trade routes around the coast. They are helped by Maya craftworkers. Long-distance trade has already been taking place in Mesoamerica for hundreds of years.

1011–1063 The Mixtecs are ruled by the leader Eight Deer, in the area of Oaxaca. The Mixtecs are master goldsmiths.

AD800   AD900   AD1000   AD1100

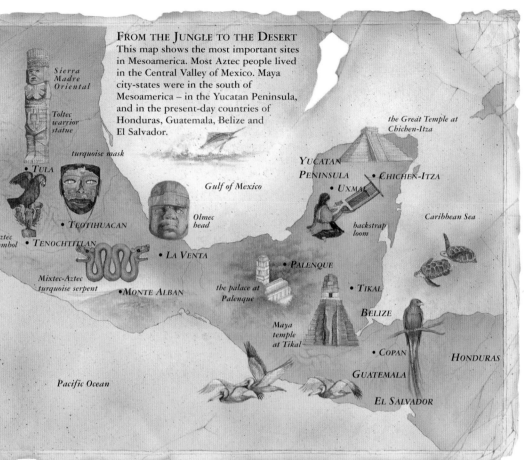

FROM THE JUNGLE TO THE DESERT

This map shows the most important sites in Mesoamerica. Most Aztec people lived in the Central Valley of Mexico. Maya city-states were in the south of Mesoamerica – in the Yucatan Peninsula, and in the present-day countries of Honduras, Guatemala, Belize and El Salvador.

Sierra Madre Oriental

Toltec warrior statue

turquoise mask

• TULA

• TEOTIHUACAN

Aztec symbol

• TENOCHTITLAN

Mixtec-Aztec turquoise serpent

Olmec head

• LA VENTA

•MONTE ALBAN

Gulf of Mexico

the Great Temple at Chichen-Itza

YUCATAN PENINSULA

• CHICHEN-ITZA

• UXMAL

backstrap loom

Caribbean Sea

• PALENQUE

the palace at Palenque

• TIKAL

BELIZE

Maya temple at Tikal

• COPAN

HONDURAS

GUATEMALA

EL SALVADOR

Pacific Ocean

1100 Aztecs leave their homeland in the dry, semi-desert land to the north of Mexico and travel southwards in search of a new place to live.

Aztec settlers

1168 The Chichimec people from central Mexico destroy the city of Tula and end Toltec power.

Aztec warrior

*c.*1200 Aztecs arrive in central Mexico. They find Tepanecs, Culhuas and Acolhuacans living there. At first, the Aztecs work as soldiers and slaves for these people, but they grow strong and fight against their masters.

*c.*1220 A new Maya city is founded at Mayapan.

1300 The Mixtec civilization begins to thrive in Oaxaca, southern Mexico.

1325 Aztecs found the city of Tenochtitlan on an island in the centre of Lake Texcoco, central Mexico.

1350 Aztecs begin to build *chinampas* (gardens) around Lake Texcoco.

1372–91 The first-known Aztec ruler, Acamapichtli, reigns.

eagle on cactus, the symbol of Tenochtitlan

AD1200

AD1300

AD1400

Mesoamerican History Makers

FAME IN MAYA AND AZTEC times usually came with power. We know the names of powerful Aztec and Maya rulers, and sometimes of their wives. However, very few ordinary people's names have been discovered.

Rulers' names were written in a codex (book) or carved on a monument to record success in battle or other great achievements. Scribes also compiled family histories, in which rulers often claimed to be descended from gods. This gave them extra religious power. Aztec and Maya rulers made sure their names lived on by building huge palaces, amazing temples and tombs.

Some of the most well-known Mesoamerican rulers lived at a time when their civilization was under threat from outsiders. Explorers from Europe have left us detailed accounts and descriptions of the rulers they met.

MAYA RULER
This statue shows a ruler from the Maya city of Kabah, in Mexico. Most Maya statues were designed as symbols of power, rather than as life-like portraits.

ROYAL TOMB
This pyramid-shaped temple was built to house the tomb of Lord Pacal. He ruled the Maya city-state of Palenque from AD615 to 684. Its walls are decorated with scenes from Pacal's life.

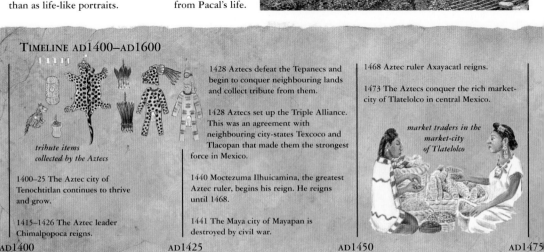

TIMELINE AD1400–AD1600

tribute items collected by the Aztecs

1400–25 The Aztec city of Tenochtitlan continues to thrive and grow.

1415–1426 The Aztec leader Chimalpopoca reigns.

1428 Aztecs defeat the Tepanecs and begin to conquer neighbouring lands and collect tribute from them.

1428 Aztecs set up the Triple Alliance. This was an agreement with neighbouring city-states Texcoco and Tlacopan that made them the strongest force in Mexico.

1440 Moctezuma Ilhuicamina, the greatest Aztec ruler, begins his reign. He reigns until 1468.

1441 The Maya city of Mayapan is destroyed by civil war.

1468 Aztec ruler Axayacatl reigns.

1473 The Aztecs conquer the rich market-city of Tlatelolco in central Mexico.

market traders in the market-city of Tlatelolco

AD1400   AD1425   AD1450   AD1475

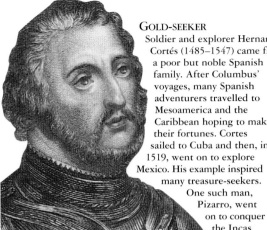

GOLD-SEEKER

Soldier and explorer Hernando Cortés (1485–1547) came from a poor but noble Spanish family. After Columbus' voyages, many Spanish adventurers travelled to Mesoamerica and the Caribbean hoping to make their fortunes. Cortes sailed to Cuba and then, in 1519, went on to explore Mexico. His example inspired many treasure-seekers. One such man, Pizarro, went on to conquer the Incas of Peru.

BETWEEN TWO WORLDS

Malintzin (far right above) was from a Mesoamerican state hostile to the Aztecs. She was of vital help to the Spanish conquerors because she spoke the Aztec language and quickly learned Spanish. The Spanish called her Doña Marina.

THE LAST EMPEROR

Aztec emperor Moctezuma II (above right) ruled from 1502 to 1520. He was the last emperor to control the Aztec lands. Moctezuma II was a powerful warrior and a good administrator, but he was tormented by gloomy prophecies and visions of disaster. He was captured when Cortés and his soldiers invaded the capital city of Tenochtitlan in 1519. The following year he was stoned in a riot whilst trying to plead with his own people.

1481–1486 Aztec ruler Tizoc reigns.

1486 Aztec ruler Ahuitzotl begins his reign.

1487 The Aztecs' Great Temple in Tenochtitlan is finished. Twenty thousand captives are sacrificed at a special ceremony to consecrate it (make it holy).

1492 The European explorer Christopher Columbus sails across the Atlantic Ocean to America.

Columbus lands

1502 Columbus sails along the coast of Mesoamerica and meets Maya people.

a comet appears in the sky

1502–1520 Moctezuma II reigns. During his reign, a comet appears in the sky. Aztec astronomers fear that this, and other strange signs, mean the end of the world.

1519 Hernando Cortés, a Spanish soldier, arrives in Mexico. A year later, Cortés and his soldiers attack Tenochtitlan. Moctezuma II is killed.

1521 The Spanish destroy Tenochtitlan.

1525 Spain takes control of Aztec lands.

1527 Maya lands are invaded by the Spanish.

1535 Mexico becomes a Spanish colony.

1600 War and European diseases wipe out 10 million Aztecs, leaving fewer than a million, but the Aztec language and many customs live on. By 1600, between 75% and 90% of Maya people are also dead, but Maya skills, beliefs and traditions survive.

Spanish soldier

AD1500   AD1525   AD1600

The First North Americans

DESCENDANTS OF THE ANASAZIS, who were among the earliest known North American Indians, have colourful tales of their origins. One story tells how their ancestors climbed into the world through a hole. Another describes how all of the tribes were created from a fierce monster who was ripped apart by a brave coyote. The early history of the many nations or tribes is not clear, though archaeological finds have helped to build a picture of their way of life. If you could step back to before 1500, you would find that the United States and Canada were home to hundreds of different Indian tribes. Each had its own leader(s) and a distinctive language and culture. Some tribes were nomadic, some settled permanently in large communities. Remains of pottery, woodcarvings and jewellery show how many of the North American peoples developed expert craft skills.

KEEPING THE PAST ALIVE
Descendants of the different tribes survive throughout North America, passing down stories and traditions to new generations. This boy in Wyoming is dressed in ceremonial costume for a modern powwow. He is helping to preserve his tribe's cultural history.

BRIDGING THE GAP
Archaeological evidence suggests that the first American Indians travelled from Asia. They crossed ice and land bridges formed at the Bering Strait around 13,000BC or earlier. From here, they moved south, some settling along the coasts.

TIMELINE 32,000BC–AD1400

Most historians believe that hunters walked to North America from Siberia. Evidence suggests there may have been two migrations – one around 32,000BC, the second between 28,000BC and 13,000BC. Some historians think there may have been earlier ancient populations already living there. More research is needed to support this theory. The hunters spread out, each group, or tribe, adapting their way of life to suit their environment. Later, some gave up the nomadic hunting life and began to settle as farmers.

serpent mound of the Hopewell culture

3000BC Inuit of the Arctic are probably the last settlers to come from Asia.

1000BC Early cultures are mound builders such as the Adena and later, the Hopewell people. The Hopewell are named after the farmer on whose Ohio land their main site was found.

1000BC Farming cultures develop in the South-west with agricultural skills brought in from Mexico.

black and yellow maize

AD200 (or before) There is evidence of maize being grown by the mound-building people, probably introduced from Mexico.

300BC–AD1450 Cultures, such as the Hohokam, use shells as currency.

AD700–900 Pueblo people bury their dead with black and white painted pots.

burial pot

3000BC

300BC

FALSE FACE

Dramatic, carved masks were worn by several tribes to ward off evil spirits thought to cause illnesses. This one is from the Iroquois people. It was known as a False Face mask because it shows an imaginary face. False Face ceremonies are still performed in North America today.

BUCKSKIN RECORD

Tales of events were painted on animal skins, such as this one, created by an Apache. The skins serve as a form of history book. North American Indians had no real written alphabet, so much of the evidence about their way of life comes from pictures.

DIGGING UP EVIDENCE

Hopewell Indians made this bird from hammered copper. It dates back to around 300BC and was uncovered in a burial mound in Ohio. The mounds were full of intricate trinkets buried alongside the dead. Finds like this tell us about the crafts, materials and customs of the time.

ANCIENT TOWN

Acoma (right) is one of the oldest continuously inhabited traditional Pueblo settlements in the South-west. It is still partly inhabited by Pueblo descendants. The Pueblo people were given their name by Spaniards who arrived in the area in 1540. *Pueblo* is a Spanish word meaning village. It was used to describe the kind of tribe that lived in a cluster of houses built from mud and stone. Flat-roofed homes were built in terraces, two or three storeys high.

AD700 Mound-building cultures build temples at Cahokia near the Mississippi. The city holds the largest population in North America before the 1800s.

AD900 Earliest Anasazis (ancient people) on the Colorado Plateau live in sunken pit homes. Later they build their homes above the ground but keep pit dwellings as kivas, which are their religious buildings.

kiva (underground temple) of the Anasazis

AD982 First Europeans reach Greenland (north-east of Canada) under the Viking, Eirik the Red.

1002 Leif Eiriksson lands in Newfoundland, Canada, and creates the first European settlements.

Vikings arrive

1100 The Anasazi people move into the mountains, building settlements in cliffs.

Mesa Verde, a cliff palace

1200 The Calusa in Florida are skilful carvers and craftsmen who trade extensively.

1270s–1300 Anasazis abandon many of their prehistoric sites and stone cities – many move eastwards.

1300 Beginnings of the Pueblo tribes (Hopi and Zuni) in the South-west. Many of these are descendants of the Anasazis.

AD1400

Inhabiting a Vast Land

THE FIRST NORTH AMERICANS were hunters who followed musk oxen, bison and other animals to the grassland interior of the huge continent. Early settlements grew up in the rugged, hostile terrain of the South-west where three dominant cultures evolved. The Mogollon (Mountain People) are thought to be the first South-west dwellers to build houses, make pottery and grow their own food from around 300BC. The Hohokam (Vanished Ones) devised an extensive canal system to irrigate the desert as early as 100BC, while the Anasazi (Ancient Ones) were basket makers who built their homes high among the cliffs and canyons.

orca (killer whale)

In contrast, the eastern and midwestern lands abounded with plant and animal life. Here, tribes such as the Adena (1000BC to AD200) and the Hopewell (300BC to AD700), created huge earth mounds to bury their dead. The central Great Plains was home to over 30 different tribes, who lived by hunting bison. In the far north, the Inuit had a similar existence, relying on caribou and seals for their food and clothes. Europeans began to arrive around AD982 with the Vikings. Then in the 1500s, Spanish explorers came looking for gold, land and slaves. Over the next 400 years, many other foreign powers laid claim to different parts of the land. By 1910, the native population was at its lowest, about 400,000, and many tribes had been forced from their homelands on to reservations.

TRIBAL HOMELANDS

In the 1400s, there were more than 300 tribes, or nations, spread across North America (between two and three million people). These are often divided into ten cultural areas based on the local environment:
1 Arctic
2 Subarctic
3 Woodlands
4 South-east
5 Great Plains
6 South-west
7 Great Basin
8 Plateau
9 North-west Coast
10 California

TIMELINE AD1400–1780

Columbus

1400 Apaches arrive in the South-west, probably by two routes – one from the Plains after following migrating buffalo, the other via the Rockies.

1492 Christopher Columbus sails from Spain to the Bahamas where he meets the peaceful, farming Arawaks.

1510 The powerful Calusas of Florida abandon their ancient centre, Key Marco, possibly after hearing of foreign invaders.

1513 Calusas drive off Ponce de León, a Spanish explorer.

1541 Zuni people get a first glimpse of horses when Spain's Francisco Vasquez de Coronado travels to the South-west.

1541 Caddo people of the Plains oppose Spanish Hernando de Soto's soldiers.

1542 The large Arawak population that Columbus first encountered has been reduced to just 200 people. Ten years later the Arawaks die out through mistreatment.

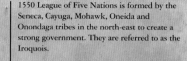

shell wampum belt celebrates the League of Five Nations

1550 League of Five Nations is formed by the Seneca, Cayuga, Mohawk, Oneida and Onondaga tribes in the north-east to create a strong government. They are referred to as the Iroquois.

1585 Sir Walter Raleigh reaches the north-east coast and, ignoring the rights of the Secotan natives, claims the land for the English, calling it Virginia.

1590 Raleigh and John White return to Virginia, but the colony has disappeared. White draws pictures documenting Secotan life.

AD1400   AD1540   AD1550   AD1595

BAFFIN
ISLAND

seal

NEWFOUNDLAND

1

Hudson Bay

Inuit with igloo

*Inuit
fisherman*

2

Cree

QUEBEC

Chipewyan canoe

Cree

Plains Cree

Blackfoot   Hidatsa

Plains Ojibwa

Mandan

Ojibwa

Algonquin

Huron

beaver

Tsimshian

9

8   *salmon*

Crow

Western Sioux

Pawnee

maize

Sioux

Chippewa

Menominee

3   New York

Iroquois

Algonquian
groups

Washington

Nootka

Nez Perce

Shoshone

Arapaho

Powhatan

N

Salish

Ute

Washoe

Cayuse

Yurok

10   Paiute
basket-make

*Cheyenne warrior
hunting bison*

Hopewell mound

Secotan
village

Hopi
katchina
doll

Osage

Cherokee
village of Echota

Chickasaw

Choctaw   Creek

Chumash

Navajo
hogans

NEW
MEXICO

5   Wichita

Comanche

4

Natchez   Seminole

eagle

Los Angeles   Mohave

Apache

TEXAS

Catawba

Miami

6

Pueblo village

Missouri River

Mississippi River

Kiowa camp

1598 Juan de Onate founds the first
Spanish colony on Pueblo Indian land.

1600s Shoshone acquire
horses from the South-
west (brought there
by Spanish
invaders) and they
spread across the
Great Plains.

horses on the Plains

1607 Jamestown colony is founded on
Powhatan land.

1607 Pamunkey members of the Powhatan
Confederacy take John Smith prisoner.

1620 The
Mayflower
Pilgrims
arrive on the
east coast and are
helped by the
Wampanoag.

1650 Guns from European
traders (at first flintlocks,
later rifles) begin to take the
place of traditional weapons.

1707 A Russian expedition
reaches North-west Coast to
discover that it is inhabited.

willow bow

*coup
stick*

rifle

1722 League of Five
Nations increases to six when the
Tuscarora join the group.

1750 Sioux tribes move to the Plains.

1774 Juan Perez sails to the North-
west Coast and takes it for Spain.
European diseases almost wipe
out the Haida people.

1771 Five missions are set up
on Chumash land, California to
try to convert North Americans to
Christianity (this leads to a revolt
in 1824).

Haida totem pole

AD1620   AD1710

INHABITING A VAST LAND 73

Shapers of History

MANY NORTH AMERICAN Indians who have earned a place in history lived around the time that Europeans reached North America. They became famous for their dealings with explorers and with the white settlers who were trying to reorganize the lives of Indian nations. Some tribes welcomed the new settlers. Others tried to negotiate peacefully for rights to their own land. Those who led their people in battles, against the settlers, became the most legendary. One of these was Geronimo, who led the last defiant group of Chiricahua Apaches in their fight to preserve the tribe's homeland and culture.

POCAHONTAS (1595–1617)
The princess became a legend, and the topic of a Disney film, for protecting English Captain John Smith against her father, Chief Powhatan. The English took Pocahontas captive to force Powhatan's people to agree to their demands. She married John Rolfe, an English soldier, and in 1616 left for England with their baby. She never returned, as she died of smallpox, in Gravesend, Kent, aged 22.

CORNPLANTER (died 1796)
In the 1700s, Cornplanter was a chief of the Iroquois. He was a friend to the Americans and fought on their side in the Revolution of 1776–85. The land of Cornplanter's tribe was spoiled but his people were given a reservation for their help. Many Iroquois people fought on the side of the British which split the group.

Opechancanough, Powhatan

Black Hawk, Sauk

Geronimo, Apache

Pontiac, Ottawa

Lapowinsa, Lenape

TIMELINE AD1780–1924

1783 The colonists (settlers) sign a treaty with Britian which recognizes their independence and calls them Americans. The tribes are never regarded as American.

1788 The Chinook in the North-west have their first encounter with Europeans when they meet Englishman John Mears.

1789 Explorers encounter Kutchin and other Subarctic tribes, who later set up trade with the Hudson's Bay Company (formed in 1831).

1795 Tecumseh refuses to sign the Treaty of Greenville giving up Shawnee land.

William Clark and Meriwether Lewis

1803 The US federal government buys Mississippi land from the French, squeezing out the Indians even more.

1804 Sacawagea guides Lewis and Clark on the first overland journey from Mississippi to the Pacific Coast.

1830–40s Painters such as Frederic Remington, George Catlin and Karl Bodmer, document lifestyles of the Plains Indians.

1832 Sauk chief, Black Hawk, leads a final revolt against the US and is defeated.

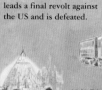

George Catlin painting a Mandan chief

1848 Discovery of gold in California.

coming of the train

1848–58 Palouse tribe of the Plateau resist white domination, refusing to join a reservation.

AD1780   AD1803   AD1848

TECUMSEH (died 1813)

A great chief of the Shawnees, Tecumseh, tried to unite tribes of the Mississippi valley, Old North-west and South against the United States. He even fought for the British against the US in the 1812–14 war. The picture shows his death.

SARAH WINNEMUCCA (1844–1891)

Sarah was from the Paviotso Paiutes of northern Nevada. Her grandfather escorted British Captain John Fremont in his exploration of the West in the 1840s. But in 1860 her mother, sister and brother were all killed in the Paiute War against white settlers. Sarah acted as a mediator between her people and the settlers to help improve conditions. She later wrote a book, Life Among the Paiutes, telling of the suffering of the tribe and her own life.

SITTING BULL (1831–1890)

The Hunkpapa Sioux had a spiritual leader, a medicine man known as Sitting Bull. He brought together sub-tribes of the Sioux and refused to sign treaties giving up the sacred Black Hills in South Dakota. He helped to defeat General Custer at Little Bighorn.

Oscelo, Seminole

Red Cloud, Sioux

Chief Joseph

PROTECTING THEIR TRIBES

These eight North American chiefs are some of the most famous. Not all fought. Lapowinsa of Delaware, was cheated out of land when he signed a contract allowing settlers as much land as they could cover in a day and a half. Pontiac traded with the French but despised English intrusion. Chief Joseph tried to negotiate peacefully for land for the Nez Perce tribe but died in exile. Red Cloud successfully fought to stop gold seekers invading Sioux hunting grounds.

1850 The Navajo sign their third treaty with the US but hostilities continue.

1850s–80s Railways open up the West to settlers.

1864 The Long Walk – Navajo people and animals are massacred by US troops, their homes burned. Survivors are forced to walk 500km to Fort Sumner.

1864 Sand Creek Massacre – 300 Cheyenne women and children are killed by US soldiers.

Sand Creek Massacre

1876 General Custer is killed by Sioux warriors in the Battle of Little Bighorn.

1886 Surrender of Geronimo to the US. He is a prisoner for many years.

1890 Ghost dance springs up as Sioux tribes mourn their dead – it worries the white settlers who see it as provocation.

1890 Sitting Bull is killed at Standing Rock (a Sioux reservation) by Indian police hired by the US.

1890 Sioux chief Big Foot and many of his tribe are killed in the Massacre of Wounded Knee. This ends the Sioux's struggle for their homelands.

buffalo coin

1924 US citizenship granted to American Indians and marked by a coin bearing a buffalo.

ghost dance shirt

AD1870

AD1924

Gods, Beliefs & Ceremonies

Questions of life and death have inspired humans to call upon a colourful pageant of gods, myths and legends, produce extraordinary art, and enact weird and wonderful rituals. Travel through time and across the world to trace myths of creation, destruction and the afterlife – from the mummies of ancient Egypt to the sky spirits of the native North Americans.

Religion, Ritual and Myth

Throughout the world, in different centuries, people have expressed their religious beliefs through prayers, ceremonies, offerings, festivals, drama, music and dancing. We do not know precisely what the ancestors of modern humans thought or felt. However, archaeologists have found evidence of burial rituals dating from more than half a million years ago. Sites discovered in France and the Zagros Mountains in Iran show carefully buried bodies with animal horns and bones around them. If people took the trouble to honour the remains of the dead, they may have believed that a person's spirit lived on, in this world or another one, after their body had decayed. People who hunted for food painted pictures of animals they wanted to find. The paintings may have been for decoration. Some experts believe that they may have been a way in which people tried to contact powerful spirits from the natural world.

Prehistoric goddess figurines may have been worshipped as symbols of fertility by early Stone Age people.

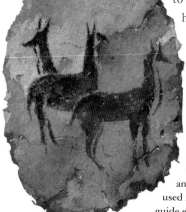

It is now believed that cave paintings of animals may have been used in magic ceremonies to guide early hunters or promote fertility.

Rituals and human activities such as art, magic, myth and ceremonies provide clues to past beliefs. They show us that people gradually developed more complex ways of

Timeline 500,000–2000bc

*c.*500,000bc Early humans living in China perform rituals using the skulls of dead people. This suggests that they either honour the dead person's spirit or fear it.

*c.*75,000bc People in the Middle East start burying some of their dead. They may have believed that a person's spirit lived on, in this world or another one, after their body had decayed.

*c.*30,000bc Cave-paintings in Europe show men and women living as hunter-gatherers trying to make contact with powerful spirits from the natural world, to guide and protect them.

*c.*10,000bc People migrate to live in all parts of North and South America. Over the centuries, Native Americans develop many

Animal cave painting

religious beliefs. Some are shared among them all, such as reverence for the natural world, and belief in shamans – magic healers who can communicate with the spirit world. Others relate to each peoples' own lifestyle and homeland.

Shamanic mask worn for special rituals

500,000bc   30,000bc   10,000bc   9000bc

explaining the world around them. Many rituals were linked to key stages in peoples' lives, such as birth, death, becoming an adult or important community events. When people began to farm and live in settled villages, from around 8000BC, religion reflected a close relationship with the plants and the seasons. The Aztecs of Mexico, the Celts of Europe and the Incas of Peru made objects of goddesses who symbolized fertility. Offerings were made to "mother earth" in the hope that in return, divine help would be given to ensure successful crops. Chinese customs encouraged hard work, order and respect on earth as this created a harmony between heaven, earth and human beings.

The Inca earth goddess, shown on this gold plate, played an important role in the beliefs of farming peoples, living in the windswept Andes mountains.

Religions bind societies together. Many settlements grew into market towns, dependent on trade and craftwork and often became centres of religion, too. In Egypt, Greece and Aztec Mexico, cities were homes to priests and scribes, who guarded religious knowledge and contained splendid temples for worshipping gods. Festivals in India, China and South America, were opportunities for people to celebrate the gods and natural events, such as the coming of spring or the harvest. As societies grew, people began to ask questions about what religion meant to them personally. What is the meaning of life? Why does

During Egyptian ceremonies, priests had to pour sacred water over offerings made to the gods to purify them.

*c.*8000BC People begin to live in settled farming villages. New religious beliefs develop, based on the close relationship between farmers, the land, growing plants and the seasons.

*c.*5000BC People begin to live in towns. They build splendid temples for their gods, and to pay for

Stonehenge, a prehistoric stone circle, may have been used for worship

priests to say prayers and make sacrifices (offerings) on the community's behalf.

*c.*3100–30BC The ancient Egyptians worship many gods and goddesses, build magnificent temples, and preserve dead bodies by mummification, so that their spirit will live on after death.

*c.*2300–500BC The civilizations of Akkad, Sumer, Babylon and Assyria flourish in Mesopotamia (Iraq). Their people worship gods of the sun and moon, and special gods and goddesses who protected their cities and kings.

Sun worshipper

8000BC   5000BC   3000BC   2000BC

suffering exist? What happens after death? Does God exist?

Many religions had human versions of their gods on earth. The pharaohs of Egypt and the emperors of China were worshipped as gods. In tribal North America, shamans (healers) had the most important role in the community because they communicated with the spiritual world, thought to control people's daily lives.

In the ancient world, many – rather than one – gods were worshipped. Around 600BC, religious leaders appeared in several regions of the world including the Buddha in India and Zoroaster in Persia (Iran). Leaders taught that fulfilment lay beyond this world, in heaven, or in seeking unity with a single God.

People at Holi, the Hindu spring festival, throw coloured powders over each other.

Philosophers (thinkers), such as Plato in ancient Greece and Confucius in China, began to discuss with their followers the best way to live. Collections of holy scriptures, such as the Hindu Upanishads from India and the Jewish Bible (Torah), were written down to guide believers. This tradition was continued in the 1st century AD by the followers of Jesus of Nazareth (Christians) and, in the 7th century AD by the prophet Mohammed from Arabia. Mohammed taught Muslims to follow the Quran, a holy text that was believed to be the actual word of God.

Confucius lived at a time of great change in China. He taught people to respect their elders and to work hard.

TIMELINE 1600BC–AD1500

c.1600–1122BC The Shang dynasty rules China. People honour the spirits of dead ancestors, and make offerings. They foretell the future by consulting oracle bones.

c.1200–600BC The earliest Hindu holy texts, called

Chinese fireworks

Vedas, are written in Sanskrit, the language of the Aryan people who migrate to India at this time.

c.800BC–AD100 The Celts are powerful in Europe. They honour nature gods, and make human sacrifices to them. They believe in magic, and are guided by learned priests, called druids.

c.604BC Birth of Laozi, religious teacher who founded the Daoist religion in China.

c.600–200BC Peak of ancient Greek civilization. The Greeks honour a family of 12 gods, who live on Mount Olympus, and resemble human beings, but possess great powers.

c.563–483BC Life of Indian religious leader Siddartha Gautama, known as "Buddha" (the enlightened one). After his death, his teachings spread to many parts of Asia.

c.551–479BC Life of Confucius, moral and ethical teacher in China.

1600BC   800BC   600BC   500BC

This section explores the main religious beliefs from around the world. It starts with the earliest evidence of ceremonies and rituals, and moves through time to see how religions developed in different ways from land to land. The religions of ancient Egypt, Greece and Rome, the Inca, Maya and Aztec peoples of Central and South America, with their many gods, have disappeared with the civilizations that created them. But some ancient tribal beliefs and ceremonies survive to this day in parts of Africa, the Americas, Australia and Asia.

The Celts worshipped their various gods in the form of sculpted images. This clenched-fisted bearded god appears on a large metal bowl.

You will be able to see how religious beliefs have played an important role in everyday life through the ages. You will be able to compare the ways in which people expressed their faith and depicted their gods – in paintings, music and festivals, legends, and traditions that can still be seen today. Most of all, you will have a sense of the rich and varied ways in which people have tried to explain the existence of good and evil, and the reasons for life and death.

The Egyptian pyramids remain a legacy to some of the great beliefs of the past. The Egyptians believed their pharaohs were gods who lived after their bodies had died. They built the pyramids to safeguard their bodies and buried them with their treasures to be used in the afterlife.

*c.*500BC–300AD Roman power spreads in Europe. The Romans worship most Greek gods, but give them Roman names, and also family gods of their own.

Shiva, the Hindu god of creation and destruction AD200 Hinduism is widespread in India. Hindus honour one of two gods, Vishnu or Shiva, as lord of creation.

AD570–632 Life of the Prophet Mohammed, who founded the faith of Islam. This spread from Arabia and is one of the leading world religions.

*c.*AD700–1100 The Vikings are powerful in Europe. They worship many gods and heroes, and their rich collection of myths and legends explains how the world was created and how it will end.

*c.*AD960 Christianity starts to spread through the Viking lands.

1469–1539 Life of Guru Nanak, founder of the Sikh religion in India.

1487 Aztecs sacrifice 20,000 captives to consecrate (make holy) the great new temple in their capital city, Tenochtitlan.

Aztec blood sacrifices

AD200   AD500   1400   1500

Stone Age Beliefs

WE CAN ONLY GUESS at the beliefs of Stone Age people, the earliest ancestors to modern humans. These were the Neanderthal people who lived from 120,000 to 33,000 years ago in Europe and Asia. There is evidence that they were burying their dead, which suggests that they believed in a spirit world. They probably worshipped the spirits of the animals they hunted and other natural things. They made paintings and engravings on rocks and in caves, which may have a magical or religious purpose.

ANCIENT BURIAL
The skull of the skeleton from this burial found in France has been scattered with red ochre earth. Red may have represented blood or life for Stone Age people. Bodies were often buried on their sides, with their knees pulled up to their chins. Tools, ornaments, food and weapons were put in the graves. Later Stone Age people built elaborate tombs for their dead.

Stone Age people probably thought illnesses and accidents were caused by evil spirits. It may have been the job of a shaman (witch doctor), to speak to the spirits and interpret what should be done.

As farming spread and settlements grew into towns, more organized religions began. Shrines decorated with religious pictures have been found at Çatal Hüyük in Turkey, the site of a well-preserved town dating from around 7000BC.

RITUAL ANTLERS
These antlers are from a red stag and were found at Star Carr in England. Some experts think that antlers were worn by a kind of priest called a shaman, perhaps in a coming-of-age ceremony or to bring good luck in that season's hunt.

CLAY GODDESS
This female figure is made from clay and was found at Pazardzik in Bulgaria. Many prehistoric societies worshipped images of the Earth Goddess, or Great Mother. As the mother of the world, she gave life to plants, animals and humans, and so ensured the future of the human race.

TREPANNING

Cutting a hole in a person's head is called trepanning. It was practised in prehistoric times from about 5000BC. A sharp flint tool was used to cut a hole in the skull in order to let illness escape from the body. Several skulls have been found that show the hole starting to close – evidence that some patients even survived the blood-curdling procedure!

SPELLS AND POTIONS

In many hunter-gatherer societies today, a shaman (witch doctor) can speak with the spirits from the world of the dead. In cultures such as that of the Amazonian Indians, shamen also administer potions from plants to cure illness. They use plants such as quinine, coca and curare. Stone Age people probably behaved in a similar way. There is evidence that neolithic farmers in north-western Europe grew poppies and hemp, possibly for use in magic potions and rituals.

poppy

ANCESTOR WORSHIP

Before the people of Jericho in the Near East buried their dead, they removed the skulls. This skull found in Jericho dates from about 6500BC. These were covered with plaster and painted to look like the features of the dead person. Cowrie shells were used for eyes. Some experts believe that this was done as a form of ancestor worship.

RITUAL DANCE

A modern painting shows a traditional Australian Aboriginal dance. Traditional ceremonies are an important part of Aboriginal life. Evidence of them has been found on prehistoric sites in Australia. Aboriginal beliefs are designed to maintain the delicate balance between people and their environment.

City Gods of Mesopotamia

As SETTLEMENTS GREW INTO TOWNS AND CITIES, religious rituals became more complex. Some of the first cities in the world developed in Mesopotamia, most of which is now modern-day Iraq. Each city had it's own guardian god and temples were built especially for that god. There were often temples dedicated to members of the god's family, too. The Sumerians, Assyrians, Babylonians and Akkadian-speaking peoples who lived in Mesopotamia worshipped the same gods and goddesses, but had different names for them. The Sumerians called the Moon-god Nanna, but in Akkadian his name was Sin. The chief Sumerian god was called Enlil, who was often also referred to as King, Supreme Lord, Father, or Creator. According to one Sumerian poem, no one was allowed to look at Enlil, not even the other gods. The Sumerian kings believed that they had been chosen by Enlil.

The god's chief sanctuary was at the city of Nippur. Legends tell that when the Nippur temple was raided by the army of the King of Agade, Enlil was so angry that he caused the Agade dynasty to end.

POWERFUL GODDESS
This statue of a goddess was found in pieces at the palace of Mari on the River Euphrates. Two goddesses like her, pouring water from vases, were part of a scene on the palace courtyard walls. The painting showed a king being invested with royal power by Ishtar, the goddess of love and war.

BEFORE THE GOD
A scene on a 4000-year-old seal shows an official called Lamabazi being led into the presence of a great god by a lesser god. The great god is sitting on the throne, and before him is a brazier for burning incense. Lamabazi is holding his hand in front of his face as a sign of respect for the god.

IN THE BEGINNING
Marduk was the god of Babylon. He is shown here standing on his mushushshu (snake dragon). In the *Epic of Creation*, a Babylonian story about how Marduk created the world, he fought against a female monster, Tiamat, and her son, Kingu. After Marduk had killed them, the other gods made him their king. Marduk then brought the rest of creation into existence. He made models of human beings by mixing some clay with the blood of Kingu and then brought them to life.

CLUES TO IDENTITY

Most of our ideas about what the Mesopotamian gods and goddesses looked like come from their pictures on cylinder seals. This one shows Ishtar, the goddess of love and war, carrying her weapons. She is accompanied by a lion, which was her sacred animal. Shamash, the sun god, is recognizable by the flames coming from him, as he rises between two mountains. Ea the water god, has streams of water gushing from his shoulders.

FERTILE MIND

Nisaba was originally a goddess of fertility and agriculture, although she later became the goddess of writing. Good harvests were very important to the people of Mesopotamia, and almost everyone ate barley bread and dates. This carving of Nisaba shows her covered with plants. She is wearing an elaborate headdress composed of a horned crown and ears of barley. Flowers sprout from her shoulders, and she is holding a bunch of dates.

GOD OF ASSYRIA

Ashur was the chief god of the Assyrians. It was thought that he was the god who chose the Assyrian kings and went before them into battle. He is often symbolized by the same horned cap as Enlil, the chief Sumerian god. Sometimes he is shown standing on a winged bull or on a mushushshu (snake dragon) like Marduk, the god of Babylon. Both gods were honoured in New Year festivals when their priests slapped the reigning king's face, pulled his ears and made him bow low. The king then said he had served his people properly and was re-crowned for another year.

Bible Links to Mesopotamia

Floods

A tale like the Old Testament story of Noah's Ark was found in the library at Nineveh. King Utnapishtim was warned that the god Enlil was going to send a flood and was told to make a boat and take his family, all the animals and craftsworkers on board. It rained for seven days and seven nights. When it stopped, the king sent out birds to see if the water had gone down. The goddess Ishtar put her necklace in the sky as a sign that this would never happen again.

WHILE THE MESOPOTAMIANS HAD MANY GODS, a faith based on one god developed among the Jews in the area. Many of the people, places and events in the Jewish holy scriptures (the Old Testament of the Bible) are also told in Mesopotamian history. Several laws and customs relating to marriage and adoption mentioned in the Old Testament are like those of Mesopotamia. Abraham, the father of the Israelite and Arab nations, lived in the Sumerian city of Ur before setting off for the Promised Land. The prophet Jonah was instructed by God to go to the Assyrian city of Nineveh, and the Jewish people were exiled from their Promised Land to Babylon. Assyrian records often include kings and events mentioned in the Old Testament.

One Assyrian king, Shalmaneser III, records his victory at the Battle of Qarqar in Syria. He says he fought against 12 kings, one of whom was Ahab of Israel. This is the first time a king of Israel appears in the history of another country.

Desert Journey

Abraham, the father of the Jewish and Arab nations, travels from the Sumerian city of Ur to the country God has promised his people. In this painting of the 1800s, Abraham is leading a wandering existence in a desert landscape with his flock of sheep moving from one area to another in search of grazing ground for his animals. However, there would have been no camels at the time he is thought to have lived, about 2000BC. They were not used for transport in Mesopotamia until about 1000BC.

BLACK OBELISK

The man bowing in front of the Assyrian king, Shalmaneser III, could be Jehu, King of Israel. Israel had been an enemy of Assyria, but Jehu has decided to change sides and become an ally of Assyria. The picture appears on the Black Obelisk, which tells of Shalmaneser III's conquests at war. The writing says that the gifts of the Israelite king are being presented to show his loyalty and win Shalmaneser's approval.

WAR CORRESPONDENTS

The Bible reports that the Assyrian king Sennacherib laid siege to Jerusalem when Hezekiah was king of Judah. It says he withdrew from the siege when an angel attacked his army. In Sennacherib's version of events on this clay prism (a hollow tablet), he does not say he was defeated or that he captured Jerusalem. All he says is that he shut Hezekiah up like a bird in a cage.

EXILE IN BABYLON

The great Babylonian king of the 500s BC was Nebuchadnezzar II who took over many parts of the ancient world that had formerly been part of the Assyrian Empire. In 597BC he attacked Jerusalem, the chief city of the kingdom of Judah, a scene imagined here by a medieval painter. At the end of a successful siege, he took the king, his courtiers, the army and all the craftworkers to Babylon. There they spent many years far from home, a time known among Jewish people as the Exile. Nebuchadnezzar took treasures from the temple in Jerusalem as booty. He appointed another king, Zedekiah, to rule in Jerusalem. Nebuchadnezzar returned some years later when Zedekiah rebelled and punished him severely.

Pharaoh Gods

THE ANCIENT EGYPTIANS believed that the ordered world in which they lived had been created out of chaos. They carried out rituals to prevent chaos and darkness from returning. The pharaohs were honoured as god-kings because it was believed the spirit of the gods lived in them. They looked after the everyday world for the gods. Over 2,000 gods were worshipped in ancient Egypt. Many gods were linked to a particular region. The mighty Amun was the god of Thebes. Some gods appeared as animals – Sebek the water god was a crocodile. Gods were also connected with jobs and interests. The hippopotamus goddess, Tawaret, looked after babies and childbirth.

Many ordinary Egyptians understood little about the religion of the court and nobles. They believed in magic, local spirits and superstitions.

HORUS
Horus the falcon god was the son of Isis. He was god of the sky and protector of the reigning pharaoh. The name Horus meant 'He who is far above'. Here he holds an *ankh*, the symbol of life. The holder of an *ankh* had the power to give life or take it away. Only pharaohs and gods were allowed to carry them.

LOTUS FLOWER
The lotus was a very important flower to the Egyptians. This sacred symbol was used to represent Upper Egypt.

THE GODDESS NUT
Nut, covered in stars, was goddess of the heavens. She is often shown with her body stretched across the sky. The Egyptians believed that Nut swallowed the Sun each evening and gave birth to it the next morning. She was married to the Earth god, Geb, and gave birth to the gods Isis and Osiris.

AMUN OF THEBES

Amun was originally the god of the city of Thebes. He later became popular throughout Egypt as the god of creation. By the time of the New Kingdom, Amun was combined with other powerful gods such as Ra, god of the Sun, and became known as Amun-Ra. He was believed to be the most powerful god of all. Amun is sometimes shown as a ram.

HOLY BEETLES

Scarabs are beetles that were sacred to the ancient Egyptians. Pottery or stone scarabs were used as lucky charms, seals, or as ring decorations. The base of these scarabs was often inscribed with stories telling of some great event.

OSIRIS, KING OF THE UNDERWORLD

The great god Osiris stands dressed as a king. He was one of the most important gods in ancient Egypt, the master of life and the spirit world. He was also the god of farming. Egyptian tales told how Osiris was murdered and cut into pieces by his brother Seth, the god of chaos. Anubis, the jackal-headed god of embalming, gathered the pieces together and his sister, Isis, brought Osiris back to life.

CAT MUMMIES

The Egyptians worshipped gods in the forms of animals from the Old Kingdom onwards. The cat goddess Bastet was said to be the daughter of the great Sun god, Ra. Cats were so holy to the Egyptians that at one time many of them were embalmed, wrapped in linen bandages and preserved as mummies. It is thought that bronze cat figures and these mummified cats were left as offerings to Bastet at her temple.

MIW THE CAT

Cats were holy animals in ancient Egypt. They even had their own god! The Egyptians' love of cats dated back to the early farmers who tamed cats to protect stores of grain from mice. Cats soon became popular pets. The Egyptian word for cat was *miw*, which was rather like a mew or miaow!

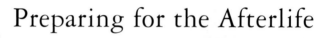

Preparing for the Afterlife

THE EGYPTIANS believed that the dead would need to use their bodies in the next life. They discovered that bodies buried in the desert were often preserved in the dry sand. The bodies dried out and became mummified. Over the ages, the Egyptians became experts at preserving bodies by embalming them.

The methods of mummification varied. The process usually took about 70 days. The brains were hooked out through the nose and the other organs were removed and placed in special jars. Only the heart was left so that it could be weighed in the next life. The body was embalmed by being dried out with salty crystals of natron. Afterwards it was stuffed and covered with oils and ointments and then wrapped in bandages. The mummy was then placed inside a series of coffins in the shape of the body.

MUMMY CASE
This beautiful gold case contains the mummy of a priestess. Once the embalmed body had been wrapped in bandages it was placed in a richly decorated coffin. Both the inside and outside would be covered in spells to help the dead person in the underworld. Sometimes more than one coffin was used. The inner coffins would be of brightly painted or gilded wood (*as left*) and the outer coffin would be a stone sarcophagus.

CANOPIC JARS
Special jars were used to store the body's organs. The human-headed jar held the liver. The baboon jar contained the lungs. The stomach was put in the jackal-headed jar and finally the guts were placed in the falcon-headed jar.

CANOPIC JARS

You will need: self-drying clay, rolling pin and board, ruler, modelling tool, sandpaper, masking tape, acrylic paint (white, blue, green, yellow, black), water pot and brush.

1 Roll out ³/₄ of the clay and cut out a circle about 7cm in diameter. This is the base of the jar. Now roll out thin strips of clay. Coil these from the base to make the sides.

2 Carefully press out the bumps between the coils until the sides of the jar are smooth and round. Finally trim the top of the jar with a modelling tool.

3 Now make a lid for the jar. Measure the size needed and cut out a circle of the remaining clay. Mould it into a dome. Model the head of a baboon on to the lid.

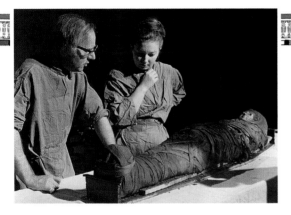

Beneath the Bandages

Unwrapping a mummy is a delicate operation. Today, archaeologists can use scanning or X-ray equipment to examine the mummies' bodies. It is possible to tell what food they once ate, the work they did and the illnesses they suffered from. X-rays also show the stuffing used to replace the internal organs.

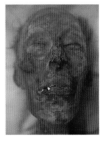

Ramesses II

This is the unwrapped head of the mummy of Ramesses II. Wadding was placed in his eye sockets to stop the natron (preserving salts) from destroying his features.

The Opening of the Mouth Ceremony

The last ritual before burial was led by a priest wearing the mask of the god Anubis. The human-shaped coffin was held upright and its face was touched with magical instruments. This ceremony enabled the mummy to speak, see and hear in the next world.

It was believed that any part of a person's body could be used against them. For this reason the organs were removed and stored in canopic jars. Spells written on the jars protected them.

4 Hapy the baboon guarded the mummy's lungs. Use the modelling tool to make the baboon's eyes and long nose. Leave the lid in a warm place to dry.

5 When both the jar and the lid are completely dry, rub them down with sandpaper until they are smooth. The lid should fit snugly on to the jar.

6 It is now time to paint your jar. Use the masking tape to protect the baboon's face and to help you get the stripes straight. Follow the colours in the picture above.

7 Paint hieroglyphs down the front of the jar as shown. Use the design shown above to help you. The canopic jar is now ready for the funeral.

Grand Temples of Egypt

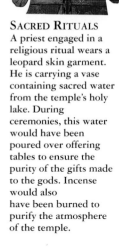

MASSIVE TEMPLES were built in honour of the Egyptian gods. Many can still be seen today. They have great pillars and massive gates, courtyards and avenues of statues. Once, these would have led to a shrine that was believed to be the home of a god.

Ordinary people did not gather to worship in an Egyptian temple as they might today in a church. Only priests were allowed in the temples. They carried out rituals on behalf of the pharaoh, making offerings of food, burning incense, playing music and singing. They had complicated rules about washing and shaving their heads, and some had to wear special clothes such as leopard skins. Noblewomen served as priestesses during some ceremonies. Many priests had little knowledge of religion and just served in the temple for three months before returning to their normal work. Other priests studied the stars and spells.

There were many religious festivals during which the god's shrine would be carried to other temples in a great procession. This was when ordinary Egyptians joined in worship. Offerings of food made to the gods were given back to the people for public feasting.

SACRED RITUALS
A priest engaged in a religious ritual wears a leopard skin garment. He is carrying a vase containing sacred water from the temple's holy lake. During ceremonies, this water would have been poured over offering tables to ensure the purity of the gifts made to the gods. Incense would also have been burned to purify the atmosphere of the temple.

KARNAK
This painting by David Roberts shows the massive temple of Karnak as it appeared in 1850. It still stands just outside the modern town of Luxor. The temple's most important god was Amun-Ra. The site also includes courts and buildings sacred to other gods and goddesses, including Mut (a vulture goddess, wife of Amun) and Khons (the Moon god, son of Amun). The Great Temple was enlarged and rebuilt over about 2,000 years.

ANUBIS THE EMBALMER
A priest wears the mask of Anubis to embalm a body. This jackal-headed god was said to have prepared the body of the god Osiris for burial. He and his priests had strong links with mummies and the practice of embalming.

TEMPLE OF HORUS
A statue of Horus, the falcon god, guards the temple at Edfu. There was a temple on this site during the New Kingdom. However, the building that still stands today dates back to the period of Greek rule. This temple was dedicated to Horus and his wife, the cow goddess Hathor. Inside the temple there are stone carvings showing Horus fighting the enemies of Osiris, his father.

KALABSHA TEMPLE
The Kalabsha temple was one of the largest temples in Lower Nubia. In the 1960s, the Aswan Dam was built and Lower Nubia was flooded. Many monuments such as the temples at Abu Simbel and Philae had to be moved. The temple at Kalabsha was dismantled, and its 13,000 blocks of stone were moved to New Kalabsha, where it was rebuilt.

GATEWAY TO ISIS
The temple of Philae (*above*) was built in honour of Isis, the mother goddess. Isis was worshipped all over Egypt and in many other lands, too. Massive gateways called pylons guard the temple of Philae. Pylons guard the way to many Egyptian temples and were used for special ceremonies.

Religions of India

MANY RELIGIONS DEVELOPED IN INDIA. The Aryan people, who settled in northern India from around 1500BC, had customs which influenced India's later beliefs. In 500BC, a spiritual leader called the Buddha founded Buddhism. This religion was dominant for the next 700 years. In time, the Aryan religion evolved into Hinduism. Many beliefs were the same, but Hinduism discouraged the practice of making animal sacrifices, and introduced new gods to replace the Aryan deities. Gradually, Hinduism took over from Buddhism, and has been India's dominant religion ever since.

In the two main types of Hinduism – Vaishnavism and Shaivism – Hindus believe that one god (Vishnu or Shiva) rules the universe. From AD1000, some worshipped the goddess Devi instead. As a result, Hindu mythology seems to have many different gods, but to most Hindus, they are versions of Vishnu, Shiva or Devi.

TERRIFYING GOD
Shiva appears in the form of a terrifying being wielding a trident. At times, Shiva is associated with the destructive forces of the universe and commands demonic beings, called ganas.

HAPPY GOD
The conch shell and the discus are the symbols of the god Vishnu, who is often shown with blue skin. Vishnu mostly brings happiness, preservation and kingship. He stands on a lotus flower.

MAKE A GARLAND OF FLOWERS
You will need: Tissue paper in orange, yellow, red, pink and white, pencil, scissors, PVA glue, paintbrush, length of string, darning needle.

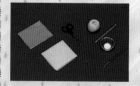

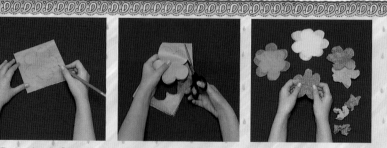

1 Draw simple flower shapes on to sheets of coloured tissue paper. If you like, you can lay the sheets of paper in layers, one on top of the other.

2 Using scissors, cut out your flower shapes. Take care not to tear the tissue paper. Cut the same number of flowers in each colour.

3 Scrunch up the tissue flower shapes with your hands. Then uncrumple them, but don't smooth them out too much.

GANESHA

The elephant god, Ganesha, is the son of Shiva. He is god of wisdom and prosperity and is known for his love of sweets. Ganesha is always shown travelling with a rat.

KRISHNA AND RADHA

The god Krishna was an incarnation of Vishnu on earth. Krishna was born as a cowherder. In his youth, he is said to have been adored by many women, but his favourite was Radha. The love of Radha and Krishna is the theme of many Hindu religious songs.

GODDESS OF DEATH AND WAR

Shiva's wife had many forms. The fiercest was Kali, goddess of death. Here, she holds an array of weapons in her many arms. Kings often worshipped Kali before going into battle.

Hindus make garlands of fresh flowers to wear at festivals to honour their gods.

4 Glue the flower shapes together loosely in layers to make larger, single flowers. Use eight layers of tissue paper for each finished flower.

5 Now gently fluff up the layers of tissue paper with your fingers. This will make your flowers look much more impressive.

6 Measure a length of string that is long enough to go around your neck. Start to thread the flowers on to the string to make a garland.

7 Thread all the tissue flowers on to the length of string. When you have secured all the flowers, tie a double knot in the string to finish.

Islam Reaches India

THE MUSLIM RELIGION, called Islam – which means submission to God – was founded in Arabia (present-day Saudi Arabia) by a man named Mohammed in AD622. It spread quickly into the countries around Arabia, and nearly 400 years later, reached India.

In AD1007 Sultan Mahmud, the Muslim leader of the city of Ghazni in Afghanistan, started a series of attacks on northern India to loot the rich temples there. More Islamic leaders followed his example, and by AD1206, Muslim Turks from Central Asia had founded a new kingdom, or Sultanate, based in the city of Delhi. The Delhi Sultanate ruled the region for 300 years.

Islam gradually spread among ordinary Indian people. Islamic sufis (mystics) played an important role in spreading the message of God's love for all people. They worshipped in a very emotional style at their countryside shrines, in a way that the Hindu peasants could understand. By the 1700s, nearly a quarter of India's population was Muslim. They showed great tolerance to other religions and cultures, especially the Hindu faith.

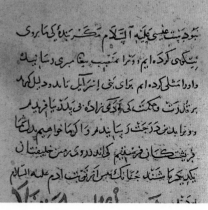

BEAUTIFUL WRITING
This page is from a Persian commentary on the holy book of Muslims, the *Quran*. Muslims were not allowed to represent images, such as humans, animals or flowers, in art. Instead they developed calligraphy (the art of beautiful writing).

SEAFARING SETTLERS
The Indian Ocean was controlled by Muslim traders from about AD700. They arrived along the south-western coast of India on their way to Indonesia and China, and were among the earliest Muslims to settle in India. These traders followed Muslim law. Different Muslim laws spread in India through further Muslim invasions from Turkey and Afghanistan in the 1100s and 1200s.

FROM TEMPLE TO MOSQUE

The Quwat al-Islam, a large mosque in Delhi, was built out of parts of destroyed temples of older faiths. It has two architectural features that were introduced to India by Islam. One feature is the arch, the other is the use of mortar for sticking bricks together. The mosque was built by the Delhi Sultanate in 1193.

HOLY MEN

Sufis (mystics) gather together to pray. Sufism was a type of Islam that preached that people's souls can communicate to God through ecstatic music, singing and dancing. Sufism came into prominence in Persia in the AD900s. By about 1100 it had also gained a foothold in the north-west of India.

FAMILY TOMB

A man cycles towards a tomb of one of the later Sultans of Delhi. The tomb is in the gardens of the Lodi family, the last rulers of the Delhi Sultanate. The last Lodi Sultan was defeated in battle by the Mughal prince Babur, in 1526.

SUFI SHRINE

This tomb-shrine, or dargah, in Rajgir, honours a famous sufi saint. Sufi teachers were called pirs, or shaikhs. They often had a large number of followers.

Sikhs of India

A S ISLAM SPREAD through northern India, Hinduism and Islam existed side by side. In the Punjab region of northern India, a new religion emerged that had elements of both. It was called Sikhism, and was founded by a man called Guru (teacher) Nanak (1469–1539). Sikhism rejected the strict Hindu caste system and adopted the Islamic idea that all people are equal before God, but kept many aspects of Hindu ritual. Sikhs worshipped in temples called gurdwaras (abode of the gurus). After Nanak, there were nine more gurus. The fifth, Arjan, founded the Golden Temple at Amritsar, which later became the holiest of all gurdwaras. He also wrote the Sikh holy book, or *Adi Granth*.

In the 1600s, the Muslim Mughal rulers in Delhi became concerned about the growth of this new religion. They began to persecute the Sikhs and killed Arjan and another guru. The tenth guru, Gobind Singh, decided that Sikhs should protect themselves and founded a military order called the khalsa. Members carried a comb and dagger, wore a steel bangle, breeches, and did not cut their hair. Sikh men took the title Singh (lion). After the death of Gobind Singh in 1708, there were no more gurus, but Sikhs continued to live by the teachings of the *Adi Granth*.

LETHAL TURBAN
A Sikh war turban is decorated with weapons that could be removed and used against the enemy during battle. Metal throwing rings could slice heads off, while 'claws' were for disembowelling people.

THE GOLDEN TEMPLE
The greatest Sikh temple is the Golden Temple in the Sikh holy city of Amritsar. The temple was built by Guru Arjan Singh (1581–1606). Its white marble walls and domes are decorated with gold. The city of Amritsar is named after the lake that surrounds the temple. Sikhs worship in their temples in large congregations (groups). Free kitchens are attached to Sikh temples, where all can eat.

SYMBOLIC COMB

This close-up picture of a Sikh turban shows the kangha, a comb that is pinned to the centre. The kangha is one of the five signs of the Sikh religion. Sikh men do not cut their hair – another sign of Sikhism.

THE SACRED BOOK

The *Adi Granth* is the sacred book of the Sikhs. Its text was compiled by Guru Arjan Singh in the late 1500s. After the death of the last teacher, Guru Gobind Singh, Sikhs came to accept these scriptures as the symbol of God. They took over the role of the teacher from the Gurus.

A MILITARY MAHARAJA

The Maharaja Ranjit Singh (1799–1838) holds court. The water tank of the Golden Temple can be seen in the background. Ranjit Singh led the Sikh army to victory against Afghan warlords and the collapsing Mughal Empire. He established a separate Sikh kingdom in the Punjab region of India.

AN ABLE WARRIOR

A Sikh soldier sits on a cushion in this portrait from the 1800s. When the British ruled India, they recruited many Sikhs into their army. Sikhs were regarded as one of India's most warlike peoples.

Festivals and Ceremonies in India

R ITUAL CEREMONIES in India go back to Aryan times (1500BC), when there were fire sacrifices throughout the year. After the growth of Buddhism, priests developed a set of rites for important events such as marriages, caste initiations and funerals, which Hindus then used for centuries. Many temple festivals developed too. Some, such as Navaratri and Dasara, honoured fierce goddesses. Diwali was a festival of lights in honour of the goddess Lakshmi. In spring, people played games at the fertility festival of Holi.

Generally, Muslims had fewer and less elaborate rituals. Islamic festivals included Eid al-Fitr after Ramadan, the month of fasting, and Eid al-Adha to commemorate Abraham's attempted sacrifice of his son, Isaac. Muslims also adopted some of the customs and practices of the Hindus.

HANDY HENNA
Using henna to mark the hands and feet was a common practice in India, and is still part of marriage ceremonies. Henna is a plant extract that is mixed into a paste with water and used to make patterns on the skin. The paste dyes the skin red.

A FESTIVAL OF FUN
The Vasantotsava (or modern Holi) was a festival of play and courtship which took place in the spring. Men and women threw coloured powders and squirted coloured waters over one another with syringes as they ran about the streets and gardens of the city.

TABLA DRUM

You will need: A2 sheet of thick card, measuring tape, scissors, pair of compasses, pencil, sticky tape, strips of newspaper, flour and water or wallpaper paste, bowl, fine sandpaper, calico fabric, bradawl, red-brown and blue paint, paintbrushes, darning needle, twine, PVA glue.

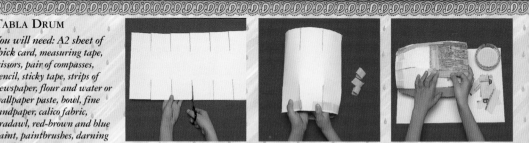

1 Cut out a card rectangle 55 x 21 cm. Cut slits along both long edges. Use the compasses to measure a card circle with a diameter of 16 cm. Cut out the circle.

2 Roll the rectangle to form a cylinder with a diameter of 16 cm and tape. Tape the slits so that the drum tapers at each end. Tape the circle to one end.

3 Cover the cylinder with 3 layers of newspaper strips soaked in paste or flour and water. Leave it to dry between layers. Smooth the edges with sandpaper.

CEREMONY AROUND THE FIRE

A bride, with her face covered, is led into the marriage pandal (ceremonial awning), which is covered with mango and lime leaves to bring good luck. The bride will follow her husband around the fire. Hindu marriages still take place in the home around a sacrificial fire, and are administered by a Brahmin priest.

END OF FASTING

Muslim men take part in Eid festivities, in Bombay. Muslim men pray in public congregations at a mosque and give zakat (gifts) to the poor. Then they celebrate with friends and families.

PILGRIMAGE TO MECCA

Muslim pilgrims travel by camel to the city of Mecca, in Arabia (modern Saudi Arabia). Muslims must travel to Mecca once in their lifetime, if possible. The journey is called the haj.

The tabla drum was played at ceremonies and festivals.

DEATH OF AN IMAM

A passion play with music and drumming is enacted in the streets to celebrate Muharram, the first month of the Muslim calender. For Shia Muslims, the tenth day of Muharram is one of dramatic public mourning to commemorate the death of an imam (spiritual leader) named Husain.

4 Cut a circle of calico with a diameter of 25 cm. Prick holes around the edge with a bradawl. Paint the tabla with two coats of red-brown paint.

5 Thread the needle with a long piece of twine and knot. Place the calico over the tabla's open end. Push the needle and thread through a hole in the calico.

6 Pass the twine across the base and through a hole on the other side of the fabric. Pull the twine tight, to stretch the fabric. Repeat all the way around the tabla.

7 Paint a pattern on to the calico. Then apply a coat of watered down PVA glue. This will help to shrink the calico and pull it tight over the tabla.

Chinese Religions

"THREE TEACHINGS FLOW INTO ONE" is an old saying in China. The three teachings are Daoism, Confucianism and Buddhism. In China they gradually merged together over the ages.

The first Chinese peoples believed in various gods and goddesses of nature, in spirits and demons. The spirit of nature and the flow of life inspired the writings that are said to be the work of Laozi (born *c.*604BC). His ideas formed the basis of the Daoist religion.

The teachings of Kong Fuzi (Confucius) come from the same period of history but they stress the importance of social order and respect for ancestors as a source of happiness. At this time another great religious teacher, the Buddha, was preaching in India. Within 500 years, Buddhist teachings had reached China and by the Tang dynasty (AD618–906), Buddhism was the most popular religion. Islam arrived at this time and won followers in the north-west. Christianity also came into China from Persia, but few Chinese were converted to this religion until the 1900s.

THE MERCIFUL GODDESS
Guanyin was the goddess of mercy and the bringer of children. She was a holy figure for all Chinese Buddhists.

DAOISM – A RELIGION OF HARMONY
A young boy is taught the Daoist belief in the harmony of nature. Daoists believe that the natural world is in a state of balance between two forces – yin and yang. Yin is dark, cool and feminine, while yang is light, hot and masculine. The two forces are combined in the black and white symbol on the scroll.

PEACE THROUGH SOCIAL ORDER
Kong Fuzi (Confucius) looks out on to an ordered world. He taught that the well-being of society depends on duty and respect. Children should obey their parents and wives should obey their husbands. The people should obey their rulers, and rulers should respect the gods. All of the emperors followed the teachings of Confucianism.

FREEDOM FROM DESIRE

Chinese monks carved huge statues of the Buddha from rock. Some can be seen at the Mogao caves near Dunhuang, where temples were built as early as AD366. The Buddha taught that suffering is caused by our love of material things. Buddhists believe that we are born over and over again until we learn to conquer this desire.

ISLAM IN CHINA

This is part of the Great Mosque in Xian (ancient Chang'an), built in the Chinese style. The mosque was founded in AD742, but most of the buildings in use today date from the Ming dynasty (1368–1644). Islam first took root in China in about AD700. Moslem traders from Central Asia brought with them the Koran, the holy book of Islam. It teaches that there is only one god, Allah, and that Mohammed is his prophet.

TEMPLE GUARDIANS

Gilded statues of Buddhist saints ward off evil spirits at Puningsi, the Temple of Universal Peace, near Chengde. The temple was built in 1755 in the Tibetan style. It is famed for its Mahayana Hall, a tower roofed in gilded bronze.

Celebrations in China

THE CHINESE FESTIVAL best known around the world today is the New Year or Spring Festival. Its date varies according to the traditional Chinese calendar, which is based on the phases of the moon. The festival is marked by dancers carrying a long dragon through the streets, accompanied by loud, crackling firecrackers to scare away evil spirits. The festival has been celebrated for over 2,000 years and has always been a time for family feasts and village carnivals. The doorways of buildings are traditionally decorated with handwritten poetry on strips of red paper to bring luck and good fortune for the coming year.

Soon after New Year, sweet dumplings made of rice flour are prepared for the Lantern Festival. Paper lanterns are hung out to mirror the first full moon of the year. This festival began during the Tang dynasty (AD618–906). In the eighth month of the year, the autumn full moon is marked by the eating of special moon cakes.

Chinese festivals are linked to agricultural seasons. They include celebrations of sowing and harvest, dances, horse races and the eating of specially prepared foods.

DANCING ANIMALS
Chinese New Year parades are often headed by a lion (*shown above*) or dragon. These are carried by dancers accompanied by crashing cymbals.
The first month of the Chinese calendar begins on the first full moon between 21 January and 19 February.

HORSE RACING
The Mongols, who invaded China in the 1200s, brought with them their love of horses and superb riding skills. Today, children as young as three years old take part in horse-racing festivals in northern China and Mongolia. Archery and wrestling competitions are also regularly held.

MAKE A LANTERN

You will need: thick card, pencil, ruler, scissors, compasses, glue and brush, red tissue paper, blue paint, paintbrush, water pot, thin blue and yellow card, wire, tape, bamboo stick, torch, fringing fabric.

Using the measurements above, draw the 10 pieces on to thick card (pieces not drawn to scale). Cut out pieces with scissors.

1 Using compasses, draw an 8cm diameter circle in the middle of one of the end pieces. Cut out the circle with scissors. Glue on the 4 sides, as shown.

2 Glue together the frame pieces. Then glue the end pieces on to the frame. When dry, cover frame with red tissue paper. Glue one side at a time.

DRAGON BOATS

In the fifth month of the Chinese year, races are held in the Dragon Boat festival. This is in memory of a famous statesman called Qu Yuan, who drowned himself in 278BC when his advice to his ruler was ignored. Rice dumplings are eaten at the Dragon Boat festival every year in his memory.

CHINESE LANTERNS

Elaborate paper lanterns brighten up a wedding in the 1800s during the Qing dynasty. Lanterns were also strung up or paraded on poles at other private celebrations and during Chinese festivals.

Light up your lantern by placing a small torch inside it. Decorate with a fringe. Now you can join in Chinese celebrations!

3 Paint top of lantern blue. Cut borders out of blue card. Glue to top and bottom of frame. Stick a thin strip of yellow card to bottom border.

4 Make 2 small holes opposite each other at top of lantern. Pass the ends of a loop of wire through each hole. Bend and tape ends to secure wire.

5 Make a hook from thick card. Split end opposite hook. Glue and wrap around bamboo stick. Hang lantern by wire loop from hook.

Ancient Japanese Faith

Almost all Japanese people in history followed a very ancient religious faith called Shinto. Shinto means the way of the gods. It developed from a central idea that all natural things had a spiritual side. These natural spirits – called *kami* in Japanese – were often kindly, but could be powerful or even dangerous. They needed to be respected and worshipped. Shinto also encouraged the worship of ancestors, spirits who could guide, help and warn. Special priests, called shamans, made contact with the spirits by chanting, fasting, or by falling into a trance.

Shinto spirits were honoured at shrines that were often built close to sites of beauty or power, such as waterfalls or volcanoes. Priests guarded the purity of each shrine, and held rituals to make offerings to the spirits. Each Shinto shrine was entered through a *torii* (large gateway) which marked the start of the sacred space. *Torii* always had the same design – they were based on the ancient perches of birds waiting to be sacrificed.

At the Shrine
A priest worships by striking a drum at the Grand Shrine at Izu, one of the oldest Shinto shrines in Japan. A festival is held there every August, with processions, offerings and prayers. An *omikoshi* (portable shrine) is carried through the streets, so that the spirits can bring blessings to everyone.

Offerings to the Spirits
Worshippers at Shinto shrines leave offerings for the *kami* (spirits) that live there. These offerings are neatly wrapped barrels of *sake* (rice wine). Today, worshippers also leave little wooden plaques with prayers on them.

Votive Dolls
You will need: self-drying clay, 2 balsa wood sticks (12cm long), ruler, paints, paintbrush, water pot, modelling clay, silver foil, red paper, gold paper, scissors, pencil, glue stick, optional basket and dowelling stick.

1 Place a ball of clay on the end of each of the balsa sticks. On one of the sticks, push the clay down so that it is 5mm from the end. This will be the man.

2 Paint hair and features on the man. Stand it up in modelling clay to dry. Repeat with the woman. Cover the 5mm excess stick on the man's head in foil.

3 Take two pieces of red paper, 6.5cm x 14cm and 6cm x 10cm. Fold them in half. Take two pieces of gold paper, 10.5cm x 10cm and 1cm x 7cm. Fold in half.

LUCKY GOD
Daikoku is one of seven lucky gods from India, China and Japan that are associated with good fortune. In Japan, he is the special god of farmers, wealth, and of the kitchen. Daikoku is recognized by both Shinto and Buddhist religions.

HOLY VOLCANO
Fuji-San (Mount Fuji) has been honoured as a holy place since the first people arrived in Japan. Until 1867, women were not allowed to set foot on Fuji's holy ground.

FLOATING GATE
This *torii* at Miyajima (Island of Shrines), in southern Japan, is built on the seashore. It appears to float on the water as the tide flows in. Miyajima was sacred to the three daughters of the Sun.

In some regions of Japan, dolls like these are put on display in baskets every year at Hinamatsuri (Girls' Day), on 3 March.

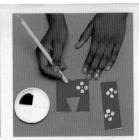

4 Take the folded red paper (6.5cm x 14cm). This is the man's *kimono*. Cut a triangular shape out of the bottom. Cut a neck hole out at the folded end.

5 Dip the blunt end of the pencil in white paint. Stipple a pattern on to the red paper. Add the central dots using the pencil tip dipped in paint.

6 Slip the man's head and body into the red paper *kimono*. Then take the larger piece of gold paper and fold around the stick, as shown. Glue in place.

7 Now stick the gold paper (1cm x 7cm) on to the woman's *kimono*, in the middle. Slip the woman's head and body into the *kimono*. Glue in place.

Gods of Ancient Greece

THE GODS OF THE ANCIENT GREEKS had many human characteristics. They looked like ordinary people and felt emotions that led them to quarrel and fall in love. However, the gods also had magical powers and were immortal (they could live forever). With these powers, the gods could become invisible, or disguise themselves, or turn people into animals. The gods were thought to influence all parts of human life. They were kept busy with requests for help, from curing illness to ensuring a victory in war. In order to keep on the right side of the gods, the Greek people made sacrifices, left offerings and said prayers. Communities financed the building of temples, such as the Parthenon in Athens. They paid for priests to look after the buildings and to organize festivals in honour of the gods.

WINGED MESSENGER
Hermes was the god of eloquence and good luck. He was known for his mischievous and adventure-seeking nature. Zeus made him a messenger to the gods, to try and keep him occupied and out of trouble.

KING OF THE GODS
Zeus ruled over earth and heaven from Mount Olympus, (a real place on the border of Macedonia). He was thought to be a fair god who upheld order and justice. Wrongdoers could be punished with thunderbolts thrown by him.

WILD GODDESS
Artemis was the goddess of wild places and animals, hunting and the moon. She was a skilful archer, whose arrows caused death and plagues. The power to heal was another of her attributes.

PARTHENON
You will need: two pieces of white card 62cm by 38.5cm, ruler, black felt-tip pen, shoebox, scissors, blue, red and cream paint, paintbrush, PVA glue, piece of red corrugated card (approximately 39cm x 28.5cm), masking tape, craft knife, 160cm of balsa wood.

1 Draw a horizontal line across the centre of the card. Place the shoebox in the middle. Draw around it. Draw a second box 7cm away from this.

2 Draw a third box 2cm away from the second. Extend the lines of the second box to meet the third, to form four tabs, one in each corner.

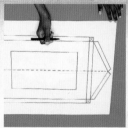

3 To make the ends of the roof, draw half a diamond shape along the edge of the second box. Add on two rectangular tabs 1cm deep.

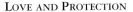

SYMBOLS

Each god and goddess was thought to be responsible for particular aspects of daily life. Each was represented by a symbol. Wheat symbolized Demeter, goddess of living things. Dionysus, god of the vine and wine, was appropriately represented by grapes.

wheat   grapes

GRAPES OF JOY

The god Dionysus was admired for his sense of fun. As god of fertility, the vine and wine, he was popular with both male and female worshippers. However, his followers were too enthusiastic for some city-states which banned celebrations in his name.

LOVE AND PROTECTION

Aphrodite was the goddess of love and beauty. Her vanity was instrumental in causing one of the biggest campaigns in Greek folklore, the Trojan War. Aphrodite promised to win Paris (son of the king of Troy) the love of the most beautiful mortal woman in the world – Helen. In return, Paris was to name Aphrodite as the most beautiful of all the goddesses. However, Helen was already married to the king of Sparta. When she left him to join Paris, the Greeks declared war on Troy. A bloodthirsty war followed in which heroes and gods clashed.

A POWERFUL FAMILY

Hera was the wife of Zeus and goddess of marriage. She was revered by women as the protector of their married lives. Her own marriage was marked by conflicts between herself and her husband. Her jealousy of rivals for her unfaithful husband's affections led her to persecute them. She was also jealous of Heracles, who was Zeus' son by another woman. Hera sent snakes to kill Heracles when he was a baby. Fortunately for Heracles, he had inherited his father's strength and killed the snakes before they harmed him.

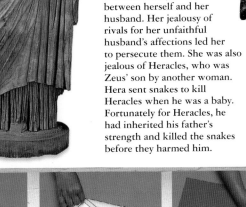

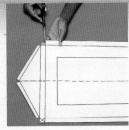

4 Repeat step 3 for the other end of the roof. Cut out both ends of the roof and cut into the four corner tabs. Get your painting equipment ready.

5 Turn the roof piece over. Draw and then paint the above design on to each end piece. Paint a blue, 1cm margin along each side. Leave to dry.

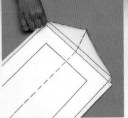

6 Turn the card over. Fold up all the sides of the second box. Fold in each corner tab and glue to its adjoining side. Fold down the rectangular tabs.

7 Cut the piece of red corrugated card in half. Stick them together with tape, along the unridged side. Turn them over and fold along the middle.

Temples and Festivals in Greece

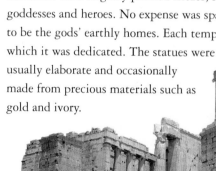

FESTIVALS TO HONOUR THE GODS were important public occasions in ancient Greece. At the heart of each festival was a temple. At festival time, people flocked to the cities from the countryside. The greatest festivals were occasions of splendour and celebration. They involved processions, music, sports, prayers, animal sacrifices and offerings of food, all of which took place at the temple.

The earliest Greek temples were built of wood, and none have survived. Later, temples built from stone echoed the simplicity of tree trunks in their columns and beams. The finest temples were made from marble. They were often decorated with brightly painted friezes, showing mythical stories of gods, goddesses and heroes. No expense was spared because temples were thought to be the gods' earthly homes. Each temple housed a statue of the god to which it was dedicated. The statues were usually elaborate and occasionally made from precious materials such as gold and ivory.

A Woman's Role
This vase in the shape of a woman's head was made about 600BC, probably for a temple dedicated to Apollo, the handsome god of music. Religion was one of the few areas of life outside the home in which women were allowed to take an active part. They served as priestesses in some cults and were often thought to have the gift of seeing into the future.

Grand Entrance
The monumental gateway to the temple complex at the Acropolis in Athens was called the Propylaea. The temple beside it honoured the city's guardian goddess, Athena.

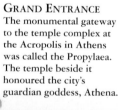

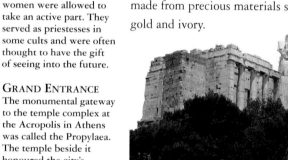

8 Glue the ends of the corrugated card to the folded up edges of the painted card. Leave to dry. This piece forms the roof to your temple.

9 Draw around the shoebox, on to the second piece of card. Draw another box 7cm away. Cut it out, leaving a 1cm border. This is the temple base.

10 Ask an adult to help you with this step. Cut out 32 columns from balsa wood. Each must be 5cm in height. Paint them cream and leave to dry.

11 Mark eight points along each edge of the second box by drawing around a column piece. Draw them an equal distance from each other.

A BIRTHDAY PARADE

A parade of horsemen, chariots and people leading sacrificial animals all formed part of the procession of the Panathenaic festival. This was held once a year, in Athens, to celebrate the goddess Athena's birthday. Every fourth year, the occasion involved an even more elaborate ceremony which lasted for six days. During the festivities, the statue of Athena was presented with a new robe.

A TEMPLE FOR THREE GODS

The Erectheum was built on the Acropolis, looking down on Athens 100 m below. Unusually for a Greek temple, it housed the worship of more than one god: the legendary king Erectheus; Athena, guardian goddess of the city of Athens, and Poseidon, god of the sea. The columns in the shape of women are called caryatids.

BUILDING MATERIALS

Big buildings, such as temples, were often put up near a quarry or navigable water. Limestone was the most commonly used stone, and pine and cypress the commonest woods. Costly marble and cedar were reserved for temples and palaces.

marble

limestone

pine

THE LION'S MOUTH

This gaping lion is actually a waterspout from an Athenian temple built in about 570BC. Although rainfall in Greece is low, waterspouts were necessary to allow storm water to drain off buildings with flat roofs. The lion was chosen as a symbol of strength and power.

12 Draw a door on to a short end of the shoebox. Glue the roof on to the top of the shoebox. Paint the 1cm border on the temple base, blue.

13 Glue the columns into place, between the roof and the base. Dab glue on to their ends. Position them on the circles marked out in step 11.

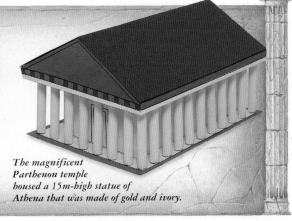

The magnificent Parthenon temple housed a 15m-high statue of Athena that was made of gold and ivory.

The Ancient Greek Underworld

PEOPLE IN ANCIENT GREECE lived only about half as long as people in the West do today. It was common for sickly children to die in infancy. Large numbers of men were killed in battle, women often died in childbirth and epidemics could wipe out whole communities.

Most Greeks believed that after death, their souls roamed the Underworld, a cold and gloomy region where the wicked were sent to be punished. Achilles, the hero in the Greek epic poem, *The Odyssey,* says, "I'd rather be a common labourer on earth working for a poor man than lord of all the legions of the dead". Few people were thought good enough to be sent to the Isles of the Blessed. If they were, they could spend eternity amusing themselves with sports and music. People who had led exceptional lives (such as the hero Heracles) were destined to become gods and live on Mount Olympus, the home of the gods.

When someone died, their body was either buried or cremated. The Greeks believed that only when the body or ashes had been covered with earth, could its spirit leave for the Underworld. Graves contained possessions for use in the afterlife, and women left offerings of food and drink at the graveside to help the spirits.

FRAGRANT FAREWELL
Graves were sometimes marked with lekythoi, white clay flasks holding a perfumed oil that had been used to anoint the body. The lekythoi were usually painted with farewell scenes, funerals or images of the dead.

FOOD FOR THOUGHT
The tradition of leaving food at gravesides began in Mycenaean times. Then people could be buried with their armour, cooking pots and even pets and slaves to accompany them. By 300BC the Greeks were leaving food such as wine and eggs at gravesides as nourishment for the dead.

wine

eggs

A DIVE INTO THE UNKNOWN
The figure on the painting above is shown leaping from life into the ocean of death. The pillars were put up by Heracles to mark the end of the known, living world. This diver was found painted on the walls of a tomb.

TUG OF LOVE

This painting from a vase shows Persephone with her husband, Hades, ruler of the underworld. Hades dragged Persephone from earth down to the Underworld. Her distraught mother, the goddess Demeter, neglected the crops to search for her. Zeus intervened and decided that Persephone would spend six months of every year with her mother and the other six with Hades. Whenever her daughter returned in spring, Demeter would look after the crops. However, Demeter grew sad each time her daughter went back to the Underworld and wintertime would set in.

LAST JOURNEY

The body of a dead person was taken from the home to the grave by mourners bearing tributes. To express their grief, they might cut off their hair, tear at their cheeks with their nails until blood flowed, and wear black robes. If there was a funeral feast at the graveside, the dishes were smashed afterwards and left there.

ROYAL TOMB

Women were less likely to be honoured by tombstone portraits than men. Philis, seen above, was an exception to this rule, possibly because she was the daughter of a powerful Spartan king. Athens enforced a law against extravagant tombs. No more than ten men could be employed for any more than three days to build one.

Roman Gods

WHEN THE ROMANS conquered Greece in 146BC, they adopted many of the ancient Greek gods. Some gods were renamed in Latin, the language of the Roman Empire. Jupiter (Zeus in Greek), the sky god, was the most powerful god. Venus (Aphrodite) was the goddess of love, Mars (Ares) was the god of war, Ceres (Demeter) goddess of the harvest and Mercury god of merchants. Household gods protected the home. Splendid temples were built in honour of the gods, and special festivals were held during the year, with processions, music, offerings and animal sacrifices. The festivals were often public holidays. The mid-winter festival of Saturnalia, in honour of Saturn, lasted up to seven days. As the Roman Empire grew, many Romans adopted the religions of other peoples, such as the Egyptians and the Persians.

CHIEF GOD
Jupiter was the chief god of the Romans. He was the all-powerful god of the sky. The Romans believed he showed his anger by hurling a thunderbolt to the ground.

DIANA THE HUNTRESS
Diana was the goddess of hunting and the Moon. In this detail from a floor mosaic, she is shown poised with a bow and arrow, ready for the hunt. Roman gods were often the same as the Greek ones, but were given different names. Diana's Greek name was Artemis.

ONE TO ALL
The Pantheon in Rome was a temple to all the gods. It was built between AD118 and 128. Its mosaic floor, interior columns and high dome still remain exactly as they were built.

A TEMPLE TO THE GODS

You will need: thick stiff card, thin card, old newspaper, scissors, balloon, PVA glue, ruler, pencils, masking tape, drinking straws, acrylic paints, paintbrush, water pot, Plasticine.

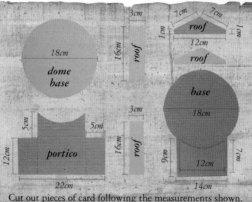

3cm · 7cm · 7cm
1cm · *roof* · 1cm
12cm
roof

18cm · 16cm · *roof*
dome base

base
18cm

3cm
16cm · *roof*
5cm · 5cm
12cm · *portico*
9cm · 12cm · 7cm
22cm · 14cm

Cut out pieces of card following the measurements shown.

1 Blow up the balloon. Cover it in strips of newspaper pasted on with glue. Keep pasting until you have a thick layer. Leave to dry. Then burst the balloon and cut out a dome.

PRIESTS OF ISIS

The Egyptian mother-goddess Isis had many followers throughout the Roman Empire. This painting shows priests and worshippers of Isis taking part in a water purification ceremony. The ceremony would have been performed every afternoon.

BLESS THIS HOUSE

This is a bronze statue of a *lar* or household god. Originally gods of the countryside, the *lares* were believed to look after the family and the home. Every Roman home had a shrine to the *lares*. The family, including the children, would make daily offerings to the gods.

MITHRAS THE BULL-SLAYER

Mithras was the Persian god of light. He is shown here, in a marble relief from a temple, slaying a bull. This bull's blood was believed to have brought life to the Earth. The cult of Mithras spread through the whole Empire, and was particularly popular with Roman soldiers. However, only men were allowed to worship Mithras.

The Pantheon was built of brick and then clad in stone and marble. Its huge dome, with a diameter of over 43m, was the largest ever constructed until the 1900s.

2 Put the dome on its card base and draw its outline. Cut out the centre of the base to make a halo shape. Make a hole in the top of the dome. Bind the pieces together, as shown.

3 Glue together the base pieces. Cut a piece of thin card long enough to go round the base circle. This will be the circular wall. Use masking tape to hold the portico in shape.

4 Cut some straws into eight pieces, each 6cm long. These will be the columns for the entrance colonnade. Glue together the roof for the entrance. Secure with tape.

5 Glue together the larger pieces, as shown. Position each straw column with a small piece of Plasticine at its base. Glue on the entrance roof. Paint your model.

Protectors of Celtic Tribes

THERE ARE MANY surviving traces of Celtic religion, in descriptions by Roman writers, in carvings and statues, in place names, in collections of religious offerings and in myths and legends. Yet there are many things we do not know or fully understand about Celtic beliefs. This is because the Celts believed that holy knowledge was too important to be written down. It seems almost certain, however, that they worshipped gods who protected the tribe and gave strength in war, and goddesses who protected homes and brought fertility. Some gods were associated with the sky, and some goddesses with the earth. Gods and spirits controlled the elements and natural forces, such as water and thunder. They were given different names in different parts of the Celtic world, which covered large areas of central and north-western Europe. Gods and goddesses were worshipped close to water and in groves of trees. The Celts believed that dreadful things would happen if they did not make sacrifices of their most valuable possessions, including living things, to the gods.

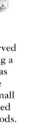
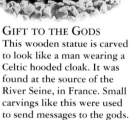

GIFT TO THE GODS
This wooden statue is carved to look like a man wearing a Celtic hooded cloak. It was found at the source of the River Seine, in France. Small carvings like this were used to send messages to the gods.

HANDS HELD HIGH
From the Gundestrup bowl, this bearded god holds his hands up. Such a gesture may have been used by druids (Celtic priests) when praying. The clenched fists are a sign of power.

MAKE THE GUNDESTRUP BOWL

You will need: plastic bowl, silver foil, scissors, cardboard strip 12 cm x 84 cm, felt-tip pen, plasticine, PVA glue, double-sided tape, bradawl, paper fasteners.

1 Find a plastic bowl that measures about 26 cm in diameter across the top. Cover the bowl on the inside and outside with silver foil.

2 Use the pair of scissors to trim any excess foil, as shown. Ensure that you leave enough foil to turn over the top edge neatly.

3 Divide the card into six sections. Leave 3 cm at the end of the card. Draw a god figure in each section. Make a plasticine version of the figure. Glue it on top.

BURIED IN A BOG

The remains of this Celtic man were found in a peat bog in northern England. He died some time between AD1 and AD200. He was sacrificed by being killed in three different ways, having been strangled, had his throat cut, and struck on the head. Like the three-mothers carving, this shows the Celts' use of the number three for religious purposes.

HORSES AND WAR

According to Roman writers, Epona was the Celtic goddess of war. Epona was worshipped by many Roman soldiers who spent time on duty in Celtic lands. This Roman-style carving shows Epona with a horse. It was found in northern France.

HUMAN SACRIFICE

Celtic priests, called druids, sometimes sacrificed human beings and animals as offerings to the gods. This scene from the Gundestrup bowl shows a giant-sized figure, maybe a god, holding a human sacrifice.

The famous Gundestrup bowl, which inspired your model, was made in eastern Europe some time between 200BC and 1BC. It was found many years later in a Danish bog.

THREE MOTHERS

To the Celts, the number three was a sign of power, so they often portrayed their gods and goddesses in triple form. This stone carving shows three mother-goddesses. It was made in Britain, probably between AD50 and AD400. The figures stand for the three female qualities of strength, power and fertility.

4 Cover both sides of the card strip and the plasticine figures with glue. Then cover with silver foil. Make sure that the foil is well glued to the figures.

5 Stick double-sided tape to the back of the foil-covered strip along the bottom and side edges. This will be used to join the sides of the bowl.

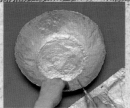

6 Make holes with a bradawl every few centimetres through the bottom of the strip. Make matching holes along the top of the bowl, as shown.

7 Attach the strip to the bowl with the double-sided tape. Stick the ends together, as shown. Secure by putting paper fasteners through both sets of holes.

Annual Celtic Festivals

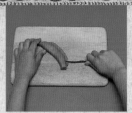

As FARMERS, the Celts needed to be able to measure time, so that they would know when to plough their fields and sow their crops. The Celtic year (354 days) was divided into 12 months, each 29 or 30 days long. Every two-and-a-half years, an extra month was added, so that the calendar kept pace with the natural seasons. The Celts marked the passing of time by holding religious festivals. Samain (1 November) was the most important. It was the beginning of the Celtic year, and was a time for sacrifices and community gatherings. It was a dangerous time, when spirits walked the earth. Samain has survived today in Christian form as All Souls' Day, and Hallowe'en. Imbolc (1 February) marked the beginning of springtime and fertility. Beltane (1 May) was observed by lighting bonfires. Their smoke had purifying powers, and was used to kill pests on cattle. The final festival of the year was Lugnasad (1 August).

GODDESS AND SAINT
This statue is of the Celtic goddess Brigit (later known as St Brigit in Ireland) who was honoured at the Imbolc festival. The Celts believed that she brought fertility and fresh growth. She was also the goddess of learning, and had healing powers.

HOLY DAYS
Celtic calendars were kept by druids (priests). They believed that some days were fortunate, while others brought bad luck. This picture, painted about 150 years ago, shows how one artist thought a druid might look. However, it is mostly imaginary.

MAKE A PIG
You will need: modelling clay, board, modelling tool, ruler, 4 x balsa-wood sticks, metallic paint, paintbrush.

1 Make the body of the pig by rolling a piece of modelling clay into a sausage shape roughly 13 cm x 3.5 cm. Make a head shape at one end.

2 With your thumb and index finger, carefully flatten out a ridge along the back of the pig. The ridge should be about 1 cm high.

3 Now use the modelling tool to make a pattern along the ridge section. The pattern should have straight vertical lines on both sides of the ridge.

CLEVER GOD

Archaeologists think that this stone head, found in North Wales, may represent Lug, the Celtic god of all the arts. According to legend, Lug was clever at everything. He was honoured at Lugnasad, the fourth and final festival of the Celtic year when offerings were made to all the earth spirits and goddesses, to ask them for a plentiful harvest.

MISTLETOE AND OAK

Both mistletoe and oak were sacred to the Celts. Druids made sacrifices at wooden temples or in sacred oak groves. Even the druids' name meant "knowledge of the oak". Mistletoe was magic and mysterious. It could only be cut with a golden sickle. Mistletoe growing on oak trees was the most holy and powerful of all.

mistletoe

oak tree leaves

DRUID CEREMONY

This picture from the 1800s shows an imaginary view of druids at a Celtic religious ceremony. We have very little detailed information about how these ceremonies were performed. According to Roman writers, there were three different kinds of druids, each with different duties. Some were soothsayers, who told the future and issued warnings. Some held sacrifices. Some wrote and performed songs in honour of the gods.

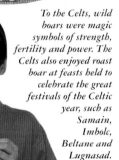

To the Celts, wild boars were magic symbols of strength, fertility and power. The Celts also enjoyed roast boar at feasts held to celebrate the great festivals of the Celtic year, such as Samain, Imbolc, Beltane and Lugnasad.

4 Roll out four legs roughly 4.5 cm long. Push a balsa-wood stick into each leg. Leave about 1 cm of balsa wood exposed, as shown.

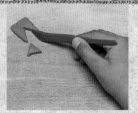

5 Now roll out a small amount of modelling clay. Cut out two triangular shapes using your modelling tool. These will be the pig's ears.

6 Carefully attach the ears on either side of the pig's head. Mould them on using a little water and your modelling tool, as shown.

7 Attach the legs to the pig, pushing the balsa wood sticks into the body. Leave the modelling clay to dry. When it is dry, paint the whole pig.

Gods of the Vikings

THOR'S HAMMER
This lucky charm from Iceland shows Thor. He used his magic hammer to fight the giants. Thor was strong and brave.

THE VIKINGS believed that the universe was held up by a great ash tree called Yggdrasil. The universe was made up of several separate worlds. Niflheim was the underworld, a misty realm of snow and ice. The upper world was Asgard, home of the gods. Its great hall was called Valholl (Valhalla), and it was here that warriors who died bravely in battle came to feast. The world of humans was called Midgard. It was surrounded by a sea of monsters and linked to Asgard by a rainbow bridge. Beyond the sea lay Utgard, the forest home of the Giants, deadly enemies of the gods.

WORSHIPPING FREYA
This silver charm shows Freya. She was the goddess of love and marriage and was particularly popular in Sweden. Freya was the sister of Frey, the god of farming. It was also believed that when women died, Freya would welcome them into the next world. In *Egil's Saga*, a dying woman says "I have not eaten and shall not till I am with Freya".

The Vikings believed in many gods. They thought that Odin, father of the gods, rode through the night sky. Odin's wife was Frigg (a day of the week – Friday – is named after her) and his son was Baldr, god of the summer Sun. Powerful, red-bearded Thor was the god of thunder. Like many of the Vikings themselves, he enjoyed laughing, but was quick to anger. The twins Frey and Freya were god and goddess of fertility and love. Trouble was stirred up by Loki, a mischief-making god.

BALDR IS SLAIN
Stories tell how the wicked Loki told the blind god Hod to aim a mistletoe spear at Baldr, god of the Sun and light.

MAKE A LUCKY CHARM

You will need: thick paper or card, pencil, scissors, self-drying clay, board, felt-tip pen, modelling tool, rolling pin, fine sandpaper, silver acrylic paint, brush, water pot, a length of cord.

1 Draw the outline of Thor's hammer onto thick paper or card and cut it out. Use this as the pattern for making your lucky charm, or amulet.

2 Place a lump of the clay on the board and roll it flat. Press your card pattern into the clay so that it leaves an outline of the hammer.

3 Remove the card. Use a modelling tool to cut into the clay. Follow around the edge of the imprint as shown, and peel away the hammer shape.

ODIN

One-eyed Odin was the wisest god. He had two ravens called Hugin, meaning thought, and Mugin, meaning memory. Each day the ravens flew across the world. Every evening they flew back to Odin to perch on his shoulders and report to him the deeds that they had seen.

SLEIPNIR

Odin rode across the sky on Sleipnir, a grey, eight-legged horse. A pair of wolves travelled with Odin. In this carved stone from Sweden, Odin and Sleipnir are arriving at Valholl. They would have been welcomed by a *valkyrie*, or servant of the gods, bearing wine for Odin to drink.

Vikings wore lucky charms or amulets to protect themselves from evil. Many of the charms, such as this hammer, honoured the god Thor.

4 Model a flattened end to the hammer, as shown. Use a modelling tool to make a hole at the end, to thread the cord through when it is dry.

5 Use the end of a felt-tip pen, a pencil or modelling tool to press a series of patterns into the clay, as shown. Leave the clay to dry and harden.

6 When the amulet is dry, smooth any rough edges with sandpaper. Paint one side silver. Leave it to dry before painting the other side.

7 When the paint has dried, take enough cord to fit your neck and thread it through the hole in the hammer. Cut it with the scissors and tie a knot.

Vikings Convert to Christianity

BY THE BEGINNING of the Viking Age, most of western Europe had become Christian. The early Vikings despised the Christian monks for being meek and mild. The warriors looted church treasures on their raids and murdered many priests or sold them into slavery. However, over the years, some Vikings found it convenient to become Christian. This made it easier for them to trade with merchants in western Europe and to hire themselves out as soldiers with Christian armies.

Christian missionaries went to Scandinavia from Germany and the British Isles. Monks from Constantinople preached to the Vikings living in the Ukraine and Russia. They soon gained followers. In about 960, King Harald Bluetooth of Denmark became a Christian. In 995, Olaf Tryggvason, a Christian king, came to the throne of Norway. He pulled down many of the shrines to the old gods. In 1000 the Viking colonists on Iceland also voted to become Christian. The new faith spread from there to Greenland. Sweden was the last Viking country to become Christian. People gave up worshipping pagan gods in the old temples of the settlement at Uppsala.

NEW FAITH
This silver crucifix was found in the Gotland region of Sweden. It is nearly 1,000 years old. It shows Christ wearing breeches, like those worn by Viking men.

STAVE CHURCH
This Christian church is made of staves, or split tree trunks. It was built in Gol, in Norway, in about 1200. The very first Christian churches in Scandinavia were built in this way. When the wooden foundations rotted away, the churches were rebuilt.

SIGN OF THE CROSS
This stone was raised at Jelling in Denmark by King Harald Bluetooth, in honour of his parents. It dates from about 985. The stone marks a turning-point in Viking history – the conversion of the Danes to Christianity. One side of the stone shows a dragon-like beast fighting with a snake. The other side is a Christian scene (*above*), showing Jesus on the cross.

crucifix

Thor's hammer charms

CHOICE OF GODS

The mould below was made from a soft mineral called soapstone. It was used to shape metal pendants 1,000 years ago. The mould could produce both hammer-of-Thor designs and crosses (_above_). The two religions – the old and the new – existed side-by-side for many years in the Viking world. It was a long time before Christianity really took hold. Many of the early converts to Christianity still turned to Thor for help in the heat of battle.

mould

BAPTISM IN A BARREL

The Danish king, Harald Bluetooth, was converted to Christianity in about 960. This gold altar piece shows Harald being baptized in a barrel of holy water by Bishop Poppo. Harald went on to build a Christian church on the ancient site of the royal burial mound at Jelling.

AGAINST EVIL

Is this a silver cross, or a hammer-of-Thor charm with a dragon's head? Perhaps it was both. It was certainly intended to protect the wearer from evil and bad luck. Even after they became Christians, the Vikings remained very superstitious people. Helgi the Lean is described in a Viking saga as believing in Christ 'yet he still asked Thor for help on sea voyages and when facing danger'.

STONE CROSS

This cross is from Kirkinner Church, in Scotland. It is about 1,000 years old. Its carving shows a mixture of Anglian and Norwegian Viking styles. The Christians in Britain, France and Germany were horrified by the Vikings' pagan religion, and they tried to persuade them to give it up. Eventually, Viking kings saw that becoming Christian could make them more powerful.

Spirits in North America

To North American Indian tribes, everything in the world had a soul or spirit that was very powerful and could help or harm humans. They believed that the changing seasons and events surrounding them were caused by different spirits. Spirits had to be treated with respect, so prayers, songs, chants and dances would be offered to please them. The most important spirit to Sioux tribes was Wakan Tanka, the Great Spirit or Great Mysterious, who was in charge of all other spirits. The Navajo tribes believed in the Holy People. These were Sky, Earth, Moon, Sun, Hero Twins, Thunders, Winds and Changing Woman. Some tribes believed in ghosts. Western Shoshonis, Salish (Flathead) people and Ojibwas considered ghosts to be spirit helpers who acted as bodyguards in battle. The leader of ceremonies was the shaman (medicine man) who conducted the dances and rites. He also acted as a doctor. The shamans of California would treat a sick person by sucking out the pain, spitting it out and sending it away.

CHARMED LIFE
A whale's tusk was used to carve this Inuit shaman's charm. Spirits called tuneraks were thought to help the angakok, as the Inuit shaman was called, in his duties. The role of shaman was passed from father to son. In Padlimuit, Copper and Iglulik tribes, women could also be shamans.

BEAR NECESSITIES OF LIFE
This shaman is nicknamed Bear's Belly and belonged to the Arikara Plains tribe. Shamans were powerful, providing the link between humans and spirits. After years of training, they could cure ill health, tell the future or speak to the dead.

MAKE A RATTLE

You will need: thick card, pencil, ruler, scissors, masking tape, compasses, PVA glue, brush, two balsa wood strips 2–3cm wide and about 18cm long, raffia or string, air-drying clay, barbecue stick, cream, black, orange/red and brown paint, paintbrushes, water pot, black thread, needle.

1 Cut two pieces of card 1.5cm wide, one 46cm long and one 58cm long. Cover both in masking tape. Make holes about 3cm apart along the strips.

2 Bend each strip into a ring. Glue and tape the ends together to make two rings. Fix the two strips of balsa wood into a cross to fit across the large ring.

3 Glue the two sticks together then strap them with raffia or string. Wrap the string round one side then cross it over the centre. Repeat on all sides.

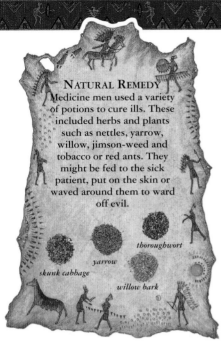

NATURAL REMEDY

Medicine men used a variety of potions to cure ills. These included herbs and plants such as nettles, yarrow, willow, jimson-weed and tobacco or red ants. They might be fed to the sick patient, put on the skin or waved around them to ward off evil.

thoroughwort

yarrow

skunk cabbage

willow bark

THE HAPPY COUPLE

Menominee people of the Woodlands made these dolls to celebrate the marriage of a couple. The miniature man and woman were tied face to face to keep husband and wife faithful. Dolls feature in the customs of many tribes, not least the Hopi and Zuni of the Southwest. Their katchina dolls are spirits shown in the form of animals, humans or plants.

MEDICINE BAGS

Crystals, animal parts, feathers and powders made of ground up plants and vegetables might be inside these bundles. They were used to make cures and spells by a shaman (medicine man) of the Winnebago tribe from the Woodlands.

SACRED BIRD

Rattles such as this Thunderbird rattle from the Northwest Coast were considered sacred objects and carved with the images of spirits. They were made of animal hoofs, rawhide or turtle shells, and filled with seeds or pebbles. Some were hand held, others were put on necklaces.

Rattles were an important part of any ceremony. In some tribes only shamans could hold one.

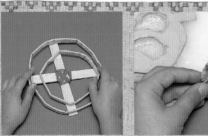

4 Glue the two card rings on to the cross, as here. The larger ring sits on the outer ends of the cross. The smaller one is roughly 1–2cm inside of that.

5 Roll out the modelling clay to a 1cm thickness. Cut out 20 to 30 semicircle shapes to resemble penguin beaks. Use a stick to make a hole at one end.

6 When the beaks are dry, paint them cream. Leave to dry. Paint the tips black then paint red or orange stripes. Next, paint the two rings brown.

7 Thread the black cotton through the hole in a painted beak, then tie it through one of the holes in the rings. Repeat with each beak, filling both rings.

American Indian Purifying Rites

S WEATING PURIFIED THE BODY AND MIND according to North American Indians. The Sioux called it "fire without end". The sweat was one of the most important and ancient of all North American religious rituals. They were among the first people to use heat to cleanse the body. But for tribe members, it was not simply a question of hygiene. The sweat lodge rite was performed before and after other ceremonies to symbolize moving into and out of a sacred world. Warriors prepared their spirits before the Sun Dance ceremony by taking a sweat bath. This was a dance to give thanks for food and gifts received during the year, and often featured self-mutilation. Sweats were also taken as a medical treatment to cure illness, and as a rite of passage through a stage in life such as from childhood to adulthood. A young boy who was about to make his transition into warrior-life was invited to spend time with the tribe's males. They would offer him the sacred pipe, which was usually smoked to send prayers. This was called Hunka's ceremony and showed the tribe's acceptance that the boy was ready. Some warrior initiation rites were brutal – such as the Mandan's custom of suspending young men by wooden hooks pierced through their chest, or scarring them, known as Okipa. Both girls and boys prepared for passing into adolescence by spending time alone and fasting (not eating).

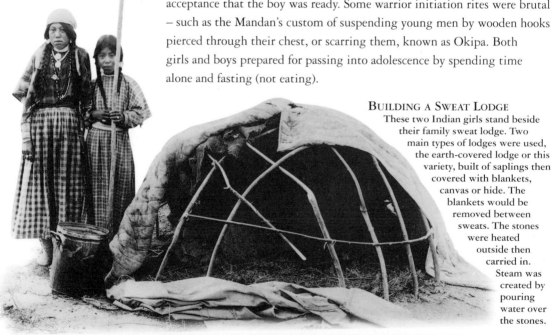

STEAM AND SMOKE
A holy man, such as this Pima shaman, would be in charge of sweats. Prayers and chants were offered and the sacred pipe was passed around each time the door was opened.

BUILDING A SWEAT LODGE
These two Indian girls stand beside their family sweat lodge. Two main types of lodges were used, the earth-covered lodge or this variety, built of saplings then covered with blankets, canvas or hide. The blankets would be removed between sweats. The stones were heated outside then carried in. Steam was created by pouring water over the stones.

BATHS IN EARTH

An Indian crawls out from an earth-covered sweat lodge for air. Six to eight people could sit around the hot stones inside, depending on the size of the sweat lodge. Males and females would both take part in sweats but it was customary to do so separately. In some tribes, families built their own family lodges and some larger sweat lodges were also used as homes or temples. Sticks and wood formed the frame. This was covered in mud or clay. The fire would be built in the lodge causing a dry heat. It was dark, stuffy and hot, similar to the saunas used in Europe. However, a sweat lodge was used to cleanse the spirit as well as the skin.

CLEANSED AND REFRESHED

Herbs, such as sweetgrass and cedar, were often put on the hot stones inside a sweat lodge. When the water was poured over the stones, the smell and essence of the herbs were released into the lodge with the steam. Herbs helped to clear the nasal passages. They could also be selected to treat particular ills. As the heat from the steam opened up the skin's pores, the herbs could enter the body and work at the illness or help purify the spirit. Sweating removed toxins (poisons in the body) and, the Indians believed, forced out disease.

GROWING UP

A young Apache girl is dressed up for a modern tribal ceremony. The lives of North American Indians were filled with rituals to mark each milestone in a person's life or important tribal events. There were ceremonies for birth, for becoming an adult or to mark changing seasons.

INSTRUMENTS TELL A STORY

This Tsimshian rattle has been involved in many ceremonies. Tribes had a vast amount of ceremonial objects, from rattles to headdresses, clothing and wands. Their decorations were usually of spiritual significance. In some tribes, the frog was respected since it would croak when danger was near. Others believed that their long tongues could suck out evil. A frog also features in the creation myths of the Nez Perce.

Shamans in the Arctic World

LONG BEFORE CHRISTIAN MISSIONARIES arrived in the Arctic, local people had developed their own beliefs. Arctic people thought that all living creatures possessed a spirit or *inua*. When an animal died, its spirit lived on and was reborn in another creature. Powerful spirits were thought to control the natural world, and these invisible forces influenced people's everyday lives. Some spirits were believed to be friendly towards humans. Others were malevolent or harmful. People showed their respect for the spirits by obeying taboos – rules that surrounded every aspect of life. If a taboo was broken the spirits would be angered. People called shamans could communicate with the spirit world. Shamans had many different roles in the community. They performed rituals to bring good luck in hunting, predicted the weather and the movements of the reindeer herds and helped to heal the sick. They worked as doctors, priests and prophets, all rolled into one.

SHAMAN AND DRUM
An engraving from the early 1800s shows a female shaman from Siberia. Most, but not all, shamans were male. Shamans often sang and beat on special drums, such as the one shown above, to enter a trance. Some drums had symbols drawn on them and helped the shamans to predict the future.

TUPILAK CARVING
This little ivory carving from Greenland shows a monster called a *tupilak. Tupilaks* were evil spirits. If someone wished an enemy harm, he might secretly make a little carving similar to this, which would bring a real *tupilak* to life. It would destroy the enemy unless the person possessed even more powerful magic to ward it off.

SHAMAN'S DRUM

You will need: ruler, scissors, thick card, PVA glue, glue brush, masking tape, compass, pencil, shammy leather, brown paint, paint brush, water pot, brown thread or string

1 Cut out two strips of thick card, each strip measuring 77 cm long and 3 cm wide. Glue the two strips together to give the card extra thickness.

2 Once the glue has dried, use masking tape to cover the edges of the double-thickness card. Try to make the edges as neat as possible.

3 Using a compass, draw a circle with a 24 cm diameter on a piece of shammy leather. Cut it out, leaving a 2 cm strip around the edge of the circle.

HERBAL MEDICINES

An Innu woman collects pitcher plants that she will use to make herbal medicines. In ancient times, shamans acted as community doctors. They made medicines from plants and gave them to sick people to heal them. They also entered trances to soothe angry spirits, which helped the sick to recover from their illness.

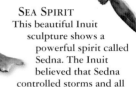

SEA SPIRIT

This beautiful Inuit sculpture shows a powerful spirit called Sedna. The Inuit believed that Sedna controlled storms and all sea creatures. If anyone offended Sedna, she withheld her blessing and hunting was poor. Here Sedna is portrayed with a mermaid's tail and accompanied by a narwhal and two seals. This very delicate carving has been made from a piece of reindeer antler.

MAGIC MASK

This mask is from Arctic North America. It was worn by Inuit shamans during a special ritual to communicate with the spirit world. Shamans wore wooden masks similar to this one. They also wore headdresses. Each mask represented a powerful spirit. The shaman would call on the spirit by chanting, dancing and beating on a special drum.

Shamans' drums were made of deerskin stretched over a round wooden frame. The shaman sometimes drew pictures of people, animals and stars on the side of the drum.

4 Using your fingers, curve the strip of card, as shown above. Make sure you curve the card slowly so that it does not crease.

5 Glue the card onto the circle. Ask someone to help keep the shammy leather stretched as you go. Tape the ends of the card together.

6 Make cuts 3 cm apart along the edge of the excess shammy leather towards the card, as shown above. Glue the edges to the cardboard ring.

7 Paint the card with dark brown paint and leave it to dry. Decorate the drum with thick brown thread or string by tying it around the edges.

Aztec Myths and Omens

THE AZTECS OF CENTRAL AMERICA lived in constant fear that their world might come to an end. Ancient legends told that this had happened four times before. Each time, the world had been born again. Yet Aztec priests and astrologers did not believe that this would happen next time. If the world ended again, it would be forever. The souls of all Aztec people would be banished to a dark, gloomy underworld. The Wind of Knives would cut the flesh from their bones, and living skeletons would feast and dance with the Lord of the Dead. Then the Aztecs would vanish forever when they reached Mictlan (hell). The Maya people told similar stories about the underworld – which they called Xibalba (the Place of Fright) in a great epic poem, the *Popol Vuh*. This poem featured two brothers, called the Hero Twins.

Aztec legends also told that the end of the world would be heralded by strange signs. In AD1519, these gloomy prophecies seemed to be coming true. Ruler Moctezuma II had weird, worrying dreams. Astronomers also observed eclipses of the Sun and a moving comet with a fiery tail.

FEATHERED SERPENT
Quetzalcoatl was an ancient god-king. His name meant feathered-serpent. He was worshipped by many Mesoamerican people, but especially by the Toltecs. They believed that he had sacrificed himself to help his people. A Toltec legend said that one day he would return, heralding the end of the world.

HEROES AND LEGENDS
This ball court is in Copan, Guatemala. The ball-game featured in many Maya legends about the Hero Twins. They were skilled ball-game players and also expert hunters with deadly blow guns.

CREATURES OF LEGEND

This Maya bowl is decorated with a picture of a spider-monkey. Many different kinds of monkeys lived in the rainforests of Mesoamerica. Monkey-gods played an important part in Maya myths and legends. Because monkeys were quick and clever, the Maya believed that monkey-gods protected clever people, such as scribes.

THE NEW FIRE CEREMONY

Every 52 years, the Aztecs believed that the world might come to an end. To stop this happening, they held a special ceremony. People put out their fires and stayed indoors. At sunset, priests climbed to the top of a hill and waited for the planet Venus to appear in the sky. At the moment it appeared, a captive was sacrificed to the gods. His heart was ripped out and a fire lit in his chest. The priests then sent messengers all over the Aztec lands, carrying torches to relight the fires. People then believed the world was safe for another 52 years.

HEAVENLY MESSENGER

Ruler Moctezuma is shown here observing the brilliant comet that appeared in the Mexican sky in 1519. Priests and Aztec people carefully studied the stars for messages from the gods. They remembered the old Toltec legend that said one day, the god Quetzalcoatl would return and bring the world to an end.

AZTEC HERITAGE

Many Aztec and Maya traditions still survive today. Millions of people speak Nahuatl (the Aztecs' language) or Maya languages. Aztec and Maya beliefs have mingled with Christian traditions to create new religious festivals. The most famous of these festivals is the Day of the Dead. Families bring presents of flowers and sweets shaped like skulls to their ancestors' graves.

Blood Sacrifices of Mesoamerica

MESOAMERICAN PEOPLE, such as the Aztecs and Maya, believed that unless they made offerings of blood and human lives to the gods, the Sun would die and the world would come to an end. Maya rulers pricked themselves with cactus thorns and sting-ray spines, or drew spiked cords through their tongues to draw blood. They pulled out captives' fingernails so the blood flowed. Aztecs pricked their ear-lobes each morning and collected two drops of blood to give to the gods. They also went to war to capture prisoners. On special occasions, vast numbers of captives were needed for sacrifice. It was reported that 20,000 victims were sacrificed to celebrate the completion of the Great Temple at Tenochtitlan in 1487. It took four days to kill them all. Mesoamerican temples were tombs as well as places of sacrifice. Rulers and their wives were buried inside. Each ruler aimed to build a great temple as a memorial to his reign.

TEMPLE TOMB
Pyramid Temple 1 at Tikal was built in the AD700s as a memorial to a Maya king. Nine stone platforms were built above the burial chamber, to create a tall pyramid shape reaching up to the sky.

HOLY KNIFE
This sacrificial knife has a blade of a semi-precious stone called chalcedony. It was made by Mixtecs from south Mexico. Mesoamerican priests used finely decorated knives of flint, obsidian and other hard stones to kill captives for sacrifice. These were trimmed to be as sharp as glass.

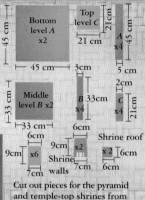

A PYRAMID TEMPLE

You will need: pencil, ruler, thick card, scissors, PVA glue, glue brush, masking tape, thin strips of balsa wood, thin card, corrugated card, water bowl, paintbrushes, paints.

Bottom level A x2 — 45 cm — 45 cm
Top level C — 21 cm — 21 cm
A x4 — 45 cm
3cm — 5 cm
Middle level B x2 — 33 cm — 33 cm
B 33cm x4 — 2cm
C x4 — 21 cm
6cm — 9cm — Shrine roof
9cm x6 — 9cm x2 — x2 6cm
Shrine walls 7cm — 7cm — 6cm — 6cm

Cut out pieces for the pyramid and temple-top shrines from thick card, as shown above.

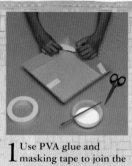

1 Use PVA glue and masking tape to join the thick card pieces to make three flat boxes (A, B and C). Leave the boxes until the glue is completely dry.

2 From the remaining pieces of card, make the two temple-top shrines, as shown. You could add extra details with strips of balsa wood or thin card.

SKULL SHRINE

Rows of human skulls, carved in stone, decorate this shrine outside the Aztecs' Great Temple in the centre of Tenochtitlan. Most Aztec temples also had skull-racks, where rows of real human heads were displayed. They were cut from the bodies of sacrificed captives.

RELIGIOUS GIFTS

Mesoamerican people also made offerings of food and flowers as gifts to the gods. Maize was a valuable gift because it was the Mesoamerican people's most important food. Bright orange marigolds were a sign of the Sun, on which every person's life depended.

maize

marigolds

PERFECTION

The ideal victim for human sacrifice was a fit and healthy young man.

HUMAN SACRIFICE

This Aztec codex painting shows captives being sacrificed. At the top, you can see a priest cutting open a captive's chest and removing the heart as an offering to the gods.

This model is based on the Great Temple that stood in the centre of Tenochtitlan.

3 Glue the boxes, one on top of the next. Cut out pieces of card the same size as each side of your boxes. They should be about 1– 2cm wide. Stick down, as shown.

4 Cut out two strips of card 2cm x 26cm. Glue them to a third piece of card 14cm x 26cm. Glue corrugated card 9.5cm x 26cm in position, as shown.

5 Stick the staircase to the front of the temple, as shown. Use a ruler to check that the staircase is an equal distance from either side of the temple.

6 Paint the whole temple a cream colour to look like natural stone. Add details, such as carvings or wall paintings, using brightly coloured paint.

Inca Feasts and Celebrations

IN COMMON WITH OTHER CENTRAL AMERICAN PEOPLE, the Incas loved to celebrate the natural world and its changing seasons. They marked them with special festivals and religious rituals. Some celebrations were held in villages and fields, others took place at religious sites or in the cities. It is said that the Incas had as many as 150 festivals each year. The biggest festival of all was *Inti Raymi*, the Feast of the Sun. It was held in June, to mark midwinter in the southern part of the world. *Qapaq Raymi*, the Splendid Festival, was held in December to mark the southern midsummer. This was when boys were recognized as adult warriors or young nobles. Crop festivals included the Great Ripening each February, the Earth Ripening each March and the Great Cultivation each May. The sowing of new maize was celebrated in August. The Feast of the Moon, held in September, was a special festival for women, while the Day of the Dead, in November, was a time to honour one's ancestors.

FEAST OF THE SUN
The Quechua people of Peru have revived the ancient festival of *Inti Raymi*. They gather each year at Sacsahuaman fortress, Cuzco, to celebrate the light and warmth of the Sun during the southern midwinter. In Inca times, a golden bowl was raised to the rising Sun. The Sun's rays would be used to make fire.

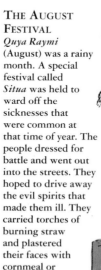

BRINGER OF RAIN
Drought was feared throughout the Empire, especially in the dry lands of the coast. If rain failed to fall, the life-giving irrigation channels dried up. In desperation, people visited the temples of Apu Illapu, bringer of rain. The priests made offerings and sacrifices, and the pilgrims prayed. The purpose of most Inca ceremonies and festivals was to prevent disaster and to ensure that life carried on.

THE AUGUST FESTIVAL
Quya Raymi (August) was a rainy month. A special festival called *Situa* was held to ward off the sicknesses that were common at that time of year. The people dressed for battle and went out into the streets. They hoped to drive away the evil spirits that made them ill. They carried torches of burning straw and plastered their faces with cornmeal or llama blood.

DANCERS AND MASKS

Drums, music and dance were always an important part of *Inti Raymi*, the Sun Festival. The Incas played rattles and whistles, drums and hand-drums, flutes and panpipes to help them celebrate the festival. Musicians played all day long without taking a break, and some of their ancient tunes are still known. Today, masks representing the Spanish invaders are added to the festivities. The modern festival proves that the old way of life has not been forgotten. Modern Peruvians are proud of their Inca past.

THE EMPEROR'S DAY

The modern festival of *Inti Raymi* attracts thousands to Cuzco. In the days of the Incas, too, nobles poured into the Inca capital from every corner of the Empire. Their aim was to honour the emperor as much as the Sun god. They came carrying tributes from the regions and personal gifts, hoping for the Emperor's favour in return.

FIESTA TIME

A drawing from the 1700s shows Peruvian dancers dressed as devils. Many of them are playing musical instruments or carrying long whips. After the conquest, festivals were known by the Spanish term, *fiestas*, and officially celebrated Christian beliefs. However, many of the festivities were still rooted in an Inca past. The dances and costumes often had their origins in Inca traditions.

Politics, Society & Leadership

Learn about the development of power and control, and the growth of cities, laws and governments in different civilizations. Travel through history to investigate how societies were organized and led from the top. A wide range of leadership styles are revealed, from ancient warrior kings and tribal chieftains to god-kings, pharaohs and imperial dynasties.

Keeping Control

IMAGINE WHAT it would be like if there were no rules at school, or no one had ever told you how to behave or what to do! When human beings live or work together, they work out basic rules about how to behave. This saves arguing all the time, and makes sure that jobs for the good of everyone, such as cleaning, get done. Often, we can work out for ourselves how to be sociable – to behave with other people. But rules may also be made by leaders and teachers. Throughout history, there have been leaders who used their experience and wisdom to guide, teach and organize – or govern – others in the best possible way. There have also been many cruel and greedy tyrants whose interest lay in increasing their own power and wealth rather than the good of the people.

The first humans lived very simply, in small family groups. There were no chiefs or rulers. The leaders were the strongest and fittest. Each group was only concerned with survival.

People live or work together at all sorts of different levels – from little groups such as your family or your class at school to the school itself and the community in which it lives. At each new level, there are additional sets of rules, and more leaders –

The warrior kings of Mycenae in ancient Greece ruled from 1500BC. They lived in palaces enclosed by massive walls, called citadels. Administrators and the rest of the population lived outside the walls.

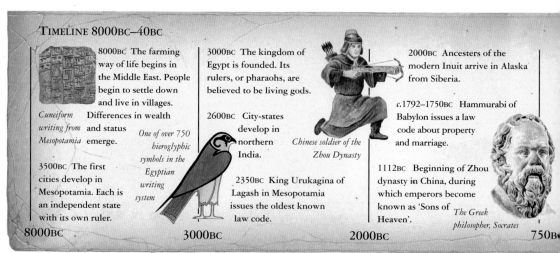

TIMELINE 8000BC–40BC

8000BC The farming way of life begins in the Middle East. People begin to settle down and live in villages.

Cuneiform writing from Mesopotamia

Differences in wealth and status emerge.

3500BC The first cities develop in Mesopotamia. Each is an independent state with its own ruler.

3000BC The kingdom of Egypt is founded. Its rulers, or pharaohs, are believed to be living gods.

2600BC City-states develop in northern India.

One of over 750 hieroglyphic symbols in the Egyptian writing system

2350BC King Urukagina of Lagash in Mesopotamia issues the oldest known law code.

Chinese soldier of the Zhou Dynasty

2000BC Ancesters of the modern Inuit arrive in Alaska from Siberia.

*c.*1792–1750BC Hammurabi of Babylon issues a law code about property and marriage.

1112BC Beginning of Zhou dynasty in China, during which emperors become known as 'Sons of Heaven'.

The Greek philosopher, Socrates

8000BC   3000BC   2000BC   750B

from the grown-ups in a family and the teachers and head teacher in a school, to the prime minister or president of a country. A number of people organized in this way is called society. Throughout history, society has become more and more complex as populations have grown. In this book you will be able to see how society evolved in different ways around the world, and how the leaders in various cultures and civilizations, controlled or governed their peoples.

In the beginning, it was all very simple. In prehistoric times, people hunted animals and picked plants for food. There was rarely any food to spare. A few related families lived together in small bands called clans.

Viking communities were at first small and tribal, hemmed in by high mountains. Land for big settlements to develop was limited. Some Viking chieftains conquered other tribes and built up kingdoms.

Everyone knew one another, and looked to the oldest and most experienced people in the clan for advice and decisions. Where there was water and fertile land, though, people learned how to farm and began to settle in permanent homes. Some farmers were more successful than others. They could use their wealth to control or persuade others. In this way, differences of status or rank developed. The Celts, for example, were made up of many tribes, each of which

Among tribal peoples, such as the Celts and Vikings, fighting for new land was a way of life and survival. Their warriors were important and respected members of tribal society. Those who were good at leading people often became chieftans.

A triumphal arch, built to celebrate a Roman victory

500BC   300BC   40BC

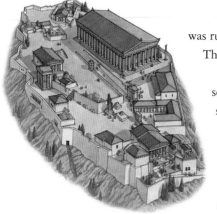

was ruled by a chief. Below the chief came warriors and then priests. Then came the farmers and last of all, the unpaid slave labour.

Although they were powerful, chiefs and kings in these simple societies had to listen to their followers or they lost their support. Like many other rulers throughout history, Celtic leaders rewarded their warriors with gifts to keep them loyal.

The Celtic tribes were scattered, and remained small and clan-based. In the fertile valleys of big rivers in the Middle East, China, India and Egypt, though, there were the resources, the climate and the space for settlements to expand.

Encouraging belief in powerful gods was one way of keeping citizens in order. In Athens, temples to the guardian goddess Athena dominated the city from the rocky Acropolis. Many public festivals were held there.

Great cities, with populations of tens of thousands, and a huge range of peoples and skills, grew up. Organizing such large communities was far too much for the ruler alone. Administrators, clerks and specialist advisers were needed to help decide how their cities and lands should be run. These groups of rulers and advisers were the first governments.

Rulers of early civilizations and cultures had to work hard at holding on to their power. The kings of city-states in Mesopotamia, the pharaohs of ancient Egypt and the Incas of South America promoted the idea that they were appointed by the gods, or even took on godly status themselves. Many leaders

In the Islamic world, it was not only scholars like these who had to study. Every Muslim had to learn the Arabic language so that they could read the laws laid down in the Koran.

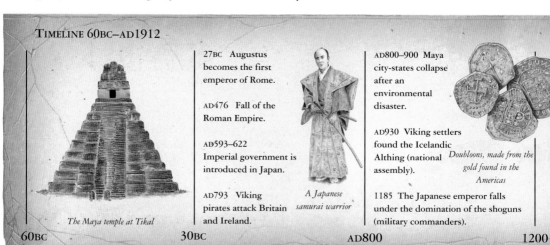

TIMELINE 60BC–AD1912

The Maya temple at Tikal

27BC Augustus becomes the first emperor of Rome.

AD476 Fall of the Roman Empire.

AD593–622 Imperial government is introduced in Japan.

AD793 Viking pirates attack Britain and Ireland.

A Japanese samurai warrior

AD800–900 Maya city-states collapse after an environmental disaster.

AD930 Viking settlers found the Icelandic Althing (national assembly).

Doubloons, made from the gold found in the Americas

1185 The Japanese emperor falls under the domination of the shoguns (military commanders).

60BC   30BC   AD800   1200

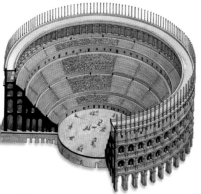

Roman emperors staged increasingly bloodthirsty gladiatorial games in the Colosseum in Rome. The events showed off the emperor's power and impressed the people. The stadium held up to 50,000 spectators.

ruled by fear, threatening dreadful punishments if they were disobeyed. Others won over those who might be useful by handing out riches, land or status.

Mesopotamian rulers were among the first to issue a formal set of rules, or laws, which the inhabitants of their city-states had to follow. The laws were inscribed on stone pillars – together with the punishments for breaking them – and erected in public places so that everyone could see them.

Those who made the rules were the few – the rich, the powerful or those who had inherited leadership from their fathers before them. The ordinary citizen did not have a say in how society was run. Then the Athenian Greeks introduced the idea of democracy, a system of government that allowed members of the community to vote. Most governments in the Western world today are democratically elected (chosen). The Romans developed a type of government called a republic. The United States and France are two countries that are run as republics today with democratically elected representatives. You can look at the different forms of government around the world today, and then see how they began and developed through history.

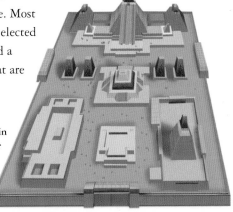

Maya rulers were buried in temple complexes. Each ruler aimed to build a fine temple as a memorial to his reign. The complex included areas for playing ball games.

Himeji castle, Japan

c.1200 The legendary emperor Manco Capac founds the Inca Empire.

1325 Foundation of the Aztec Empire.

1407 Building of the Chinese emperors' palace, the Forbidden City, in Beijing begins.

1521 The Spanish under Cortés conquer the Aztecs.

1526 The Mughals under Babur begin to conquer India.

1532 The Spanish under Pizarro conquer the Incas.

1687 Mughal empire reachest its peak under Aurangzeb.

1868 In Japan the shogunate falls and the emperors are returned to power.

1912 China becomes a republic after the last emperor is deposed.

Body of a Chinese princess in a jade suit

1400   1600   1912

Beginnings of Social Structure

IN STONE AGE TIMES, there were very few people in the world. Experts estimate that the world's population in 13,000BC was about eight million. Today it is nearly six billion – 750 *thousand* times as many. We can guess how Stone Age people lived together by looking at hunter-gatherer societies that still exist today in South America and the Pacific.

Groups of families lived together in clans. All the members of each clan were related to each other, usually through their mother's family or by marriage. Clans were large enough to protect and feed everyone, but not so large that they were unmanageable. All the members of a clan, including children, were involved in finding and gathering food for everyone. Clans were probably also part of larger tribes, which may have met up at certain times of year, such as for a summer hunt. The members of a tribe shared a language and a way of life. When people learned how to farm, populations increased and societies began to be organized in more complicated ways.

MOTHER GODDESSES
Eight thousand years ago, this clay sculpture from Turkey may have been worshipped as a goddess of motherhood. Families were often traced through the female line because mothers give birth, so everyone knew who the babies belonged to. The fathers were not always known.

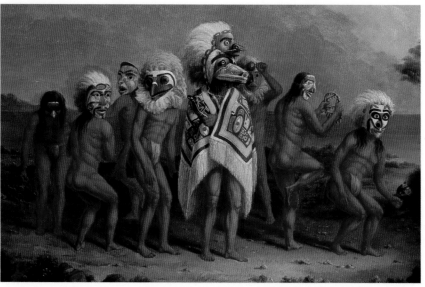

SHAMAN LEADERS
This painting from the 1800s shows Native American shamans performing a ritual dance. Shamans were the spiritual leaders of their tribes. They knew the dances, chants, prayers and ceremonies that would bring good luck and please the spirits. Shamanism is found in hunter-gatherer societies around the world today and was practised in prehistoric times.

TRIBAL CHIEF

This man is a Zulu chief from South Africa. His higher rank is shown by what he wears. In prehistoric times, tribes might have been ruled by chiefs or councils of elders. An old man buried at Sungir in Russia around 23,000BC was probably a chief. His body was found richly decorated with fox teeth and beads made of mammoth ivory.

SCENES FROM LONG AGO

Paintings on cliff walls in the Sahara Desert in Africa show hippopotamuses being hunted and herders tending cattle. Other images show a woman pounding flour, ceremonies and a family with a dog. They show that, in 6000BC, it was a fertile area with organised communities.

FINE FIGURE

Between 3000 and 2000BC, some of the finest prehistoric sculpture was made on the Cycladic Islands of Greece. This figurine is made of ground marble and shows a slender woman with her arms folded above her waist. Finely worked sculpture was a sign that a society had become more complex than a simple clan. There were more people with more specialized jobs, and more free time.

A TRADITIONAL WAY OF LIFE

The man on the right is helping a boy prepare for his coming-of-age ceremony in Papua New Guinea. Traditional ways of life are still strong in that country, where there are many remote tribes. In some villages, all the men live together, rather than with their wives and children. This allows them to organize their work, such as hunting, more easily.

Legendary Kings of Mesopotamia

GIANT ATTACK
The giant Humbaba guarded the Cedar Forest, far away, in Lebanon. His voice was like thunder, his breath was fire, and he could hear the faintest noise from the ends of the earth. To test their courage, Gilgamesh and Enkidu decided to kill this monster. They were terrified by the giant's dreadful face and taunting words, but finally cut off his head with one stroke.

FROM AROUND 3000BC, the people of Mesopotamia lived in walled cities. Each city had its own ruler and guardian god. The rulers wanted to be remembered for ever, by the wonderful temples and palaces they had built, or by having their deeds and battle victories carved into stone pillars called stelae.

Some of the world's oldest stories are about Gilgamesh, king of one of Sumer's most important cities in around 2700BC. Stories and poems about him passed from the Sumerian people to those who lived in the Babylonian and Assyrian empires. Finally, in the 7th century BC, the Assyrians wrote down all these exciting stories on to clay tablets. The *Epic of Gilgamesh* was stored in the great libraries of King Ashurbanipal of Assyria, where it was discovered by archaeologists over 100 years ago. Gilgamesh was not a good king at first, so the gods created Enkidu, a wild, hairy man, to fight him. The king realized he had met his match, and the two then became good friends and went everywhere together.

THE BULL OF HEAVEN
Ishtar, the goddess of love and war (on the left), tries to stop Enkidu and Gilgamesh from killing the Bull of Heaven. Ishtar had fallen in love with the hero-king, and she wanted to marry him. Gilgamesh knew that the goddess was fickle, and turned her down. Ishtar was furious and asked her father, Anu the sky god, to give her the Bull of Heaven so she could take revenge on Gilgamesh. The Bull was a deadly beast who had the power to bring death and long-term misery to the city of Uruk. The two friends fought and killed the bull. Enkidu (on the right) hung on to its tail, as Gilgamesh delivered the death blow with his sword.

THE CITY OF URUK

There is very little of Uruk left today, but it was a very important city when Gilgamesh was king. The city had splendid temples dedicated to Anu, the sky god, and his daughter Ishtar who fell in love with Gilgamesh. The king also built a great wall round the city. When his friend Enkidu died, Gilgamesh was heartbroken, and also frightened because he realized he would die one day, too. He wanted to live for ever. In the end, he decided that creating a beautiful city was his best chance of immortality. He would be remembered for ever for creating the fine temples and massive walls of Uruk.

LASTING FAME

The figures on this stone vase from Uruk probably show Gilgamesh. The king found the lasting fame he wanted because his name lived on in stories and legends, and in statues and carvings such as this.

THE PLANT OF ETERNAL LIFE

This massive stone carving of a heroic figure found in the palace of King Sargon II may be of Gilgamesh. Sargon II created the world's first empire by conquering all the cities of Sumer, Mari and Ebla. Gilgamesh set out to find Utnapishtim, the ruler of another Sumerian city who was said to have found the secret of eternal life. The way was long and dangerous, and led into the mountains where lions prowled. After a terrifying walk in total darkness, Gilgamesh emerged on the other side of the mountain into the garden of the gods. Beyond the garden were the Waters of Death, but our hero found a ferryman to take him safely across. At last he met Utnapishtim, who told him he would never die if he found a plant that grew on the sea bed. Gilgamesh tied stones on his feet, dived into the sea and picked the plant. However, on the way home, he stooped down to drink at a pool. A water snake appeared and snatched the plant. With it went Gilgamesh's hope of immortality.

Kingly Duties in Mesopotamia

The KINGS OF MESOPOTAMIA considered themselves to have been chosen by the gods. For example, Ur-Nanshe of Lagash (2480BC) said that he was granted kingship by Enlil, chief of the gods, and Ashurbanipal (669BC) claimed he was the son of the Assyrian god, Ashur, and his wife, Belit. The Mesopotamian kings ran the state on the god's behalf. Even in the Assyrian Empire, when the kings had grand titles such as 'King of the Universe', they still felt they were responsible to the gods for the well-being of their people. Another of their titles was 'Shepherd'. This meant they had to look after their people, just as a shepherd tends his flock.

AUTHORITY
An onyx mace was carried by the Babylonian kings of Mesopotamia as a symbol of authority. At New Year, the king laid the mace before the statue of the chief god, Marduk. When he picked it up again, it meant he would reign for another year.

SUN GOD TABLET FROM SIPPAR
Kings had to see that temples and statues of the gods were kept in good repair. This tablet shows King Nabu-apla-iddina of Babylon being led into the presence of the god Shamash. The story on the tablet tells us that the king wanted to make a new statue of the god. He was meant to repair the old one but it had been stolen by enemies. Fortunately a priest found a model of the statue that could be copied.

MAKE A FLY WHISK
You will need: calico fabric, pencil, ruler, PVA glue and brush, scissors, thick card, paints and paintbrushes, newspaper.

1 Draw long leaf shapes about 45cm long on to the calico fabric with the pencil. Paint the shapes with watered down PVA glue. Leave to dry.

2 Cut out the leaf shapes. Make a card spine for the centre of each leaf as shown, thicker at the bottom than at the top, and glue them on.

3 Paint the leaves in gold, yellow and red paints on both sides. Add fine detail by cutting carefully into the edge of each leaf using the scissors.

FIGHTING FOR THE GODS

Kings believed that they were commanded by the gods to conquer other cities and states in their name. In this relief, King Sennacherib is sitting on his throne receiving the booty and prisoners taken after the city of Lachish had fallen. The king devoted a whole room in his palace at Nineveh to the story of this siege. He also made war on Babylon and completely devastated the city. In 612BC the Babylonians had their revenge. They destroyed the city of Nineveh and hacked out Sennacherib's face on this sculpture.

EXPLORATION AND DISCOVERY

Another mark of good kingship was the expansion of knowledge. King Shalmaneser III sent an expedition to find the source of the River Tigris (pictured here). His men set up a stela (a carved monument) to record the discovery and made offerings to the gods to celebrate. Many Mesopotamian kings were learned men. They collected clay tablets to make great libraries or built up collections of exotic plants and animals.

Fly whisks made of long thin leaves or feathery reeds kept the flies away from the king. They could also be used as a fan to keep him cool.

4 Draw two identical handle shapes on to the stiff card. They should be about 22cm long and 10cm wide at the top. Cut out the shapes with the scissors.

5 Tear up newspaper strips and dip into glue. Wrap the strips around the edges of the two handles to fasten them together. Leave the top of the handle unglued.

6 Decorate the handle with gold paint. Leave to dry. Paint decorative details on to the gold with black paint using a fine paintbrush.

7 Glue the bottoms of the leaves and push them into the top of the handle, between the two pieces of cardboard. Spread the leaves well apart.

Running the Assyrian Empire

FROM THE BEGINNING of the 800s BC, the country of Assyria in the north of Mesopotamia began to grow into a vast empire. The land was divided into provinces that were named after the main city, such as Nineveh, Samaria or Damascus. Every city had a governor who made sure that taxes were collected, called up soldiers in times of war, and supplied workers when a new palace or temple was to be built. The governor made sure that merchants could travel safely, and he was also responsible for law and order. If the king and his army passed through the province, the governor supplied them with food and drink. A vast system of roads connected the king's palace with governors' residences and the important cities of the Empire.

ENFORCED REMOVAL
Conquered people were banished from their homelands, and forced to go and live in Assyria. These people were from Lachish, near Jerusalem, and were moved to the Assyrian city of Nineveh. The men were used as forced labour in the limestone quarries.

THE KING'S MEN
An Assyrian king was constantly surrounded by bodyguards, astrologers and other members of the court. There were also visitors such as provincial governors who helped the king run the Empire. The King's servants included scribes to write down orders, messengers to deliver them and an attendant to hold a parasol. In this picture King Ashurnasirpal is celebrating a successful bull hunt with priests and musicians.

MAKE A PARASOL

You will need: pencil, coloured card 60cm x 60cm, scissors, masking tape, paints in bright colours and paintbrushes, white card, string or twine, glue, dowel.

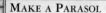

1 Draw a circle on the coloured card measuring roughly 60cm across. Cut out the circle with the scissors keeping the edge as neat as possible.

2 Cut a slit from the edge of the circle to the centre. Pull one edge of the slit over the other to make a conical shape. Secure with masking tape.

3 Paint your parasol with red paint. Leave to dry. Then paint stripes in lots of different shades of orange and red from the top to the bottom.

Towards a New Life

Defeated people camp out en route to a new life in Assyria. The Assyrian Empire grew so big, that it could take months to travel back from a newly won territory. Conquered people were usually kept together in families and given homes in the countryside. Often they were set to work to cultivate more land.

Keeping Accounts

Assyrian scribes at the governor's palace at Til Barsip on the River Euphrates make a note of taxes demanded by the king. Taxes were exacted not only from the local Assyrian people, but also from the conquered territories. They could be paid in produce, such as grain, horses or cattle, and wine.

Kings were accompanied by an attendant carrying a sunshade, which was probably made of fine woollen material and decorated with tassels.

Useful Tribute

Conquered people had to give tributes such as horses to the Assyrian king, as well as food for the animals. The horses swelled the chariot and cavalry units in the Assyrian army. The best-bred and strongest horses came from the foothills of the Zagros Mountains to the east of Assyria.

4 Cut 20 oval shapes about 5cm by 4cm from the white card. Cover with a base colour of gold. Leave to dry, then paint with bright designs.

5 Use the scissors to make holes around the edge of the parasol and in the ovals. Attach the ovals to the parasol with twine, knotting it as shown.

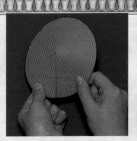

6 Cut a small circle out of coloured card measuring 10cm across. Make a slit to the centre, and pull one edge over the other as before. Paint the small cone gold.

7 Glue it to the top of the parasol. Paint the handle with gold paint and allow to dry. Attach it to the inside of the parasol using plenty of masking tape.

The Pharaohs of Egypt

THE WORD PHARAOH comes from the Egyptian *per-aa*, which meant 'great house' or 'palace'. It later came to mean the man who lived in the palace, the ruler. Pictures and statues show pharaohs with special badges of royalty, such as crowns, headcloths, false beards, sceptres and a crook and flail held in each hand.

The pharaoh was the most important person in Egypt. He was the link between the people and their gods, and therefore had to be protected and cared for. The pharaoh's life was busy. He was high priest, chief law-maker, commander of the army and in charge of the country's wealth. He had to be a clever politician, too. The ancient Egyptians believed that on his death, the pharaoh became a god. Pharaohs were usually men, but women sometimes ruled Egypt as Queen Hatshepsut did, when her husband Thutmose II died and his son was still a child. A pharaoh could take several wives. Within royal families, it was common for fathers to marry daughters and for brothers to marry sisters. Sometimes pharaohs married foreign princesses in order to make an alliance with another country.

THE CROOK AND FLAIL
These emblems of the god Osiris became badges of royal authority. The crook stood for kingship and the flail for the fertility of the land.

flail

crook

MOTHER GODDESS OF THE PHARAOHS
Hathor was worshipped as the mother goddess of each pharaoh. Here she is shown welcoming the pharaoh Horemheb to the afterlife. Horemheb was a nobleman who became a brilliant military commander. He was made pharaoh in 1323BC.

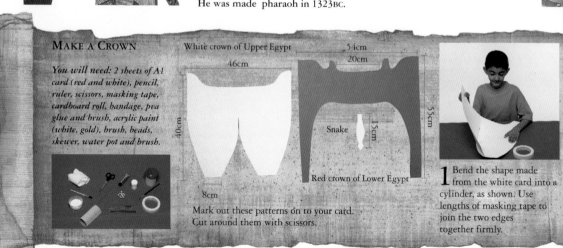

MAKE A CROWN

You will need: 2 sheets of A1 card (red and white), pencil, ruler, scissors, masking tape, cardboard roll, bandage, pva glue and brush, acrylic paint (white, gold), brush, beads, skewer, water pot and brush.

White crown of Upper Egypt

54cm

46cm

20cm

40cm

Snake

15cm

55cm

8cm

Red crown of Lower Egypt

Mark out these patterns on to your card. Cut around them with scissors.

1 Bend the shape made from the white card into a cylinder, as shown. Use lengths of masking tape to join the two edges together firmly.

RAMESSES MEETS THE GODS

This painting shows the dead pharaoh Ramesses I meeting the gods Horus (left) and Anubis (right). Pharaohs had to pass safely through the afterlife. If they did not, the link between the gods and the world would be broken forever.

THE QUEEN'S TEMPLE

This great temple (*below*) was built in honour of Queen Hatshepsut. It lies at the foot of towering cliffs at Deir el-Bahri, on the west bank of the Nile near the Valley of the Kings. The queen had the temple built as a place for her body to be prepared for burial. Pyramids, tombs and temples were important symbols of power in Egypt. By building this temple, Hatshepsut wanted people to remember her as a pharaoh in her own right.

HATSHEPSUT

A female pharaoh was so unusual that pictures of Queen Hatshepsut show her with all the badges of a male king, including a false beard! Here she wears the pharaoh's crown. The cobra on the front of the crown is the badge of Lower Egypt.

The double crown worn by the pharaohs was called the pschent. *It symbolized the unification of the two kingdoms. The white section at the top (hedjet) stood for Upper Egypt, and the red section at the bottom (deshret) for Lower Egypt.*

2 Tape a cardboard roll into the hole at the top. Plug its end with a ball of bandage. Tape the bandage in position and glue down the edges.

3 Wrap the white section with lengths of bandage. Paint over these with an equal mixture of white paint and glue. Leave the crown in a warm place to dry.

4 Now take the shape made from the red card. Wrap it tightly around the white section, as shown, joining the edges with masking tape.

5 Now paint the snake gold, sticking on beads as eyes. When dry, score lines across its body. Bend the snake's body and glue it to the crown, as shown.

High Society in Egypt

EGYPTIAN PALACES were vast complexes. They included splendid public buildings where the pharaoh met foreign rulers and carried out important ceremonies. Members of the royal family lived in luxury in beautiful townhouses with painted walls and tiled floors near the palace.

The governors of Egypt's regions also lived like princes, and pharaohs had to be careful that they did not become too rich and powerful. The royal court included large numbers of officials and royal advisors. There were lawyers, architects, tax officials, priests and army officers. The most important court official of all was the vizier, who carried out many of the pharaoh's duties for him.

The officials and nobles were at the top of Egyptian society. But most of the hard work that kept the country running smoothly was carried out by merchants and craft workers, by farmers, labourers and slaves.

GREAT LADIES
Ahmose-Nefertari was the wife of Ahmose I. She carries a lotus flower and a flail. Kings could take many wives. It was common for them to have a harem of beautiful women.

A NOBLEMAN AND HIS WIFE
This limestone statue shows an unknown couple from Thebes. The man may have worked in a well-respected profession, as a doctor, government official or engineer. Noblewomen did not work but were quite independent. Any property that a wife brought into her marriage remained hers.

THE SPLENDOURS OF THE COURT
This is the throne room of Ramesses III's palace at Medinet Habu, on the west bank of the Nile near Thebes. Pharaohs often had many palaces, and Medinet Habu was one of Ramesses III's lesser ones. Surviving fragments of tiles and furniture give us an idea of just how splendid the royal court must have been. A chamber to one side of the throne room is even believed to be an early version of a shower cubicle!

RELAXATION

Ankherhau (above), a wealthy overseer of workmen, relaxes at home with his wife. They are listening to a harpist. Life was pleasant for those who could afford it. Kings and nobles had dancers, musicians and acrobats to entertain them. Cooks worked in their kitchens preparing sumptuous meals. By comparison, ordinary people ate simple food, rarely eating meat except for the small animals they caught themselves.

HAIR CARE

The royal family was waited on by domestic servants who attended to their every need. Here (left), the young Queen Kawit, wife of the pharaoh Mentuhotep II, has her hair dressed by her personal maid. Although many of the female servants employed in wealthy households were slaves, a large number of servants were free. This meant that they had the right to leave their employer at any time.

Rulers of India

Over the centuries, India has been ruled by leaders from many different lands, cultures and religions. Their titles and the symbolic objects that surrounded them are often a clue to their roles and beliefs. From the time of the emperor Ashoka, around 250BC, the ruler became known as *cakravartin* (wheel-turner). The wheel was a Buddhist symbol for the world, so this suggested that the king made the world go round. Objects that were symbols of royalty included sceptres, crowns and yak-tail fans. The most important object was the *chatra* (umbrella), which signified the king's protection of his realm. Hindu *maharajadhirajas* (kings) developed the idea that the god Vishnu lived within them. When Islam arrived in the 1300s, the sultans showed their obedience to the caliph (the head of Islam in Baghdad) by taking titles such as *nasir* (helper). Rulers in the Mughal Empire (1526-1857), took Persian titles such as *padshah* (emperor).

DISPLAY OF POWER
A Mughal emperor rides through the city on top of an elephant, a symbol of royalty. Kings often processed through their cities to display their power and majesty. They were always followed by attendants and courtiers.

THE MARKS OF A KING
A picture of the foot of Hindu ruler Rama bears images of a lotus, conch shell, umbrella, fly whisk and other royal symbols. People believed that a world-ruling king was born with features such as these on their soles and palms. Rama was said to be a wise and good ruler. He was later deified (made into a god).

MAKE A CHAURI
You will need: strip of corrugated cardboard measuring 3cm x 25cm, raffia, scissors, sticky tape, PVA glue, 20 cm length of dowel, modelling clay, paint in gold and a contrasting colour, paintbrushes, foil sweet wrappers.

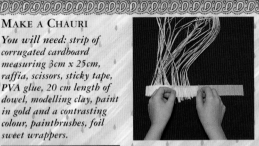

1 Put the strip of card on a covered, flat surface. Cut strips of raffia. Carefully tape the strands of raffia to the card. Leave your chauri to dry.

2 Wrap the card and raffia around the dowel, and glue it in place. Keep the card 2 cm from the top, so that the dowel supports the raffia.

3 Tape the card and raffia band firmly in place to make sure that it will not come undone when you use your whisk. Leave the whisk to dry.

A KING'S HALO
The king in this procession has a halo surrounding his head. From Mughal times, rulers were thought to be blessed with the divine light of wisdom. This was represented in pictures by a halo.

ROYAL CUSHION
Raja Ram Singh of Jodhpur sits with his nobles. Only the king was allowed to sit on a cushion. The Rajputs were kings of northern India who fought against Muslim invaders in the first millennium AD. In the Mughal Empire, they were important military allies of the Muslims.

ROYAL RAMA
Rama was a Hindu king, believed to be the earthly representative of the god Vishnu. He is with his wife Sita and his brothers. He holds a bow, a symbol of courage. Attendants hold other symbols of royalty.

The fly whisk was a symbol of a Hindu king's power.

4 Make lots of small beads from modelling clay. Glue these on to the dowel in a circle, about 2.5 cm below the strip of card. Leave to dry.

5 Paint the dowel and beads with two coats of gold paint. Leave it to dry. Then paint a pattern on the strip of card and the dowel, in different colours.

6 When the paint is dry, glue bits of coloured foil paper to your chauri. The more decorations you add, the more it will look like a real chauri.

The Mughal Empire

I N 1526, A PRINCE called Babur invaded India from the north-west. He swept across the country with a powerful army and soon arrived in Delhi. The city was the heart of the Sultanate, the kingdom that Islamic invaders had founded 300 years before. Babur defeated the Sultanate and founded the Mughal Empire. It was the last important dynasty of India before the British arrived in the 1700s.

Babur's grandson, Akbar was a great Mughal leader from 1556 to 1605. Although a Muslim, he was tolerant of other religions and took Hindu princesses as his wives. Forty years later, the warlike Mughal ruler Aurangzeb returned to a stricter form of Islam and expanded the Empire. The Mughals were patrons of the arts, and built glorious palaces,

gardens and tombs. Many of India's most precious works of art date from this era. Persian was the language of their court, but they also spoke Urdu, a mixture of Persian, Arabic and Hindi.

ORDERLY COURTIERS
Mughal nobles had to take part in court rituals. They had to arrive punctually at court, and line up in rows. Dress and posture were very important. The cummerbund tied around the waist and the turban were signs of self-control. Courtiers guarded the palace strictly in turn.

THE FIRST MUGHAL EMPEROR
Babur defeats Ibrahim Lodi, the last sultan of Delhi, at the Battle of Panipat in 1526. Babur invaded India because he was unable to recapture his own homeland in Samarkand.

MAKE A LACQUERED STORAGE BOX
You will need: pencil, ruler, sheets of card, scissors, sticky tape, newspaper, wallpaper paste or flour and water, bowl, fine sandpaper, paint in white and bright colours, paintbrushes, non-toxic varnish.

1 Scale up the shape shown here to the size you want your box to be and copy the shape on to card. Cut out the shape and fix the edges with sticky tape to form a box.

2 Draw 4 card triangles with sides the same length as the top of the box. Tape the triangles together to form a pyramid and cut off the top.

3 Add newspaper strips to the paste, or flour and water, to make papier mâché. Cover the box and lid with three layers of papier mâché. Dry between layers.

A POEM IN STONE

The Mughal emperor Shah Jahan commemorated his wife Mumtaz Mahal (who died in childbirth) by building this magnificent mausoleum. It was built between 1631 and 1648, and came to be known as the Taj Mahal. It is built of white marble from Rajasthan. The Taj Mahal is one of the most magnificent buildings in the world, and is the high point of Mughal art.

JADE HOOKAH

This Mughal period *hookah* (pipe) is made from precious green jade. During Mughal times, the culture of the court reached a high point in Indian history. Many fine objects and ornaments like this were made.

Lacquered boxes were popular with women of the royal court for storing jewellery.

RED PALACE

The Red Fort in Agra is one of the palaces built by Akbar. The Mughal emperors broke with the tradition of kings living in tents, and built sumptuous residences in their capital cities.

 4 When the papier mâché is dry, smooth any rough edges with sandpaper. Add squares of cardboard as feet. Paint the box and the lid white.

 5 Allow the painted box and lid to dry. Draw a pattern on to the box and lid. You could copy the pattern shown here, or use your own design.

6 Paint the lid and the box, including the feet, with brightly coloured paints. Use the pattern that you have drawn as a guide. Leave to dry.

7 To finish, paint the box and lid with a coat of non-toxic varnish. Leave to dry completely, then add a final coat of varnish. Your storage box is now finished.

Lives of the Chinese Rulers

THE FIRST CHINESE RULERS lived about 4,000 years ago. This early dynasty (period of rule) was known as the Xia. We know little about the Xia rulers, because Chinese history of this time is mixed up with ancient myths and legends. Excavations have told us more about the Shang dynasty rulers about 1,000 years later. They were waited on by slaves and had fabulous treasures.

During the next period of rule, the Zhou dynasty, an idea grew up that Chinese rulers were Sons of Heaven, placed on the throne by the will of the gods. After China became a powerful, united empire in 221BC, this idea helped keep the emperors in power. Rule of the Empire was passed down from father to son. Anyone who seized the throne by force had to show that the overthrown ruler had offended the gods. Earthquakes and natural disasters were often taken as signs of the gods' displeasure.

Chinese emperors were among the world's most powerful rulers ever. Emperors of China's last dynasty, the Qing (1644–1912), lived in luxurious palaces that were cut off from the world. When they travelled through the streets, the common people had to stay indoors.

WHERE EMPERORS PRAYED
There are beautifully decorated pillars inside the Hall of Prayer for Good Harvests at Tiantan in Beijing. An emperor was a religious leader as well as a political ruler. Each New Year, the emperor arrived at the hall at the head of a great procession. The evening was spent praying to the gods for a plentiful harvest in the coming year.

TO THE HOLY MOUNTAIN
This stele (inscribed stone) is located on the summit of China's holiest mountain, Taishan, in Shandong province. To the ancient Chinese, Taishan was the home of the gods. For over 2,000 years the emperors climbed the carved steps to the temple to offer prayers.

IN THE FORBIDDEN CITY
The vast Imperial Palace in Beijing is best described as 'a city within a city'. It was built between 1407 and 1420 by hundreds of thousands of labourers under the command of Emperor Yongle. Behind its high, red walls and moats were 800 beautiful halls and temples, set among gardens, courtyards and bridges. No fewer than 24 emperors lived here in incredible luxury, set apart from their subjects. The Imperial Palace was also known as the Forbidden City. Ordinary Chinese people were not even allowed to approach its gates.

'WE POSSESS ALL THINGS'

This was the message sent from Emperor Qianlong to the British King George III in 1793. Here the emperor is being presented with a gift of fine horses from the Kyrgyz people of Central Asia. By the late 1800s, Chinese rule took in Mongolia, Tibet and Central Asia. All kinds of fabulous gifts were sent to the emperor from every corner of the Empire, as everyone wanted to win his favour.

RITUALS AND CEREMONIES

During the Qing dynasty, an emperor's duties included many long ceremonies and official receptions. Here in Beijing's Forbidden City, a long carpet leads to the ruler's throne. Officials in silk robes line the steps and terraces, holding their banners and ceremonial umbrellas high. Courtiers kneel and bow before the emperor. Behaviour at the royal court was set out in the greatest detail. Rules decreed which kind of clothes could be worn and in which colours.

CARRIED BY HAND

The first Chinese emperor, Qin Shi Huangdi, is carried to a monastery high in the mountains in the 200s BC. He rides in a litter (a type of chair) that is carried on his servants' shoulders. Emperors always travelled with a large following of guards and courtiers.

Japan's Emperors of the Sun

THE JAPANESE PEOPLE began to live in villages in about 300BC. Over the next 600 years, the richest and most powerful of these villages became the centres of small kingdoms, controlling the surrounding lands. By about AD300, a kingdom based on the Yamato Plain in south-central Japan became bigger and stronger than the rest. It was ruled by chiefs of an *uji* (clan) who claimed to be descended from the Sun goddess. The chiefs of the Sun-clan were not only army commanders. They were priests, governors, law-makers and controllers of their people's treasure and food supply as well. Over the years, their powers increased.

By around AD500, Sun-clan chiefs from Yamato ruled over most of Japan. They claimed power as emperors, and organized lesser chiefs to work for them, giving them noble titles as a reward. Each emperor chose his own successor from within the Sun-clan, and handed over the sacred symbols of imperial power – a jewel, a mirror and a sword. If a male successor to the throne was too young to rule, an empress might act for a time as regent.

Descendants of these early emperors still rule Japan today, although their role is purely ceremonial. In other periods of Japan's history, too, the emperors had very little power. Some did play an active part in politics, while others spent their time shut away from the outside world.

HANIWA FIGURE
From around AD300-550, clay *haniwa* figures were put around tombs. Statues of soldiers, servants and animals were placed in an emperor's tomb to look after him in his next life.

NARA
This shrine is in the ancient city of Nara. Originally called Heijokyo, Nara was founded by Empress Gemmei (ruled AD707–715) as a new capital for her court. The city was planned and built in Chinese style, with streets arranged in a grid pattern. The Imperial Palace was situated at the northern edge.

FANTASTIC STORIES

Prince Shotoku (AD574–622) was descended from the imperial family and from another powerful clan, the Soga. He never became emperor, but ruled as regent for 30 years on behalf of Empress Suiko. Many fantastic stories were told about him. One was that he was able to speak as soon as he was born. It was also said that he could see into the future. More accurate reports of Shotoku's achievements list his introduction of a new calendar, and his reform of government, based on Chinese ideas. He was also a supporter of the new Buddhist faith, introduced from China.

LARGEST WOODEN STRUCTURE

The Hall of the Great Buddha at Nara was founded on the orders of Emperor Shomu in AD745. The whole temple complex is said to be the largest wooden structure in the world. It houses a bronze statue of the Buddha, 16m tall and weighing 500 tonnes. It was also designed to display the emperor's wealth and power. There is a treasury close to the Hall of the Great Buddha, built in AD756. This housed the belongings of Emperor Shomu and his wife, Empress Komyo. The treasury still contains many rare and valuable items.

BURIAL MOUNDS

The Yamato emperors were buried in huge, mound-shaped tombs surrounded by lakes. The largest, built for Emperor Nintoku, is 480m long. From above, the tombs have a keyhole-shaped layout. Inside, they contain many buried treasures.

THE SUN GODDESS

The Sun goddess Amaterasu Omikami is shown emerging from the earth in this print. She was both honoured and feared by Japanese farmers. One of the emperor's tasks was to act as a link between the goddess and his people, asking for her help on their behalf. The goddess's main shrine was at Ise, in central Japan. Some of its buildings were designed to look like grain stores – a reminder of the Sun's power to cause a good or a bad harvest.

Keeping Control in Japan

I**N EARLY JAPAN**, everyone, from the proudest chief to the poorest peasant, owed loyalty to the emperor. However, many nobles ignored the emperor's orders – especially when they were safely out of reach of his court. There were plots and secret schemes as rival nobles struggled to influence the emperor or even to seize power for themselves.

Successive emperors passed laws to try to keep their nobles and courtiers under control. The most important new laws were introduced by Prince Shotoku (AD574–622) and Prince Naka no Oe (AD626–671). Prince Naka considered his laws to be so important that he gave them the name *Taika* (Great Change). The Taika laws created a strong central government, run by a Grand Council of State, and a well-organized network of officials to oversee the 67 provinces.

DANCE
A Bugaku performer makes a slow, stately movement. Bugaku is an ancient form of dance that was popular at the emperor's court over 1,000 years ago. It is still performed today.

POLITE BEHAVIOUR
A group of ladies watches an archery contest from behind a screen at the edge of a firing range. The behaviour of courtiers was governed by rigid etiquette. Noble ladies had to follow especially strict rules. It was bad manners for them to show their faces in public. Whenever men were present, the ladies crouched behind a low curtain or a screen, or hid their faces behind their wide sleeves or their fans. When travelling, they concealed themselves behind curtains or sliding panels fitted to their ox-carts. They also often left one sleeve dangling outside.

THE SHELL GAME
You will need: fresh clams, water bowl, paintbrush, gold paint, white paint, black paint, red paint, green paint, water pot.

1 Ask an adult to boil the clams. Allow them to cool and then remove the insides. Wash the shells and leave them to dry. When dry, paint the shells gold.

2 Carefully pull each pair of shells apart. Now paint an identical design on to each of a pair of clam shells. Start by painting a white, round face.

3 Add features to the face. In the past, popular pictures, such as scenes from the *Tale of Genji,* were painted on to the shell pairs.

NOBLES AT COURT

Two nobles are shown here riding a splendid horse. Noblemen at the imperial court spent much of their time on government business.

They also practised their riding and fighting skills, took part in court ceremonies, and read and wrote poetry.

THE IMPERIAL COURT

Life at court was both elegant and refined. The buildings were exquisite and set in beautiful gardens. Paintings based on the writings of courtiers show some of the famous places they enjoyed visiting.

THE FUJIWARA CLAN

Fujiwara Teika (1162–1241) was a poet and a member of the Fujiwara clan. This influential family gained power at court by arranging the marriages of their daughters to young princes and emperors. Between AD724 and 1900, 54 of the 76 emperors of Japan had mothers who were related to the Fujiwara clan.

A LOOK INSIDE

This scroll-painting shows rooms inside the emperor's palace and groups of courtiers strolling in the gardens outside. Indoors, the rooms are divided up by silken blinds and the courtiers sit on mats and cushions.

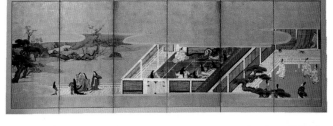

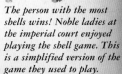

4 Paint several pairs of clam shells with various designs. Make sure that each pair of shells has an identical picture. Leave the painted shells to dry.

5 Turn all your shells face down and mix them up well. Turn over one shell then challenge your opponent to pick the matching shell to yours.

6 If the two shells do not match, turn them over and try again. If they do match, your opponent takes the shells. Take it in turns to challenge each other.

The person with the most shells wins! Noble ladies at the imperial court enjoyed playing the shell game. This is a simplified version of the game they used to play.

Japanese Military Power

IN 1159, a bloody civil war, known as the Heiji War, broke out in Japan between two powerful clans, the Taira and the Minamoto. The Taira were victorious in the Heiji War, and they controlled the government of the country for 26 years. However, the Minamoto rose again and regrouped to defeat the Taira in 1185.

Yoritomo, leader of the Minamoto clan, became the most powerful man in Japan and set up a new headquarters in the city of Kamakura. The emperor continued to act as head of the government in Kyoto, but he was effectively powerless. For almost the next 700 years, until 1868, military commanders such as Yoritomo, rather than the emperors, were the real rulers of Japan. They were known by the title *sei i tai shogun* (Great General Subduing the Barbarians).

SHOGUN FOR LIFE
Minamoto Yoritomo was the first person to take the title shogun and to hand the title on to his sons. In fact, the title did not stay in the Minamoto family for long because the family line died out in 1219. But new shogun families soon took its place.

FIRE! FIRE!
This scroll-painting illustrates the end of a siege during the Heiji War. The war was fought between two powerful clans, the Taira and the Minamoto. The rival armies set fire to buildings by shooting burning arrows and so drove the inhabitants out into the open where they could be killed.

MAKE A KITE
You will need: A1 card, ruler, pencil, dowelling sticks tapered at each end (5 x 50cm, 2 x 70cm), masking tape, scissors, glue, brush, thread, paintbrush, paints, water pot, paper (52cm x 52cm), string, bamboo stick.

1 Draw a square 50cm x 50cm on card with a line down the centre. Lay the dowelling sticks on the square. Glue the sticks to each other and then tape.

2 When the glue has dried, remove the masking tape. Take the frame off the card. Bind the corners of the frame with the strong thread.

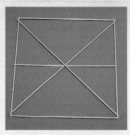

3 Now position your two longer dowelling sticks so that they cross in the middle of the square. Glue and then bind the corners with the strong thread.

DYNASTY FOUNDER

Tokugawa Ieyasu (1542-1616) was a noble from eastern Japan. He was one of three powerful warlords who brought long years of civil war to an end and unified Japan. In 1603 he won the battle of Sekigahara and became shogun. His family, the Tokugawa, ruled Japan for the next 267 years.

RESTING PLACE

This mausoleum (burial chamber) was built at Nikko in north-central Japan. It was created to house the body of the mighty shogun Tokugawa Ieyasu. Three times a year, Ieyasu's descendants travelled to Nikko to pay homage to their great ancestor.

UNDER ATTACK

Life in Nijo Castle, Kyoto, is shown in great detail on this painted screen. The castle belonged to the Tokugawa family of shoguns. Like emperors, great shoguns built themselves fine castles, which they used as centres of government or as fortresses in times of war. Nijo Castle was one of the finest buildings in Japan. It had 'nightingale' floors that creaked loudly when an intruder stepped on them, raising the alarm. The noise was made to sound like a bird call.

Kites were sometimes used for signalling during times of war. The Japanese have also enjoyed playing with kites for over 1,000 years.

4 Paint a colourful kite pattern on to the paper. It is a good idea to tape the edges of the paper down so it does not move around or curl up.

5 Draw light pencil marks 1cm in from the corners of the paper on all four sides. Carefully cut out the corners of the paper, as shown.

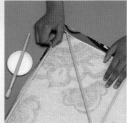

6 Glue the paper on to the kite frame. You will need to glue along the wooden frame and fold the paper over the edge of the frame. Leave to dry.

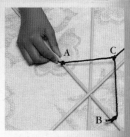

7 Tie a short length of string across the centre of the kite frame (A to B). Knot a long kite string on to it as shown (C). Wind the string on the bamboo.

Imperial Life in Japan

IT WAS THE CUSTOM for each Japanese ruler to build a new palace when he or she came to power. But in AD710, the Empress Gemmei built a whole new city, at Nara. It became the government centre for all Japan.

In AD794, Emperor Kammu decided to build a city that would be bigger and even more beautiful than Nara. He moved his imperial court to a new site, called Heian-kyo. Kammu based the plans for his new capital on the great Chinese city of Chang'an (modern Xian). The whole city was laid out as a rectangle, with main streets running at right angles to one another. The emperor's palace was in the north of the city, and courtiers lived in elegant *shinden* (single-storey villas) close by. Workers and lower officials lived on the outskirts. Heian-kyo (modern Kyoto) was home to the Japanese emperors for over 1,000 years, until 1868 when Emperor Meiji came to power. Its royal and noble inhabitants became known as the people who lived in the clouds, because they lived shut away from ordinary, everyday life.

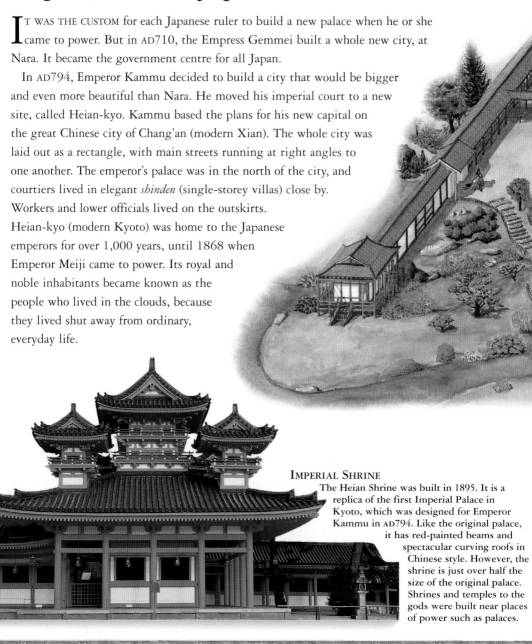

IMPERIAL SHRINE
The Heian Shrine was built in 1895. It is a replica of the first Imperial Palace in Kyoto, which was designed for Emperor Kammu in AD794. Like the original palace, it has red-painted beams and spectacular curving roofs in Chinese style. However, the shrine is just over half the size of the original palace. Shrines and temples to the gods were built near places of power such as palaces.

LIFE IN A SHINDEN

In *Heian-kyo*, nobles and courtiers lived in splendid *shinden* (houses) like this one. Each *shinden* was designed as a number of separate buildings, linked by covered walkways. It was usually set in a landscaped garden, with artificial hills, ornamental trees, bridges, pavilions and ponds. Sometimes a stream flowed through the garden – and through parts of the house, as well. The various members of the noble family, and their servants, lived in different parts of the *shinden*.

GOLDEN PAVILION

This is a replica of the Kinkakuji (Temple of the Golden Pavilion). The original was completed in 1397 and survived until 1950. But, like many of Kyoto's old wooden buildings, it was destroyed by fire. The walls of the pavilion are covered in gold leaf. The golden glow is reflected in the calm waters of a shallow lake.

SILVER TEMPLE

The Ginkakuji (Temple of the Silver Pavilion) in Kyoto was completed in 1483. Despite its name, it was never painted silver, but left as natural wood.

THRONE ROOM

The Shishinden Enthronement Hall is within the palace compound in Kyoto. The emperor would have sat on the raised platform (left) while his courtiers bowed low before him. This palace was the main residence for all emperors from 1331 to 1868.

Organized Government in Greece

Ancient Greece was made up of about 300 separate city states. Some were no bigger than villages, while others centred around cities such as Sparta or Athens. Each city state was known as a *polis* (from which we take our word politics) and had its own laws and government. In the 4th century BC, the Greek philosopher Aristotle wrote that there were various types of government. Autocracy was power held by one person. This might be a monarch, on account of his royal birth, or a tyrant who had siezed power by force. Oligarchy was government by a few people. These might be aristocrats who assumed control by right of noble birth, or a group of rich and powerful people. Democratic government was rule by many and was only practised in Athens. It gave every male citizen the right to vote, hold public office or serve on a jury. However, women, slaves and foreigners were not counted as full citizens.

BEHIND THE SCENES
Women were not allowed to take an active part in politics in ancient Greece. However, some played an important role behind the scenes. One such woman was Aspasia, a professional entertainer. She met and became mistress to Pericles, one of the most influential Athenian statesmen of the 5th century BC. Pericles confided in his mistress about affairs of state. He came to rely on her insight and wisdom in his judgement of people and situations.

SET IN STONE
The laws of the city of Ephesus were carved on stone tablets in both Greek and Latin. The Greeks believed that their laws had to be clearly set in stone and seen by everyone if all citizens were to be expected to obey them.

VOTING TOKENS
You will need: pair of compasses, thin card, pencil, ruler, scissors, rolling pin, cutting board, self-hardening clay, modelling tool, balsa wood stick 5cm long, piece of drinking straw 5cm long, bronze-coloured paint, paintbrush, water pot.

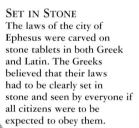

1 Make two templates. Use a pair of compasses to draw two circles, on a piece of thin card. Make each one 4cm in diameter. Cut them out.

2 Use a rolling pin to roll out the clay to 3cm thickness. Use a modelling tool to cut around the card circles into the clay. Press down hard as you do this.

3 Make a hole in the centre of each clay circle. Use the balsa wood to make one hole (innocent token). Use the straw to make the other hole (guilty token).

PEOPLE POWER

Solon the Lawgiver was an Athenian statesman and poet who lived from 640 to 559BC. Around 594BC, he served as chief magistrate. He gave Athens new laws that enabled more people to take part in politics. His actions prevented a civil war from breaking out between the few nobles in power and the people who suffered under their rule.

VOTE HERE

This terracotta urn was used to collect voting tokens. They were used in Athens when votes needed to be taken in law courts or when the voters' intentions needed to be kept secret. Each voter put a bronze disc in the urn to register his decision. Normally, voting was done by a show of hands, which was difficult to count precisely.

FACE TO FACE

The ruins of this council chamber at Priene in present-day Turkey show how seating was arranged. The tiered, three-sided square enabled each councillor to see and hear clearly all of the speakers involved in a debate. Even in the democracies of ancient Greece, most everyday decisions were taken by committees or councils and not by the assembly of voters.

4 Write a name on the innocent token using the modelling tool. Carefully push the balsa stick through the hole. Leave it to dry.

5 Write another name on the guilty token using the modelling tool. Carefully push the drinking straw through the hole. Leave it to dry.

6 Wait until the clay tokens are dry before painting them. The original tokens were made from bronze, so use a bronze-coloured paint.

Jurors were issued with two tokens to vote with. A hollow centre meant that the juror thought the accused was guilty. A solid centre meant that the juror thought the accused was innocent.

Inequality in Greece

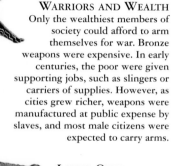

GREEK SOCIETY WAS DIVIDED by a strict social structure that was enforced by its governments. Most city states were ruled by a small group of people (oligarchy). Two exceptions were the powerful cities of Sparta and Athens. Sparta held on to its monarchy, while Athens introduced the first democratic government in history. In the city of Athens, all citizens could vote and hold office. However to be a citizen, it was necessary to be an adult male, born in the city itself. Even so-called democratic Athens was ruled by a minority of the people who lived there. The treatment of *metics* (foreign residents), women, slaves and children was just the same as in other city states.

Women had no legal rights and rarely took part in public life. Metics had to pay extra taxes and serve in the army, but could not own land or marry an Athenian. The Athenians felt uneasy about the large number of metics living in their city, but depended upon their skills.

Slaves made up half the population of Athens. Most of them had been born to slaves, were prisoners of war or captives of pirates. Even native Greeks could become slaves by falling into debt, but they were freed once the debt was paid off.

WARRIORS AND WEALTH

Only the wealthiest members of society could afford to arm themselves for war. Bronze weapons were expensive. In early centuries, the poor were given supporting jobs, such as slingers or carriers of supplies. However, as cities grew richer, weapons were manufactured at public expense by slaves, and most male citizens were expected to carry arms.

A WOMAN'S PLACE

Greek women spent their lives at home. On this vase, made about 450BC, a woman ties her sandal before going out. As she has attendants, she must be wealthy. Poor women would leave the house to fetch water, work in the fields or shop in the market. Women with slaves, like this one, might leave the home to visit relatives or to pray at a shrine or temple.

LOVED ONES

A young girl and her pet dog are seen on this tombstone from the 4th century BC. The likely expense of such a detailed carving suggests that she was dearly loved. Not all children were cherished. Girl babies, and sick babies of either sex, were often left outside to die. Some were underfed and fell victim to diseases. Greek law required children to support their parents in old age. Childless couples were always keen to adopt, and sometimes rescued abandoned children.

CRAFTSMAN

This smith could be a slave working in a factory owned by a wealthy man. Most craftsmen were slaves, ex-slaves or *metics* (foreign residents). They were looked down upon by other citizens. If a master owned a talented slave, he might set the slave up to run his own business. In return, the master would receive a share of the profits. This smith might also have been a free, self-employed man, with his own workshop and a slave or two working as his assistants.

PATH TO POWER?

Being able to read and write in ancient Greece was not an automatic key to success. The Greek alphabet could be learned quite easily. Even slaves could become highly educated scribes. However, illiterate men were unlikely to hold high positions, except perhaps in Sparta, where written records were rarely kept. Although women were denied the right to a formal education, they were often able to read and write enough to keep a record of household stores.

ENSLAVED BY LANGUAGE

This Roman bottle is made in the shape of an African slave girl's head. The Greeks also owned slaves. The Greek philosopher Aristotle argued that some people were "naturally" meant to be slaves. His opinion was shared by many of his countrymen. He felt that this applied most obviously to people who did not speak Greek. Slaves were treated with varying degrees of kindness and hostility. Some were worked to death by their owners, but others had good jobs as clerks or bailiffs. A few hundred slaves were owned by the city of Athens and served as policemen, coin-inspectors and clerks of the court.

Rulers of Rome

I**N ITS EARLY DAYS**, the city of Rome was ruled by kings. The first king was said to be Romulus, the founder of the city in 753BC. The last king, a hated tyrant called Tarquinius the Proud, was thrown out in 509BC. The Romans then set up a republic. The Senate, an assembly of powerful and wealthy citizens, chose two consuls to lead them each year. By 493BC, the common people had their own representatives – the tribunes – to defend their rights in the Senate. In times of crisis, rulers could take on emergency powers and become dictators. The first Roman emperor, Augustus, was appointed by the Senate in 27BC. The emperors were given great powers and were even worshipped as gods. Some lived simply and ruled well, but others were violent and cruel. They were surrounded by flatterers, and yet were in constant fear of their lives.

TRIUMPHAL PROCESSION
When a Roman general won a great victory, he was honoured with a military parade called a triumph. Cheering crowds lined the streets as the grand procession passed by. If a general was successful and popular, the way to power was often open to him. Probably the most famous Roman ruler of all, Julius Caesar, came to power after a series of brilliant military conquests.

STATE SACRIFICE
Roman emperors had religious as well as political duties. As *pontifex maximus*, or high priest, an emperor would make sacrifices as offerings to the gods at important festivals.

DEADLY FRUIT

figs

Who killed Augustus, the first Roman emperor, in AD14? It was hard to say. It might have been a natural death... but then again, it might have been caused by his wife Livia. She was said to have coated the figs in his garden with a deadly poison. Roman emperors were much feared, but they were surrounded by enemies and could trust no one, least of all their own families.

GUARDING THE EMPEROR

The Praetorian Guards were the emperor's personal bodyguards. They wore special uniforms, were well paid and they were the only armed soldiers allowed in the city of Rome. They became very powerful and sometimes took power into their own hands. Guards assassinated the emperor Caligula and elected Claudius to succeed him.

In Rome, wreaths made from leaves of the laurel tree were worn by emperors, victorious soldiers and athletes. The wreath was a badge of honour. The Romans copied the idea from the ancient Greeks.

WREATH OF HONOUR

You will need: tape measure, garden wire, pliers, scissors, clear tape, green ribbon, bay or laurel leaves (real or fake).

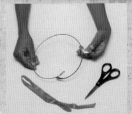

1 Measure around your head with the tape measure. Cut some wire the same length, so the wreath will fit you. Bend the wire as shown and tape the ribbon round it.

2 Start to tape the leaves by their stems on to the wire, as shown above. Work your way around to the middle of the wire, fanning out the leaves as you go.

3 Then reverse the direction of the leaves and work your way around the rest of the wire. Fit the finished wreath to your head. Hail, Caesar!

Masters and Slaves in Rome

ROMAN SOCIETY was never very fair. In the early days of the Republic, a group of rich and powerful noble families, called the patricians, controlled the city and the Senate. A citizen who wanted his voice heard had to persuade a senator to speak on his behalf. Over the centuries the common citizens, known as plebeians, became more powerful. By 287BC, they shared equally in government. Eventually, in the days of the Empire, even people of humble birth could become emperor, provided they were wealthy or had the support of the army. Emperors always feared riots by the common people of Rome, so they tried to keep the people happy with handouts of free food and lavish entertainments. Roman women could not vote. Most had little power outside the family, but some were successful in business or influenced political events through their husbands. Slaves had very few rights, even though Roman society was dependent on their labour. Prisoners of war were sold as slaves, Many were treated cruelly and revolts were common.

A ROMAN CONSUL
This is a statue of a Roman consul, or leader of the Senate, in the days of the Republic. At first, only members of the noble and wealthy class could be senators. However, under the emperors, the power and influence of the Senate slowly grew less.

LIFE AS A SLAVE
The everyday running of the Empire depended on slavery. This mosaic shows a young slave boy carrying fruit. In about AD100, a wealthy family might have had as many as 500 slaves. Some families treated their slaves well, and slaves who gave good service might earn their freedom. However, many more led miserable lives, toiling in the mines or labouring in the fields.

SLAVE TAG
This bronze disc was probably worn like a dog tag around the neck of a slave. The Latin words on it say: 'Hold me, in case I run away, and return me to my master Viventius on the estate of Callistus'. Slaves had few rights and could be branded on the forehead or leg as the property of their owners.

COLLECTING TAXES

This stone carving probably shows people paying their annual taxes. Officials counted the population of the Empire and registered them for paying tax. Money from taxes paid for the army and running the government. However, many of the tax collectors took bribes, and even emperors seized public money to add to their private fortunes.

ARISTOCRATS

This Italian painting of the 1700s imagines how a noble Roman lady might dress after bathing. Wealthy people had personal slaves to help them bathe, dress and look after their hair. Household slaves were sometimes almost part of the family, and their children might be brought up and educated with their owner's children.

Celtic Societies

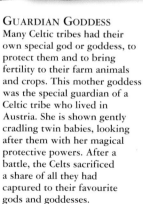

THE CELTS WERE NEVER a single, unified nation. Instead there were many separate tribes throughout Europe. Greek and Roman writers recorded many Celtic tribal names, for example, the Helvetii (who lived in Switzerland) and the Caledones (who lived in Scotland). Tribes sometimes made friendly alliances with one another, or with a stronger power such as Rome. This usually happened when a tribe was threatened by invaders or at war. Within each tribe, there were many clans. These were families who traced their descent from a single ancestor, and who shared ties of loyalty and a family name.

Each tribe was headed by a king (or chieftain). His task was to lead men in battle and on raids, and to maintain peace and prosperity. Kings were chosen from rich noble families. Senior noblemen were expected to support the king and to lead their own bands of warriors. Druids (Celtic priests) and bards (well-educated poets) also came from noble families. Farmers and craftworkers ranked lower, but they were highly valued for their important skills. There were also servants and slaves.

GUARDIAN GODDESS

Many Celtic tribes had their own special god or goddess, to protect them and to bring fertility to their farm animals and crops. This mother goddess was the special guardian of a Celtic tribe who lived in Austria. She is shown gently cradling twin babies, looking after them with her magical protective powers. After a battle, the Celts sacrificed a share of all they had captured to their favourite gods and goddesses.

PROUD LEADER

This stone statue of a Celtic king or chieftain from Gaul (modern France) was made around 50BC. He is dressed ready to lead his tribe into war, in a chainmail tunic and a magic torc. His torc (neck ornament) is an indication of high rank, but we have no idea who he actually was.

Religious support, knowledge, rituals

Protection and offerings

Gifts and prestige

Loyalty and help in battle

Chieftains

Protection and offerings

Religious support

Druids and bards

Farmers and craftworkers

Nobles and warriors

Religious support

Respect and offerings

Respect and manpower

Protection and access to land

THE STRUCTURE OF SOCIETY

All the different groups within Celtic society had an important part to play. They relied on one another to survive. This diagram shows what each different group gave to society, and what it received in return. Chieftains offered leadership and inspired loyalty. Nobles and warriors protected the tribe from attack. Farmers and craftworkers produced food and goods. Druids and bards provided religious support and celebrated tribal pride. The lowest social rank was held by labourers and slaves. They did jobs that were often hard and dirty.

TRIBAL COIN

Many Celtic tribes issued coins, marked with their own special design. This coin was made for the Catuvellauni tribe who lived in southern England. It shows a warrior on horseback riding into battle brandishing a carnyx (war-trumpet). It was designed to tell everyone what a brave and warlike people the Catuvellauni were.

SLAVE CHAIN

Chains like these were used to stop slaves running away. The round iron bracelets, joined by links of heavy metal, were fastened round a slave's wrists or ankles and locked shut. Slavery was never very important in Celtic society. There were many more free people than slaves. However, slaves were used for dirty, difficult, dangerous work (for example, in the salt mines at Hallstatt, Germany).

Viking Rulers and Freemen

MOST VIKINGS WERE KARLS (freemen) who owned some land and a farm, and went to sea for raids and adventures. Other karls were merchants, ship builders or craft workers. The free Vikings used *thralls* (slaves) as labourers and servants on farms and in workshops. Many Vikings were slave-traders. Prisoners who had been captured on raids all over Europe were sold as thralls. Viking society allowed thralls few rights. Their children were slaves as well.

STRONG RULERS
This king is a piece in a chess set from the Isle of Lewis, Scotland. Viking kings were often violent men who were hungry for power. They led their men into battle and fought with them to the bitter end.

The most powerful and wealthy Vikings were chieftains or *jarls* (earls). They controlled large areas in Norway and Sweden, and some jarls became local kings. Viking kings became more powerful as they conquered new lands and united them into kingdoms. By 900, Harald Finehair, King of Vestfold, had brought all of Norway under his control. Denmark had always been ruled by a single person, and in the reign of Harald Bluetooth, government became even more centralized. Yet the early Vikings had been quarrelsome and proud people, who bridled against any centralized control. This remained true in colonies such as Iceland. Many people, including Eirik the Red, fled to Iceland to escape the law, or because they did not want to be ruled by a distant king. Iceland remained an independent republic throughout the Viking Age. However, after 1100, it was forced to recognize a Norwegian king.

FIGHTING FORCE
Karls (freemen), formed the backbone of a Scandinavian invasion force when the Normans attacked England in 1066. This scene is part of the Bayeux tapestry and shows Norman karls preparing for conquest.

FARMERS
Viking karls (freemen) built farmhouses on the Shetland islands to the north of Scotland. The search for new land to farm led many karls to travel overseas. The buildings on Shetland were made of timber, stone and turf. This Viking site is known as Jarlshof today.

LOYAL TO YOUR LORD

This reconstruction of a Viking raid is taking place on the island of Lindisfarne in northern England. Viking raiders first attacked Lindisfarne in the year 793. A typical war band would have been made up of karls (freemen). In battle, they followed their jarl (earl), into the thick of the fighting without hesitation. They formed a tight guard around him when the fighting got tough. In the early Viking days, it was more important to show loyalty to one's family or lord than to a kingdom.

DEFENSIVE FORT

King Harald Bluetooth had a series of forts built to defend the Danish kingdom in the 980s. This one is at Fyrkat, in Jutland. By the end of the Viking period, it was very rare for independent Viking chieftains to lead small bands of karls on raids.

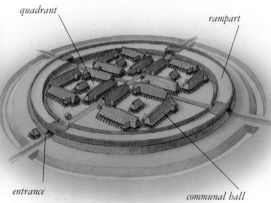

quadrant

rampart

entrance

communal hall

A RESTLESS PEOPLE

Poor farmhands prepare wool in this reconstruction showing Vikings at work. Families of all social classes left Scandinavia to settle new lands during the Viking age. They were driven by the need for land and wealth. They faced long sea voyages and years of hard work building new farms or towns.

Viking Assemblies

EACH REGION AND LAND where the Vikings settled had its own public assembly called the *Thing*, where laws and judgements were passed. The Thing met at regular intervals and was made up only of karls (freemen). Women and slaves had no right to speak there.

The Thing had great powers, and it could even decide who should be king. If someone was murdered or robbed, the victim's relatives could go to the Thing and demand justice. Everybody in the assembly considered the case. If they all agreed that a person was guilty, then judgement was passed. The person sentenced might have to pay a fine of money or other valuable goods. Sometimes the only way a dispute could be settled was by mortal combat (a fight to the death). However, mortal combat was made illegal in Iceland and Norway around AD1000. The assembly also dealt with arguments over property, marriage and divorce.

PAY UP
The Thing could order a criminal to pay the victim, in the form of money or goods. If the criminal failed to do so, he was made an outlaw. This entitled anyone to kill him.

In Iceland there was no king at all in the Viking period. Instead, an *Althing* or national assembly was held each midsummer. The Althing was a cross between a court, a parliament and a festival. It was a chance for families to come in from their isolated farmhouses and meet up with each other. The assembly approved laws that had been drafted by the jarls and elected a Law Speaker.

MEETING PLACE
The Icelandic Althing met on the Thingvellir, a rocky plain east of the city of Reykjavik. A Law Speaker read out the laws, which had been passed by a group of 39 chieftains, from the Law Rock. The Althing is the world's oldest surviving law-making assembly on record. It met from 930 until 1800 and again from 1843. Today it is Iceland's parliament.

A DIFFICULT DECISION

This carving shows an important gathering of the Althing in 1000. The assembly was split over a difficult decision – should Iceland become Christian? It was left to the Law Speaker to decide. After a lot of thought, he ruled that the country should be officially Christian, but that people who wished to worship the old gods could do so in private.

MANX LAW

An earth mound marks the site of the old Viking assembly on the Isle of Man. The Vikings who settled on the island, off the west coast of Great Britain, called this assembly field the Tynwald. This is also the name of the island's parliament today. The Tynwald still has the power to make the island's laws.

MORTAL COMBAT

A Viking duel is re-enacted today. Life was cheap in Viking times, and violent death was common. A fight to the death was an official way of settling a serious dispute, such as an accusation of murder. This system of justice was taken to England by the Normans in 1066.

LAW MAKERS

Viking chieftains would ride to Iceland's Thingvellir (Assembly Plain) from all over the island. This 19th-century painting by W.G. Collingwood shows chieftains gathering for the Althing. This assembly was held only once a year.

Aztec and Maya Social Order

T HE LAND BETWEEN North and South America, known as Mesoamerica, was never a single, united country. During the Maya (AD250-900) and later Aztec civilizations, it was divided into several, separate states. The rulers of these states often combined the roles of army commanders, law-makers and priests. Some claimed to be descended from the gods. Rulers were almost always men. Mesoamerican women – especially among the Maya – had important religious duties but rarely took part in law-making or army life. Maya rulers were called *ahaw* (lord) or *mahk'ina* (great Sun lord), and each city-state had its own royal family.

The supreme Aztec leader was called the *tlatoani* (speaker). Originally, he was elected from army commanders by the Aztec people. Later, he was chosen from the family of the previous leader. He ruled all Aztec lands, helped by a deputy called *cihuacoatl* (snake woman), nobles and army commanders. Rulers, priests and nobles made up a tiny part of society. Ordinary citizens were called *macehualtin*. Men were farmers, fishermen or craftworkers. There were thousands of slaves, who were criminals, enemy captives or poor people who had given up their freedom in return for food and shelter.

OFFICIAL HELP
This Maya clay figure shows a scribe at work. Well-trained officials, such as scribes, helped Mesoamerican rulers by keeping careful records. Scribes also painted ceremonial pottery.

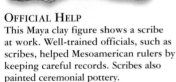

HONOUR TO THE KING
Painted pottery vases like this were buried alongside powerful Maya people. They show scenes from legends and royal palace life. Here, a lord presents tribute to the king.

MAYA NOBLEWOMAN
This terracotta figure of a Maya noblewoman dates from between AD600 and 900. She is richly attired and is protecting her face with a parasol. Women did not usually hold official positions in Mesoamerican lands. Instead noblewomen influenced their husbands by offering tactful suggestions and wise advice. Whether she was rich or poor, a woman's main duty was to provide children for her husband and to support him in all aspects of his work.

The Ruling Class

A noble is shown getting ready for a ceremony in this Aztec picture. Aztec nobles played an important part in government. They were chosen by rulers to be judges, army commanders and officials. Nobles with government jobs paid no taxes and were given a free house to live in. Noble men and women came from ancient families who were related to the rulers. It was, however, possible for an ordinary man to achieve higher rank if he fought very bravely in battle and captured four enemy soldiers alive.

War Leader

A Maya stone carving shows ruler Shield Jaguar (below left) getting ready to lead his army in AD724. He is wearing a padded tunic and holding a knife in his right hand. His wife, Lady Xoc, is handing him his jaguar headdress. Maya rulers also took part in religious ceremonies, where they offered drops of their blood to the gods in return for their help.

Men at Work

Aztec farmers are harvesting ripe cobs of maize. This painting comes from the Florentine Codex. This 12-volume manuscript was made by a Spanish friar. Codex pictures like this tell us a lot about ordinary peoples' everyday lives. Notice how simply the farmers are dressed compared to the more powerful people on these pages.

Life at the Top in Mesoamerica

THE RULERS OF EACH Maya and Aztec city-state lived in splendid palaces that were a reflection of their power and wealth. The palace of the Aztec ruler Moctezuma II in Tenochtitlan was vast. It had banqueting rooms big enough to seat 3,000 guests, private apartments, a library, a schoolroom, kitchens, stores, an arsenal for weapons, separate women's quarters, spectacular gardens and a large zoo. Etiquette around the emperor was very strict. Captains of the royal bodyguard had to approach Moctezuma barefoot, with downcast eyes, making low bows and murmuring, 'Lord, my lord, my great lord.' When they left, they had to walk backwards, keeping their gaze away from his face.

Palaces were also the government headquarters where rulers greeted ambassadors from neighbouring city-states and talked with advisors.

Rulers had the power to make strict laws. Each city-state had its own law-courts, where formidable judges had the power of life and death.

ROYAL RECORD
Maya rulers set up stelae (stone pillars) in their cities. Carved pictures recorded major people and events of their reigns. This one celebrates a Maya ruler in Copan, Honduras.

THE SEAT OF POWER
This carved jade ornament shows a seated Maya king. Aztec and Maya leaders had the final say in any decision. However, they were advised by judges, officials and scribes.

MAKE A FEATHER FAN

You will need: pencil, thick card, scissors, thin red card, green paper, double-sided tape, feathers (real or paper), masking tape, paints, paintbrushes, coloured felt, PVA glue and brush, sticky tape, coloured wool, bamboo cane.

1 Draw two rings about 45cm in diameter and 8cm wide on thick card. Cut them out. Make another ring the same size from thin red card, as above.

2 Cut lots of leaf shapes from green paper. Stick them around the edge of one thick card ring using double-sided tape. Add some real or paper feathers.

3 Cut two circles about 12cm in diameter from thin red card. Draw around something the right size, such as a reel of tape. These are for the centre of the fan.

LOCKED UP

A group of Aztec judges discusses how best to punish prisoners in the cage. Punishments were very severe. If ordinary citizens broke the law, they might be beaten or speared with cactus spines. For a second offence, they might be stoned to death.

THE RULE OF THE GODS

In this stone carving, a human face is being swallowed by a magic serpent. Royal and government buildings were often decorated with carvings like this. They signified the religious power of the ruler of a particular city.

FIT FOR A KING

An Aztec picture shows visitors at a ruler's palace. Spanish explorers in the 1500s reported that over 600 nobles visited the Aztec ruler's palace every day. They attended council meetings, consulted palace officials, asked favours from the ruler and made their views heard. It was the Aztec tradition that the ruler sat on a mat on the floor with his council.

Beautiful feather fans rather like this were used by Aztec nobles and rulers to keep themselves cool.

4 Paint a flower on one of the two smaller red circles and a butterfly on the other. Cut v-shapes from the felt and glue them to the large red ring.

5 Using sticky tape, fix lengths of coloured wool to the back of one of the red circles, as shown. Place the red circle in the centre of the ring with leaves.

6 Tape the lengths of wool to the outer ring to look like spokes. Coat the ring with PVA glue and place the second card ring on top, putting a cane in between.

7 Use double-sided tape to stick the second red circle face up in the centre. Glue the red ring with felt v-shapes on top of the second thick card ring.

Inca Lords of the Sun

THE INCAS WERE ORIGINALLY a tribal people of the Peruvian Andes in the 1100s. As the tribes grew in size, strong leaders began to take control. Under them, the Incas began to conquer neighbouring lands in the 1300s. During the 1400s, the mighty Inca Empire had developed.

The Inca emperor was called *Sapa Inca* (Only Leader). He was regarded as a god, a descendant of the Sun. He had complete power over his subjects, and was treated with the utmost respect at all times, but was always on his guard. There were many rivals for the throne among his royal relations. Each emperor had a new palace built for himself in the royal city of Cuzco. Emperors were often veiled or screened from ordinary people.

The empress, or *Quya* (Star), was the emperor's sister or mother. She was also thought to be divine and led the worship of the Moon goddess. The next

emperor was supposed to be chosen from among her sons. An emperor had many secondary wives. Waskar was said to have fathered eighty children in just eight years.

RELIGIOUS LEADERS
Sacrifices of llamas were made to the gods each month, at special festivals and before battle. The *Sapa Inca* controlled all religious activities. In the 1400s, the emperor Wiraqocha Inka declared that worship of the god Wiraqocha, the Creator (after whom he was named), was more important than worship of Inti, the Sun god. This made some people angry.

A CHOSEN WOMAN
Figurines of young girls were originally dressed, but the specially made clothes have perished or been lost over the years. Chosen girls (*akllakuna*), were educated for four years in religion, weaving and housekeeping. Some became the emperor's secondary wives or married noblemen. Others became priestesses or *mamakuna* (virgins of the Sun).

MAKE AN EMPEROR'S FAN
You will need: pencil, card, ruler, scissors, paints in bright colours, paintbrush, water pot, masking tape, wadding, PVA glue, hessian or sackcloth, needle, thread, string or twine.

1 Draw a feather shape 18cm long on to card and cut it out. The narrow part should be half of this length. Draw around the shape on card nine times.

2 Carefully paint the feathers with bright colours. Use red, orange and yellow to look like rainforest birds. Allow the paint to dry completely.

3 Cut out each feather and snip along the sides of the widest part to give a feathery effect. When the paint is dry, paint the other side as well.

COMMANDER IN CHIEF

The emperor sits on his throne. He wears a tasselled woollen headdress or *llautu*, decorated with gold and feathers, and large gold earplugs. He carries a sceptre. Around him, army chiefs await their orders. Emperors played an active part in military campaigns and relied on the army to keep them in power.

COOL SPRINGS

At Tambo Machay, to the south of Cuzco, fresh, cold water is channelled from sacred springs. Here, the great Pachakuti Inka Yupanki would bathe after a hard day's hunting.

THE LIVING DEAD

The dead body of an emperor, preserved as a mummy, is paraded through the streets. When each emperor died, his palace became his tomb. Once a year, the body was carried around Cuzco amid great celebrations. The picture is by Guamán Poma de Ayala, who was of Inca descent. In the 1600s, he made many pictures of Inca life.

Feathers from birds of the tropical forests to the east of the Andes were used to make fans for the emperor.

4 Hold the narrow ends of the feathers and spread out the tops to form a fan shape. Use masking tape to secure the ends firmly in position.

5 Cut a rectangular piece of wadding 9cm high and long enough to wrap the base of the feathers several times. Use glue on one side to keep it in place.

6 Cut a strip of hessian or sackcloth about 5cm wide. Starting at the base of the feathers, wrap the fabric around the stems. Hold it in place with a few stitches.

7 Wind string or twine firmly around the hessian to form the fan's handle. Tuck in the ends and use glue at each end to make sure they are secure.

Controlling Inca Society

FAMILY CONNECTIONS PLAYED an important part in royal power struggles and in everyday social organization in the Inca world. The nobles were grouped into family-based corporations called *panakas*. Members of each *panaka* shared rights to an area of land, its water, pasture and herds. Linked to each *panaka* was a land-holding *ayllu* (or clan) – a group of common people who were also related to each other.

The Incas managed to control an empire that contained many different peoples. Loyal Incas were sent to live in remote areas, while troublemakers from the regions were resettled nearer Cuzco, where they could be carefully watched. Conquered chiefs were called *kurakas*. They and their children were educated in Inca ways and allowed to keep some of their local powers.

The Inca system of law was quite severe. State officials and *kurakas* (conquered chiefs) acted as judges. Those who stole from the emperor's stores of grain, textiles and other goods faced a death sentence. Torture, beating, blinding and exile were all common punishments. The age of the criminal and the reason for the crime were sometimes taken into account.

A CLEVER CALCULATOR
One secret of Inca success was the *quipu*. It was used by government officials for recording all kinds of information, from the number of households in a town to the amount of goods of various kinds in a warehouse. The *quipu* was a series of strings tied to a thick cord. Each string had one or more colours and could be knotted. The colours represented anything from types of grain to groups of people. The knots represented numbers.

ONE STATE, MANY PEOPLES
The ancestors of these Bolivian women were subjects of the Incas. The Inca Empire was the largest ever known in all the Americas. It included at least a hundred different peoples. The Incas were clever governors and did not always try to force their own ideas upon other groups. Conquered peoples had to accept the Inca gods, but they were allowed to worship in their own way and keep their own customs.

A ROYAL INSPECTION

The Inca emperor Topa Inka Yupanki inspects government stores in the 1470s. In the Inca world, nearly all grain, textiles and other goods were produced for the State and stored in warehouses. Some extra produce might be bartered, or exchanged privately, but there were no big markets or shops.

PUBLIC WORKS

Labourers build fortifications on the borders of the Inca Empire. People paid their taxes to the Inca State in the form of labour called *mit'a*. This might be general work on the land. Men were also conscripted to work on public buildings or serve in the army. The Spanish continued to operate the *mit'a* as a form of tax long after they conquered the Inca Empire.

OLLANTAYTAMBO

This building in Ollantaytambo, in the Urubamba Valley, was once a State storehouse for the farm produce of the region. Ollantaytambo was a large town, which was probably built about 550 years ago. It protected the valley from raids by the warriors who lived in the forests to the east. Buildings dating from the Inca Empire were still being lived in by local people when the American archaeologist Dr Hiram Bingham passed through in 1911.

Levels of Inca Society

INCA SOCIETY was strictly graded. At the top were the *Sapa Inca* and his *Quya*. The High Priest and other important officials were normally recruited from members of the royal family.

If noblemen were loyal to the emperor, they might receive gifts of land. They might be given gold or a beautful *akllakuna* as a wife. They could expect jobs as regional governors, generals or priests. Lords and ladies wore fine clothes and were carried in splendid chairs, called litters.

Next in rank were the conquered non-Inca rulers and chiefs, the *kurakas*. They were cleverly brought into the Inca political system and given traditional honours. They served as regional judges.

Most people in the Empire were peasants. They were unable to leave their villages without official permission. They had no choice but to stay and toil on the land, sending their produce to the government stores.

CRAFT AND CLASS
A pottery figure from the Peruvian coast shows a porter carrying a water pot on his back. In the Inca Empire, craft workers such as potters and goldsmiths were employed by the State. They formed a small middle class. Unlike peasants they were never made to do *mit'a* (public service).

A TRUE NOBLEMAN
This man's headdress sets him apart as a noble or possibly a high priest. The model dates from a pre-Inca civilization 1,500-2,000 years ago. The Incas absorbed many different cultures into their own civilization.

MAKE A WATER POT

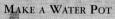
You will need: self-drying clay, cutting board, rolling pin, ruler, water, water pot, acrylic paints, paintbrush.

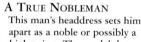

1 Roll out a piece of clay on the board. Make a circle about 17cm in diameter and 1cm thick. This will form the base of your water pot.

2 Roll some more clay into long sausages, about as fat as your little finger. Dampen the base with water and carefully place a sausage around the edge.

3 Coil more clay sausages on top of each other to build up the pot. Make each coil slightly smaller than the one below. Water will help them stick.

A PEASANT'S LIFE

A woman harvests potatoes near Sicuani, to the south of Cuzco. Then, as now, life was hard for the peasant farmers of the Andes. Both men and women worked in the fields, and even young children and the elderly were expected to help. However, the Inca State did provide some support for the peasants, supplying free grain in times of famine.

PLUGGED IN

Earplugs like this one, made of gold, turquoise and shell, were worn as a badge of rank. Inca noblemen wore such heavy gold earplugs that the Spanish called them *orejones* (big ears). Noblewomen wore their hair long, covered with a head-cloth.

LAND AND SEASONS

One third of all land and produce belonged to the emperor, one third to the priests and one third to the peasants. It was hardly a fair division. A peasant's life, digging, planting and harvesting, was ruled by the seasons. Each new season was celebrated by religious festivals and ceremonies.

Children were expected to help their parents by fetching water from the wells and mountain springs.

4 When you reach the neck of the pot, start making the coils slightly bigger again to form a lip. Carefully smooth the coils with wet fingertips.

5 Use two more rolls of clay to make handles on opposite sides of the pot. Smooth out the joints carefully to make sure the handles stay in place.

6 Leave the clay to dry completely. Then paint the pot all over with a background colour. Choose an earthy reddish brown to look like Inca pottery.

7 Leave the reddish brown colour to dry. Use a fine paintbrush and black paint to draw Inca designs on the pot like the ones in the picture above.

Tribes in North America

FROM AROUND 3000BC, many different tribal societies developed throughout North America, from the Apaches in the South to the Inuits of the far North. A single tribe might be as small as ten families or number thousands. Tribes came together in times of war, for ceremonies and for trading, or to form powerful confederacies (unions). Some Algonquin people formed the Powhatan Confederacy and controlled the coast of present-day Virginia. In the South-east, the Creek, Seminole, Cherokee, Choctaw and Chickasaw were known by Europeans as the 'Five Civilized Tribes' because their system of law courts and land rights developed from European influences.

MAGNIFICENTLY COSTUMED
American Horse of the Oglala Sioux wears a double-trail war bonnet. His painted shirt shows he was a member of the Ogle Tanka'un or Shirt Wearers, who were wise and brave.

COMMITTEE MEETING
A Sioux council gathers to hear the head chief speak. Councils were made up of several leaders or chiefs. They elected the head chief whose authority came from his knowledge of tribal lore and skill as a warrior.

MAKE A SKIN ROBE

You will need: an old single sheet (or large piece of thin cotton fabric), scissors, tape measure or ruler, pencil, large needle, brown thread, felt in red, yellow, dark blue and light blue, pva glue, glue brush, black embroidery thread (or string), red cotton thread (or other colour).

1 Take the sheet and cut out a rectangle 140cm x 60cm. Then cut out two 40cm x 34cm rectangles for the arms. Fold the main (body) piece in half.

2 At the centre of fold, draw a neckline 22cm across and 6cm deep. Cut it out. Roll fabric over at shoulders and stitch down with an overlapping stitch.

3 Open the body fabric out flat and line up the arm pieces, with the centre on the stitched ridge. Stitch the top edge of the arm pieces on to the body.

WOMEN IN SOCIETY

The Iroquois women attended council meetings, but in most tribes women did not join councils or become warriors. Women held a respected place in society. In many tribes, such as the Algonquan, people traced their descent through their mother. When a man married, he left his home to live with his wife's family.

DISPLAYS OF WEALTH

Potlatch ceremonies could last for several days. The gathering was a big feast celebrated by tribes on the Northwest Coast. Gifts were exchanged. The status of a tribe was judged by the value of the gifts.

IN COMMAND

This chief comes from the Kainah group of Blackfoot Indians. The Kainah were also known by Europeans as the Blood Indians because of the red face paint they wore. The Blackfoot headdress had feathers that stood upright as opposed to the Sioux bonnet which sloped backwards sometimes, with trailing eagle feathers.

FEATHER PIPE OF PEACE

North American Indians had a long tradition of smoking pipes. Plants were often smoked for religious and ritual reasons. Early peace talks involved passing around a pipe for all to smoke to show they had good intentions of keeping agreements.

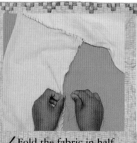

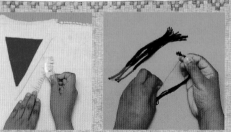

4 Fold the fabric in half again to see the shirt's shape. Now stitch up the undersides of the sleeves. The sides of the shirt were usually not sewn together.

5 Your shirt is ready to decorate. Cut out strips and triangles of felt and glue them on to the shirt. Make fringes by cutting into one side of a felt strip.

6 Make fake hair pieces by cutting 8cm lengths of black thread and tying them together in bunches. Wind red thread tightly around the top, as here.

7 Glue or sew the fake hair (or scalplocks) on to your shirt. You can follow the pattern we used as shown in the picture (top), or create your own.

Survival of a Tribal Tradition

Sᴏᴍᴇ ᴛʀɪʙᴀʟ ꜱᴏᴄɪᴇᴛɪᴇꜱ have had to fight to hold on to their social structure and traditions. The North American Indian culture was nearly wiped out forever. From the 1600s onwards, settlers from Europe took over the land of North America and imposed their own laws. By 1900 the population of tribes north of Mexico had dropped from just below three million to 400,000.

The foreign settlers formed the United States of America at the end of the 1700s, but did not regard the native tribes as 'Americans'. Over the next 200 years, the US Government moved the native Indian peoples from their homelands to areas of land known as reserves or reservations. About 300 US federal reservations still exist today, some for a single tribe, others as home to a number of groups.

In the 1900s, Indians became more politically active. Tribes began to demand financial compensation for lost land. The Cherokees were awarded $15 million. Today, many reservations are governed by the tribes, although the US Government still controls a lot of surviving Indian land. Since 1970, tribes have been allowed to run their reservation schools and teach ancestral history.

Mᴏᴅᴇʀɴ Cᴇʀᴇᴍᴏɴɪᴇꜱ
This couple are joining other American Indian descendants at a powwow (tribal gathering). The meetings are popular because of a recent surge of interest in the culture of the tribes. Powwows give the people a chance to dress in traditional costume, speak their native language and learn more about their tribal history.

Tʀɪʙᴀʟ Pʀᴏᴛᴇꜱᴛ
In July 1978 these American Indians walked for five months to Washington from their reservations to protest to Congress. At protest meetings, leaders read from a list of 400 treaties – promises that the United States had made and broken. For years, many tribes tried to get back land taken from them. In 1992, Navajo and Hopi tribes were given back 1.8 million acres of their land in Northern Arizona to be divided between the tribes.

Sᴏᴅᴀ Bᴀʀ Sᴛᴏᴘ
A Seminole family enjoy sodas in 1948 in a Miami store. Tribes gradually adapted to the American ways of life, but some kept their own customs and dress. Seminoles were forced from Florida to Oklahoma in 1878. Almost 300 refused to leave the Everglades and around 2,000 live there today.

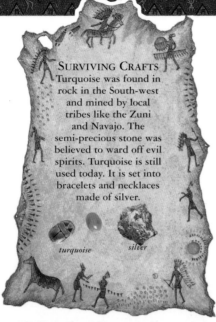

SURVIVING CRAFTS
Turquoise was found in rock in the South-west and mined by local tribes like the Zuni and Navajo. The semi-precious stone was believed to ward off evil spirits. Turquoise is still used today. It is set into bracelets and necklaces made of silver.

turquoise   *silver*

THE TOURIST TRAIL
A traditional Inuit scene of snowshoes propped outside an igloo. Most people in Alaska and Greenland live in modern, centrally heated homes. However, the ancient skills of building temporary shelters from ice bricks still survive. They are passed down to each generation and occasionally used by hunters or tourists keen to experience North American Indian customs.

CHEERLEADING CHIEF
Dressed in full ceremonial costume, this North American Indian helps conduct celebrations at a football stadium. It is a way of raising awareness of the existence of tribes. The cheerleading is not far removed from a war chief's tribal role of encouraging warriors in battle.

STITCHING THE PAST
Traditional American Indian crafts are still made today. The method of curing hides has remained the same. No chemicals are used during the tanning process and the scraping is still done by hand. However, styles of the crafts had already changed to suit the European market in the 1600s when traders brought in new materials.

TRADITIONAL SKILLS
An Indian craftsman produces beautiful jewellery in silver and turquoise. Zuni and Navajo people were among the finest jewellery makers in this style. Other tribes, such as the Crow, are famous for their beadwork.

Travel, Conquest & Warfare

Methods of transport and the need to conquer new territory led to the spread of ideas around the world. Journey through history and find out how people got around, where and why they travelled, and how they fought for land. Discover why people wanted to conquer new territories, and how existing technologies were used for transport and weapons.

Breaking New Frontiers

EARLY HUMANS WERE ALWAYS on the move, searching for wild animals and plants for food. They had to walk everywhere. They had not learned how to tame such animals as wild oxen or asses to carry them. But then, the hunter-gatherers did not feel the need to develop new methods of transport, because they did not have much to carry around.

Gradually, some humans learned how to cultivate wild grasses into reliable crops. They built permanent shelters in the fertile river valleys and farmed there. They wanted and needed to find out how to grow better food, and to store and transport it. Life was no longer the scrabble for survival that it had been for their earliest ancestors.

They had time to work out how to make improvements. New and better methods of transport and travel were used in peacetime and in war.

Populations increased in the fertile farmlands. People moved in search of new places to live, and with this, came the need to

Primitive humans were hunter-gatherers. They were always on the move, looking for food. They had not learned how to tame animals that could be ridden or used to pull vehicles.

The Polynesians roamed the ocean of the South Pacific seeking new islands to settle. Over 2,000 years ago they could navigate the seas successfully, and travel over vast expanses of empty ocean in sail-powered canoes.

TIMELINE 100,000–200BC

100,000 years ago. Nomadic bands of hunter-gatherers migrate north out of Africa into the Middle East in search of new hunting grounds.

50,000 years ago. The ancestors of the Aborigines become the earliest people to build boats or rafts when they sail from Asia to Australia.

Early humans used their upright stance to gather berries

10,000BC Humans discover every continent except ice-covered Antarctica.

8000BC Beginning of farming in the Middle East.

4500BC The first Mesopotamian sailing ships are built.

3800BC Metal weapons, made of bronze, come into use in the Middle East.

3500BC The first wheeled vehicles are made in Mesopotamia.

3000BC Age of the oldest surviving large ships, discovered buried in the desert in Egypt.

1500BC War chariots are used by the Assyrians and Egyptians to carry archers into battle.

bronze spearheads

100,000BC   10,000BC   3500BC   2500BC

travel. As people travelled to lands already settled by others, they had to fight to win new territory. Both travel and war led to the spread of new inventions and ideas, and the incentive to create ever better transport and weapons.

Farming communities were producing more goods than they needed for themselves. Surplus produce could be transported to other regions and traded. With

Horsedrawn chariots could travel fast over the battlefield. The Hittites, who lived in a region that is now part of modern Turkey, were among the first to use horses in warfare. They made the chariot one of the most feared weapons of war around 1600 to 1200BC.

expansion and trade, came the need for faster, safer and more reliable methods of travel. Farmers tamed animals such as the horse and ox for carrying goods and people from place to place, and then realized that the animals could also pull ploughs to till the soil.

About 6,000 years ago, the Mesopotamians harnessed the wind by hoisting sails on their boats. Sailing in the open ocean is dangerous even in today's yachts. Imagine then what it must have been like for Phoenician traders, who, from about 850BC, were sailing from the eastern Mediterranean into the Atlantic Ocean.

Expert horsemen were at an advantage over footsoldiers. Persian soldiers had horses that were strong and nimble, and the rider could wield a weapon from a height.

Sometimes, people wanted to travel and conquer just because they were greedy. A successful farmer might fancy taking over someone else's land just to increase the size of his own farm and give him more wealth and power. A neighbouring tribe or region

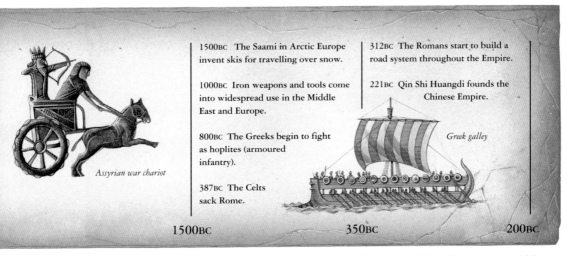

1500BC The Saami in Arctic Europe invent skis for travelling over snow.

1000BC Iron weapons and tools come into widespread use in the Middle East and Europe.

800BC The Greeks begin to fight as hoplites (armoured infantry).

387BC The Celts sack Rome.

312BC The Romans start to build a road system throughout the Empire.

221BC Qin Shi Huangdi founds the Chinese Empire.

Greek galley

Assyrian war chariot

1500BC   350BC   200BC

might have something another tribe wanted such as fertile soil, timber or metal. Conflict was an inevitable result. Celts and Vikings fought over cattle and land. Monarchs and emperors fought for control of whole countries.

Unfortunately it is often a war that provides the spur to technological improvements. If you want to win a race or a battle, you make sure you have the best equipment. The warlike Hittites were among the first to ride horses into battle and use iron weapons. Their country in south-eastern Europe (present day Turkey) was landlocked, and they fought for control of ports and trade in the Mediterranean Sea. The Mesopotamians upgraded the solid-wheeled cart into an effective war chariot with spoked wheels.

Early Egyptian life centred on the River Nile, so the Egyptians were experts in making river boats. Later, they wanted to trade farther afield and built seagoing boats like this one with huge sails.

Both trade and empire-building encouraged the spread and exchange of ideas and technology. European invaders introduced the horse to America in the 1500s, which completely transformed how North American Indians hunted, travelled and fought. Phoenician traders and Greek adventurers

In the Crusades, a series of conflicts between Christians and Saracen Muslims during the Middle Ages, the knights of both sides fought on horseback. The Europeans also picked up some useful ideas on castle and weapon design from their foes.

Timeline 200BC–AD1900

191BC–AD43 The Romans conquer the Celts in northern Europe.

AD476 Fall of the Western Roman Empire. The Eastern Empire survives until 1453.

AD793 Viking pirates begin to attack Britain and Ireland.

AD800 The Chinese build their first large ships, called junks, with many masts and proper rudders.

Viking longship

AD969 Gunpowder is used in war for the first time, in China.

AD1000 The Viking Leif Eriksson becomes the first European to reach America.

1100 Samurai warriors become important in warfare in Japan.

Chinese fireworks

200BC   AD800   AD900   AD1300

took their shipbuilding
expertise throughout the
Mediterranean and beyond.
The superb metalworking
crafsmanship of the Saracen
Muslims east of the Mediterranean,
spread to northern Europe.

Roman galleys were used mostly for
war. They had picked up the galley
design from the Greeks. Oarpower
allowed for manoeuvrability in
close combat.

   The geography of a country shapes the way in
which its transport and warfare develops. The
Greeks were great seafarers partly because of their
endless coastline, but also because there was a limited
amount of fertile land in their rugged country. The Vikings,
trapped in narrow coastal strips beneath the mountains of
Scandinavia, built ships that crossed the Atlantic Ocean to America. They were also fearsome

warriors. The Incas in South America had a major road
network and wheeled toys, but no wheeled vehicles. As
in the mountains of Japan, walking over steep, narrow
tracks was faster and safer than wheeled transport.

   As you turn these pages, you will see how different
countries and cultures travelled and conquered –
and developed transport and weapons.

The Spanish went to Mesoamerica greedy for Aztec gold. The
Aztecs were fierce fighters but no match for the Spanish,
on horseback, with their gunpowder and steel.

1492 Columbus
'discovers'
America while
searching for a
route to China.

1521 The Spanish
under Cortes
conquer the
Aztecs.

Christopher Columbus

1526 The Mughals begin to
conquer India.

1532 The Spanish
under Francisco
Pizarro conquer
the Incas.

1607 The
English begin to
settle in Virginia
in North America.   *Francisco Pizzaro*

1776 The United States declares
independence from Britain.

1868 The Tokugawa
dynasty of shoguns
comes to an end
in Japan.

1890 The 'Battle' of
Wounded Knee ends
the Indian Wars in the
United States. Native
Indians are confined
to reservations.

a Huron brave

AD1500   AD1800   AD1900

BREAKING NEW FRONTIERS   201

Stone Age People on the Move

THE EARLIEST MEANS of transport, apart from travelling on foot, was by boat. The first people to reach Australia, around 50,000BC, probably paddled log or bamboo rafts across the open ocean. Later Stone Age peoples made skin-covered coracles, kayaks (canoes) hollowed from tree trunks and boats made from reeds. Wooden sledges or *travois* (triangular platforms of poles lashed together) were dragged to carry goods and people overland. People pushed logs to act as rollers beneath very heavy objects such as rocks. The taming of horses, donkeys, camels and oxen revolutionized land transport. The first roads and causeways in Europe were built around the same time. By about 3500BC, the wheel had been invented in Egypt and Mesopotamia.

HORSE'S HEAD
This rock engraving of a horse's head comes from a cave in France. Some experts think that horses may have been tamed as early as 12,000BC. There are carvings that appear to show bridles around the heads of horses, although these could indicate manes.

CORACLE
A man fishes from a coracle, one of the oldest boat designs. Made of animal hide stretched over a wooden frame, the coracle may have been used since about 7600BC.

MAKE A MODEL CANOE
You will need: card, pencil, ruler, scissors, PVA glue, glue brush, masking tape, self-drying clay, double-sided sticky tape, chamois leather, pair of compasses, thread, needle.

canoe top
—20cm—
canoe top
—10cm—
canoe base
—20cm—
canoe base
—10cm—

1 Cut card to the size of the templates shown on the left. Remember to cut semicircles from the long edge of both top pieces.

2 Glue the bases together and the tops together. Use masking tape to secure them as they dry. Join the top to the base in the same way.

STONE BRIDGE

Walla Brook bridge on Dartmoor is one of the oldest stone bridges in Britain. Bridges make travelling easier, safer and more direct. The first bridges were made by placing tree trunks across rivers, or by laying flat stones in shallow streams.

SAILING BOATS

Skin-covered boats called *umiak* were used by the Inuit of North America. The figure at the back is the helmsman, whose job is to steer the boat. The other figures are rowing the oars. The ancient Egyptians were among the first people to have sailing boats – for moving around on the River Nile.

KAYAK FRAME

This wooden frame for a kayak was made by an Inuit fisherman. It has been built without any nails. The joints were lashed together with strips of leather. Canoes like this have been in use for thousands of years.

Inuit kayaks give clues about how Stone Age boats may have looked. The outsides were covered with skin.

3 Draw three circles the size of the holes in the top, with smaller circles inside. Cut them out. Make clay rings the same size.

4 Cover the clay and the card rings with double-sided tape. These rings form the seats where the paddlers will sit.

5 Cover your canoe with chamois leather, leaving holes for seats. Glue it tightly in place so that all the cardboard is covered.

6 Use a needle and thread to sew up the edges of the leather on the top of the canoe. Position and fix the seats and oars.

Egyptian Sailpower

THE ANCIENT EGYPTIANS were not great seafarers, although their ships did sail through the Mediterranean and the Red Sea, and may even have reached India. Generally, though, they mostly kept to coastal waters and became experts at river travel. The River Nile was Egypt's main road, and all kinds of boats travelled up and down. Simple boats made from papyrus reed were used for fishing and hunting. Barges transported stones to temple building sites, ferries carried people and animals across the river. There were trading vessels and royal pleasure boats. Egypt had little timber, so wooden ships had to be built from cedar imported from Lebanon in the eastern Mediterranean.

THE FINAL VOYAGE

Archaeologists have found many well-preserved pictures and models of boats in tombs. People believed that the boats carried the mummified body of a pharaoh to its final resting place on the west bank of the Nile, and carried the dead person's spirit into the Underworld.

ALL ALONG THE NILE

Wooden sailing boats with graceful, triangular sails can still be seen on the River Nile today. They carry goods and people up and down the river. The design of the *felucca* has changed since the time of the ancient Egyptians. The sails on early boats were tall, upright and narrow. Later designs were broader, like the ones shown above. In Egypt, most people lived in the fertile valley of the River Nile. The river has always been the main route of communication and transport.

MAKE A BOAT

You will need: a large bundle of straw 30cm long, scissors, string, balsa wood, red and yellow card, PVA glue and brush.

1 Divide the straw into five equal bundles and then cut three of them down to 15cm in length. Tie all five bundles securely at both ends and in the middle, as shown.

2 Take the two long bundles and tie them together at one end as shown. These bundles will form the outer frame of the boat. Put them to one side.

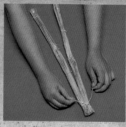

3 Next take the three short bundles of straw and bind them together at both ends. These will form the inner surface of the straw boat.

STEERING ROUND SAND BANKS

A wooden tomb model shows a boat from 1800BC with high, curved ends. Long steering oars kept the boat on course through the powerful currents of the flooding river. Timber was the main material for building large boats, but designs were similar to those of the simple reed vessels used for fishing.

FINAL VOYAGE

These boats are making a pilgrimage to Abydos. This was the city of Osiris, the god of death and rebirth. Mummies were taken here by boat. Ships and boats played a major part in the religious beliefs of the Egyptians. Ra the Sun god travelled on a boat across the sky to bring in each new day. In October 1991, a fleet of 12 boats dating from about 3000BC was found at Abydos near Memphis. The boats were up to 30m long and had been buried beneath the desert sands. They are the oldest surviving large ships in the world.

SIGN OF THE NORTH

The hieroglyph below means boat. It looks a bit like the papyrus reed vessels. This sign later came to mean north. Boats floated downstream with the current from south to north, and used sail power to travel the other way.

Early boats were made from papyrus reeds. These were bound with string made from reed fibres.

4 Next push the short bundles into the centre of the long pair firmly. Tie the bundles together with string at one end, as shown.

5 Bring the rear of the long pair of bundles together and tie them securely, as shown. Bind the whole boat together with string.

6 Thread a string lengthwise from one end to the other. The tension on this string should give the high curved prow and stern of your boat.

7 Finally, cut the card and glue it to the balsa sticks to make the boat's paddle and harpoon. Boats like these were used for fishing and hunting hippos.

Sailing in the Mediterranean

GALLEYS WERE SAILED and rowed in Mediterranean waters for hundreds of years, from the heyday of Phoenician traders around 1000–572BC to the merchant galleys of Venice in the 1400s. Roman galleys were very similar to the earlier Greek vessels. When the wind was favourable, a big, square sail could be set for extra speed. Continuous power, though – whatever the weather – and manoeuvrability in battle – came from one or more rows of oars. A standard Roman war galley had 270 oarsmen below deck.

Most goods, especially heavy cargoes of food or building materials, were moved around the Roman Empire by water. Barges were used on rivers.

CONTAINERS
A large pottery jar called an amphora is being taken from one ship to another. Merchant ships were deeper, heavier and slower than galleys. They had bigger sails and longer oars. They were usually sailed, as they were too heavy to be rowed.

AT THE DOCKS
This wall painting from the port of Ostia shows a Roman merchant ship being loaded. Heavy sacks of grain are being carried on board. You can see the two large steering oars at the stern (rear) of the ship.

Seafaring in the Mediterranean was dangerous, mainly because of storms and piracy. The Greeks built the first lighthouse at Alexandria around 300BC, and the Romans built many around their empire.

ROLLING ON THE RIVER
Wine and other liquids were sometimes stored in barrels. These were transported by river barges, like the one in this carving. Barrels of wine would be hauled from the vineyards of Germany or southern France to the nearest seaport.

MAKE AN AMPHORA

You will need: large sheet of thin card, ruler, two pencils, scissors, corrugated cardboard – two circles of 10cm and 20cm in diameter, two strips of 40cm x 30cm and another large piece, masking tape, pva glue, old newspaper, paintbrush, reddish-brown acrylic paint, water pot.

1 Cut two pieces of card – 5cm and 38cm in depth. Tape the short piece to the small circle. Curl the long piece to make the neck. Make two holes in the side and tape it to the large circle.

2 Roll up the strips of corrugated cardboard. Bend them, as shown, fitting one end to the hole in the neck and the other to the cardboard. Fix in place with glue and tape.

3 Cut a piece of card, 40cm square. Roll it into a cylinder shape. Cut four lines, 10cm long, at one end, so it can be tapered into a point, as shown. Bind with tape.

SAILING OFF TO BATTLE

A Roman war galley leaves harbour on its way to battle. A helmsman controlled a war galley's steering and shouted orders down to the oarsmen below deck. Slaves manned the oars, and there was a separate fighting force on board. This galley has three banks (layers) of oars and is called a trireme (meaning three oars). An underwater battering ram stuck out from the bow (front) of Greek and Roman war galleys. During battle, the mast was lowered, as the ship was easier to manoeuvre under oarpower. The galley rammed the enemy ship to disable it. Then the soldiers boarded to fight man to man.

In the ancient world, amphorae were used to transport wine and oil and fish sauce. The jars could be easily stacked in the ship's hold. Layers of brushwood provided padding.

4 To give the amphora a more solid base, roll up a cone of corrugated cardboard and stick it around the tapered end. Push a pencil into the end, as shown. Tape in position.

5 Stick the neck on to the main body. Cover the whole piece with strips of newspaper brushed on with glue. Leave to dry. Repeat until you have built up a thick layer.

6 When the paper is dry, paint the amphora. Roman amphorae were made of clay, so use a reddish-brown paint to make yours look like it is clay. Leave to dry.

Overland in China

THE ANCIENT CHINESE EMPIRE was linked by a network of roads used only by the army, officials and royal messengers. A special carriageway was reserved for the emperor. Ordinary people travelled along dusty or muddy routes and tracks.

China's mountainous landscape and large number of rivers meant that engineers became expert at bridge-building. Suspension bridges of rope and bamboo were built from about AD1 onwards. A bridge suspended from iron chains crossed the Chang Jiang (Yangzi River) as early as AD580. A stone arch bridge of AD615 still stands today at Zhouxian in Hebei province.

Most people travelled by foot, and porters carried great loads on their backs or balanced on shoulder poles. Single-wheeled barrows were useful too, 1,000 years before they were invented in the West. China's small native ponies were interbred with larger, stronger horses from central Asia sometime after 100BC. This provided fast, powerful mounts that were suitable for messengers and officials, and could also pull chariots and carriages. Mules and camels were the animals used on the trade routes of the north, while shaggy yaks carried loads in the high mountains. Carts were usually hauled by oxen.

HEADING OUT WEST
Chinese horsemen escort the camels of a caravan (trading expedition). The traders are about to set out along the Silk Road. This trading route ran all the way from Chang'an (Xian) in China to Europe and the lands of the Mediterranean.

RIDING ON HORSEBACK
A Chinese nobleman from about 2,000 years ago reins in his elegant horse. Breaking in the horse would have been difficult, as the rider has no stirrups and could easily be unseated. Metal stirrups were in general use in China by AD302. They provided more stability and helped the rider control his horse.

CARRIED BY HAND
A lazy landowner of the Qing Dynasty travels around his estates. Wealthy people were often carried in a litter (a portable chair). An umbrella shades the landowner from the heat of the summer sun.

CAMEL POWER
Bactrian (two-humped) camels were originally bred in central Asia. They could endure extremes of heat and cold for long distances without water. This toughness made them ideal for transporting goods through the mountains and deserts of the Silk Road.

HAN CARRIAGE
During the Han Dynasty (202BC–AD 220), three-horse carriages were used by the imperial family only. This carving from a tomb brick probably shows a messenger carrying an important order from the emperor.

TRAVELLING IN STYLE
Han Dynasty government officials travelled in stylish horse-drawn carriages. New breeds of large strong horses became a status symbol for the rich and powerful. The animals were considered celestial (heavenly). The Han civilization developed around the Huang He (Yellow River). Han people invented the chariot by 1500BC, around 500 years later than in Mesopotamia.

The Chinese Afloat

FROM EARLY IN CHINA'S history, the country's rivers, lakes and man-made canals were its main highways. Fishermen propelled small wooden boats with a single oar or pole at the stern. These small boats were often roofed with mats, like the sampans (meaning 'three planks') still seen today. Large, wooden, ocean-sailing ships called junks were either keeled or flat-bottomed, with a high stern and square bows. Matting sails were stiffened with strips of bamboo.

By the 1st century AD, the Chinese had built the first ships with rudders instead of steering oars, and soon went on to make ships with several masts. In the 1400s, admirals Zheng He and Wang Jinghong led expeditions to South-east Asia, India, Arabia and East Africa. The flagship of their 300-strong naval fleet was over five times the size of the largest European ships of the time.

IN FULL SAIL
Junks were a type of sailing vessel used by merchants in the East and South China seas. They were also used by pirates. The China seas could be blue and peaceful, but they were often whipped into a fury by typhoons (tropical storms).

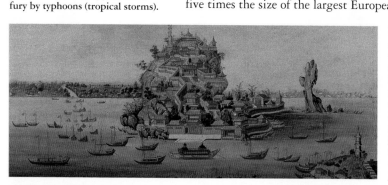

RIVER TRAFFIC
All sorts of small trading boats were sailed or rowed along China's rivers in the 1850s. River travel had always been difficult and could be dangerous. The Huang He (Yellow River) often flooded and changed course. The upper parts of China's longest river, the Chang Jiang (Yangzi River), were rocky and had powerful currents.

MAKE A SAMPAN

You will need: ruler, pencil, thick and thin card, scissors, glue and brush, masking tape, 6 wooden barbecue sticks, string, thin yellow paper, paint (black, dark brown), paintbrush, water pot.

39cm
1cm
Runner A (x2)

33.5cm
Side B (x2)
5cm
15cm

Base C (x2)   7cm   Base D
15cm   18cm

Floor E   7cm   Floor F (x2)
10cm   7cm   Edge G (x2)   4cm
6.5cm   1cm

Cut pieces B, C, D and G from thick card. Cut pieces A, E, and F from thin card.

1 Glue base pieces C and D to side B, as shown. Hold the pieces with masking tape while the glue dries. When dry, remove the masking tape.

2 Glue remaining side B to the boat. Stick runner A pieces to top of the sides. Make sure the ends jut out 2.5cm at the front and back of the boat.

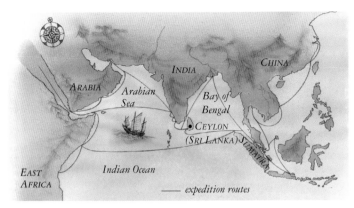

expedition routes

THE VOYAGES OF ZHENG HE

Chinese admirals Zheng He and Wang Jinghong carried out seven fantastic voyages of exploration between 1405 and 1433. This map shows how far and wide they travelled on these expeditions. Their impressive fleets included over 60 ships crewed by about 27,000 seamen, officers and interpreters. The biggest of their vessels was 147m long and 60m wide.

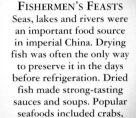

FISHERMEN'S FEASTS

Seas, lakes and rivers were an important food source in imperial China. Drying fish was often the only way to preserve it in the days before refrigeration. Dried fish made strong-tasting sauces and soups. Popular seafoods included crabs, prawns and squid.

dried fish

dried squid

THE FISHING TRIP

A fisherman poles his boat across the river in the 1500s. The bird shown in the picture is a tamed cormorant, used for catching the fish. The cormorant was normally attached to a line, with a ring around its neck to prevent it from swallowing the fish.

To add the finishing touch to your sampan, make a boatman and oar to propel the vessel through the waterways.

3 Glue floor E to centre of base. Add floor F pieces to the ends of the base, as shown. Stick edge G pieces in between the ends of the runners.

4 Bend 2 barbecue sticks into 10cm high arches. Cut 2 more sticks into five 10cm struts. Glue and tie 2 struts to sides of arches and 1 to the top.

5 Repeat step 4 to make a second roof. To make roof matting, cut thin yellow paper into 1cm x 10cm strips. Fold strips in half and stick to roofs.

6 Paint boat and roofs. Allow to dry. Glue the matting strips to the roofs, as shown. When the glue is dry, place roofs inside the boat.

Over the Mountains of Japan

J APAN IS A RUGGED and mountainous country. Until the 1900s, the only routes through the countryside were narrow, winding tracks. Paths and fragile wooden bridges across deep gullies and streams were often swept away by landslides or floods.

During the Heian period (from around AD794), wealthy warriors rode fine horses, while important officials, wealthy women, children and priests travelled in lightweight wood and bamboo carts. The carts were pulled by oxen and fitted with screens and curtains for privacy. If the route was impassable for ox-carts, wealthy people were carried on palanquins (lightweight portable boxes or litters). Ordinary people usually travelled on foot.

During the Tokugawa period (1600–1868) the shoguns (military rulers) encouraged new road building as a way of increasing trade and keeping control of their lands. The Eastern Sea Road ran for 480km between Kyoto and the shogun's capital, Edo, and took 20-30 days to travel on foot. Some people said it was the busiest road in the world.

BEASTS OF BURDEN
A weary mother rests with her child and ox during their journey. You can see that the ox is loaded up with heavy bundles. Ordinary people could not afford horses, so oxen were used to carry heavy loads or to pull carts.

SHOULDER HIGH
Noblewomen on palanquins (litters) are being taken by porters across a deep river. Some women have decided to disembark so that they can be carried across the river. Palanquins were used in Japan right up to the Tokugawa period (1600–1868). Daimyos (warlords) and their wives might be carried the whole journey to or from the capital city of Edo in a palanquin.

HUGGING THE COASTLINE

Ships sail into harbour at Tempozan, Osaka. The marks on the sails show the company that owned them. Cargo between the shogun's city of Edo and Osaka was mostly carried by ships that hugged the coastline.

CARRYING CARGO

Little cargo-boats, such as these at Edobashi in Edo, carried goods along rivers or around the coast. They were driven through the water by men rowing with oars or pushing against the river bed with a long pole.

STEEP MOUNTAIN PATHS

Travellers on mountain paths hoped to find shelter for the night in villages, temples or monasteries. It could take all day to walk 16km along rough mountain tracks.

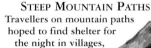

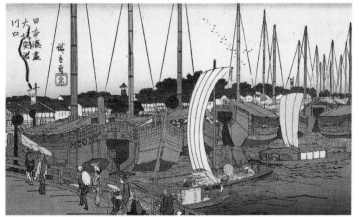

IN THE HARBOUR

Sea-going sailing ships, laden with cargo, are shown here at anchor in the harbour of Osaka, an important port in south-central Japan. In front of them you can see smaller river-boats with tall sails. Some families both lived and worked on river-boats.

Viking Specialities

IT WAS OFTEN QUICKER for the Vikings to travel around the coast than over the icy mountains. However, they used horses for carrying baggage and pulling wheeled carts and wagons over their wooden causeways. Sledges hauled goods over grass as well as ice and snow. The Vikings became best known, however, for their shipbuilding skills. Longships were designed for ocean voyages and warfare. They were up to 23m long but were shallow enough to row on rivers. A single oak beam was used for the keel – the backbone of the ship. Planks were caulked (made watertight) with wool or animal hair and coated with a tar made of pine resin. Oar holes ran the length of the ship, and there was a broad steering oar at the stern (back). The large square or rectangular sail was made of heavy woollen or linen cloth.

The Vikings also made broad-beamed cargo and trading vessels and small rowing and sailing boats.

DRAGON SHIPS
The hulls were clinker-built. This means that long, wedge shaped strakes (planks) were nailed to the frame so that they overlapped.

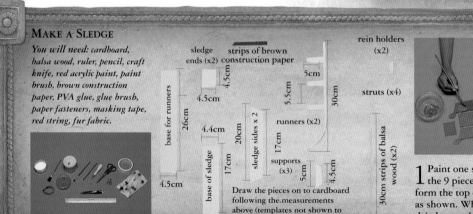

MAKE A SLEDGE

You will need: cardboard, balsa wood, ruler, pencil, craft knife, red acrylic paint, paint brush, brown construction paper, PVA glue, glue brush, paper fasteners, masking tape, red string, fur fabric.

sledge ends (x2)
strips of brown construction paper
rein holders (x2)
base for runners 26cm
4.5cm
4.5cm
4.4cm
5cm
5.5cm
30cm
struts (x4)
runners (x2)
base of sledge
17cm
20cm
sledge sides x 2
17cm
supports (x3)
5cm
4.5cm
4.5cm
30cm strips of balsa wood (x2)

Draw the pieces on to cardboard following the measurements above (templates not shown to scale). Ask an adult to cut them out with a craft knife.

1 Paint one side of each of the 9 pieces that will form the top of the sledge, as shown. When they have dried, turn them over and paint the other side.

MODERN VIKINGS

In recent years modern replicas of longships have proved to be strong, fast and easy to sail. The planking bends well to the waves and the ships are light enough to be hauled overland.

PUTTING TO SEA

A longship put to sea with a crew of 30 or more fighting men. In Greek and Roman galleys, there was a separate fighting force. The Vikings, though, were both warriors and sailors. They sometimes slung their round shields along the side of the ship.

Many Viking sledges were designed to be pulled by horses and were often finely carved.

SHIPS' TIMBERS

In the Viking Age, much of northern Europe was still densely forested. In most places there was no shortage of timber for building or repairing longships. Oak was always the shipbuilders' first choice of wood, followed by pine, beech and ash.

beech

oak

2 Cut several strips of brown construction paper. Arrange them to form diamond patterns along the sides of the sledge. Trim and glue in place.

3 Ask an adult to make cuts with a craft knife. Push paper fasteners through to form patterns. Glue the top of the sledge. Hold it together with masking tape.

4 While you wait for the top to dry, glue the 8 pieces that form the base of the sledge together. Glue the 2 rein holders on the top of the base.

5 Paint the base red. When it is dry, brush plenty of glue on to it and carefully stick on the top. Leave it to dry. Attach the reins and trim with fur fabric.

Wheel-less in Mesoamerica

THE AZTEC AND MAYA PEOPLE of Central America knew about wheels and built an intricate system of roads – but they did not make wheeled transport of any kind. Carriages and carts would not have been able to travel through dense rainforests, along steep, narrow mountain tracks or the raised causeways that linked many cities.

Most people travelled on foot, carrying goods on their backs. Porters carried heavy loads with the help of a *tumpline*. This was a broad band of cloth that went across their foreheads and under the bundles on their backs, leaving their arms free. Rulers and nobles were carried in portable beds, called litters.

On rivers and lakes, Mesoamericans used simple dug-out boats. Maya sailors travelled in huge wooden canoes that were able to make long voyages, even in the rough, open sea.

CARRIED HIGH
A Maya nobleman is shown being carried in a litter (portable bed) made from jaguar skins. Spanish travellers reported that the Aztec emperor was carried in the same way. When the emperor walked, blankets were spread in front of him so that his feet did not touch the ground.

MEN OR MONSTERS?
Until the Spaniards arrived with horses in 1519, there were no animals big and strong enough to ride in the Mesoamerican lands. There were horses in America in prehistoric times, but they died out around 10,000BC. When the Aztecs saw the Spanish riding, they thought the animals were monsters – half man, half beast.

MAKE A WHEELED DOG

You will need: board, self-drying clay, 4 lengths of thin dowel about 5cm long and 2 lengths about 7cm long, water bowl, thick card, scissors, PVA glue, glue brush, paintbrush, paint, masking tape.

1 Roll a large piece of clay into a fat sausage to form the dog's body. Push the 5cm pieces of dowel into the body to make the legs. Leave to dry.

2 Cover the dowel legs with clay, extending the clay 2cm beyond the end of the dowel. Make a hole at the end of each leg with a piece of dowel. Leave to dry.

3 Push the dowel through the holes in the legs to join them horizontally. Make the dog's head and ears from clay. Join them to the body using water.

HARDWORKING PORTERS

This engraving from the 1900s shows Aztec slaves and commoners carrying loads for Spanish conquerors. Being a porter was very hard work. They were expected to cover up to 100km per day, carrying about 25–30kg on their backs. Like most Mesoamerican people, they travelled these long distances barefoot.

BY BOAT

The city of Tenochtitlan was built on artificial islands on a lake. Transport around the city was by flat-bottomed boat. The boats ferried people and transported fruits and vegetables to market. Dug-out canoes made from hollowed-out tree trunks were popular too.

AZTEC WATERWAYS

The Aztecs paddled their canoes and flat-bottomed boats on Lake Texcoco. Today most of this lake has dried up. The lakeside *chinampas*, where they grew food and flowers, have almost disappeared. This photograph shows modern punts sailing along one of the last remaining Aztec waterways between the few *chinampas* that survive.

Toys such as this dog are proof that the wheel was known in Mesoamerica. Wheeled vehicles were not suitable for rugged Mesoamerican land.

4 Cut four circles 3.5cm in diameter from card to make wheels. Pierce a hole in the centre of each. Make the holes big enough for the dowel to fit through.

5 Make four wheels from clay, the same size as the card wheels. Glue the clay and card wheels together. Make holes through the clay wheels and leave to dry.

6 Paint the dog's head, body, legs and wheels with Aztec patterns. When the paint is dry, give the dog a thin coat of PVA glue to act as a varnish.

7 Fit the wheels on to the ends of the dowels that pass through the dog's legs. Wrap strips of masking tape around the ends to stop the wheels falling off.

Arctic Travel

DURING THE WINTER, the surface of the Arctic Ocean freezes and snow covers the land. In the past, sledges were the most common way of travelling over the ice and snow. They were made from bone or timber lashed together with strips of hide or whale sinew. They glided over the snow on runners made from walrus tusks or wood. Arctic sledges had to be light enough to be pulled by animals, yet strong enough to carry an entire family and its belongings. In North America, huskies pulled the sledges. In Siberia and Scandinavia, however, reindeer were used.

From ancient times, Arctic peoples have needed skis and snowshoes to travel over snow. Skis are thought to have been invented by the Saami people of Lapland more than 3,500 years ago. Snowshoes enabled Arctic hunters to stalk prey without sinking into deep snowdrifts.

REINDEER SLEDGES
Three reindeer stand by a family and their sledge in Siberia. In Arctic Russia and Scandinavia, reindeer were commonly used to pull sledges. Small, narrow sledges carried just one person. Larger, wider models could take much heavier loads.

HITCHING A DOG TEAM
A husky team struggles up a hill in eastern Greenland. Traditionally, the traces (reins) that connected the dogs to the sledge were made of walrus hide. Different Arctic cultures used one of two arrangements to hitch the dogs together. Some people hitched them in the shape of a fan. Others hitched the dogs in pairs in a long line.

MAKE A MODEL SLEDGE
You will need: thick card, balsa wood, ruler, pencil, scissors, PVA glue, glue brush, masking tape, compass, barbecue stick, string, shammy leather, brown paint, paint brush, water pot.

Template C x 8 — 18 cm / 4 cm
Template D x 1 — 18 cm / 8 cm
Template B x 4 — 21 cm / 8 cm
Template E x 1 — 18 cm / 3 cm
Template A x 4 — 61 cm / 54 cm / 5 cm / 6.5 cm

Using the shapes above for reference, measure out the shapes on the card (use balsa wood for template C). Cut the shapes out using your scissors. You will need to make 4 A templates, 4 B templates, 8 C templates (balsa wood), 1 D template and 1 E template. Always remember to cut away from your body when using scissors.

1 Glue 2 A templates together. Repeat this for the other 2 A templates. Repeat this with the 4 B templates. Cover all the edges with masking tape.

SNOWSHOES

Snowshoes are used to walk across deep snowdrifts without sinking into the snow. They spread the person's weight across a large area. To make the snowshoe, thin, flexible birch saplings were steamed to make them supple. The saplings were then bent into the shape of the snowshoe frame. Some shoes were rounded but others were long and narrow. The netting was woven from long strips of animal hide.

birch sapling

snowshoes

rawhide thongs

MAN'S BEST FRIEND

This picture, painted around 1890, shows an Inuit hunter harnessing one of his huskies. Huskies were vital to Inuit society. On the hunt, the dogs helped to nose out seals hiding in their dens. They hauled heavy loads of meat back to camp.

SAAMI SKIS

The Saami have used skis for thousands of years. Early skis were made of wood and the undersides were covered with strips of reindeer skin. The hairs on the skin pointed backwards, giving the skier grip when walking uphill.

LET SLEEPING DOGS LIE

A husky's thick coat keeps it warm in temperatures as low as −50°C. These hardy animals can sleep peacefully in the fiercest of blizzards. The snow builds up against their fur and insulates them.

Inuit hunters used wooden sledges pulled by huskies to hunt for food over a large area. The wood was lashed together with animal hide or sinew.

2 Using a compass, make small holes along the top edge of the glued A templates. Use the end of a barbecue stick to make the holes a little larger.

3 Glue the balsa wood slats C in position over the holes along the A templates as shown above. You will need to use all 8 balsa wood slats.

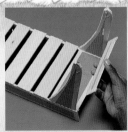

4 Carefully glue the B templates and the E and D templates to the end of the sledge, as shown above. Allow to dry, then paint the model.

5 Thread string through the holes to secure the slats on each side. Decorate the sledge with a shammy-covered card box and secure it to the sledge.

Early Conflicts in Mesopotamia

THE CITY-STATES of Mesopotamia were frequently at war with one another. Usually, the disputes were local affairs over pieces of land or the ownership of canals. Later, powerful kings created empires and warred with foreign countries. King Sargon of Agade, for example, subdued all the cities of Sumer and then conquered great cities in northern Syria. Assyria and Babylonia were often at war in the first millennium BC. The walls of Assyrian palaces were decorated with reliefs (painted carvings) that celebrate battle scenes.

The Mesopotamians were among the first people to invent the wheel. They put this to good use in chariot warfare and wheeled siege machines.

WHEELED ADVANTAGE
An Assyrian king charges along in his chariot at a lion hunt. Chariots were also used to ride into battle. The Assyrians perfected the art of chariot warfare, which gave them a big advantage over enemies who were fighting on foot.

IN THE BEGINNING
A model of a very early chariot, about 4,000 years old, shows the first wheel designs of solid wood. By the time of the Assyrian Empire, about 900-600 BC, war chariots had spoked wooden wheels with metal rims.

THE KING'S GUARDS
A panel from the palace of the Persian kings at Susa shows a long procession of king's guards. The guards are armed with spears, and carry quivers full of arrows. King Cyrus of Persia conquered Babylon in 539BC.

MAKE A CHARIOT
You will need: pen, cardboard, scissors, paints and paintbrushes, flour, water and newspaper to make papier mâché, glue, masking tape, 2 x dowel 16cm long, card tubes, needle, 4 cocktail sticks.

1 Cut four circles about 7cm in width out of the card. Use the scissors to make a hole in the centre of each circle. Enlarge the holes with a pen.

2 Cut out two sides for the chariot 12cm long x 8cm high as shown, one back 9 x 8cm, one front 9 x 15cm, one top 9 x 7cm and one base 12 x 9cm.

3 Trim the top of the front to two curves as shown. Stick the side pieces to the front and back using masking tape. Stick on the base and top.

SLINGS AND ARROWS
Assyrian foot-soldiers used rope slings and stone balls the size of modern tennis balls. Others fired arrows while sheltering behind tall wicker shields. They wore helmets of bronze or iron and were protected by metal scale armour and leather boots.

GOING INTO BATTLE
Sumerian chariot drivers charge into battle. A soldier armed with spears stands on the footplate of each chariot ready to jump off and fight. They are all protected by thick leather cloaks and helmets. The chariots were drawn by onegars (wild asses).

STORMING A CITY
Many Assyrian fighting methods can be seen in the palace reliefs at the city of Nimrud. In this scene, the Assyrians storm an enemy city which stands on a hill. A siege engine with spears projecting from the front breaks down the walls. Attacking soldiers climbed the walls with the help of siege ladders, and they were protected by archers.

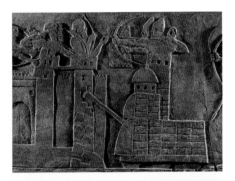

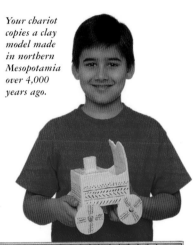

Your chariot copies a clay model made in northern Mesopotamia over 4,000 years ago.

4 Roll up a piece of newspaper to make a cylinder shape 3cm long, and attach it to the chariot. Attach the cardboard tubes to the bottom of the chariot.

5 Mix a paste of flour and water. Dip newspaper strips into the paste to make papier mâché. Cover the chariot with layers of papier mâché. Leave to dry.

6 Paint the whole chariot cream. Add detail using brown paint. Paint the wheels, too. Make a hole with the needle in each end of the dowels.

7 Insert a cocktail stick in the dowel, add a wheel and insert into the tube. Fix another wheel and stick to the other end. Repeat with the other wheels.

EARLY CONFLICTS IN MESOPOTAMIA 221

Indian Armies

CONFLICT WAS A FACT OF LIFE in India from the time when people invaded from central Asia around 1750BC. At first, tribes fought and stole each others' cattle. Gradually, empires grew and warfare became more elaborate. By the time of the emperor Ashoka in 250BC, armies were divided into four parts – infantry (footsoldiers), cavalry (horses), chariots and elephants. The infantry was the core of all Indian armies, but was often made up of poorly trained peasants. Elephants were symbols of royalty, majesty and prestige.

In the first millennium AD, when the Turks invaded, chariots became less important. This was because the Turks had excellent horses and could use bows on horseback. Soon, all Indian armies copied them and developed a top-grade cavalry. The first recorded use of gunpowder in Indian warfare was in the 1400s. Later, the Mughals combined field artillery (guns) with cavalry and elephants.

UNEQUAL CONTEST
A mounted warrior and a footsoldier attack each other. From the 1200s, nobles preferred to fight on horseback. Footsoldiers faced a height disadvantage when fighting mounted soldiers. The horsemen could also use swords as well as bows.

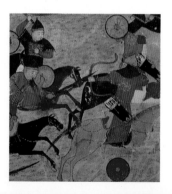

SUPERIOR WARRIOR
A Mongol warrior draws his bow and aims behind him as he rides. The Mongols were great fighters, especially on horseback. In 1398, they devastated Delhi and took many of its citizens as slaves.

MUGHAL HELMET

You will need: strips of newspaper, flour and water or wallpaper paste, bowl, inflated balloon, scissors, fine sandpaper, thin card, sticky tape or PVA glue, gold and black paint, paintbrushes, 20 x 10 cm piece of black card, ruler.

1 Soak the newspaper in the paste or flour and water. Cover half the balloon with three layers of newspaper. Leave to dry between layers.

2 When dry, burst the balloon and remove it. Smooth edges of helmet with sandpaper. Wrap a strip of card around the base. Fix with tape or glue.

3 Place a longer piece of card inside the helmet. It should be long enough to cover your ears and neck. Glue or tape it into position and trim to fit.

LIGHT PROTECTION

A Hindu warrior on horseback prepares to hurl his spear. Warriors had little armour besides shields. They often wore ornaments and lucky charms.

FORTIFIED CHAIR

A king at war travels in a fortified howdah (chair) on an elephant's back. The combination of howdah and elephant was like the armoured tank of modern warfare. The best elephants for army use came mainly from eastern and southern India, and Sri Lanka.

BEST WEAPON

The Hindu footsoldier's favoured weapons were the bow and arrow, and the sword. However, they also fought with maces, lances, spears and daggers.

FINE WEAPONRY

This Mughal dagger handle is inlaid with gold and jewels. Weapons were often crafted from the finest materials.

A Mughal warrior wore a plumed helmet to protect his head in battle.

4 Paint the entire helmet with two coats of gold paint, using a medium-sized paintbrush. Allow the paint to dry completely between coats.

5 Add detail with black paint and a fine paintbrush. You could use a Mughal pattern like the one shown here, or design your own.

6 Cut narrow slits 5 mm apart in the black card. Leave 5 cm uncut at the bottom of the card. Cover this patch with glue and roll the card up tightly.

7 When the glue is dry, fix the plume to the top of your helmet with glue, or you can cut a small hole in the helmet and push the plume through.

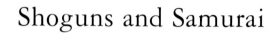

Shoguns and Samurai

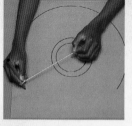

BETWEEN 1185 AND 1600 there were a great many wars throughout Japan. Rival warlords fought to become shogun – the title held by the military ruler. Some former emperors also tried, unsuccessfully, to restore imperial rule. During this troubled time in Japanese history, emperors, shoguns and daimyo all relied on armies of well-trained samurai to fight their battles. The samurai were highly trained warriors from noble families. Members of each samurai army were bound by a solemn oath, sworn to their lord. They stayed loyal from a sense of honour – and because their lord gave them rich rewards. The civil wars ended around 1600, when the Tokugawa dynasty of shoguns came to power. From this time onwards, samurai spent less time fighting, and served instead as officials and business managers.

Riding off to War
Painted in 1772, this samurai general is in full armour. A samurai's horse had to be fast, agile and strong enough to carry the full weight of the samurai, his armour and his weapons.

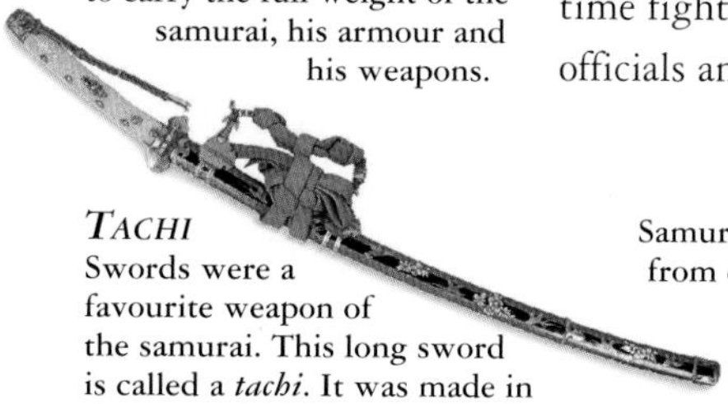

Tachi
Swords were a favourite weapon of the samurai. This long sword is called a *tachi*. It was made in the 1500s for ceremonial use by a samurai.

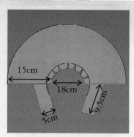

Metal Helmet
Samurai helmets like this were made from curved metal panels, carefully fitted together, and decorated with elaborate patterns. The jutting peak protected the wearer's face and the nape-guard covered the back of the neck. This helmet dates from around 1380.

Samurai Helmet
You will need: thick card, pin, string, felt-tip pen, ruler, scissors, tape measure, newspaper, bowl, water, PVA glue, balloon, petroleum jelly, pencil, modelling clay, bradawl, paper, gold card, paints, brush, water pot, glue brush, masking tape, paper fasteners, 2 x 20cm lengths of cord.

1 Draw a circle 18cm in diameter on card using the pin, string and felt-tip pen. Using the same method, draw two larger circles 20cm and 50cm.

2 Draw a line across the centre of the three circles using the ruler and felt-tip pen. Draw tabs in the middle semi-circle. Add two flaps as shown.

15cm
18cm
5cm
5.5cm

3 Now cut out the neck protector piece completely, as shown above. Make sure that you cut around the tabs and flaps exactly.

PROTECTIVE CLOTHING

This fine suit of samurai armour dates from the Tokugawa period (1600–1868). Armour gave the samurai life-saving protection in battle. High-ranking warriors wore suits of plate armour, made of iron panels, laced or riveted together and combined with panels of chain mail or rawhide. Lower-ranking soldiers called *ashigaru* wore thinner, lightweight armour, made of small metal plates. A full suit of samurai armour could weigh anything up to 18kg.

SURCOAT FINERY

For festivals, ceremonies and parades samurai wore surcoats (long, loose tunics) over their armour. Surcoats were made from fine, glossy silks, dyed in rich colours. This example was made during the Tokugawa period (1600–1868). Surcoats were often decorated with family crests. These were originally used to identify soldiers in battle, but later became badges of high rank.

MAKING BOWS

Japanese craftworkers are busy at work making bows, around 1600. The bow was the Japanese warrior's most ancient weapon. Bows were made of wood and bamboo and fired many different kinds of arrow.

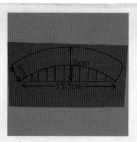

4 Draw the peak template piece on another piece of card. Follow the measurements shown in the picture. Cut out the peak template.

5 To make papier-mâché, tear the newspaper into small strips. Fill the bowl with 1 part PVA glue to 3 parts water. Add the newspaper strips.

6 Blow up the balloon to the size of your head. Cover with petroleum jelly. Build up three papier-mâché layers on the top and sides. Leave to dry between layers.

7 When dry, pop the balloon and trim. Ask a friend to make a mark on either side of your head.

Instructions for the helmet continue on the next page...

Honour Among Samurai

Samurai were highly trained warriors who dedicated their lives to fighting for their lords. However, being a samurai involved more than just fighting. The ideal samurai was supposed to follow a strict code of behaviour, governing all aspects of his life. This code was called *bushido* (the way of the warrior). *Bushido* called for skill, self-discipline, bravery, loyalty, honour, honesty, obedience and, at times, self-sacrifice. It taught that it was nobler to die fighting than to run away and survive.

Many samurai warriors followed the religious teachings of Zen, a branch of the Buddhist faith. Zen was introduced into Japan by two monks, Eisai and Dogen, who went to China to study in the 1100s and 1200s and brought Zen practices back with them. Teachers of Zen encouraged their followers to meditate (to free the mind of all thoughts) in order to achieve enlightenment.

THE TAKEDA FAMILY

The famous daimyo (warlord) Takeda Shingen (1521–1573), fires an arrow using his powerful bow. The influential Takeda family owned estates in Kai province near the city of Edo and kept a large private army of samurai warriors. Takeda Shingen fought a series of wars with his near neighbour, Uesugi Kenshin. However, in 1581, the Takeda were defeated by the army of General Nobunaga.

SWORDSMEN

It took young samurai many years to master the skill of swordsmanship. They were trained by master swordsmen. The best swords, made of strong, springy steel, were even given their own names.

8 Place clay under the pencil marks. Make two holes – one above and one below each pencil mark – with a bradawl. Repeat on the other side.

9 Fold a piece of A4 paper and draw a horn shape on to it following the design shown above. Cut out this shape so that you have an identical pair of horns.

10 Take a piece of A4 size gold card. Place your paper horns on to the gold card and draw around them. Carefully cut the horns out of the card.

11 Paint the papier-mâché helmet brown. Paint a weave design on the neck protector and a cream block on each flap. Leave to dry.

OFF TO WAR
A samurai warrior (on horseback) and foot-soldiers set off for war. Samurai had to command and inspire confidence in others, so it was especially important for them to behave in a brave and honourable way.

MARTIAL ARTS
Several sports that people enjoy playing today have developed from samurai fighting skills. In aikido, players try to throw their opponent off-balance and topple them to the ground. In kendo, players fight one another with long swords made of split bamboo. They score points by managing to touch their opponent's body, not by cutting or stabbing them!

kendo   *aikido*

SURVIVAL SKILLS
Samurai had to know how to survive in wild countryside. Each man carried emergency rations of dried rice. He also used his fighting skills to hunt wild animals for food.

ZEN
The Buddhist monk Rinzai is shown in this Japanese brush and ink scroll-painting. Rinzai was a famous teacher of Zen ideas. Many pupils, including samurai, travelled to his remote monastery in the mountains to study with him.

Samurai helmets were often decorated with crests made of lacquered wood or metal. These were mounted on the top of the helmet.

12 Bend back the tabs on the peak piece. Position it at the front of the helmet. Stick the tabs to the inside with glue. Hold in place with tape.

13 Now take the neck protector. Bend back the front flaps and the tabs. Glue the tabs to the helmet, as shown. Leave the helmet to dry.

14 Stick the horns to the front of the helmet. Use paper fasteners to secure, as shown. Decorate the ear flaps with paper fasteners.

15 Thread cord through one of the holes made in step 8. Tie a knot in the end. Thread the other end of the cord through the second hole. Repeat on the other side.

Greek Fighting Forces

ALL GREEK MEN were expected to fight in their city's army. In Sparta the army was on duty all year round. In other parts of Greece men gave up fighting in autumn so that they could bring in the harvest and make the wine. The only full-time soldiers were the personal bodyguards of a ruler and mercenaries who fought for anyone who paid them. Armies consisted mainly of hoplites (armoured infantry), cavalry (soldiers on horseback) and a group of foot soldiers armed with stones and bows and arrows. The hoplites engaged in hand-to-hand combat and were the most important fighting force. The cavalry was less effective because riders had no stirrups. This made charging with a lance impossible, as the rider would fall off on contact. Instead horsemen were used for scouting, harassing a beaten enemy and carrying messages.

HARD HELMET
This bronze helmet from the city of Corinth was fashioned to protect the face. It has guards for the cheeks and the bridge of the nose. Iron later replaced bronze as the main metal for weapons.

BOWMEN
The Greek army usually employed Scythian archers from north of the Black Sea to fight for them. Archers were useful for fighting in mountainous countryside if they were positioned above the enemy. Some Greek soldiers did fight with bows and arrows. They fought in small units known as *psiloi*. But most of the soldiers in these units could only afford simple missile weapons, such as a javelin or slings from which they shot stones.

WARRIOR GREAVES
You will need: clear film, bowl of water, plaster bandages, sheet of paper, kitchen paper, scissors, cord, gold paint, paintbrush.

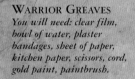

1 Ask a friend to help you with steps 1 to 3. Loosely cover both of your lower legs (from your ankle to the top of your knee) in clear film.

2 Soak each plaster bandage in water. Working from one side of your leg to the other, smooth the bandage over the front of each leg.

3 Carefully remove each greave. Set them on some paper. Dampen some kitchen paper and use it to smooth the greaves down. Leave them to dry.

A RARE SIGHT IN BATTLE

Chariots were not often used in Greek warfare. They could only be used on plains. There were usually two people in the chariot, one to drive it and the other to fight from the back.

FIGHTING FORCES

Tin and copper were used to make bronze, the main material for weapons and armour. Bronze is harder than pure copper and, unlike iron, does not rust. As there was no tin in Greece, it was imported from faraway lands.

copper   tin

MIDDLE CLASS FOOT SOLDIERS

The hoplite fighting force was made up of middle-class men who could afford to arm themselves. A hoplite's armoury consisted of a shield, helmet, spear, sword and greaves. Helmets were made of bronze and were usually crested with horsehair. The body was protected by a bronze cuirass – a one-piece breast- and back-plate. Underneath this, there was a leather cuirass. Shields were usually round and decorated with a symbol.

4 Trim the edges of the greaves, to make them look neat. Measure four lengths of cord to fit around your leg, below the knee and above the ankle.

5 Turn the greaves on to their front. Lay the cord in place at the point where you want to tie them to your leg. Fix them into place using wet bandages.

6 Leave the plaster bandages to dry, with the cord in place. Now paint each greave with gold paint. Once they are dry, tie them on.

Greaves were attached to the lower leg to protect it in battle. They were worn by hoplites.

Legions of Romans

T HE ARMY OF THE EARLY ROMAN EMPIRE was
divided into 28 groups called legions. Each of
these numbered about 5,500 soldiers. The legion
included mounted troops and foot-soldiers. They
were organized into cohorts of about 500 men, and
centuries, of about 80 men – even though centuries
means 'hundreds'. Each legion was led into battle
by soldiers carrying standards. These were
decorated poles that represented the honour and bravery of the legion.

The first Roman soldiers were called up from the wealthier families
in times of war. These conscripts had to supply their own weapons.
In later years, the Roman army became paid professionals, with
legionaries recruited from all citizens. During the period of the Empire,
many foreign troops also fought for Rome as auxiliary soldiers.

Army life was tough and discipline was severe. After a long march
carrying heavy kits, tents, tools and weapons,
the weary soldiers would have to dig camp
defences. A sentry who
deserted
his post would
be beaten to death.

AT WAR
Trajan's Column in Rome
is decorated with scenes from the
Dacian wars. These were fought in
the region of present-day Romania.
Scenes like these can tell us much
about Roman soldiers,
the weapons they
used, their enemies
and their allies.

A LEGIONARY
This bronze statue of
a legionary is about
1,800 years old.
He is wearing a
crested parade
helmet and the
overlapping bronze
armour of the period.
Legionaries underwent
strict training and were
brutally disciplined.
They were tough soldiers
and quite a force to be
reckoned with.

ON HORSEBACK
Roman foot-soldiers were
backed up by mounted
troops, or cavalry. They
were divided into groups,
of 500 to 1,000, called *alae*.
The cavalry were amongst
the highest paid of
Roman soldiers.

RAISING THE STANDARD

The Emperor Constantine addresses his troops, probably congratulating them on a victory. They are carrying standards, emblems of each legion. Standards were decorated with gold eagles, hands, wreaths and banners called *vexilla*. They were symbols of the honour and bravery of the legion and had to be protected at all costs.

A ROMAN FORT

The Roman army built forts of wood or stone all over the Empire. This fort is in southern Britain. It was built to defend the coast against attacks by Saxon raiders from northern Europe. Today, its surrounding area is called Porchester. The name comes from a combination of the word port and *caster*, the Latin word for fort.

HADRIAN'S WALL

This is part of Hadrian's Wall, which marks the most northerly border of the Roman Empire. It stretches for 120km across northern England, almost from coast to coast. It was built as a defensive barrier between AD122 and 128, at the command of the Emperor Hadrian.

Equipped to Kill

ROMAN SOLDIERS were renowned for their effective weapons. A legionary carried a dagger called a *pugio*, a short iron sword called a *gladius*, which was used for stabbing and slashing, and a javelin, or *pilum*. In the early days of the Empire, a foot-soldier's armour was a mail shirt, worn over a short, thick tunic. Officers wore a cuirass, a bronze casing that protected the chest and back, and crests on their helmets to show their rank. By about AD35, the mail shirt was being replaced by plate armour, in which iron sections were joined by hooks or leather straps. Early shields were oval, and later ones were oblong with curved edges. They were made of layers of wood glued together, covered in leather and linen. A metal boss, or cover, over the central handle could be used to hit an enemy who got too close.

ROMAN SOLDIERS
Artists over the ages have been inspired by the battles of the Roman legions. They imagined how fully armed Roman soldiers might have looked. This picture shows a young officer giving orders.

HEAD GEAR
Roman helmets were designed to protect the sides of the head and the neck. This cavalry helmet is made of bronze and iron. It would have been worn by an auxiliary, a foreign soldier fighting for Rome, sometime after AD43. Officers wore crests on their helmets, so that their men could see them during battle.

ROMAN ARMOUR

You will need: tape measure, A1-size sheets of silver card (one or two, depending on how big you are), scissors, pencil, PVA glue, paintbrush, 2m length of cord, compass.

1 Measure yourself around your chest. Cut out three strips of card, 5cm wide and long enough to go round you. Cut out some thinner strips to stick these three together.

2 Lay the wide strips flat and glue them together with the thin strips, as shown above. The Romans would have had leather straps to hold the wide metal pieces together.

3 When the glue is dry, bend the ends together, silver side out. Make a hole in the end of each strip and thread the cord through, as shown above.

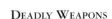

DEADLY WEAPONS

These iron spearheads were found on the site of an old Roman fort near Bath, in Britain. The wooden shafts they were on rotted long ago. Roman soldiers carried both light and heavy spears. The lighter ones were used for throwing, and the heavier ones were for thrusting at close range.

TORTOISE TACTICS

Siege tactics were one of the Roman army's great strengths. When approaching an enemy fortress, a group of soldiers could lock their shields together over their heads and crouch under them. Protected by their shields, they could safely advance toward the enemy. This was known as the *testudo* (tortoise), formation. During a siege, iron bolts and large stones were hurled over fortress walls by giant catapults.

SWORDS

Both short and long swords were kept in scabbards. This spectacular scabbard was owned by an officer who served the Emperor Tiberius. It may have been given to him by the emperor himself. It is elaborately decorated in gold and silver.

4 Cut a square of card as wide as your shoulders. Use the compass to draw a 12cm diameter circle in the centre. Cut the square in half and cut away the half circles.

5 Use smaller strips of card to glue the shoulder halves together, leaving a neck hole. Cut out four more strips, two a little shorter than the others. Attach them in the same way.

Put the shoulder piece over your head and tie the chest section round yourself. Now you are a legionary ready to do battle with the enemies of Rome. Metal strip armour was invented during the reign of the Emperor Tiberius, AD14-37. Originally, the various parts were hinged and were joined together either by hooks or by buckles and straps.

Celts versus Romans

THE ROMANS HAD TO DO some hard fighting to win over new lands for their empire. The Celts were among their fiercest foes. There were Celtic tribes scattered throughout central and northern Europe. They shared similar languages and customs – and resistance against Roman rule! The first major conflicts began soon after 400BC, when migrating bands of Celts from France arrived in northern Italy. Then, in 387BC, Celtic warriors attacked the city of Rome itself. To the Romans, the Celts were savage, barbarian and brutal, compared with their own people. However, Roman soldiers were impressed by the courage and ferocity of Celtic warriors, and the fast, two-horse chariots that the chiefs rode into battle. The Romans soon discovered that most of the Celtic troops were no match for their well-organized, disciplined way of fighting, or for their short, stabbing swords. Once ordinary Celtic warriors saw their hero chiefs dead on the battlefield, they panicked. They either hurled themselves recklessly towards the Romans, and were easily killed, or else retreated in confusion and despair.

It took many years for the Romans to conquer all the Celtic tribes, but in the end, they succeeded.

ROMANS RIDING HIGH
This tombstone was carved as a memorial to a Roman soldier named Flavinus. He served as a standard-bearer in a cavalry regiment that was sent to enforce the Roman conquest of Britain in about AD50. The carving shows his horse trampling a Celtic warrior under its hoofs. The warrior has hair stiffened with lime to make him look more fierce. Despite their courage, Celtic foot soldiers had little chance of surviving a Roman cavalry charge.

CAPTIVE CELTS
Once captured by the Romans, Celtic men, women and children were either killed or sold as slaves. This painting dates from the 1800s and shows captive Celts in Rome. The artist has invented some details of the Celts' clothes and hairstyles. After success in war, the Romans paraded captured prisoners through the city.

TRIUMPH AND DEFEAT

Two Celts, captured and in chains, are depicted on a Roman triumphal arch. The arch was built around AD25 in southern France. It commemorates a Roman victory against the rebellious Gauls. The sculptor has shown the Gauls as the Romans imagined them, looking wild and ragged, and dressed in shaggy fur.

ENEMIES ON COINS

The Romans chose to show a Celtic warrior in his battle chariot on this Roman coin. They admired certain aspects of the Celtic civilization and were proud to have conquered such a people.

JULIUS CAESAR

Roman army commander Julius Caesar was very ambitious. He used his success against the Celts in France to help advance his political career in Rome. In 44BC, he declared himself "Dictator (sole ruler) for Life". He wrote a book describing his campaigns against the Celts. Although it paints a hostile picture of the Celtic people, Caesar's book has become one of the most important pieces of evidence about Celtic life. This silver coin shows Julius Caesar, represented as an elephant, crushing Gaul (France).

WALLED FRONTIER

In AD122, the Roman emperor, Hadrian, gave orders for a massive wall to be built across northern England. Its purpose was to mark the border between lands ruled by Rome and lands further north in Scotland, where Celtic chiefs still had power. Roman soldiers were stationed at forts built at intervals along the wall. They kept a look out for Celtic attackers, but also met, traded with, and sometimes married, members of the local Celtic population who lived and worked close to the wall.

Celts Fight Back

THE CELTS RELIED ON THEIR STRENGTH – and their weapons – to survive in battle. Their heavy iron swords were used for cutting and slashing. They were carried in decorated scabbards made of bronze, wood or leather. Spears and javelins were lighter. They were used for stabbing at close quarters or for throwing at an enemy many metres away. Round pebbles, hurled by cloth or leather slings, could also be deadly weapons. Archaeologists have found huge stockpiles of pebbles at Celtic hill forts. Wooden clubs were used by warriors to bludgeon their enemies in battle, but were also used for hunting birds.

For protection, Celtic warriors carried a long shield, usually made of wood and leather. Normally, Celtic men wore a thigh-length tunic over baggy trousers but, in battle, they often went naked except for a torc (twisted metal ring) around the neck and a metal helmet. This nakedness was a proud display of physical strength – even the Celts' enemies admired their tall, muscular physique. The Celts believed that torcs gave magical protection. Their helmets, topped with magic crests, gave them extra height and made them look frightening.

CHAIN MAIL
The Celts sometimes used flexible chest coverings of chain mail in battle. Several burial sites have yielded actual chain mail such as that shown above, found in St Alban's, England. However, most of the time, the Celts went into battle naked.

UNDRESSED TO KILL
This gold pin is decorated with the figure of a naked Celtic warrior, armed with sword, shield and helmet. One ancient writer described a Celtic warrior's weapons: "A long sword worn on the right side, and a long shield, tall spears and a kind of javelin. Some also use bows and slings. They have a wooden war club, which is thrown by hand with a range far greater than an arrow …"

MAKE A SHIELD

You will need: felt-tip pen, card 77cm x 38cm, scissors, ruler, pair of compasses, bottle top, bradawl, leather thongs, paper fasteners, sticky tape, drink carton lid, plasticine, PVA glue, paint, paintbrushes, dowling rod 75cm long.

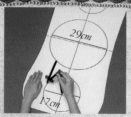

1 Draw a shield shape on to card. The shield should have rounded corners and curve in slightly on each of the long sides, as shown. Cut out.

2 Draw a vertical and a horizontal line through the centre of the shield. Add a large circle in the centre and two smaller circles either side, as shown.

3 With a felt-tip pen draw a typical Celtic design inside the circles, as shown. Use the bottle top and compasses to help you create your design.

SPANISH SHIELDS

The design of weapons and armour varied in different Celtic lands. These Celts are carrying small, round shields that originated in Spain. Shields were made from wood and leather. All Spanish warriors usually fought with a short, single-edged sword, called a *falcata*.

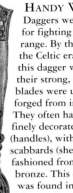

HANDY WEAPON

Daggers were used for fighting at close range. By the end of the Celtic era, when this dagger was made, their strong, sharp blades were usually forged from iron. They often had finely decorated hilts (handles), with scabbards (sheaths) fashioned from softer bronze. This dagger was found in the River Thames, London.

BRAIN GUARD

Helmets were usually made of iron, padded inside with cloth and covered on the outside by a layer of bronze. The high, domed shape protected the wearer's skull. The peaked front kept slashing sword blows away from the eyes.

SHARP AND DEADLY

Celtic weapons were fitted with sharp metal blades, designed to cause terrible injuries. This bronze spear-point was made in Britain in about 1400BC, using techniques that were still employed by the Celts a thousand years later. Celtic metalworkers used moulds to make tools and weapons. Molten bronze was poured into the mould. Once the bronze object was cold and hard, rough edges were polished away, using coarse sand.

Shields were a speciality of craft workshops in southern England. A shield was one of a Celtic warrior's most prized possessions.

4 Use the bradawl to make two holes between the large and smaller circles, as shown. Thread the leather thongs through the holes.

5 With the bradawl, make small holes for the decorative paper fasteners. Push the paper fasteners through the holes and tape the ends on the back.

6 Stick the drink carton lid into the centre of the large circle. Roll long, thin plasticine snakes. Glue them along the lines of your decorative pattern.

7 Paint the front of the shield bronze. When dry, turn over and stick the dowling rod down the back. Use tape to secure. Tie the leather thongs.

The Fall of the Celts

CELTIC POWER in Europe lasted for around 800 years. It started to decline because other peoples grew strong enough to make their own claims for power and land. The first and most formidable of these were the well-trained, well-equipped soldiers of the Roman Empire. They had driven Celtic settlers from northern Italy in 191BC and from Spain in 133BC. After long campaigns led by their brilliant general, Julius Caesar, the Romans finally conquered France in 51BC. They invaded southern Britain in AD43, and at first met with resistance, such as the revolt led by the Celtic queen, Boudicca. Nevertheless, by AD61, the Romans controlled southern Britain, and they ruled there until AD410. However, they never managed to conquer the whole of the British Isles. Parts of Scotland and Ireland continued under Celtic rule until about AD1100. As Roman power weakened, new groups of migrants arrived, mostly from the north, to settle in the former Celtic lands.

These invaders included many peoples with strong armies and vibrant cultures of their own, such as the Visigoths, the Angles and Saxons, the Franks and the Vikings.

GREAT CONQUEROR
Julius Caesar (*c.*100–44BC) led the Roman armies that conquered the Celts in France. He fought and won a series of battles, known as the Gallic Wars, between 58BC and 51BC. He also hoped to conquer Britain and Germany, but a political crisis in Italy forced him to return to Rome.

ROMAN STYLE
After the Romans conquered Britain in AD43, a new, mixed civilization grew up which combined both Roman and Celtic traditions. Although some Celtic chieftains rebelled against Roman rule, others decided to co-operate with the Romans, and served as local governors. They built splendid country houses, known as villas, which were decorated in the Roman style with beautiful mosaic floors such as this one.

THE VISIGOTHS

This jewelled, golden crown was made for the Visigothic kings of Spain to give as a religious offering. The Visigoths were a people from northern Europe. Celtic lands in Spain were conquered by the Romans in 133BC, and then by the Visigoths in about AD400. Even so, many Celtic skills, such as the art of fine metalworking, survived and were passed down by successive generations of settlers.

KING OF THE FRANKS

The Romans ruled France until about AD400. Northern France was then taken over by the Franks, a people from southern Germany. The Frankish kings built up a powerful empire in former Celtic France. Their most successful and powerful ruler was King Charlemagne (left), who reigned from AD771 to 814.

SAXON KING

This fine, metal helmet was made for an Anglo-Saxon warrior king. The king was buried at Sutton Hoo, on the east coast of England, the land that Boudicca once ruled. The Angles and Saxons came from southern Denmark and north-western Germany. They settled in southern England, where they established seven separate kingdoms.

VIKING WARRIORS

The Vikings were sailors, raiders and traders who came from Scandinavia. They first attacked Britain around AD790. Soon afterwards, Viking settlers came to live in many parts of the British Isles and northern France. This tombstone shows two Viking warriors with round shields.

THE FALL OF THE CELTS 239

Viking Raids and Piracy

IN AD793, A BAND of heavily armed Vikings ran
their longships ashore on Lindisfarne (an island
off the north-east coast of England). It was the site of
a Christian monastery. The monks tried in vain to
hide their precious crosses, silver chalices and bibles,
but the Vikings axed them down. They set fire to the
buildings and sailed away with their loot.

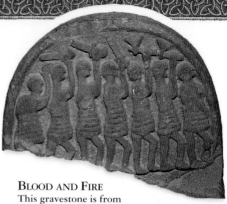

BLOOD AND FIRE
This gravestone is from
Lindisfarne. It shows fierce Viking warriors
armed with swords and battle axes.

This was the start of the period in which the Vikings
spread terror around western Europe. They began by
attacking easy targets, such as villages, monasteries or other ships. They took away cattle, grain,
chests of money and church bells that could be melted down. They also took women, and prisoners as
slaves. Booty was shared among members of the crew. Soon the Vikings were attacking the largest
and richest cities in Europe. In AD846, they sacked (raided), the cities of Hamburg and Paris. King
Charles the Bald of France had to pay the Viking leader Ragnar Hairy-Breeks over three tonnes of
silver to leave. From AD865 onwards, the English kings were also forced to pay over huge sums of

money, called Danegeld.
Like gangsters, the Vikings
returned time after time,
demanding more money –
as well as land on which
they could settle.

INVADING VIKINGS
This painting shows Danish
Vikings invading Northumbria.
The raiders soon realized how
easy it was to attack neighbouring
lands. They began to set up year-
round war camps on the coasts.
Soon they were occupying large
areas of territory and building
their own towns.

SAFE AND SOUND

Viking gold, silver and jewellery were locked in beautiful caskets and chests. This copy of a Viking chest is made of walrus ivory and gilded bronze.

ST CUTHBERT

This picture from the Middle Ages shows St Cuthbert praying in the sea. Cuthbert was one of Lindisfarne's most famous monks. He was made a saint on his death in AD687. In AD875, when the Danish Vikings attacked the island, the monks fled inland to safety, carrying St Cuthbert's remains.

BUILT FROM THE RUINS

In AD793 the Vikings sacked the monastery on Lindisfarne, an island off the coast of northeast England. Afterwards, the religious buildings lay in ruins. The new priory pictured here was built between 1100 and 1200. The stones used to build it were taken from the ruins left by the Vikings. Today, only bare stones remain to remind visitors of the original monastery and its terrible fate.

TREASURE HOARD

Part of a Viking treasure hoard was found in a chest in Cuerdale, England. It included about 40kg of chopped-up silver, fine brooches and coins from many places that the Vikings had raided. They had sailed west to North America, south to Spain, and via European rivers to Constantinople (modern Istanbul).

The Taking of America

THE VIKINGS WERE THE first Europeans to travel to North America. Later explorers, who arrived around 500 years later, made a bigger impact. They claimed the land for their own countries and set up colonies of settlers. Commissioned by Queen Isabella of Spain, the Italian explorer Christopher Columbus landed in the Bahamas in 1492, and declared the land as Spanish territory. Spaniard Ponce de León landed in Florida in 1512, and Hernando Cortés had conquered the Aztec peoples of Central America by 1521. Tales of mountains of gold in the Southwest lured a Spanish expedition headed by Vasquez de Coronado. He encountered many native American Indian tribes, but never found gold.

The native peoples were forced from their homelands, taken captive or killed in their thousands. European explorers and colonists never regarded them as equals. They tried to force tribes to change their lifestyles and beliefs and made them adapt their traditional crafts to suit European buyers.

EARLY VISITORS
Erik the Red, the Viking king, sailed to Greenland around AD982. He was probably in search of new trading partners. His son Leif later sailed to Newfoundland and established a settlement at a place now called L'Anse aux Meadows. A trade in furs and ivory was set up with northern Europe.

SETTING SAIL
Columbus and his crew prepare to set sail from Spain in 1492 in search of a trade route to India. He never reached Asia, but landed on San Salvador in the Bahamas. The Arawaks there thought that Columbus and his men came from the sky and greeted them with praise. Columbus set about claiming the islands for the Spanish Empire. He made many of the natives slaves.

A DISTANT LAND

This map from around 1550 shows a crude European impression of North America. Henry II of France ordered Descallier, a royal cartographer, to make a map of what middle and North America looked like. The French were keen to gain land there. Jacques Cartier, a French navigator, spent eight years exploring the St Lawrence River area. He made contact with the native American Huron communities. He wrote to the king that he hoped the Indians would be "easy to tame".

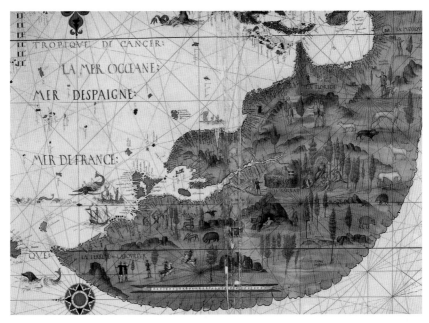

MAN WITH A MISSION

A Plains Indian views a missionary with suspicion. Eastern tribes were the first to meet French missionaries whom they called "Black Robes". In California, Indians were forced to live and work in Spanish mission villages.

SAY A LITTLE PRAYER

Young Indian girls dressed in European clothes have been separated from their families and tribal customs. Europeans could not understand the North American Indians' society and religious beliefs. They wanted to convert them to Christianity, by force if necessary. In many areas, children were taken away from their people and sent to white boarding schools, given European names and taught European religion, language and history.

Aztec Power Struggles

TOTONAC TRIBUTE
Ambassadors from lands conquered by the
Aztecs came to Tenochtitlan to deliver the
tribute demanded from their rulers. This
painting shows splendidly dressed
representatives of the Totonac people
meeting Aztec tax collectors. The Totonacs
lived on the Gulf coast of Mexico, in Veracruz.
Here they are shown offering tobacco, fruit and
vanilla grown on their lands. They hated and
feared the Aztecs.

WAR WAS ESSENTIAL to the survival of the
Aztecs in Central America. They had invaded
from the north from around AD1200, winning new
territory by fighting the people who already lived there.
From then on, the Aztecs relied on war to keep control
and to win more land and cities to keep them rich.
They forced the people they conquered to pay tributes of
crops, treasures and other goods in return for being left
in peace. The big Aztec cities such as Tenochtitlan
needed steady supplies of tribute to feed their citizens.
Without such riches won from war, the whole empire
would have collapsed. War was also a useful source of
captives, who could be sacrificed to the gods. The
Aztecs sacrificed thousands of people each year,
believing that this would win the gods' help.

Each new Aztec ruler traditionally began his reign
with a battle. The Empire grew rapidly during the
1400s until it included most of Mexico. Conquered
cities were often controlled by garrisons of Aztec soldiers
and linked to the government in Tenochtitlan by large
numbers of officials, such as tax collectors and scribes.

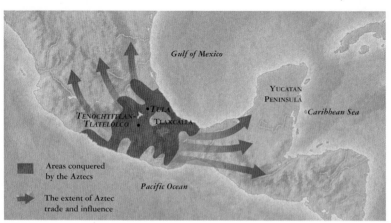

Gulf of Mexico

YUCATAN
PENINSULA

Caribbean Sea

TULA
TENOCHTITLAN
TLATELOLCO • TLAXCALLA

Pacific Ocean

■ Areas conquered
by the Aztecs

➤ The extent of Aztec
trade and influence

AZTEC LANDS
This map shows the area
ruled by the Aztecs in 1519.
Conquered cities were
allowed to continue with
their traditional way of life,
but had to pay tribute to
Aztec officials. The Aztecs
also put pressure on two
weaker city states, Texcoco
and Tlacopan, to join with
them in a Triple Alliance.
One nearby city-state,
Tlaxcalla, refused to
make an alliance with the
Aztecs and stayed
fiercely independent.

CANNIBALS

One of the Aztecs' most important reasons for fighting was to capture prisoners for sacrifice. In this codex picture, we can see sacrificed bodies neatly chopped up. In some religious ceremonies, the Aztecs ate the arms and legs of sacrificed prisoners.

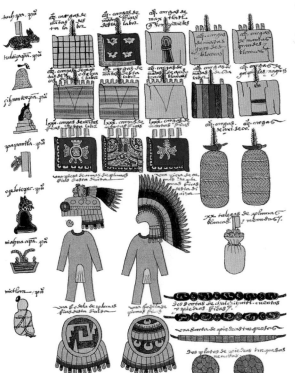

FROM HUMBLE BEGINNINGS

Aztec settlers are shown on their difficult trek through northern Mexico. The Aztecs built up their empire from humble beginnings in a short time. They first arrived in Mexico some time after AD1200. By around 1400, they had become the strongest nation in central Mesoamerica. To maintain their position, they had to be constantly ready for war. The Aztecs invented many legends to justify their success. They claimed to be descended from earlier peoples living in Mexico, and to be specially guided by the gods.

TRIBUTE LIST

The Aztecs received vast quantities of valuable goods as tribute each year. Most of the tribute was sent to their capital city of Tenochtitlan. Aztec scribes there drew up very detailed lists of tribute received, like the one on the left. Among the goods shown are shields decorated with feathers, blankets, turquoise plates, bracelets and dried chilli peppers.

End of the Aztec and Maya

AGAINST THE AZTECS
This picture comes from *The History of the Indies*. It was written by Diego Duran, a Spanish friar who felt sympathy for the Aztecs. Spanish soldiers and their allies from Tlaxcalla are seen fighting against the Aztecs. Although the Aztecs fought bravely, they had no chance of defeating Spanish soldiers mounted on horseback and armed with guns.

In 1493, explorer Christopher Columbus returned to Spain from his pioneering voyage to the Bahamas off the coast of Mesoamerica. He told tales of a 'new world' full of gold. Excited by Columbus' stories, a group of Spanish soldiers sailed to Mexico in 1519, hoping to make their fortunes. They were led by a nobleman called Hernando Cortés. Together with the Aztecs' enemies, he led a march on the Aztec city of Tenochtitlan. For the next two years, the Aztecs fought to keep their land. They drove the Spaniards out of Tenochtitlan in May 1520, but in 1521, Cortés attacked the city again, set fire to its buildings and killed around three-quarters of the population. In 1535, Mexico became a colony, ruled by officials sent from Spain.

Similar events happened in lands controlled by the Maya people in the south of Mesoamerica, but more slowly. The Spanish landed there in 1523, but did not conquer the last independent city-state, Tayasal, until 1697.

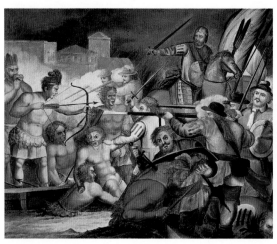

A SAD NIGHT
On 6 May 1520, Spanish soldiers massacred Aztecs gathered for a religious festival in Tenochtitlan. The citizens were outraged and attacked the Spaniards, many of whom died. During this night, the emperor Moctezuma II was stoned to death, probably by Aztecs who believed he had betrayed them. Cortés called this the *Noche Triste* (sad night).

THE END OF AZTEC POWER
This Aztec picture shows the surrender of Cuauhtemoc, the last Aztec king, to Cortés. After Moctezuma II died in 1520, the Aztecs were led by two of Moctezuma's descendants – Cuitlahuac, who ruled for only one year, and Cuauhtemoc. He was the last king and reigned until 1524.

RUNNING FOR THEIR LIVES

This illustration from a Spanish manuscript shows Aztec people fleeing from Spanish conquerors. You can see heavily laden porters carrying stocks of food and household goods across a river to safety. On the far bank, mothers and children, with a pet bird and dog, hide behind giant cactus plants.

WORKING LIKE SLAVES

Spanish settlers in Mexico took over all the Aztec and Maya fields and forced the people to work as farm labourers. They treated them cruelly, almost like slaves. This modern picture shows a Spanish overseer giving orders.

AFTER THE CONQUEST

Mexican artist Diego Rivera shows Mesoamerica after the Spanish conquest. Throughout the 1500s and 1600s, settlers from Spain arrived there. They drove out the local nobles and forced ordinary people to work for them. Spanish missionaries tried to replace local beliefs with European customs and Christianity. In Tenochtitlan, the Spaniards pulled down splendid Aztec palaces and temples to build churches and fine homes for themselves. You can see gangs of Aztec men working as labourers in the background of this picture.

Holding on to an Empire

THE INCA PEOPLE were one of many small tribes living in the Andes Mountains of Peru. In the 1200s, though, they began to take over other tribes and lands. By the 1400s, the Inca Empire covered 3,600km of the Andes and the coast. The Incas numbered only about 40,000, but they controlled a population of 12 million. They hung on to their power by military force. Borders were defended by a string of forts, and cities became walled refuges when the surrounding countryside was under attack. The permanent army of some 10,000 elite troops, could be increased substantially by those serving their *mit'a*, a system of enforced labour.

TAKE THAT!
This star may have looked pretty, but it was deadly when whirled from the leather strap. It was made of obsidian, a glassy black volcanic rock. Inca warriors also fought with spikes set in wooden clubs. Some troops favoured the *bolas*, corded weights that were also used in hunting. Slings were used for scaring birds. However, in the hands of an experienced soldier, they could bring down a hail of stones on enemies and crack their heads open.

WAITING FOR THE CHARGE
A Moche warrior goes down on one knee and brings up his shield in defence. He is bracing himself for an enemy charge. All South American armies fought on foot. The horse was not seen in Peru until the Spanish introduced it.

IN THE BARRACKS
Many towns of the Inca Empire were garrisoned by troops. These restored barrack blocks at Machu Picchu may once have housed soldiers serving out their *mit'a* (enforced labour for the State). They would have been inspected by a high-ranking general from Cuzco. During the Spanish invasion, Machu Picchu may have been a base for desperate resistance fighters.

MAKE AN INCA HELMET
You will need: scissors, cream calico fabric, ruler, balloon, PVA glue, paintbrush, paints, water pot, yellow and black felt, black wool.

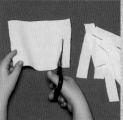

1 Cut the fabric into strips about 8cm x 2cm as shown in the picture. You will need enough to cover the top half of a blown-up balloon three times.

2 Blow up the balloon to the same size as your head. Glue the strips of fabric over the top half. Leave each layer to dry before adding the next.

3 When the last layer is dry, pop the balloon and carefully pull it away. Use scissors to trim round the edge of the helmet. Paint it a reddish orange.

KINGS OF THE CASTLE

The massive fortress of Sacsahuaman at Cuzco was built on a hill. One edge was formed by a cliff and the other defended by massive terraces and zigzag walls. When the Spanish invaded in the 1500s, they were awestruck by Sacsahuaman's size and defences. The Incas regarded warfare as an extension of religious ritual. Sacsahuaman was certainly used for religious ceremonies. Some historians claim that the Inca capital was laid out in the shape of a giant puma, with Sacsahuaman as its head.

SIEGE WARFARE

An Inca army takes on the enemy at Pukara, near Lake Titicaca. Most South American cities were walled and well defended. Siege warfare was common. The attackers blocked the defenders' ways of escape from the town. After the Spanish Conquest in 1536, Inca rebels under Manko Inka trapped Spanish troops in Cuzco and besieged them for over a year.

Inca helmets were round in shape and made of wood or cane. They were decorated with braids and crests.

4 Take the felt. Measure and cut a 3cm yellow square, a yellow circle with a diameter of 3cm, a 9cm yellow square and a 5.5cm black square.

5 Glue the felt shapes on to the helmet as shown above. Glue a 2cm-wide strip of yellow felt along the edge of the helmet to neaten the edge.

6 Take 12 strands of black wool, each 30cm long. Divide them into 3 hanks of 4 strands. Knot the ends together, then plait to the end.

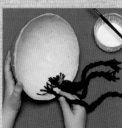

7 Knot the end of the finished braid. Make two more. Glue them inside the back of the helmet. Wait until it is dry before trying it on.

Spaniards Eclipse the Inca Sun

THE WORD OF GOD?
When emperor Ataw Wallpa met the Spanish invaders in Cajamarca, he was approached by a Christian priest called Vincente de Valverde. The priest raised a Bible and said that it contained the words of God. Ataw Wallpa grabbed the book and listened to it. No words came out, so he hurled it to the ground. The Spanish were enraged, and the invasion began.

IN 1532, SPANISH SOLDIERS UNDER their commander Francisco Pizarro, landed in Peru, greedy for gold. In November, they met the Inca emperor, Ataw Wallpa, in the great square of Cajamarca. The *Sapa Inca* (Only Leader) was riding in a litter that was covered in feathers. Surrounding him, his troops glinted with gold. The sound of conch trumpets and flutes echoed around the buildings. The Spanish were amazed by the sight; the Incas looked uneasily at the strangers with their strange, fidgeting horses.

Within an hour, thousands of Incas were killed, and their emperor was in the hands of the Spanish. Ataw Wallpa offered to raise a ransom for his release, and he filled a whole room with silver and gold. Even so, in the summer of 1533, the Spanish accused Ataw Wallpa of treason, and he was garrotted (executed by strangulation). Inca resistance to the Spanish continued for another 39 years, but South American civilization had changed for ever that day.

CONQUEST AND SLAVERY
The Incas were fierce fighters, but they stood no chance against the guns and steel of the Spanish. Their defeat was a disaster for all the native peoples of the Americas. Many were murdered, enslaved or worked to death in the mines. The Spanish became wealthy at the expense of the native peoples.

"SANTIAGO!"
Before the 1532 meeting with Ataw Wallpa in the great square of Cajamarca, the Spanish invader Francisco Pizarro had hidden troops behind buildings. When he shouted the pre-arranged signal of *"Santiago!"* (St James), they began to shoot into the crowd. Chaos broke out as the emperor was seized and taken prisoner.

TEARS OF THE MOON
In 1545, the Spanish discovered silver at Potosí in the Bolivian Andes and began to dig mines. The wealth was incredible, but the working conditions were terrible. Local people were forced to work as slaves. Mule trains carried the silver northwards to Colombian ports, making Spain the richest country in the world.

DESCENDANTS OF THE EMPIRE
Christians of native Andean and mixed descent take part in a procession through the city of Cuzco. In the Andes, over the past few hundred years, many Inca traditions, festivals and pilgrimages have become mixed up with Christian ones. Indigenous peoples today make up 45 per cent of the total population in Peru, 55 per cent in Bolivia and 25 per cent in Ecuador.

THE TREASURE FLEETS
· The Spanish plundered the treasure of the Incas and the minerals of the Andes. Big sailing ships called galleons carried the gold and silver back to Europe from ports in Central and South America. The region was known as the Spanish Main. Rival European ships, many of them pirates from England, France and the Netherlands, began to prey on the Spanish fleets. This led to long years of piracy on the seas. Between 1820 and 1824, Spain's South American colonies finally broke away from European rule to become independent countries, but most of the region's native peoples remained poor and powerless.

Invasion of North America

FROM 1500, NORTH AMERICA was visited by the English, French and Spanish in increasing numbers. Each country laid claim to land and established colonies of settlers. It was mainly the British and the French who stayed. The first settlements were on the east coast, but gradually spread farther inland, encountering more and more tribes of native American Indians. The Europeans introduced diseases previously unknown to the Indians. A smallpox epidemic of 1837 almost wiped out the Mandan people. Fewer than 200 people survived from a tribe that had once numbered over 2,500.

From the 1760s to 1780s, colonists fought for independence from their parent countries, and in 1783, the United States became an independent country. It doubled in size in 1803, when Louisiana Territory was bought from France for $15 million. This marked the end of French rule, and native tribes from the East could be moved west of the Mississippi River. As frontiers edged farther and farther west, more native tribes were pushed out of their homelands.

LEADING THE WAY
Sacawagea, a Shoshoni girl, guides US captains Meriwether Lewis and William Clark from Mississippi to the Pacific coast, in 1804. The journey took nearly a year. President Thomas Jefferson asked them to map out the land from the Mississippi River to the Rockies. This helped to pave the way for settlers to move to the far West.

ROLLING ACROSS THE PLAINS
From around 1850, wagon trains were signs that times were changing for the Plains tribes. Although settlers had been living in North America for around 300 years, they had mostly remained on the east coast. The US government encouraged white families to move inland.

SOD HOUSE
This is a fine example of a soddy, a house literally made from sod, or turf, cut out of the ground. Settlers had to build homes from whatever material was to hand. Life was hard for the children, they had to do chores, such as feeding chickens. If they were lucky, they went to school.

NEW TOWN

Plains Indians watch a train steaming into a new town. Land was sacred to the tribes who called it their Earth Mother. The settlers thought that the tribes wasted their land and wanted to build towns and railways on it. At first the federal government just took land for settlers. Later, they bought millions of acres of Indian land in various treaties (agreements), using force if the Indians did not agree.

PANNING FOR GOLD

A man is sifting through sand in search of gold. When gold was discovered in late 1848 in California, it started the Gold Rush. Thousands of immigrants came to the west coast from all over the world. The sheer numbers forced the tribes off their land.

TRAIN ATTACK

Plains warriors attack a train crossing their hunting grounds. The Plains tribes had always been fiercely defensive of their territory. Now they turned on the new invaders. More and more settlers were encouraged to move on to the Plains. In the 1860s, railways were constructed across Indian lands. They were built over sacred sites and destroyed buffalo hunting grounds which were essential to the tribes' livelihood. Attacks on settlers, trains and white trading posts became more frequent.

Native Americans Fight Back

WILD WEST
There were many conflicts between US soldiers and different tribes, such as this attack in the 1800s. Some attempts at peaceful talks were made. However, military records show that between 1863 and 1891, there were 1,065 fights.

WHEN THE EUROPEAN SETTLERS in North America began to fight for independence from their home countries from 1775 to 1783, some native tribes remained neutral, others took sides. Tribes who had banded together in the Iroquois League of Nations did not want to be involved in a white man's quarrel at first. They had, however, allied with the British against the French in other European wars. The League was split and eventually most of the tribes supported the British. In 1777, they ended up fighting some of their own people, the Oneidas.

Once independence had been won, the United States Government could make its own laws. In 1830, it introduced the Indian Removal Act and relocated tribes from their homelands to areas set aside for Indians called reservations. The Choctaws were relocated in 1830 to Oklahoma. They were followed by the Chickasaws, Creeks and Seminoles. Bitter battles were fought as the Indians struggled to keep their homelands. Reservation land was often less fertile and productive than the old tribal land, and some tribes faced starvation.

TRAIL OF TEARS
The heartbroken Cherokee nation is being forced to leave its homelands in 1838-39. During the trek west, rain and snow fell and soldiers made the Indians move on too quickly. It is estimated that almost 4,000 Cherokees died from exhaustion and exposure.

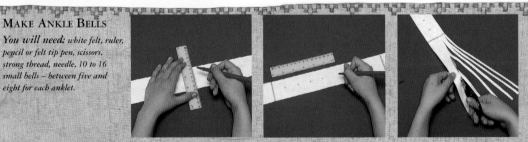

MAKE ANKLE BELLS
You will need: white felt, ruler, pencil or felt tip pen, scissors, strong thread, needle, 10 to 16 small bells – between five and eight for each anklet.

1 Cut out two strips of white felt 75cm x 5cm. Measure and mark a line across the felt strips, 24cm in from one end. Do the same at the other end.

2 Now make a series of marks in the middle section of the strips. Start 3cm away from one line, then mark every 3cm. This is where the bells will go.

3 Create the fringing at each end of the anklet. Do this by cutting into both ends of the band up to the pencilled lines. Do the same for the other anklet.

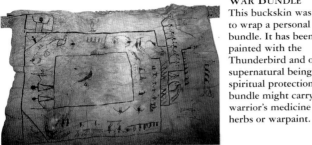

WAR BUNDLE

This buckskin was used to wrap a personal war bundle. It has been painted with the Thunderbird and other supernatural beings for spiritual protection. A bundle might carry a warrior's medicine herbs or warpaint.

THE SHIELD SURVIVED

This warrior's shield belonged to a Dakota (Sioux) warrior in the late 1800s. It may have been used in the Battle of Little Bighorn. The Sioux tribes fought in many battles with the US around that time. In 1851 their lands were defined by a treaty. Then, when gold was found in Montana, gold hunters broke the treaties by travelling through Sioux land, and war raged again.

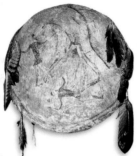

THE END OF GENERAL CUSTER

The Battle of Little Bighorn, in 1876, is counted as the last major victory of the North American Indian. Custer and his entire 7th Cavalry were defeated by Sioux sub-tribes, after they attacked an Indian village. Sadly, this made US soldiers even more brutal in their dealings with tribes.

WAR DANCE

Sioux warriors are performing a war dance. During the dance a medicine man would chant and ask for spiritual guidance and protection for warriors going into battle. Other dances were performed after a battle.

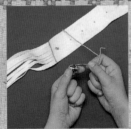
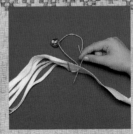

4 Thread a large needle with strong, doubled and knotted thread. Insert the needle into the fabric and pull through until the knot hits the fabric.

5 Thread the needle through the bell and slip the bell up to the felt. Then insert the needle back into the felt very near to the place it came out.

6 Push the needle through and pull tight. Knot the end (opposite side to the bell) to secure and cut away the excess thread. Repeat with the other bells.

The bells of the North American Indians were sewn on to strips of animal skins. They were tied around the ankles or just under the knees, for ceremonial dances.

NATIVE AMERICANS FIGHT BACK **255**

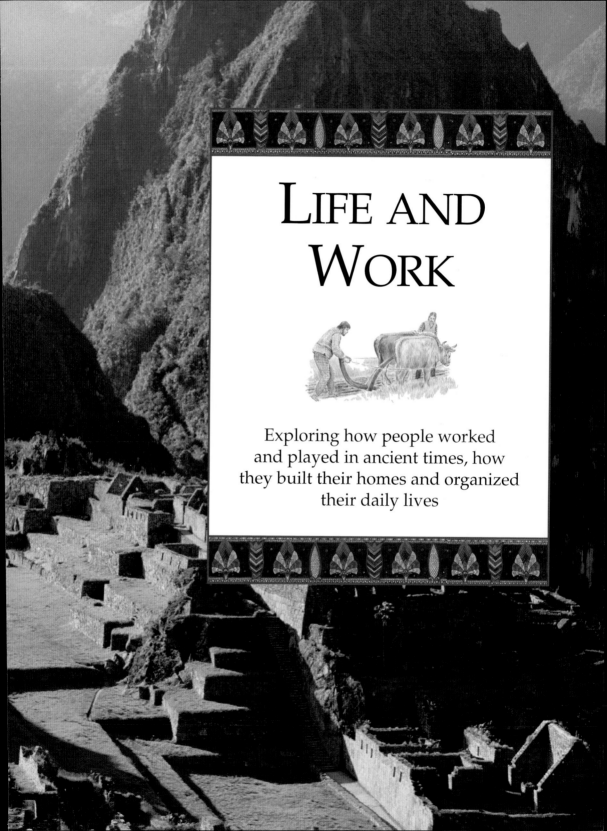

LIFE AND WORK

Exploring how people worked
and played in ancient times, how
they built their homes and organized
their daily lives

Great Themes of Everyday Life

RURAL COMMUNITIES
The first nomadic peoples began to settle around 12,000BC. They farmed the land to provide a reliable food supply for themselves and their families. Scenes such as this Chinese rice field show how little some people's lives have changed through the centuries.

When the ancient Chinese wanted to curse their enemies, they said to them: "May you live in interesting times". This referred to times of war and revolution, which, for ordinary people, meant suffering and destruction. Interesting times were bad times.

Ordinary people preferred to be left in peace, so that they could concentrate on making comfortable homes, working, having families and getting enough food to eat. This section explores the many ways of peaceful, everyday life that existed in the ancient world.

Slower Pace

Thanks to television, cheap air travel and the Internet, today we know more about people in other cultures than ever before. New ideas and fashions spread very quickly. However, in the ancient world, travel was slow and often dangerous. Many people lived their whole lives without travelling more than a few miles from their home towns and villages. Communities were isolated and developed their own styles of clothing, houses and tools. Most people probably knew nothing about how people lived in the next village – or even that other countries existed.

Creating a good home has been a priority for people for thousands of years. Humans originally evolved in equatorial Africa, where the weather is warm enough for people to live outside in every season. But even there, people needed to shelter from rain or

ANCIENT FASHIONS
Styles of dress varied from one area to another, and did not change from one year to the next, as ideas were slow to travel. Viking clothes were typically loose-fitting, and made of wool and linen. They were fastened with decorated metal clasps and buckles. Dyes were made from local plants and insects, so fabric colours also varied from place to place.

VILLAGE LIFE
A typical scene of rural life in ancient India. Most settlements were near rivers, for drinking water, bathing and irrigation.

hot sun in caves or shelters. The remains of the oldest known huts in Africa date back 300,000 years.

When people lived by hunting and gathering wild plants, they built simple homes that could be easily put up, dismantled and moved. This was because they often had to move on in search of new food sources. It was not worth building a permanent house, if they were going to have to leave it behind.

When humans started to farm for a living, people settled down and stayed in one place, probably for the rest of their lives. It became worthwhile to build more solid homes. Farming brought other changes, too. Hunter-gatherers had small families as it was difficult to find enough food. Older or weaker members of the family starved. Ancient farmers, however, had as many children as possible. There were then more hands to work the land. Members of the family could also be spared to care for the very old or very young.

MAKESHIFT HOMES
Hunter-gatherers roamed the land looking for food. They needed homes that could be moved easily. Summer tents were built by Ice Age people in Pincevant, France. They were made from animal skins, held up with wooden poles and secured with stones around the bottom.

FARMING METHODS
Sumerian farmers in the Middle East developed an ox-drawn plough around 4000BC, which replaced the hand-held plough. This meant that they could grow more food using fewer workers. Farming methods developed to suit the local environment in each area.

Widespread Farming

Farming first began about 10,000 years ago in the Middle East (also called the Near East). By 2,000 years ago, most of the world's population were farmers, although even today, the Inuits and some tribal peoples still live by hunting. Each area adapted its own farming methods, crops and domestic animals to the local climate, soil and natural environment.

In hot, dry lands, such as Mesopotamia, crops only grew successfully if irrigation canals carried water from rivers to the fields. In cool, wet areas – such as the Viking lands of northern Europe – crops did not grow well, so farmers relied more on raising domestic animals such as sheep and cattle.

Crafts and Trades

Most people in the ancient world had little choice about what they did to earn a living. Formal education was a privilege (and more often for boys than girls). Many children learned their parents' trade or occupation, and as they grew up, they took on more and more responsibilities.

By the time they reached their early teens, young people were treated as adults and might even marry.

Because most settlements were in isolated rural areas, each family learned how to make tools, cooking pots and clothes, and how to build the family home – in addition to growing crops and tending the farm animals. In larger towns, however, specialist skills and trades evolved. Builders, metalworkers, potters, bakers, brewers, shopkeepers, merchants, weavers, soldiers and administrators could all make a living supplying services and skills.

SEARCHING FOR FISH
Fishing was an important source of food in the ancient world. People who lived near rivers, lakes and coastal areas developed all kinds of fishing methods. The Aztec boy pictured uses a stick and paddles to drive fish into his net, which is woven from cactus fibre. Other peoples used hooks, lines and harpoons to catch fish.

LEARNING BY DOING
In the ancient world, children often learned their parents' trade or occupation. The budding Native American potter pictured is helping her mother to make a water vessel. By the time she reaches her teens, she will be very accomplished at her craft.

Free Time

It is easy to imagine that people in the ancient world lived a life of constant hard work. In fact, people often had more leisure time than we do today. Farmers had to work hard in the spring and autumn. In summer and winter, there was plenty of spare time. Even slaves in ancient Greece and Rome were given days off, often when there was a festival or holy day (from which the word holiday comes). People in ancient times liked to dress up for their free time and for festivals, and sometimes wore decorative clothing and jewellery.

SPORTS AND GAMES
Ancient cultures developed many sports that often had religious significance. This discus thrower was an athlete in ancient Greece, where the Olympic Games were first held in 776BC. The Olympic competitions were for men only, but the women held their own games in honour of Hera, the goddess of women.

There was no shortage of entertainment. Music, singing and dancing, storytelling, board games and all types of sport were popular everywhere. Many of the same sports are still played today. Athletic games were introduced by the ancient Greeks.

Some ancient forms of entertainment were very violent by modern standards. The Romans enjoyed gladiator shows, where two men fought each other to the death. The Mesoamericans played a ball game that was something like basketball – but the losing team was sacrificed to the gods.

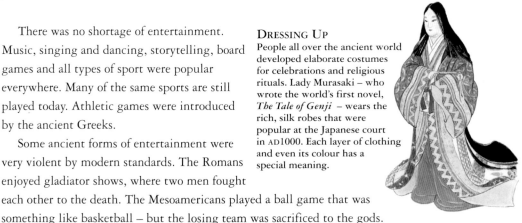

DRESSING UP
People all over the ancient world developed elaborate costumes for celebrations and religious rituals. Lady Murasaki – who wrote the world's first novel, *The Tale of Genji* – wears the rich, silk robes that were popular at the Japanese court in AD1000. Each layer of clothing and even its colour has a special meaning.

RHYTHM OF THE GODS
Music was an important part of religious celebrations. It was developed in all cultures to honour the gods and goddesses, and to mark special days of the year. The members of this Aztec orchestra play rhythms on instruments, such as conch shells, rattles and drums.

Belief in Many Gods

Religious festivals brought many opportunities for celebration. In ancient Greece, they were marked by plays, music and sports competitions.

The main religions in the world today – including Judaism, Christianity and Islam – are monotheistic, meaning that they worship only one god. This was very unusual in the ancient world, when most religions were polytheistic, with many gods. People believed that different gods watched over different activities, and had the power to help or hinder them. Some gods, such as those of the Celts and the Aztecs, were believed to demand human sacrifices in return for favours.

Life after Death

Preparing for death was an important part of most ancient religions. Some faiths, such as the Indian Hindu religion, believe in reincarnation (being reborn in a different body). Most believed in an afterlife of the spirit. The next world was often thought to be similar to earthly life. In ancient Egypt, people were buried with furniture, tools, weapons and personal belongings that would be useful on their journey. For many in the ancient world, everyday life was something that they expected to continue even after they died.

BEYOND DEATH
The Egyptians preserved the bodies of their dead by a process called mummification. They buried them in richly decorated tombs. The deceased person was then surrounded with furniture, tools, jewellery and clothes that would be useful in the afterlife.

Work, Trade & Farming

Compare the lives and skills of the
workers of the world from ancient
Egypt and Greece to the Inca Empire
and the frozen Arctic. Examine the
working lives of peasants and kings,
merchants and builders. Find out
how new jobs were created as
societies became more civilized and
trace the growth of money, crafts,
farming and worldwide trade.

From Survival to Specialization

For early farmers, farming was difficult, back-breaking work. There were only stone and wood tools to work the soil. Seeds were scattered by hand.

Our ancestors, the first humans, survived by hunting animals and gathering wild food for almost half a million years. They lived mostly as nomads, moving from place to place according to the season. They followed herds of animals or shoals of fish, and gathered nuts, berries and other wild plants. Their job was to survive – to find food, make tools and build shelters. They traded with other travelling people they encountered by exchanging useful goods they had for food, weapons or jewellery that they wanted or needed.

Around 12,000BC, the lifestyles of some hunter-gatherer communities began to change. They started to build permanent settlements close to reliable water supplies, to plant and harvest crops, and to domesticate (tame and use) animals. This change happened in different ways and at different times, from one part of the world to the other, depending on climate change and the local environment. By around 5000BC, there were farmers in almost every inhabited continent.

The development of farming

The wild auroch was the ancestor of early farm cattle. Bones found by archaeologists show that early domesticated cattle were smaller than their wild relatives.

TIMELINE 100,000–550BC

100,000BC Peoples in many different regions of the world live as hunter-gatherers.

9000BC Horses become extinct in America through over-hunting. They were reintroduced by European settlers in the AD1500s.

Early people lived as hunter-gatherers

8500BC Sheep and goats are domesticated in Mesopotamia (modern Iraq).

Sheep

8000BC The first farming villages are built in the Middle East. Long-distance trade routes develop in Europe and the Middle East.

6300BC Potatoes are cultivated in the Andes mountains of South America.

5000BC Rice is cultivated in China and South-east Asia.

4000BC Wild horses are first domesticated in Russia.

3000BC Maize is cultivated in Mesoamerica (Central America).

Maize

100,000BC   8500BC   5000BC   3000BC

has been called a revolution, because it dramatically changed how people lived and worked. Until the 1700s, most people around the world lived in small villages. They were farmers, or they found work connected with growing crops, raising animals or transporting and processing food.

In different civilizations, farmwork was organized in many different ways. Sometimes farmworkers were peasants, working for just themselves and their families. In other parts of the world, such as in Celtic Europe, ancient China and Egypt, the land was owned by a lord. Workers had to pay the landowner in service and loyalty. In ancient Egypt, Greece and Rome, these workers were often unpaid slaves.

Not everyone made their living from the land. Permanent settlements (that is, villages and later, towns) also became centres for crafts, trade and building work. Men and women survived by using special skills such as stonemasonry, carving, working with clay, metal or textiles, or by buying and selling goods made by others. Some cultures specialized in particular work. Remains of grand temples in Egypt and Central

When people worked out how to cultivate the waterlogged fields of China and South-east Asia, rice became the main crop of these areas.

This Mesopotamian clay figure of a woman holding a baby dates from c.5500BC. At this time, towns were growing into cities and craftworkers were becoming more skilled.

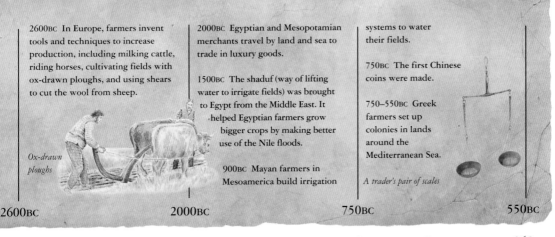

2600BC In Europe, farmers invent tools and techniques to increase production, including milking cattle, riding horses, cultivating fields with ox-drawn ploughs, and using shears to cut the wool from sheep.

2000BC Egyptian and Mesopotamian merchants travel by land and sea to trade in luxury goods.

1500BC The shaduf (way of lifting water to irrigate fields) was brought to Egypt from the Middle East. It helped Egyptian farmers grow bigger crops by making better use of the Nile floods.

900BC Mayan farmers in Mesoamerica build irrigation systems to water their fields.

750BC The first Chinese coins were made.

750–550BC Greek farmers set up colonies in lands around the Mediterranean Sea.

A trader's pair of scales

Ox-drawn ploughs

2600BC   2000BC   750BC   550BC

Tomb paintings tell us a lot about life in ancient Egypt. This painting shows how building bricks were made – by mixing clay and straw in a big, rotating pot.

America, and public buildings in Peru, show that people in those areas were expert stonemasons, even though their tools were basic. The ancient Greeks, Romans, Celts and Vikings produced many fine objects of art, including pottery, jewellery and sculptures. These were often made by craft-workers in workshops in towns.

Qin Shi Huangdi (the first Emperor in China) introduced round coins with holes. People could carry them easily on a string.

Some regions specialized in making or trading in valuable items. Silk came from China, spices from India and South-east Asia, gold from Africa, and perfumes from Arabia. Goods made or processed in villages were offered for sale at local markets. The finest products were often transported to sell in distant lands. At first, they were bartered (exchanged for other items of equal value). Business deals became much easier after coins were invented – in China around 750BC and in Lydia (modern Turkey) around 600BC.

Many towns on trading routes grew into powerful cities and became centres of organized government and trade. They were places where rulers lived, surrounded by people such as

Women often had the job of going to the market. Here, one Aztec woman in Tlatelolco is selling maize to another.

TIMELINE 635BC–AD1900

635BC The first coins in Europe were made in Lydia (modern Turkey).

c.400–300BC Celtic Europe prospers. Farmers build round-house villages. Celtic traders travel long distances to trade with the merchants from Rome and Greece. After around 200BC, the Celts build oppida (fortified towns) to trade.

c.110BC Trade begins between China, Central Asia, the Middle East and Europe along the Silk Road.

AD50 Roman traders reach India and Bengal.

AD200 The Hopewell people of North America set up trade routes.

AD250–900 The Maya prosper. Farmers grow maize, beans, squash, cacao and tropical fruits in slash-and-burn fields.

AD300 Tea is first cultivated in China.

A brazier (used to hold hot coal) made in Baghdad c.AD800, was probably brought by a Viking merchant to Scandinavia

AD750–1100 Vikings from northern Europe establish trade with merchants from the Middle East.

1325 The Aztecs of Mexico build a new capital city in the middle of a lake. They

635BC

AD50

AD750

1325

As towns grew into trading centres, rulers became responsible for governing the people and providing safe passage for merchants. Mesopotamian kings were often surrounded by other nobles who helped with running their empire or to celebrate a successful bull hunt!

servants, scribes, stonemasons, soldiers, lawyers and officials. As towns grew bigger and more complex, so did people's needs. They needed comfortable homes, public buildings and good roads. They wanted doctors, teachers and priests to look after their physical, mental and spiritual wellbeing. Over the centuries, craftworkers, entertainers and artists also came to live and work alongside merchants and craftworkers in towns. The large numbers of people living there meant that they would find willing audiences and rich patrons to support them.

In this section, you can compare how different working activities, from farming and building to textile production and craftwork, developed in different civilizations through time. You will be able to see which regions became known for particular industries and how trading links were first established between the Americas, Europe, the Middle East and South-east Asia.

Mesoamerican featherworkers wove feathers to make shields, headdresses, cloaks and fans. Mesoamerican craft goods were known for their beautiful designs.

surround it with chinampas (market-gardens) – where they grow fruit, vegetables and flowers.

1475 The Aztecs conquer the trading city of Tlatelolco, and make it the greatest market in Central America.

1540 The first European traders and missionaries arrive in Japan. European traders

Portuguese sailor

hope to find spices and rich silks. Missionaries want to spread the Christian faith throughout Japan.

1603 A long period of peace in Japan. Trade and towns expand, and new forms of art and entertainment, such as kabuki plays, develop.

1700–1900 European whaling expeditions and trading companies introduce great changes to traditional life for many people in the Arctic.

Whale hunting in the Arctic

1475　　　　　　　　　　1600　　　　　　　　　　1700　　　　　　　　　　1900

Crops in the Stone Age

I N ABOUT 8000BC, people in the Near East began growing their own food for the first time. Instead of gathering and eating the seeds of wild grasses, such as wheat and barley, they saved some of it. Then, the following year, they planted it to produce a crop. As they began to control their food sources, the first farmers found that a small area of land could now feed a much larger population. People began living in permanent settlements in order to tend their crops and guard their harvest. Over the next 5000 years, farming spread from the Near East to western Asia, Europe and Africa. Farming also developed separately in other parts of Asia around 6500BC and in America by about 7000BC.

The first farms were in hill country where wheat and barley grew naturally and there was enough rain for crops to grow. As populations increased, villages began to appear along river valleys, where farmers could water their crops at dry times of the year.

STONE TOOLS

This chipped flint is the blade of a hoe. It was used in North America between about AD900 and AD1200, but it is very similar to the hoes used by the first farmers to break up the soil. Rakes made of deer antlers were used to cover over the seeds. Ripe corn was harvested with sharp flint sickle blades.

SICKLE BLADE

Ears of ripe corn would either have been plucked by hand or harvested with sickles such as this flint sickle. The blade has been hafted, or inserted, into a modern wooden handle.

WILD RICE

Rice is a type of grass that grows in hot, damp areas, such as swamps. It was a good food source for early hunter-gatherers along rivers and coasts in southern Asia. The seeds were collected when ripe and stored for use when little other food was available. The grain could be kept for many months.

WORLD CROPS

The first plants in the world to be domesticated, or farmed, were those that grew naturally in an area. Wheat and barley grew wild in the Near East. In India, China and south-east Asia, rice was domesticated by 5000BC and soon became the main food crop. Around 3000BC in Mexico, farmers grew maize, beans and squash. Farther south in the Andes mountains, the chief crops were potatoes, sweet potatoes and maize.

maize   *butternut squash*

GRINDING GRAIN

This stone quern, or hand-mill, is 6000 years old. It was used to grind grain into a coarse flour for making porridge or bread. The grain was placed on the flat stone and ground into flour with the smooth, heavy rubbing stone. Flour made in this way often contained quite a lot of grit. To make bread, water was added to the flour. The mixture was then shaped into flat loaves, which were baked in a clay oven.

STRAIGHT TRACK

Several tracks were built across marshes between 4000 and 2000BC in southern England. In some cases these were to link settlements to nearby fields of crops. The long, thin rods used to build the track above tell us a lot about the surrounding woodlands. The trees were coppiced, which means that thin shoots growing from cut hazel trees were harvested every few years.

A STEP UP

These terraced hillsides are in the Andes mountains of Peru. In mountainous areas where rainfall was high, some early farmers began cutting terraces, or steps, into the steep hillsides. The terraces meant that every scrap of soil could be used for planting. They prevented soil from eroding, or washing away. Farmers also used terracing to control the irrigation, or watering, of their crops. One of the first crops to be cultivated in Peru was the potato, which can be successfully grown high above sea level.

Taming Animals

ABOUT THE SAME time that people began to grow crops, they also started to domesticate (tame) wild animals. Wild sheep, goats, pigs and cattle had been hunted for thousands of years before people started to round them up into pens. Hunters may have done this to make the animals easier to catch. These animals gradually got used to people and became tamer. The first animals to be kept like this were probably sheep and goats around 8500BC in the Near East.

Herders soon noticed that larger animals often had larger young. They began to allow only the finest animals to breed, so that domestic animals gradually became much stronger and larger than wild ones. As well as four-legged livestock, chickens were domesticated for their eggs and meat. In South America, the llama was kept for its meat and wool, along with ducks and guinea pigs. In south-east Asia, pigs were the most important domestic animals.

WILD CATTLE
This bull is an aurochs, or wild ox. The aurochs was the ancestor of today's domestic cattle. Taming these huge, fierce animals was much harder than keeping sheep and goats. Wild cattle were probably not tamed until about 7000BC. The aurochs became extinct in AD1627. In the 1930s, a German biologist re-created the animal by crossing domesticated breeds such as Friesians and Highland cattle.

WILD HORSES
Horses were a favourite food for prehistoric hunter-gatherers. This sculpture of a wild horse was found in Germany. It was made around 4000BC. Horses also often appear in cave art. They were probably first domesticated in Russia around 4400BC. In America, horses had become extinct through over-hunting by 9000BC. They were reintroduced by European explorers in the 1500s.

DINGOES AND DOGS

The dingo is the wild dog of Australia. It is the descendant of tame dogs that were brought to the country more than 10,000 years ago by Aboriginal Australians. Dogs were probably the first animals to be domesticated. Their wolf ancestors were tamed to help with hunting and, later, with herding and guarding. In North America, dogs were used as pack animals and dragged a *travois* (sled) behind them.

DESERT HERDERS

Small herds of wild cattle were probably first domesticated in the Sahara and the Near East. This rock painting comes from the Tassili n'Ajjer area of the Sahara Desert. It was painted in about 6000BC at a time when much of the Sahara was covered by grassland and shallow lakes. The painting shows a group of herders with their cattle outside a plan of their house.

GOATS AND SHEEP

Rock paintings in the Sahara show goats and sheep, among the first animals to be domesticated. They were kept for their meat, milk, hides and wool, and are still some of the most common farmed animals.

LLAMAS

The llama was domesticated in central Peru by at least 3500BC. It was kept first for its meat and wool, but later it was also used for carrying food and goods long distances. A relative of the llama, the alpaca, was also domesticated for its wool.

Stone Age Exchange

STONE AGE PEOPLE did not use banknotes and coins for money, as we do. Instead they bartered, or exchanged, things. When one person wanted a bowl, for example, he or she had to offer something in exchange to the owner of the bowl – perhaps a tool or ornament. Towards the end of the Stone Age, however, people began to use shells or stone rings as a kind of currency.

Even isolated hunter-gatherer groups came into contact with each other and exchanged things, such as seashells, for tools or hides. With the beginning of farming around 8000BC in the Near East, however, long-distance exchange and a more organized trading system began. New activities, such as farming, pottery and weaving, needed specialized tools, so a high value was put on suitable rocks. In western Europe, flint mines and stone quarries produced axe blades that were prized and traded over great distances. Sometimes goods were traded thousands of kilometres from where they were made.

COWRIE SHELLS
Small, highly polished cowrie shells were popular as decoration for clothes and jewellery in prehistoric times. The shells have been found scattered around skeletons in burial sites, many of which are hundreds of kilometres from the coast. Later, cowrie shells were used as money in Africa and parts of Asia.

AXES
A good strong axe was a valuable commodity. It was particularly important for early farmers, who used it to chop down trees and clear land for crops. Axe heads made of special stone were traded over wide distances.

BURIED WITH WEALTH
This communal burial on the Solomon Islands in the Pacific Ocean shows the deceased accompanied by shells and ornaments. Shells have been used for money for thousands of years – in fact, for longer and over a wider area than any currency including coins. One hoard of shells, found in Iraq, was dated before 18,000BC.

STONE TRADE

During the neolithic period there was a widespread trade in stone for axes. At Graig in Clwyd, Wales (*left*), stone was quarried from the scree slopes and taken all over Britain. The blades were roughed out on site, then transported to other parts of the country, where they were ground and polished into axe heads. Rough, unfinished axes have been found lying on the ground at Graig.

FUR TRAPPER

A modern Cree trapper from the Canadian Arctic is surrounded by his catch of pine marten pelts. Furs were almost certainly a valuable commodity for prehistoric people, especially for hunter-gatherers trading with more settled farmers. They could be traded for food or precious items such as amber or tools.

SKINS AND PELTS

White Arctic fox skins are left to dry in the cold air. In winter, Arctic foxes grow a thick white coat so that they are well camouflaged against the snow. Furs like this have traditionally been particularly valuable to Arctic people, both for the clothing that makes Arctic life possible and for trading.

Mesopotamian Trade Network

THE PEOPLE OF MESOPOTAMIA (present-day Iraq) were very enterprising and expert business people. They travelled long distances to obtain goods they needed and imported timber, metal and semi-precious stones.

Around 2000BC, the Assyrians had a widespread, long-distance trading network in Anatolia (modern Turkey). The headquarters were in the northern Mesopotamian city of Ashur, and the trade was controlled by the city government and by large family firms.

The head of a firm usually stayed in Ashur but trusted members of the family were based in Anatolian cities such as Kanesh. From here they conducted business on the firm's behalf, going on business trips around Anatolia, and collecting any debts or interest on loans. Deals were made on a credit basis – for the Assyrian families acted as money-lenders and bankers as well. On delivery, goods and transportation (the donkeys) were exchanged for silver, which was then sent back to Ashur. In about 2000BC, one Kanesh businessman failed to send back the silver, and the firm threatened to send for the police.

TROPHIES AND TAX
Carved ivory furniture and bronze bowls were often carried off after successful battles. There is little evidence of trade in Mesopotamia from 900 to 600 BC. The Assyrian kings helped themselves to anything they wanted from the people they defeated. They collected as tax whatever was needed, such as straw and fodder for horses.

TRADE TO KANESH
Donkeys or mules are still used to transport goods from one village to another in modern Iraq. When trade with ancient Turkey was at its peak, donkey caravans took large amounts of tin and textiles through the mountain passes to Kanesh. A typical load for one donkey load would usually consist of 130 minas (about 65kg) of tin (which was specially packed and sealed by the city authorities) and ten pieces of woollen cloth.

PRECIOUS THINGS

The marvellous jewellery in the Royal Graves of Ur not only demonstrates the skills of the jewellers who made it, but is also evidence that the Sumerians went in for long-distance trade. None of the materials used to make the jewellery was available in Sumer, so the precious stones had to be imported. The gold may have come from Oman, the lapis lazuli from Afghanistan and the semi-precious stones from the Indus Valley.

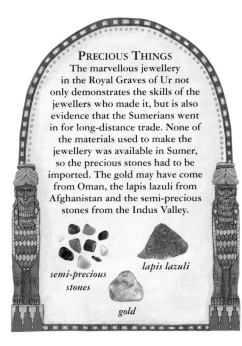

semi-precious stones

lapis lazuli

gold

STRIKING A DEAL

Two merchants make a contract. One is agreeing to supply goods for a certain amount of silver, and the other is promising to pay by a certain date. The details of a deal were written on a clay tablet and impressed with the cylinder seals of the two men. Often a copy was made and put in a clay envelope. If there was a dispute about the deal later, the envelope would be broken and the agreement checked.

LETTERS FROM KANESH

The site of the trading settlement of Kanesh, where the Assyrians did an enormous amount of business, has been excavated. A great many clay tablets have been found, many of them business letters. From these letters, it is clear that the Anatolian princes had the first pick of the goods brought by Assyrian merchants. They charged the merchants taxes on their donkey caravans. In return, the princes protected the roads and provided insurance against robbers.

CASH AND CARRY

There was no money in Mesopotamia, so goods were usually paid for in silver. Silver was measured in shekels and each shekel weighed about 8g. It was carefully weighed to make sure that the person who was paying gave an amount equal to the value of the goods he or she was buying.

Egyptian Slaves

THE PHARAOHS may have believed that it was their links with the gods that kept Egypt going, but really it was the hard work of the ordinary people. It was they who dug the soil, worked in the mines and quarries, sailed the boats on the river Nile, marched with the army into Syria or Nubia, cooked food and raised children.

Slavery was not very important in ancient Egypt, but it did exist. Most of the slaves were prisoners who had been captured during the many wars that Egypt fought with their neighbours in the Near East. Slaves were usually treated well and were allowed to own property.

PLOUGHING WITH OXEN
A model figure from a tomb shows a farmer ploughing the soil with oxen. The Egyptian farm workers' daily toil was hard. Unskilled peasant labourers did not own land and were paid little.

Many Egyptian workers were serfs. This meant that their freedom was limited. They could be bought and sold along with the estates where they worked. Farmers had to be registered with the government. They had to sell crops at a fixed price and pay taxes in the form of produce. During the season of the Nile floods, when the fields lay under water, many workers were recruited into public building projects. Punishment for those who ran away was harsh.

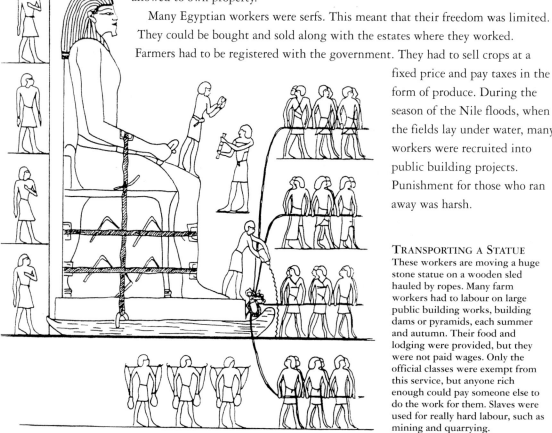

TRANSPORTING A STATUE
These workers are moving a huge stone statue on a wooden sled hauled by ropes. Many farm workers had to labour on large public building works, building dams or pyramids, each summer and autumn. Their food and lodging were provided, but they were not paid wages. Only the official classes were exempt from this service, but anyone rich enough could pay someone else to do the work for them. Slaves were used for really hard labour, such as mining and quarrying.

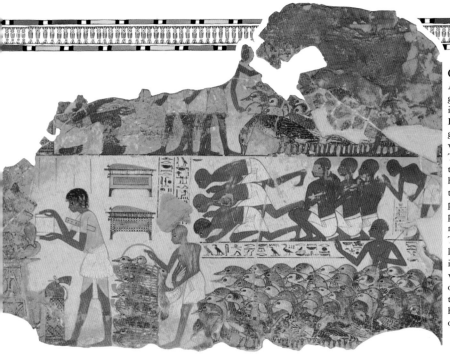

COUNTING GEESE

A farmer's flock of geese is counted out in this wall painting. Every other year, government officials visited each farm. They would count the animals to see how much tax had to be paid to the pharaoh. Taxes were paid in produce rather than money. The scribe on the left is recording this information. Scribes were members of the official classes and therefore had a higher position than other workers.

CARRYING BREAD

A woman carries a tray of loaves on her head. Most of the cooking in large houses and palaces was done by male servants, but baking bread was the job of the women. Baking was one of the few public jobs open to women.

GRINDING CORN

This model from 2325BC shows a female servant grinding wheat or barley grains into flour. She is using a stone hand-mill called a quern.

GIVE THAT MAN A BEATING

In this tomb painting, an official is shown overseeing work in the fields. Unskilled peasant farmers were attached to an estate belonging to the pharaoh, a temple or a rich landowner. Farmers who could not or would not give a large percentage of their harvest in rent and taxes to the pharaoh were punished harshly. They might be beaten, and their tools or their house could be seized as payment. There were law courts, judges and local magistrates in place to punish tax collectors who took bribes.

Along the Banks of the Egyptian Nile

HARVEST FESTIVAL
A priestess makes an offering of harvest produce in the tomb of Nakht. The picture shows some of the delicious fruits grown in ancient Egypt. These included figs, grapes and pomegranates.

FARMING TOOLS
Hoes were used to break up soil that had been too heavy for the ploughs. They were also used for digging soil. The sharp sickle was used to cut grain.

sickle   *hoes*

THE ANCIENT EGYPTIANS called the banks of the Nile the Black Land because of the mud that was washed downstream each year from Africa. The Nile flooded in June, depositing this rich, fertile mud along its valley in Egypt. The land remained underwater until autumn.

By November the ground was ready for ploughing and then sowing. Seeds were scattered on the soil and trampled in by sheep or goats. During the drier periods of the year, farmers dug channels and canals to bring water from the river to irrigate their land. In the New Kingdom (1550BC–1070BC), a lifting system called the *shaduf* was introduced to raise water from the river. The success of the farming cycle was vital. Years of low flood or drought could spell disaster. If the crops failed, people went hungry.

Farm animals included ducks, geese, pigs, sheep and goats. Cows grazed the fringes of the desert or the greener lands of the delta region, north of Egypt. Oxen were used for hauling ploughs and donkeys for carrying goods.

TOILING IN THE FIELDS
Grain crops were usually harvested in March or April, before the great heat began. The ears of wheat or barley were cut off with a sickle made of wood and sharpened flint. In some well-irrigated areas there was a second harvest later in the summer.

MAKE A SHADUF
You will need: card, pencil, ruler, scissors, pva glue, masking tape, acrylic paint (blue, green, brown), water pot and brush, balsa wood strips, small stones, twig, clay, hessian, string .
Note: mix green paint with dried herbs for the grass mixture.

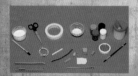

c = water tank
15cm · 2.5cm · 3cm · 2.5cm
5cm · 5cm · 9cm
c · 9cm · 9cm
23cm · 23cm · 23cm · 3.5cm · 2.5cm
a · 7cm
4cm · 3.5cm
16cm
5cm · 5c · 23cm · b · 23cm · 23cm
15cm · 8cm · 4cm
a = irrigation channel & river bank · 3.5cm · 7cm

Cut out the cardboard shapes (a), (b) and (c) as shown.

b = river

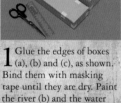

1 Glue the edges of boxes (a), (b) and (c), as shown. Bind them with masking tape until they are dry. Paint the river (b) and the water tank (c) blue and leave to dry.

HERDING THE OXEN

This New Kingdom wall painting shows oxen being herded in front of a government inspector. Cattle were already being bred along the banks of the Nile in the days before the pharaohs. They provided milk, meat and leather. They hauled wooden ploughs and were killed as sacrifices to the gods in the temples.

NILE CROPS

The chief crops were barley and wheat, used for making beer and bread. Beans and lentils were grown alongside leeks, onions, cabbages, radishes, lettuces and cucumbers. Juicy melons, dates and figs could be grown in desert oases. Grapes were grown in vineyards.

leeks   *onions*

WATERING MACHINE

The *shaduf* has a bucket on one end of a pole and a heavy weight at the other. First the weight is pushed up, lowering the bucket into the river. As the weight is lowered, it raises up the full bucket.

The mechanical lifting system called the shaduf *was invented in the Middle East. It was brought into Egypt about 3,500 years ago.*

2 Paint the river bank with the green grass mixture on top, brown on the sides and the irrigation channel blue. Next, get the balsa strips for the frame of the shaduf.

3 Glue the strips together, supporting them with masking tape and a piece of card. When dry, paint the frame brown. Glue the stones onto the water tank.

4 Use a twig for the shaduf pole. Make a weight from clay wrapped in hessian. Tie it to one end of the pole. Make a bucket from clay, leaving two holes for the string.

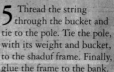

5 Thread the string through the bucket and tie to the pole. Tie the pole, with its weight and bucket, to the shaduf frame. Finally, glue the frame to the bank.

Skilled Workers in Egypt

In ancient Egypt, skilled workers formed a middle class between the poor labourers and the rich officials and nobles. Wall paintings and models show us craft workers carving stone or wood, making pottery, or working precious metals. There were boat builders and chariot makers, too.

Artists and craft workers could be well rewarded for their skills, and some became famed for their work. The house and workshops of a sculptor called Thutmose was excavated in el-Amarna in 1912. He was very successful in his career and was a favourite of the royal family.

Craft workers often lived in their own part of town. A special village was built at Deir el-Medina, near Thebes, for the builders of the magnificent, but secret, royal tombs. Among the 100 or so houses there, archaeologists found delivery notes for goods, sketches and plans drawn on broken pottery. Working conditions cannot always have been very good, for records show that the workers once went on strike. They may well have helped to rob the tombs that they themselves had built.

GLASS IN GOLD
This pendant shows the skill of Egyptian craft workers. It is in the form of Nekhbet the vulture, goddess of Upper Egypt. Glass of many colours has been set in solid gold using a technique called cloisonné. Like many other such beautiful objects, it was found in the tomb of Tutankhamun.

JEWELLERS AT WORK
Jewellers are shown at their work benches in this wall painting from 1395BC. One is making an ornamental collar while the others are working with precious stones or beads. The bow strings are being used to power metal drill bits.

A HIVE OF INDUSTRY

Skilled craftsmen are hard at work in this bustling workshop. Carpenters are sawing and drilling wood, potters are painting pottery jars, and masons are chiselling stone. A foreman would inspect the quality of each finished item.

DEIR EL-MEDINA

The stone foundations of the village of Deir el-Medina may still be seen on the west bank of the Nile. They are about 3,500 years old. In its day, Deir el-Medina housed the skilled workers who built and decorated the royal tombs in the Valley of the Kings. The men worked for eight days out of ten. The village existed for four centuries and was large and prosperous. Nevertheless, the workmen's village did not have its own water supply, so water had to be carried to the site and stored in a guarded tank.

SURVEYING THE LAND

Officials stretch a cord across a field to calculate its area. These men have been employed to survey an estate for government records.

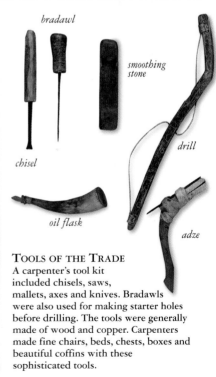

bow drill

bradawl

smoothing stone

chisel

drill

oil flask

adze

saw

axe

pull saw

TOOLS OF THE TRADE

A carpenter's tool kit included chisels, saws, mallets, axes and knives. Bradawls were also used for making starter holes before drilling. The tools were generally made of wood and copper. Carpenters made fine chairs, beds, chests, boxes and beautiful coffins with these sophisticated tools.

Egyptian Trade

A T ITS HEIGHT, the Egyptian Empire stretched all the way from Nubia, in southern Egypt, to Syria on the Mediterranean coast. The peoples of the Near East who were conquered, had to pay tribute to the pharaohs in the form of valuable goods such as gold or ostrich feathers. However, the Egyptians were more interested in protecting their own land from invasion than in establishing a huge empire. They preferred to conquer by influence rather than by war. Egyptian trading influence spread far and wide as official missions set out to find luxury goods for the pharaoh and his court – timber, precious stones or spices. Beautiful pottery was imported from the Minoan kingdom of Crete. Traders employed by the government were called *shwty*. The ancient Egyptians did not have coins, and so goods were exchanged in a system of bartering.

Expeditions also set out to the land of Punt, probably a part of east Africa. The traders brought back pet apes, greyhounds, gold, ivory, ebony and myrrh. The Egyptian Queen Hatshepsut encouraged these trading expeditions. The walls of her mortuary temple record details of them and also show a picture of Eti, the Queen of Punt.

WOODS FROM FARAWAY FORESTS
Few trees grew in Egypt, so timber for making fine furniture had to be imported. Cedarwood came from Lebanon and hardwoods such as ebony from Africa.

ALL THE RICHES OF PUNT
Sailors load a wooden sailing boat with storage jars, plants, spices and apes from the land of Punt. Goods would have been exchanged in Punt for these items. Egyptian trading expeditions travelled to many distant lands and brought back precious goods to the pharaoh. This drawing is copied from the walls of Hatshepsut's temple at Deir el-Bahri.

SYRIAN ENVOYS

Foreign rulers from Asia and the Mediterranean lands would send splendid gifts to the pharaoh, and he would send them gifts in return. These Syrians have been sent as representatives of their ruler, or envoys. They have brought perfume containers made of gold, ivory and a beautiful stone called lapis lazuli. The vases are decorated with gold and lotus flower designs. The pharaoh would pass on some of the luxurious foreign gifts to his favourite courtiers.

NUBIANS BRINGING TRIBUTE

Nubians bring goods to the pharaoh Thutmose IV – gold rings, apes and leopard skins. Nubia was the land above the Nile cataracts (rapids), now known as northern Sudan. The Egyptians acquired much of their wealth from Nubia through military campaigns. During times of peace, however, they also traded with the princes of Nubia for minerals and exotic animals.

EXOTIC GOODS

Egyptian craftsmen had to import many of their most valuable materials from abroad. These included gold, elephant tusks (for ivory), hardwoods such as ebony and softwoods such as cedar of Lebanon. Copper was mined in Nubia and bronze (a mixture of copper and tin) was imported from Syria.

ivory

ebony

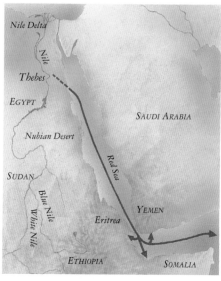

A WORLD OF TRADE

The Egyptians travelled over the Red Sea to the mysterious land of Punt. This modern map shows the voyage the traders would have made. No one is sure of the exact location of Punt, but it was probably present-day Somalia, Eritrea, Yemen or southern Sudan.

Chinese Merchants and Peasants

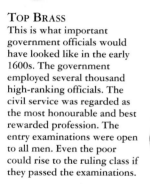

THE RIVER VALLEYS AND COASTS of China have always been among the most crowded places on earth. The thinker, Confucius, with his love of social order, had taught that this vast society could be divided into four main groups. At the top were the nobles, the scholars and the landowners. Next came the farmers, including even the poorest peasants. These people were valued because they worked for the good of the whole nation, providing the vast amounts of food necessary to feed an ever-increasing population. In third place were skilled workers and craftsmen. In the lowest place of all were the merchants, because Confucius believed they worked for their own profit rather than for the good of the people as a whole. However, the way in which Chinese society rewarded these groups in practice did not fit the theory. Merchants ended up becoming the richest citizens, lending money to the upper classes. In contrast, the highly valued peasants often led a wretched life, losing their homes to floods and earthquakes or starving in years of famine.

TOP BRASS
This is what important government officials would have looked like in the early 1600s. The government employed several thousand high-ranking officials. The civil service was regarded as the most honourable and best rewarded profession. The entry examinations were open to all men. Even the poor could rise to the ruling class if they passed the examinations.

THE IDEAL ORDER?
A government official tours the fields, where respectful peasants are happily at work. This painting shows an idealized view of the society proposed by Confucius. The district prospers and flourishes because everybody knows their place in society. The reality was very different – while Chinese officials led comfortable lives, most people were very poor and suffered great hardship. They toiled in the fields for little reward. Officials provided aid for the victims of famine or flood, but they never tackled the injustice of the social order. Peasant uprisings were common through much of Chinese history.

WORKING IN THE CLAYPITS

The manufacture of pottery was one of imperial China's most important industries. There were state-owned factories as well as many smaller private workshops. The industry employed some very highly skilled workers, and also thousands of unskilled labourers whose job was to dig out the precious clay. They had to work very hard for little pay. Sometimes there were serious riots to demand better working conditions.

DRAGON-BACKBONE MACHINE

Peasants enlist the aid of machinery to help work the rice fields. The life of a peasant was mostly made up of back-breaking toil. The relentless work was made slightly easier by some clever, labour-saving inventions. The square-pallet chain pump (*shown above*) was invented in about AD100. It was known as the dragon-backbone machine and was used to raise water to the flooded terraces where rice was grown. Men and women worked from dawn to dusk to supply food for the population.

LIFE BEHIND A DESK

Country magistrates try to remember the works of Confucius during a tough public examination. A pass would provide them with a path to wealth and social success. A failure would mean disgrace. The Chinese civil service was founded in about 900BC. This painting dates from the Qing dynasty (1644–1912). There were exams for all ranks of officials and they were very hard. The classic writings had to be remembered by heart. Not surprisingly, candidates sometimes cheated!

TOKENS OF WEALTH

Merchants may have had low social status, but they had riches beyond the dreams of peasants. They amassed wealth through money-lending and by exporting luxury goods, such as silk, spices and tea. The influence of the merchant class is reflected in the first bronze Chinese coins (*c.*250BC), which were shaped to look like knives, hoes

knife

hoe

and spades. Merchants commonly traded or bartered in these tools.

Working the Land in China

EIGHT THOUSAND YEARS AGO, most Chinese people were already living by farming. The best soil lay beside the great rivers in central and eastern China, where floods left behind rich, fertile mud. As today, wheat and millet were grown in the north. This region was mostly farmed by peasants with small plots of land. Rice was cultivated in the warm, wet south, where wealthy city-dwellers owned large estates. Pears and oranges were grown in orchards.

Tea, later to become one of China's most famous exports, was first cultivated about 1,700 years ago. Hemp was also grown for its fibres, used to make coarse cloth. During the 500s BC, cotton was introduced. Farmers raised pigs, ducks, chickens and geese, while oxen and water buffalo were used as labouring animals on the farm. Most peasants used basic tools, such as stone hoes and wooden rakes. Ploughs with iron blades were used from about 600BC. Other inventions to help farmers were developed in the next few hundred years, including the wheelbarrow, a pedal hammer for husking grain and a rotary winnowing fan.

PIGS ARE FARM FAVOURITES
This pottery model of pigs in their sty dates back about 2,000 years. Pigs were popular farm animals, as they are easy to feed and most parts of a pig can be eaten. They were kept in the city as well as in rural country areas.

FEEDING THE MANY
Rice has been grown in the wetter regions of China since ancient times. Wheat and millet are grown in the drier regions. Sprouts of the Indian mung bean add important vitamins to many dishes.

mung beans

millet

rice

wheat

CHINESE TEAS
Delicate leaves of tea are picked from the bushes and gathered in large baskets on this estate in the 1800s. The Chinese cultivated tea in ancient times, but it became much more popular during the Tang dynasty (AD618–906). The leaves were picked, laid out in the sun, rolled by hand and then dried over charcoal fires.

A HELPING HAND

A farmer uses a pair of strong oxen to help him plough his land. This wall painting found in Jiayuguan dates back to about 100BC. Oxen saved farmers a lot of time and effort. The Chinese first used oxen in farming in about 1122BC.

KEEPING WARM

This model of a Chinese farmer's lambing shed dates from about 100BC, during the Han dynasty. Sheepskins were worn for warmth, but wool never became an important textile for clothes or blankets in China.

HARVESTING RICE – CHINA'S MAIN FOOD

Chinese peasants pull up rice plants for threshing and winnowing in the 1600s. Farming methods were passed on by word of mouth and in handbooks from the earliest times. They advised farmers on everything from fertilizing the soil to controlling pests.

A TIMELESS SCENE

Peasants bend over to plant out rows of rice seedlings in the flooded paddy fields of Yunnan province, in southwest China. This modern photograph is a typical scene of agricultural life in China's warm and wet south-west region. Little has changed in hundreds of years of farming.

Chinese Silk Production

FOR YEARS, THE CHINESE tried to stop outsiders finding out how they made their most popular export – *si*, or silk. The shimmering colours and smooth textures of Chinese silk made it the wonder of the ancient world. Other countries such as India discovered the secret of silk making, but China remained the producer of the world's best silk.

Silk production probably dates back to late Stone Age times (8000BC–2500BC) in China. Legend says that the process was invented by the empress Lei Zu in about 2640BC. Silkworms (the caterpillars of a type of moth) are kept on trays and fed on the leaves of white mulberry trees. The silkworms spin a cocoon (casing) of fine but very strong filaments. The cocoons are plunged into boiling water to separate the filaments, which are then carefully wound on to reels.

A filament of silk can be up to 1,200 metres long. Several filaments are spun together to make up thread, which is then woven into cloth on a loom. The Chinese used silk to make all kinds of beautiful products. They learned to weave flimsy gauzes and rich brocades, and they then wove elaborate coloured patterns into the cloth in a style known as *ke si*, or cut silk.

PREPARING THE THREAD
A young woman winds silk thread on to bobbins in the late 1700s. Up to 30 filaments of silk could be twisted together to make silk thread for weaving. The Chinese made ingenious equipment for spinning silk into thread. They also built looms for weaving thread into large rolls of fabric. By the 1600s, the city of Nanjing alone had an estimated 50,000 looms.

LOAD THOSE BALES!
Workers at a Chinese silk factory of the 1840s carry large bales of woven silk down to the jetty. From there the woven cloth would be shipped to the city. It might be used to make a costume for a lady of the court, or else exported abroad. The Chinese silk industry reached its peak of prosperity in the mid-1800s.

THE DRAGON ON THE EMPEROR'S BACK

A scaly red dragon writhes across a sea of yellow silk. The dragon was embroidered on to a robe for an emperor of the Qing dynasty. The exquisite clothes made for the Chinese imperial court at this time are considered to be great works of art.

WINDING SILK

Silk is being prepared at this workshop of the 1600s. The workers are taking filaments (threads) from the cocoons and winding them on to a reel. Traditionally, the chief areas of silk production in imperial China were in the east coast provinces of Zhejiang and Jiangsu. Silk was also produced in large quantities in Sichuan, in the west.

MAGIC MULBERRIES

These Han dynasty workers are collecting mulberry leaves in big baskets, over 2,000 years ago. These would have been used to feed the silkworms. Silkworms are actually the larva (caterpillars) of a kind of moth. Like most caterpillars, silkworms are fussy feeders and will only eat certain kinds of plant before they spin cocoons.

MAKING SILK

Raising silkworms is called sericulture. It can be a complicated business. The caterpillars have to be kept at a controlled temperature for a month before they begin spinning their silk cocoons.

adult silkmoth and cocoons

silkmoth larva

Coins and Markets in China

THE EARLIEST CHINESE TRADERS bartered (exchanged) goods, but by 1600BC people were finding it easier to use tokens such as shells for buying and selling. The first metal coins date from about 750BC and were shaped like knives and spades. It was Qin Shi Huangdi, the first emperor, who introduced round coins. These had holes in the middle so that they could be threaded on to a cord for safe-keeping. The world's first paper money appeared in China in about AD900.

There were busy markets in every Chinese town, selling fruit, vegetables, rice, flour, eggs and poultry as well as cloth, medicine, pots and pans. In the Tang dynasty capital, Chang'an (Xian), trading was limited to two large areas – the West Market and the East Market. This was so that government officials could control prices and trading standards.

CHINESE TRADING
Goods from China changed hands many times on the Silk Road to Europe. Trade moved in both directions. Porcelain, tea and silk were carried westwards. Silver, gold and precious stones were transported back into China from central and southern Asia.

raw silk *Chinese tea*

CASH CROPS
Tea is trampled into chests in this European view of tea production in China. The work looks hard and the conditions cramped. For years China had traded with India and Arabia. In the 1500s it began a continuous trading relationship with Europe. By the early 1800s, China supplied 90 per cent of all the world's tea.

MAKE A PELLET DRUM

You will need: large roll of masking tape, pencil, thin cream card, thick card, scissors, glue and brush, 2.5cm x 30cm thin grey card, thread, ruler, needle, bamboo stick, paint (red, green and black), water pot, paintbrush, 2 coloured beads.

1 Use the outside of the tape roll to draw 2 circles on thin cream card. Use the inside to draw 2 smaller circles on thick card. Cut out, as shown.

2 Glue grey strip around one of smaller circles. Make 2 small holes each side of strip. Cut two 20cm threads. Pass through holes and knot.

3 Use the scissors to make a hole in the side of the strip for the bamboo stick. Push the stick through, as shown. Tape the stick to the hole.

THE SILK ROAD

The trading route known as the Silk Road developed during the Han dynasty. The road ran for 11,000 km from Chang'an (modern Xian), through Yumen and Kasghar, to Persia and the shores of the Mediterranean Sea. Merchants carried tea, silk and other goods from one trading post to the next.

FROM DISTANT LANDS

A foreign trader rides on his camel during the Tang dynasty. At this time, China's international trade began to grow rapidly. Most trade was still handled by foreign merchants, among them Armenians, Jews and Persians. They traded their wares along the Silk Road, bringing goods to the court at the Tang dynasty capital, Chang'an.

BUYERS AND SELLERS

This picture shows a typical Chinese market in about 1100. It appears on a Song dynasty scroll and is thought to show the market in the capital, Kaifeng, at the time of the New Year festival.

Twist the drum handle to make the little balls rattle. In the hubbub of a street market, a merchant could shake a pellet drum to gain the attention of passers by. He would literally drum up trade!

4 Tape the stick handle down securely at the top of the drum. Take the second small circle and glue it firmly into place. This seals the drum.

5 Draw matching designs of your choice on the 2 thin cream card circles. Cut out a decorative edge. Paint in the designs and leave them to dry.

6 Paint the bamboo stick handle red and leave to dry. When the stick is dry, glue the 2 decorated circles into position on top of the 2 smaller circles.

7 Thread on the 2 beads. Make sure the thread is long enough to allow the beads to hit the centre of the drum. Tie as shown. Cut off any excess.

Money and Trade in India

TRADE WITH DISTANT COUNTRIES has been important for India as far back as the ancient civilization of the Indus Valley. Later, trade routes became established up and down the length of India as well as to faraway places. Luxurious and precious goods such as spices, jewels, ebony, ivory and teak, were the main trade objects. One highly prized import was silk from China.

The first coins in India, which had very simple designs, date from about 500BC. They were probably introduced from Persia (modern Iran). By about 100BC, coins were widely used to pay for goods and services in city markets and courts, but were less common in villages, where people simply exchanged goods, a practice called bartering. Bartering remained the normal way of trading for villagers until Mughal times (from 1526).

Many different types of coins were produced, including square ones. Some had portraits of kings and gods on them, and were often inscribed with the name of the ruling king. They were made of gold, silver, copper and alloys (mixes of metals). Silver seems to have been frequently used for the best coins, but it sometimes ran short when it was in demand for making statues and ornaments instead.

HEADS OR TAILS
A king of the Gupta dynasty with a stringed instrument is shown on a gold coin dating from around AD350. Portraits of ancient Hindu royalty were most often to be found on coins. Few other likenesses, such as sculptures or carvings, exist of ancient Hindu kings.

SHELLING OUT
Cowrie shells were used as currency (money) in coastal areas. They were also used inland when precious metals were scarce. Cowries were the lowest form of coinage. In one court poem, it is said that King Ramapala of Bengal paid his army in cowrie shells.

TRADE ROAD FOR SILK
The Silk Road stretched for more than 7,000 km from China to Anatolia (modern Turkey) and beyond. It was a trade route for items such as silk, jewels and spices. Travellers along the Silk Road also brought new ideas. China and Central Asia were introduced to Buddhism, and many Chinese pilgrims came to India via the Silk Road.

TRADING IN SPICE
Saffron is an aromatic spice grown in north India. Sandalwood is a musky-smelling wood, produced mainly in the south. Both were rare and valuable, and were among India's most prized trading items. They were exported to the Middle East and to China.

ARAB TRADING VESSEL
This painting shows an Arab trading ship. The Indian Ocean became an important trading zone after the rise of Islam in the AD600s. The ocean linked the powerful empires of Arabia to eastern lands, including India, South-east Asia and China. Muslim merchants ruled the seas from the AD700s until the coming of the Europeans in the 1500s.

TRADERS TRAVELLING TOGETHER
A wall mural from Rajasthan shows a caravan (a group of merchants travelling together). Camels were ideal for travel in western Rajasthan, which is mostly desert. From Mughal times, Rajasthani merchants were famous throughout India for being good at making money.

COIN MEDALLION
A gold coin of the Mughal emperor Jahangir (1605-1627) has a portrait on one side and a Persian inscription on the other. This coin was probably not used in trade but was instead worn as a sign of the emperor's favour. Using coins as decorations – especially if the coins were made of gold – dates back to the AD100s. At that time Roman coins were made into jewellery in southern India.

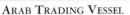

Textiles Industry in India

MAKING TEXTILES HAS ALWAYS BEEN an important activity in India. There are records of ancient Romans buying Indian cloth, so the textile trade must have been well established by then. As fabric does not last very well, there are few examples from before AD900, but sculptures show us the kinds of cotton cloth that were made. In Buddhist and Hindu sculptures, clothing is generally light and draws attention to the shape of the body.

India's textiles show a lot of different influences. Silk originally came from China, but from about AD100 it was produced in India and became an important Indian export. From about 1100, Turkish and then Persian invaders introduced floral designs. Fine carpets also began to be made following Persian traditions and styles. Some places began to specialize in the production or sale of textiles. In Mughal times (from 1526), silks and muslin (fine cotton fabric) were produced at Ahmedabad, Surat and Dhaka, while Kanchipuram, near Madras, became known for its fine silk saris. The Coromandel coast, Gujarat and Bengal all became textile export centres.

DRAPED GARMENT
A red sandstone figure from Jamalpur dates from about AD400, and shows the Buddha dressed in a fine muslin garment. Many clothes in ancient India were draped and folded rather than sewn.

SPINNING WHEEL
A woman sits at her spinning wheel. Weavers were important because Indian fabrics were in great demand in Europe.

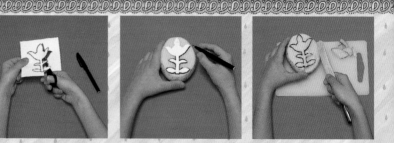

MAKE A PRINTING BLOCK

You will need: paper, felt-tipped pen, scissors, halved raw potato, blunt knife, 20 x 15 cm piece of beige calico fabric, iron, scrap paper, paints, paintbrush.

1 Copy the pattern shown here on to a sheet of paper. You can invent your own Indian design, if you prefer. Carefully cut out the pattern.

2 Place the cut-out pattern on the cut surface of the halved potato. Draw around the outline of the pattern with a felt-tipped pen.

3 Use the knife to cut away the potato around the pattern. Your pattern should be raised about 5 mm above the rest of the potato half.

PERSIAN-STYLE CARPET

This fine, wool carpet is decorated with floral patterns. In Mughal times, many fine carpets like this one were produced in India. Carpet weaving was a skill learned in the north-west of India from Persian craftworkers.

indigo block   *madder*

RED AND BLUE DYES

Dark-red dye made from the root of the madder plant and violet-blue dye made from the leaves of the indigo plant were used to dye textiles during Mughal times. Little is known about the way in which textiles were dyed in earlier times.

PRINTING COTTON CLOTH

A Punjabi man prints a pattern on to a length of cotton with a printing block. Dyes for cotton cloth were usually made from vegetables.

HUNTING COAT

This satin hunting coat has scenes and animals of the hunt embroidered on it in silk. It is typical of the type of dress worn by Mughal nobles.

Printing blocks were used in Mughal times to decorate fabric for festivals and other special occasions.

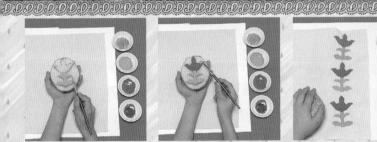

4 Ask an adult to help you to iron the fabric. Lay the ironed fabric on top of scrap paper. Apply paint to part of your printing block with a paintbrush.

5 Brush a different colour of paint on to your printing block. Give the block an even coat of paint that is not too heavy. Do not drench the block.

6 Press the printing block on to the fabric a few times. When the paint design starts to fade, apply more paint to the block with the paintbrush.

7 When the print design has dried, add some colourful details. Try out different colours on your printing block, or alter the pattern on the fabric.

Poor Soils and Hot Sun in Greece

MOST ANCIENT GREEKS lived in the countryside and worked as farmers. The mountainous landscape, poor, stony soil and hot, dry climate restricted what crops they grew and which animals they kept, but olive trees and bees flourished. Olives provided oil and bees supplied honey (the main sweetener in the ancient Greek diet) and wax. Unlike ancient Egypt and China, grain, such as barley, was difficult to grow. The land used for grain production had to be left fallow every other year to recover its fertility. Country people kept oxen to pull ploughs and drag heavy loads, and used donkeys to carry goods to market. Rural areas also produced materials used by city craftworkers, such as timber, flax for linen, horn and bone for glue, and leather.

Country living was hazardous, because droughts, floods, wolves and warfare threatened people's livelihoods. Over time, another problem developed. As forests were cut down for timber and fuel, soil erosion increased, leaving even less fertile land. The search for new agricultural land prompted the growth of Greek colonies along the shores of the Mediterranean and the Black Sea.

OLIVE HARVEST
This vase shows men shaking and beating the branches of an olive tree to bring down its fruit. Olives were eaten and also crushed to extract their oil. The oil was used for cooking, cleaning, as a medicine and a fuel for lamps.

FOOD FOR THE POT
Meat was obtained through hunting and the rearing of domesticated animals. Hunting was considered a sport for the rich, but it was a serious business for the poor, who hoped to put extra food on their tables. Simple snares, nets and slings were used to trap lizards and hares and to bring down small birds.

GONE FISHING
Many Greeks lived near water. The sea, rivers and lakes provided fish and shellfish which were their main source of protein. Fish was smoked or salted for future use. Always at the mercy of storms and shipwreck, fishermen prayed to the sea god Poseidon to save them.

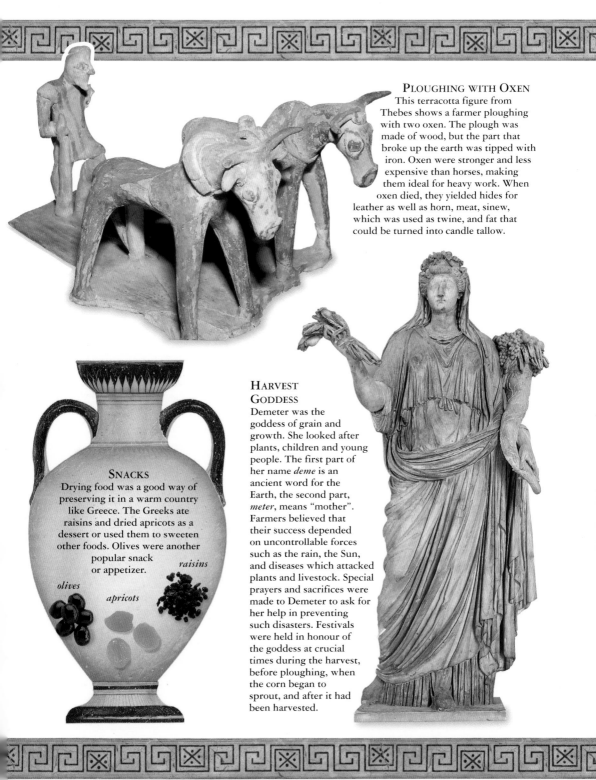

PLOUGHING WITH OXEN

This terracotta figure from Thebes shows a farmer ploughing with two oxen. The plough was made of wood, but the part that broke up the earth was tipped with iron. Oxen were stronger and less expensive than horses, making them ideal for heavy work. When oxen died, they yielded hides for leather as well as horn, meat, sinew, which was used as twine, and fat that could be turned into candle tallow.

HARVEST GODDESS

Demeter was the goddess of grain and growth. She looked after plants, children and young people. The first part of her name *deme* is an ancient word for the Earth, the second part, *meter*, means "mother". Farmers believed that their success depended on uncontrollable forces such as the rain, the Sun, and diseases which attacked plants and livestock. Special prayers and sacrifices were made to Demeter to ask for her help in preventing such disasters. Festivals were held in honour of the goddess at crucial times during the harvest, before ploughing, when the corn began to sprout, and after it had been harvested.

SNACKS

Drying food was a good way of preserving it in a warm country like Greece. The Greeks ate raisins and dried apricots as a dessert or used them to sweeten other foods. Olives were another popular snack or appetizer.

olives

apricots

raisins

Seafaring Greeks

THE MOUNTAINOUS LANDSCAPE of ancient Greece was too rocky for carts or chariots, so most people rode donkeys or walked. Sea travel was simpler – the many islands of the eastern Mediterranean made it possible to sail from one port to another without losing sight of land. Merchant ships were sailed because they were too heavy to be rowed. Greek sailors had no compasses. By day they relied on coastal landmarks and at night they navigated by the stars. However, neither method was reliable. A sudden storm could throw a ship off course or cause it to sink.

Merchant ships carried olive oil, wool, wine, silver, fine pottery and slaves. These goods were traded in return for wheat and timber, both of which were scarce in Greece. Other imported products included tin, copper, ivory, gold, silk and cotton.

COINAGE
The gold coin above shows Zeus, ruler of the gods, throwing a thunderbolt. Coins were invented in Lydia (in present-day Turkey) around 635BC, and introduced to Greece soon afterwards. Before that, the Greeks had used bars of silver and rods of iron as money. Greek coins were also made of silver, bronze and electrum, a mixture of gold and silver.

SEA GOD
Poseidon was the god of the sea, horses and earthquakes. Sailors prayed and made sacrifices to him, hoping for protection against storms, fogs and pirates. He is usually pictured holding a trident, the three-pronged spear used by Greek fishermen. At the trading port of Corinth, the Isthmian Games were held every other year in honour of Poseidon.

HARD CURRENCY
The first coins may have been used to pay mercenary soldiers, rather than for trading or collecting taxes. The earliest coins usually bore a religious symbol or the emblem of a city. Only later did they show the head of a ruler. The coin on the right shows the sea god Poseidon with his trident. The coin on the left bears the rose of Rhodes. Many countries that traded with the Greeks copied their idea of using coins for money.

SHIPPING

The ship on the right is a sail-powered merchantman. The criss-cross lines represent a wooden and rope catwalk stretched over the cargo, which was stored in an uncovered hold. Liquids such as wine and olive oil were transported and sold in long narrow pottery jars called amphorae, which could be neatly stacked in the hold. Merchant ships faced many dangers that could cause the loss of their cargo. Pirates and storms were the worst of these.

WEIGHING

Most dry goods were sold loose and had to be weighed on a scale such as this one. Officials would oversee the proceedings to make sure that they were fair. They stopped merchants and traders from cheating one another. In Athens, these officials were known as metronomoi. It was essential for merchants to familiarize themselves with the various systems of weights and measures used in different countries.

MARKET STALLS

The agora, or market place, was to be found in the center of every Greek town. Market stalls sold a wide variety of goods including meat, vegetables, eggs, cheese, and fish. Fish was laid out on marble slabs to keep it cool and fresh.

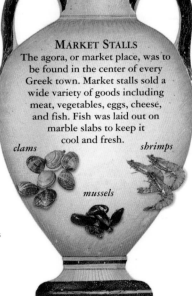

clams

shrimps

mussels

RIDING

Mountainous countryside made traveling overland difficult in Greece. The few roads that did exist were in poor condition. For most people, walking was the only way to reach a destination. Horses were usually only used by wealthy people to travel on. Donkeys and mules were used by tradesmen to transport large loads. Longer journeys were made by boat.

Ancient Greek Workshops

The artists and craftworkers of ancient Greece were admired for the quality of their work. They produced many objects of art including beautiful pottery, fine jewellery and impressive sculptures. Materials they worked with included stone, gold, silver, glass, gemstones and bronze. They also used wood, leather, bone, ivory and horn. Most goods were made on a small scale in workshops surrounding the market-place. A craftsman might work on his own or with the help of his family and a slave or two. In the larger workshops of such cities as Athens, slaves laboured to produce bulk orders of popular goods. These might include shields, pottery and metalwork, which were traded around the Mediterranean Sea for a large profit.

BULK PRODUCTION
Above is a terracotta mould, and on the right, the casting taken from it. Making a mould was a skilled and time-consuming task. Using a mould made it possible to produce items faster and more cheaply than carving each piece individually.

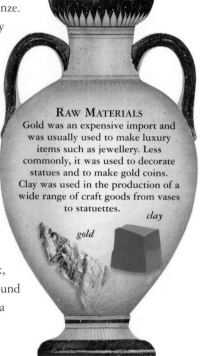

RAW MATERIALS
Gold was an expensive import and was usually used to make luxury items such as jewellery. Less commonly, it was used to decorate statues and to make gold coins. Clay was used in the production of a wide range of craft goods from vases to statuettes.

clay

gold

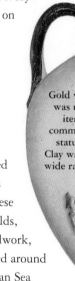

PANATHENAIC VASE
You will need: balloon, bowl, PVA glue, water, newspaper, two rolls of masking tape, black pen, scissors, sheet of paper 42cm x 30cm, card, pencil, paintbrush, black and cream paint.

1 Blow up the balloon. Cover it with two layers of papier mâché (paper soaked in one part glue, two parts water). Leave on one side to dry.

2 Using a roll of masking tape as a guide, draw and cut out two holes at the top and bottom of the balloon. Throw away the burst balloon.

3 Roll the sheet of paper into a tube. Make sure that it will fit through the middle of the roll of masking tape. Secure the tube with tape or glue.

VASE PAINTING

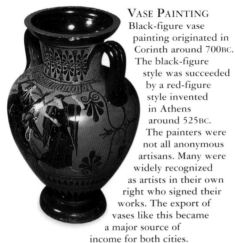

Black-figure vase painting originated in Corinth around 700BC. The black-figure style was succeeded by a red-figure style invented in Athens around 525BC. The painters were not all anonymous artisans. Many were widely recognized as artists in their own right who signed their works. The export of vases like this became a major source of income for both cities.

HOT WORK

In this scene two blacksmiths are forging metal at a brick furnace. Metal goods were expensive to produce. The furnaces themselves were fuelled by charcoal (burnt wood) which was expensive to make because wood was scarce in Greece. In addition, supplies of metal often had to be imported, sometimes from great distances. For example, tin, which was mixed with local copper to make bronze, was brought from southern Spain.

Amphorae like this one were given as prizes at the Panathenaic games. They were decorated with sporting images.

GOLD PECTORAL

This gold pectoral, made on the island of Rhodes in the 7th century BC, was meant to be worn across the breast. Gold was rare in Greece. It was usually imported at great expense from surrounding areas such as Egypt or Asia Minor.

4 Push the tube through the middle of the balloon. Tape into place. Push a roll of masking tape over the bottom of the paper tube and tape.

5 Tape the second roll of masking tape to the top of the tube. Make sure that both rolls are securely attached at either end of the paper tube.

6 Cut two strips of card, 15cm long. Attach them to either side of the vase, as seen above. Cover the entire vase with papier mâché, and leave to dry.

7 Using a pencil, copy the pattern seen on the vase in the picture above on to your vase. Carefully paint in the pattern and leave on one side to dry.

ANCIENT GREEK WORKSHOPS 301

Shopping Roman-style

IN MOST LARGE TOWNS IN THE ROMAN EMPIRE, shops spread out from the forum and along the main streets. Shops were usually small, family-run businesses. At the start of day, shutters or blinds would be taken from the shop front and goods put on display. Noise would soon fill the air as bakers, butchers, fishmongers, fruit and vegetable sellers all began crying out that their produce was the best and cheapest. Joints of meat might be hung from a pole, while ready-cooked food, grains or oils would be sold from pots set into a stone counter. Other shops sold pottery lamps or bronze lanterns, kitchen pots and pans or knives, while some traders repaired shoes or laundered cloth. Hammering and banging coming from the workshops at the back added to the clamour of a busy main street.

ROMAN MONEY
The same currency was used throughout the Roman Empire. Coins were made of gold, silver and bronze. Shoppers kept their money in purses made of cloth or leather or in wooden boxes.

GOING TO MARKET
This is a view of Trajan's Market, which was a five-storey group of shops set into a hillside in Rome. Most Roman towns had covered halls or central markets like this, where shops were rented out to traders.

A ROMAN DELICATESSEN

About 1,700 years ago this was the place to buy good food in Ostia, the seaport nearest to Rome. Bars, inns and cafés were fitted with stone counters that were often decorated with coloured marble. At lunchtime, bars like this would be busy with customers enjoying a meal.

A BUTCHER'S SHOP

A Roman butcher uses a cleaver to prepare chops while a customer waits for her order. Butchers' shops have changed very little over the ages – pork, lamb and beef were sold, and sausages were popular, too. On the right hangs a steelyard, a metal bar with a pan like a scale, for weighing the meat.

DISHING IT UP

These are the remains of a shop that sold food. Set into the marble counter are big pottery containers, called *dolia*. These were used for displaying and serving up food, such as beans and lentils. They were also used for keeping jars of wine cool on hot summer days. The containers could be covered with wooden or stone lids to keep out the flies.

Celtic Farmers of Europe

BULL'S EYE
Cattle were the most important farm animals in many Celtic lands. Oxen were used to pull carts and farm machinery, as well as for food. All cattle were highly prized, and were the main source of wealth for many farmers. Irish myths and legends tell of daring raids, when Celtic warriors galloped off to attack enemy farms and take all their cattle away.

A s FARMING PEOPLE in central and northern Europe, the Celts cleared fields, planted crops and bred livestock. They also fenced meadowland, and kept out their grazing animals until they had cut and dried the meadow grass to make hay for winter fodder. Farmers used an iron-tipped plough, pulled by oxen, to turn over the soil in their fields and prepare the ground for planting. Seeds of grain were scattered by hand on ploughed land in early spring. The crops were ready to harvest in late summer or autumn. The Celts' most important crops were wheat, oats and barley, which were cooked to make porridge, or ground into flour.

The most common farm animals were pigs, cattle, sheep and goats. In addition to producing meat, animals provided milk (used to make butter and cheese), wool (spun and woven into cloth) and hides (which were tanned to make leather). The Celts also reared ducks and geese, for meat and eggs. Manure from animals and birds was used as a fertilizer on the fields. In some areas, Celtic farmers dug pits for marl (natural lime) to spread on their land. The lime helped to fertilize the soil and make the crops grow.

SICKLE AND HOE
As crops grew in the fields, the Celtic farmer used a hoe (right) to keep the weeds down. The crops were harvested with a sharp, curved sickle (above). This hoe and sickle date from the La Tène era (450–50BC). Farming tools such as these were made by blacksmiths out of iron. Grain crops and hay were sometimes cut by an animal-drawn reaping machine, called a *vallus*. It was made of wood, with iron cutting blades.

WILD PAIR
The Celts raised pigs on their farms as well as hunting wild boar in the woods. Farm pigs were much smaller and thinner than European pigs today. They had long legs and stripy, bristly hair. In Celtic art, the boar was a symbol of great strength and power. These two little bronze pigs were probably made as offerings to the gods.

RARE BREED

The Soay sheep is an ancient breed that is rare today. It is similar to the sheep kept by Celtic farmers. It is small, nimble and hardy, and has long horns. Soay sheep do not need shearing because their fleece sheds naturally in summer. The wool can then be combed or pulled out by hand.

GRACEFUL GOOSE

This stone slab was carved in Scotland, in about AD450. It shows a goose turning round to preen its tail feathers. Geese were kept for their meat, eggs and grease. Goose grease could be rubbed on sore, dry skin, and used to soften and waterproof leather. Although the evidence has not survived, it seems likely that soft goose feathers were used to make warm bedding as well.

GOOD GRAINS

The Celts' main food crops were grains such as wheat, barley, oats and rye. These crops were harvested in late summer, heated over firepits to remove moisture, then stored in underground chambers (historians call them souterrains) for winter use.

wheat

barley

RIDGE AND FURROW

Ancient ridges and furrows in south-west England, shown in this picture, were created by later medieval farmers using techniques that may have been developed by the Celts. During the Celtic era, farmers began to move away from the light, well-drained soils on hilltops and slopes, clearing new fields on the heavier, wetter but more fertile land in valley bottoms. They invented heavy ploughs, fitted with wheels and pulled by oxen, to help cultivate this land.

Celtic Trading Routes

FOR THOUSANDS OF YEARS, different parts of Europe have been linked by long-distance trade. Well-known routes followed great river valleys, such as the Rhine, the Rhône and the Danube, or connected small ports along the coasts, from Ireland to Portugal. As early as 600BC, eastern traders from the Mediterranean claimed to have sailed through the Straits of Gibraltar and over the sea to the British Isles. After around 200BC, the Celts began to build fortified settlements as centres of government, craftwork and trade. Some grew up around existing hill forts or villages, others occupied fresh sites. The Romans called them *oppida*, the Latin word for towns. Some of the oppida were very large. For example, Manching, in southern Germany, covered about 380 ha, and its protective walls were 7 km long.

WINE LOVERS

The Celts were very fond of wine, which they imported from Italy. Roman wine merchants transported their wine in tall pottery jars called amphorae. You can see four amphorae at the back of this picture.

HIGH VALUE

Celts learned how to make coins from the Macedonians, who lived in eastern Europe. The first Celtic coins were made of pure precious metals, such as gold and silver. They were made by stamping a metal disc between two dies (moulds).

SMALL CHANGE

During the Celtic era in Europe, coins were made from alloys (mixed metals) containing only a small amount of silver or gold. These coins were much less valuable than the earlier, pure metal ones. This alloy coin was made around 100BC in western France.

MAKE A WAGON

You will need: white card, ruler, felt-tip pen, scissors, balsa wood, PVA glue, masking tape, sandpaper, pair of compasses, paint and paintbrush, drawing pins, bradawl, leather thong.

1 Take a piece of stiff white card measuring 29 cm x 16 cm. Using a ruler and felt-tip pen, draw lines 2 cm in from the edges of the card.

2 Make cuts in the corners of the card, as shown. Score along the lines and fold the edges up to make a box shape. This is the body of the wagon.

3 Take a piece of card 27 cm x 12 cm. Take two lengths of balsa wood 20 cm long. Stick them across the card, 4 cm in from the two ends.

KEY

◊ Iron
⊕ Tin
⟡ Amphorae (wine jars)
◊ Amber
⏇ Salt

LONG-DISTANCE TRADE

Celtic merchants and craftworkers in different lands were linked together by a network of trade routes, leading north-south and east-west. Few traders would have travelled the length of any one route. Instead, merchants from different countries met at trading towns. Valuable goods might be bought and sold several times along a trade route before reaching their final owner.

TOWN WALLS

Oppida were surrounded by strong, defensive walls. These ruined ones are from a Celtic town in southern France. Within the walls, houses, streets and craft workshops were laid out in well-planned, orderly rows.

This model wagon is based on the remains of funeral wagons found buried in Celtic graves. The Celts used wagons that were more roughly made but easier to steer for carrying heavy loads.

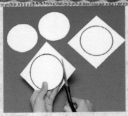

4 Take two sticks of balsa wood 26 cm and 11 cm long. Sand the end of the long stick to create a slight indent to fit against the short piece. Glue together.

5 Use the pair of compasses to draw four circles, each 10 cm in diameter, out of card. Next, carefully cut the circles out, as shown above.

6 Glue the box on to the piece of card. Attach the wheels to the balsa wood shafts by pressing a drawing pin through the centre of each wheel.

7 Make two holes in the front of the wagon with a bradawl. Thread the leather thong through the holes and attach the steering pole. Paint the wagon silver.

Long-distance Trade in Viking Times

COINS
These silver coins were found on the site of the market place in Birka. They were minted in Hedeby in around 800.

MAKING MONEY
This disc is a die – a metal stamp used to punch the design on to the face of a coin. The die is from York, in England. It has a sword design.

THE VIKINGS were very successful merchants. Their home trade was based in north European towns such as Hedeby in Denmark, Birka in Sweden and Kaupang in Norway. As they settled new lands, their trading routes began to spread far and wide. They traded in countries as far apart as Britain, Iceland and Greenland.

In about 860, Swedish Vikings opened up new routes eastwards through the lands of the Slavs. They rowed and sailed down rivers such as the Volga, Volkhov and Dniepr. Viking sailors hauled their boats around rapids and fought off attacks from local peoples. Their trade turned the cities of Holmgard (Novgorod) and Könugard (Kiev) into powerful states. This marked the birth of Russia as a nation. Merchants crossed the Black Sea and the Caspian Sea. They travelled on to Constantinople (Istanbul), capital of the Byzantine empire, and to the great Arab city of Baghdad.

Viking warehouses were crammed with casks of wine from Germany and bales of woollen cloth from England. There were furs and walrus ivory from the Arctic and timber and iron from Scandinavia. Vikings also traded in wheat from the British Isles and rye from Russia.

AMBER KING
This carved amber king is a piece from a board game. Amber was exported from the lands around the Baltic Sea. It was much prized by traders and by craftworkers, who also made it into jewellery and lucky charms.

MAKE A COIN AND DIE

You will need: self-drying clay and tool, board, rolling pin, scissors, compasses, pencil, paper, PVA glue, brush, paintbrush, bronze and silver paint.

1 Roll out a large cylinder of clay and model a short, thick handle at one end. This is the die. Leave it in a warm place to harden and dry.

2 Cut out a circle from paper. It should be about the same size as the end of the die. Draw a simple shape on the paper circle, with a pencil.

3 Cut the paper circle in half. Cut out the shape as shown. If you find it hard to cut the shape out, you could ask an adult to cut it out with a craft knife.

EASTERN CONNECTIONS

Trade networks in the East linked up with older routes, such as the "silk road" to China. Silk, jewellery and spices were brought by camel from the Far East. In Baghdad's markets, Vikings bought these things in return for furs, beeswax and slaves.

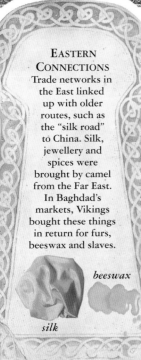

beeswax

silk

FAIR TRADING

Scales and weights were used by Viking merchants wherever they traded. Some could be folded up inside a small case.

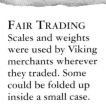

scales

walrus ivory · FINLAND
NORWAY · ASIA
SWEDEN · *furs*
slaves
SCOTLAND · *timber* · *stones*
IRELAND · *wool* · *furs*
wheat · DENMARK · *slaves*
ENGLAND · *honey* · *amber* · POLAND
pottery · *glass* · *slaves*
salt · *beeswax*
FRANCE · GERMANY
silver · *jewellery* · *silver*
wine · TURKEY · *jewellery*
EUROPE
wine · *silk* · *silk*
silver

scales

weights

TRADE MAP

The routes taken by Viking traders fanned out south and east from their homelands. As well as exotic goods from the East, everyday items such as salt, pottery and wool were brought back from western Europe.

The first coins to show Viking kings were minted in England.

4 Glue the cut paper pieces onto the end of the die with PVA glue. You may need to trim the pieces if they are too big to fit on the end.

5 Viking dies would have been made of bronze, or some other metal. Paint your die a bronze colour. Make sure you paint an even coat.

6 Roll out some more clay. Use the die to stamp an impression into the clay. This is your first coin. You can make as many as you like.

7 Use a modelling tool to cut around the edge of the coin. Make more coins from the left-over clay. Let the coins harden and dry and then paint them silver.

North American Trading

NORTH AMERICAN INDIAN TRIBES have a long tradition of trading. The Hopewell civilizations of about AD200 brought metals and other materials to their centres around the Ohio valley. The Calusas in southern Florida had a vast trade network both inland and across the sea to the Bahamas and Cuba. Many people would travel long distances to buy and sell goods at a regular meeting place. Although some tribes used wampum (shell money), most swapped their goods. People from settled villages exchanged agricultural products such as corn and tobacco for buffalo hides, baskets or eagle feathers from nomadic tribes. When European traders arrived, in the 1600s, they exchanged furs and hides for horses, guns, cotton cloth and metal tools. Early trading posts such as the Hudson's Bay Company were built by Europeans. These posts were usually on rivers which could be reached easily by canoe.

BASKETS FOR GOODS
Crafts, such as this Salish basket, were sometimes traded (or swapped) between tribes, and later with Europeans. Indians particularly wanted woollen blankets while European traders eagerly sought bison robes.

WORDS OF A WAMPUM
A Mohawk chief, King Hendrick of the League of Five Nations, was painted on a visit to Queen Anne's court in London in 1710. He holds a wampum belt made from shells. These were made to record historic events such as the formation of the League of Five Nations of the Iroquois.

COLONIAL TRADERS
A native hunter in Canada offers beaver skins to colonial fur traders in 1777. They would probably have been made into beaver hats. Beaver fur was the most important item the Woodlands tribes had to trade, as competition between European nations for animal skins was fierce. This trade was partly to blame for many tribal conflicts. The Iroquois were renowned beaver hunters who ruthlessly guarded their hunting territory.

SHELL SHOW
A Plains Indian is holding up a wampum belt decorated with shells. The belts were usually associated with the Iroquois and Algonquian tribes who used them to trade, as currency, or to record tribal history. Quahog clam shells were strung together to make a long rectangular belt with patterns showing tribal agreements and treaties. Even colonists used them as currency when there were no coins around.

SAVING SHELLS
Instead of coins, shells or beads made from shells were the main currency. They served as tokens which were swapped for goods. Blue and white shells such as clams and periwinkles were the most prized. These were strung, like beads, on to buckskin thongs.

thong   *clam shell*   *mussel shell*

TRADING POSTS
North American Indians would gather in the Hudson's Bay trading post. In return for bringing in pelts (animal furs), the Indians would be given European goods. Many would be useful such as iron tools and utensils or coloured cloth. Firearms and liquor traded from around 1650 did the tribes more harm than good. As trade increased, more trappers and hunters frequented the trading posts. Later, some of the fur trade posts became military forts and attracted settlers who built towns around them.

Arctic Trapping and Trade

BEFORE 1600, few Europeans had visited the Arctic, but those that did, returned with tales of waters teeming with whales and other sea creatures. European whaling ships were soon arriving in larger numbers to slaughter whales.

The whaling industry boomed during the 1700s and became important to the livelihoods of the Arctic people. By 1800, however, the Europeans had slaughtered so many whales that they faced extinction. As the whaling industry began to decline, European merchants soon realized that the soft fur of Arctic mammals, such as sea otters and foxes, would fetch a high price in Europe. They traded with local hunters for these skins, setting up trading posts across the Arctic. In every region, the fur trade was controlled by the nation that had explored there first. Russia controlled all trade in Alaska. Britain controlled business in Canada.

Arctic people came to rely on European trade for metal tools and weapons. Many tribes abandoned their traditional life of hunting. Instead, they trapped mammals for their skins and sold them to the merchants. Arctic people entered troubled times. Diseases previously unknown in the region, such as measles and tuberculosis, killed thousands of people.

SKINS FOR SALE
The skins of seals and Arctic foxes hang in a store in north-west Greenland. During the 1800s and early 1900s, otter, fox and mink fur became extremely popular in Europe. European merchants made huge profits from the trade but paid Arctic hunters low rates for trapping these valuable animals.

CONVENIENCE FOOD
In 1823 this tin of veal was prepared for Sir William Parry's expedition to the Arctic. European explorers, whalers and traders introduced many foods to the native Arctic peoples. Local trappers exchanged furs for food and other goods. However, some Arctic people began to rely on the food provided by the traders rather than hunting for their own food.

TRADING POST
This engraving, made around 1900, shows an Inuit hunter loading his sledge with European goods at a trading post in the far north of Canada. By the mid-1800s, fortified posts such as this had sprung up all over Arctic North America. The British Hudson Bay Trading Company, which was set up in the 1820s, became very wealthy exploiting Canada's natural resources.

ADDICTED TO ALCOHOL

Whisky was traded throughout the Arctic in the 1800s and 1900s. As well as goods made from metal, merchants introduced European foods and stimulants, such as tea, coffee, sugar, alcohol and tobacco, to the Arctic. Many Arctic hunters became addicted to spirits, such as whisky. This made them rely even more heavily on traders who could supply them with alcohol.

SCRIMSHAW

During the long Arctic nights or lengthy voyages across the ocean, European explorers, sailors and traders occupied their time carving pictures and patterns on whale bones and walrus tusks. This work was called scrimshaw. First, a design was scratched in the bone or tusk using a knife or needle. Then the artist made the picture visible by rubbing soot into the scratches.

soot

walrus tusk   scrimshaw

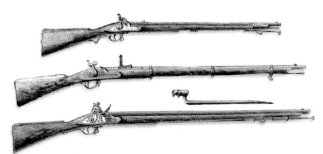

POWERFUL WEAPON

This engraving shows a number of British rifles from the 1840s. During the 1800s and 1900s, European guns and rifles transformed traditional hunting methods in the Arctic. Rifles were much more accurate than the old Arctic weapons, bows and arrows, and could target prey from a much greater distance.

GOODS FOR TRADE

Local hunters trade with Europeans in a local store in this engraving. Hundreds of metal tools and weapons were traded by Europeans in the Arctic, most often for animal skins. European merchants also bartered rifles, saws, knives, drills, axes and needles. The Inuit and other Arctic groups soon came to depend on these valuable tools and weapons.

Reclaiming Land in Mesoamerica

PEOPLE LIVING IN DIFFERENT REGIONS of Mesoamerica (Central America) during Aztec and Maya times used various methods to cultivate their land. Farmers in the rainforests grew maize, beans and pumpkins in fields they cleared by slashing and burning. They cut down thick, tangled bushes and vines, leaving the tallest trees standing. Then they burned all the chopped-down bushes and planted seeds in the ashes. As the soil was only fertile for a few years, the fields were left to turn back into forest, and new ones were cleared. Maya farmers also grew crops in raised fields. These were plots of land along the edge of rivers and streams, heaped up with rich, fertile silt dug from the riverbed.

Aztec farmers planted maize wherever they could on steep rocky hillsides or the flat valley floor. They grew their biggest crops of fruit, flowers and vegetables in gardens called *chinampas*. These were reclaimed from the marshy shallows along the shores of Lake Texcoco and around the island city of Tenochtitlan.

MAIZE GOD
This stone statue shows Yum Caax (Lord of the Forest Bushes), the Maya god of maize. It was found at Copan. All Mesoamerican people honoured maize goddesses or gods, as the crop was so important.

DIGGING STICKS
Mesoamerican farmers had no tractors, horses or heavy ploughs to help them prepare their fields. Instead, a sharp-bladed wooden digging stick, called an *uictli*, was used for planting seeds and hoeing weeds. Some farmers in Mesoamerica today find digging sticks are more efficient than the kind of spade traditionally used in Europe.

FIELD WORK
In this painting by Mexican artist Diego Rivera, Aztecs are shown using digging sticks to hoe fields of maize. You can see how dry the soil is. If the May rains failed, or frosts came early, a whole year's crop would be lost. Mesoamerican farmers made offerings to the rain god between March and October.

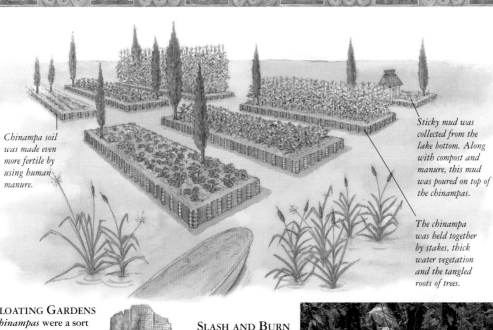

Chinampa soil was made even more fertile by using human manure.

Sticky mud was collected from the lake bottom. Along with compost and manure, this mud was poured on top of the chinampas.

The chinampa was held together by stakes, thick water vegetation and the tangled roots of trees.

FLOATING GARDENS

Chinampas were a sort of floating garden. They were made by sinking layers of twigs and branches under the surface of the lake and weighting them with stones. *Chinampas* were so productive that the government passed laws telling farmers when to sow seeds. This ensured there would be a steady supply of vegetables and flowers for sale in the market.

SLASH AND BURN

Mesoamerican farmers used a technique called slash and burn to clear land for farming. Crops grew very quickly in Mesoamerica's warm climate.

VEGETARIANS

Many ordinary Mesoamerican people survived on a largely vegetarian diet, based on maize and beans. This would be supplemented by other fresh fruits and vegetables in season. Meat and fish were expensive, luxury foods. Only rulers and nobles could afford to eat them every day.

beans

prickly pear

FOREST FRUITS

This Aztec codex painting shows men and women gathering cocoa pods from trees. Cocoa was so valuable that it was sent as tribute to Tenochtitlan.

The Mesoamerican Market

THE MARKET PLACE was the heart of many Mesoamerican cities and towns. Traders, craftworkers and farmers met there to exchange their produce. Many market traders were women. They sold cloth or cooking pots, made by themselves or their families, and maize, fruit, flowers and vegetables grown by their husbands. In big cities, such as the trading centre of Tlatelolco, government officials also sold exotic goods that had been sent to the Aztec rulers as tribute (taxes) by conquered city-states. After the Aztecs conquered Tlatelolco in 1473, it soon became the greatest market in Mesoamerica. It was reported that almost 50,000 people came there on the busiest days.

Long-distance trade was carried out by merchants called *pochteca*. Gangs of porters carried their goods. The work was often dangerous, but the rewards were great.

MERCHANT GOD
Yacatecuhtli was the Aztec god of merchants and traders. In the codex picture above, he is shown standing in front of a crossroads marked with footprints. Behind him (*right*), is a tired porter with a load of birds on his back.

MAIZE MARKET
Mesoamerican farmers grew many different varieties of maize, with cobs that were pale cream, bright yellow, or even deep blue. Their wives took the maize to market, as selling was women's work. This modern wall-painting shows Aztec women buying and selling maize in the great market at Tlatelolco. At the market, judges sat in raised booths, keeping a lookout for thieves and cheats.

MAKE A MAYA POT

You will need: self-drying clay, board, rolling pin, masking tape, modelling tool, water bowl, small bowl, petroleum jelly, PVA glue, glue brush, yellow and black paint, paintbrush, water pot.

1 Roll out the clay until it is approximately 5mm thick. Cut out a base for the pot with a modelling tool. Use a roll of masking tape as a guide for size.

2 Roll out some long sausages of clay. Coil them around the base of the pot to build up the sides. Join and smooth the clay with water as you go.

3 Model a lip at the top of the pot. Leave it to dry. Cover a small bowl with petroleum jelly. Make a lid by rolling out some clay. Place the clay over the bowl.

JOURNEY'S END
This modern painting shows merchants and porters arriving at the market city of Tlatelolco. Such travellers made long journeys to bring back valuable goods, such as shells, jade and fig-bark paper. Young men joining the merchants' guild were warned about tiredness, pain and ambushes on their travels.

SKINS
Items such as puma, ocelot and jaguar skins could fetch a high price at market.

BARTER
Mesoamerican people did not have coins. They bought and sold by bartering, exchanging the goods they wanted to sell for other peoples' goods of equal value. Costly items such as gold-dust, quetzal feathers and cocoa beans were exchanged for goods they wanted to buy.

colourful feathers   *cocoa beans*

MARKET PRODUCE
In Mexico today, many markets are still held on the same sites as ancient ones. Many of the same types of foodstuffs are on sale there. In this modern photograph, we see tomatoes, avocados and vegetables that were also grown in Aztec times. Today, as in the past, most market traders and shoppers are women.

Mesoamerican potters made their pots by these coil or slab techniques. The potter's wheel was not used at all in Mesoamerica. The pots were sold at the local market.

4 Turn your pot upside down and place it over the rolled-out clay. Trim away the excess clay with a modelling tool by cutting around the top of the pot.

5 Use balls of clay to make a turtle to go on top of the lid. When both the lid and turtle are dry, use PVA glue to stick the turtle on to the centre of the lid.

6 Roll three small balls of clay of exactly the same size for the pot's feet. When they are dry, glue them to the base of the pot. Make sure they are evenly spaced.

7 Paint the pot with Aztec designs in black and yellow. When you have finished, varnish the pot with a thin coat of PVA glue to make it shiny.

Inca Master Masons

THE ROCKS OF THE ANDES MOUNTAINS in Peru provided high quality granite for the Inca people who used them for impressive public buildings. These included temples, fortresses, palaces, holy shrines and aqueducts (stone channels for carrying water supplies). Most buildings were on a grand scale, but all were of a simple design. Many remain in place to this day.

The *mit'a* labour system provided the workforce. In the quarries, massive rocks weighing up to 120 tonnes were cracked and shifted with stone hammers and bronze crowbars. They were hauled with ropes on log rollers or sleds. On site, the stones were shaped to fit and rubbed smooth with water and sand. Smaller stone blocks were used for upper walls or lesser buildings.

Inca stonemasons had only basic tools. They used plumblines (weighted cords) to make sure that walls were straight. They had no mortar or cement, but the stones fitted together perfectly.

BUILDING THE TEMPLE

These rectangular stone blocks were part of the holiest site in the Inca Empire, the *Coricancha* (Temple of the Sun). Inca stonework was deliberately designed to withstand the earthquakes that regularly shake the region. The original temple on this site was badly damaged by a tremor in 1650.

BRINGER OF WATER

This beautifully engineered stone water-channel was built across a valley floor by Inca stonemasons. Aqueducts, often covered, were used both for irrigation and for drinking supplies. Irrigation schemes were being built in Peru as early as around 4,500 years ago.

AN INCA GRANARY

You will need: ruler, pencil, beige, dark and cream card, scissors, white pencil, paints, paintbrush, water pot, pair of compasses, masking tape, PVA glue, hay or straw.

1 Use a ruler and pencil to mark eight strips 8.5cm long and 0.25cm wide, and one strip 36cm long and 0.25cm wide on beige card. Cut them out.

2 On the dark card, draw a curved shape 34cm along the base, 11cm in height and 30cm along the top. Cut it out. Cut out a doorway 6cm high.

3 Paint another piece of card a stone colour. Leave it to dry. Cut it into "blocks" about 2cm high. Glue them one by one on to the building shape.

History in Stone

Stone walls and streets, such as these fine examples still standing in Ollantaytambo, survive to tell a story. Archaeology is much more difficult in the rainforests to the east, where timber structures rot rapidly in the hot, moist air. That is one reason we know more about the way people lived in the Andes than in the Amazon region.

A Massive Fortress

Llamas still pass before the mighty walls of Sacsahuaman, at Cuzco. This building was a fortress with towers and terraces. It also served as a royal palace and a sacred shrine. Its multi-sided boulders are precisely fitted. It is said to have been built over many years by 30,000 labourers. It was one of many public buildings raised in the reign of Pachakuti Inka Yupanki.

Inca Design

A building in Machu Picchu shows an example of typical Inca design. Inca stonemasons learned many of their skills from earlier Peruvian civilizations. Trapezoid-shaped openings that are wider at the bottom than the top are seen only in Inca buildings.

Storehouses were built of neat stone blocks. They kept precious grain dry and secure.

4 Use compasses to draw a circle 18cm across on cream card. Cut it out and cut away one quarter. Tape the straight cut edges together to form a cone.

5 Make a circle by joining the ends of the 36cm strip with masking tape. Then fix the eight 8.5cm strips around the edge and in the middle as shown.

6 Glue short lengths of straw or hay all over the cardboard cone to form the thatched roof of the granary. The thatch should all run in the same direction.

7 Join the edges of the walls with masking tape. Fold in the sides of the doorway. Place the rafters on top. The thatched roof fits over the rafters.

Science, Crafts & Technology

Amazing developments in science, technology or crafts do not come about by chance. They happen when people try to solve a problem with raw materials. Examine the inventions and engineering skills of the ancient Greeks, Romans, Aztecs and Maya, and explore the full range of human ingenuity in scientific achievements and technical innovation.

Making Life Easier

MANY OF THE ANIMALS of prehistoric times were faster, bigger, or stronger than the early humans who hunted them. The humans had one great advantage: they had bigger brains. The humans fought – and survived – by using their brains. They looked at the world they lived in and worked out how to make use of it. Their questioning, learning and understanding is what we call science. Their ability to shape and alter natural materials and turn them into tools, weapons and clothes was the beginning of technology.

The early species of human called *Homo habilis* (meaning handy man) was a pioneeer of technology. *Homo habilis* had big enough brains to work things out, and hands that could grip objects firmly. They were the first humans to make simple stone tools.

Early humans had to take meat they had hunted to the safety of a cave before other, fiercer animals came along. Smaller pieces were easier to carry.

Speed was vital. The humans found hard pebbles that they could split to reveal sharp edges to cut with. Technological breakthroughs such as this were gradually perfected and crafted into an ever-wider and more complex range of tools, all of which made human life safer and easier.

Because humans learned to make use of whatever local materials were available, they adapted to new environments instead of being confined to particular habitats like most animals. They moved all over the

The wheelbarrow was invented in China more than 1,000 years earlier than in the West. This was partly because there was a huge population of rice farmers who needed to find ways of making their back-breaking work easier.

TIMELINE 2,400,000BC–500BC

stone spearheads

2,400,000 years ago. The early human *Homo habilis* (handy man) makes the first simple tools by splitting pebbles to create sharp edges.

1,500,000 years ago. *Homo erectus* (upright man) makes hand axes, using flint, wood and bone. These are made over the next million years.

400,000 years ago. Date of the oldest surviving wooden tool a spear from Germany.

100,000 years ago. Following the evolution of *Homo sapiens* – fully modern humans – a greater variety of more sophisticated tools are made.

round-based pot from ancient Japan

8000-3000BC Farming becomes widespread in Asia, Europe and Africa. New tools are invented such as axes to clear forests, sickles for harvesting corn and grindstones for making flour. Pottery is used for cooking pots and storage containers.

6500BC The earliest known cloth is woven in Turkey.

6000BC The first metal tools and ornaments are made from copper in Turkey.

2,400,000BC   400,000BC   8000BC   6000BC

world. The settlements and civilizations that grew up were often separated by oceans, mountains and deserts, but they often went through similar stages of discovery and invention quite independently of each other. The ancient Egyptians were sailing boats at around the same time as the Mesopotamians, for example. The Chinese, far in the East, invented a decimal system of mathematics from 300BC, although they had no known communication with the ancient Egyptians who had done the same thing about 350 years earlier.

New technology often depended on the natural resources available. The earliest metalworkers were people who had noticed metal ore in the local rocks, and eventually learned how to extract it.

The speed with which science, craft and technology developed depended on what local materials were available, and how great the need for improvement was. Some Stone Age peoples became expert potters because they lived on clay deposits. At first, however, they only made little clay figures. It was many thousands of years before someone realized that clay could be made into ideal containers for food and liquid. The Chinese development of fine, waterproof pottery called porcelain, 1,000 years before the West, was helped by rich supplies of a very fine clay called kaolin. Inca tribes became brilliant at working with gold and silver because of the rich resources of these precious metals in the South American mountains. Most new technology was invented by people who worked with their hands. Ancient China was one of the most inventive civilizations ever because it

The Chinese emperor Shenb Nong described 365 medicinal plants. The study of subjects such as medicine and astronomy was often left to the upper classes. Practical inventions were made by those who worked on the land or with their hands.

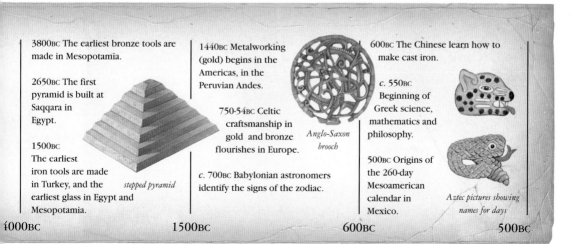

3800BC The earliest bronze tools are made in Mesopotamia.

2650BC The first pyramid is built at Saqqara in Egypt.

1500BC The earliest iron tools are made in Turkey, and the earliest glass in Egypt and Mesopotamia.

stepped pyramid

1440BC Metalworking (gold) begins in the Americas, in the Peruvian Andes.

750-54BC Celtic craftsmanship in gold and bronze flourishes in Europe.

Anglo-Saxon brooch

c. 700BC Babylonian astronomers identify the signs of the zodiac.

600BC The Chinese learn how to make cast iron.

c. 550BC Beginning of Greek science, mathematics and philosophy.

500BC Origins of the 260-day Mesoamerican calendar in Mexico.

Aztec pictures showing names for days

4000BC   1500BC   600BC   500BC

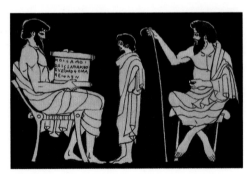

The ancient Greeks made learning a lot easier by inventing a simple alphabet. More people could read and write, so new ideas and technology spread. Ancient Greece had more scientists than any other early civilization.

was a huge country with great numbers of peasant farmers. The small, but very rich upper level of society demanded a luxurious life-style. This led to the development of fine craft skills, silk, and papermaking and printing for books.

In many civilizations, wealthy and powerful people were more interested in studying the stars and planets. Religion, astronomy and science were all closely connected in the early civilizations. The first astronomers in Babylon and Egypt believed that the movement of the stars and planets would help them discover what the gods were

The Romans were great engineers and built long, straight roads that were unsurpassed for centuries. A good road system was one way of keeping in control of their empire.

planning. Greek mathematicians such as Pythagoras believed that they could understand more about the gods through numbers.

Greed and competition acted as spurs to science, craft and technology too. The person with the most efficient plough could till more land and harvest more crops than his neighbour. The country with the most deadly and effective weapons could build empires. Knowledge, science and craft skills developed very fast in empires that could call upon the resources of all the lands under their control. The rulers also had to stay in control, which was an incentive to keep one step ahead in road and transport systems, and efficient ways of trading, language, writing, and coinage. And many kings

TIMELINE 500BC–AD1800

c. 400BC The Greek Hippocrates founds one of the earliest medical schools.

384-322BC Life of the Greek philosopher Aristotle. He is widely regarded as the founder of Western science.

Hippocrates, the Greek doctor

c. 310-230BC The Greek astronomer Aristarchus claims that the Earth goes around the Sun.

c. 200BC The Romans begin the large-scale use of concrete in building.

AD1-100 The magnetic compass is invented in China.

c. AD100 Paper is invented in China.

Chinese printed paper money

c. AD350 Maya astronomy develops in Mesoamerica.

AD605-9 The Grand Canal in China is completed.

AD800-1000 Viking craftsmanship in wood and precious metals flourishes in northern Europe.

carved prow of a Viking ship

500BC · 200BC · AD300 · AD800

and emperors, such as the Egyptian pharaohs, masterminded amazing engineering works so that they would be remembered for eternity.

Some cultures developed slowly because they did not have the way of life or the need to invent. Native peoples in North America did not invent sophisticated methods of transport because they did not have much to carry. They did develop fine craft skills, though, making use of animal hide and bones, and dyes from plants.

Although the Vikings were not great inventors, their dependence on the sea for travel and invasion meant that they developed very advanced boat-building skills.

As you read through these pages, you will be able to trace the special skills of different cultures, and discover what their particular contributions were to human knowledge. You will be able to see varying paces of technological development around the world and understand how different cultures had different priorities. Some cultures enjoyed remarkably intensive periods of technological advancement that provided the foundations of much of the science, craft and technology that make modern life easier.

New ideas and technology were spread by war. During the Crusade wars of the 11th and 12th centuries, peoples from northern Europe picked up tips on castle building and forging steel from the Muslim Saracen armies of the East.

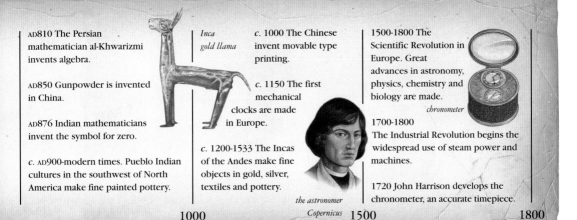

AD810 The Persian mathematician al-Khwarizmi invents algebra.

AD850 Gunpowder is invented in China.

AD876 Indian mathematicians invent the symbol for zero.

c. AD900-modern times. Pueblo Indian cultures in the southwest of North America make fine painted pottery.

Inca gold llama

c. 1000 The Chinese invent movable type printing.

c. 1150 The first mechanical clocks are made in Europe.

c. 1200-1533 The Incas of the Andes make fine objects in gold, silver, textiles and pottery.

the astronomer Copernicus

1500-1800 The Scientific Revolution in Europe. Great advances in astronomy, physics, chemistry and biology are made.

chronometer

1700-1800 The Industrial Revolution begins the widespread use of steam power and machines.

1720 John Harrison develops the chronometer, an accurate timepiece.

1000   1500   1800

The Beginning of Technology

HANDY MAN
Chipped pebbles from Tanzania in Africa are some of the oldest tools ever found. They were made by *Homo habilis,* who lived almost two million years ago. *Homo habilis* (handy man) was the first human to make stone tools.

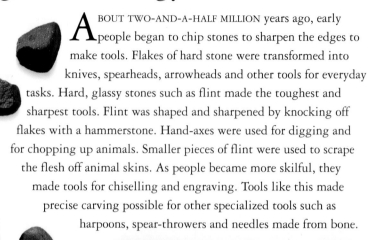

A BOUT TWO-AND-A-HALF MILLION years ago, early people began to chip stones to sharpen the edges to make tools. Flakes of hard stone were transformed into knives, spearheads, arrowheads and other tools for everyday tasks. Hard, glassy stones such as flint made the toughest and sharpest tools. Flint was shaped and sharpened by knocking off flakes with a hammerstone. Hand-axes were used for digging and for chopping up animals. Smaller pieces of flint were used to scrape the flesh off animal skins. As people became more skilful, they made tools for chiselling and engraving. Tools like this made precise carving possible for other specialized tools such as harpoons, spear-throwers and needles made from bone.

FLAKING
Some 1½ million years after *Homo habilis,* a new species of human evolved with bigger brains. Neanderthals and *Homo sapiens* were far better toolmakers. They produced pointed or oval-shaped hand-axes (*left and middle*) and chopping tools (*right*).

VALUABLE STONE
Flint was dug in this mine in England from about 2800BC. Flint was vital for survival. People would trek long distances for the stone if there were none in their area.

MAKE A MODEL AXE
You will need: self-drying clay, board, modelling tool, sandpaper, grey acrylic paint, wood stain, water pot, paintbrush, thick dowelling, craft knife, ruler, chamois leather, scissors.

1 Pull out the clay into a thick block. With a modelling tool, shape the block into an axe head with a point at one end.

2 When the clay is completely dry, lightly rub down the axe head with sandpaper to remove any rough surfaces.

3 Paint the axe head a stone colour, such as grey. You could use more than one shade if you like. Leave it to dry.

SPEAR POINT
Cro-Magnon people were top hunters, using leaf-shaped spear points to kill reindeer, wild horses, deer and woolly mammoths. They lived in Europe and Russia from around 38,000 years ago, and also learned to start fire by striking iron against flint.

STONES FOR TOOLS
The best rocks for tools were usually those that had been changed by heat. Obsidian, a glassy volcanic rock was widely used in the Near East and Mexico. It fractured easily, leaving sharp edges. In parts of Africa, quartz was made into beautiful, hardwearing hand-axes and choppers. Flint is another type of quartz. It is found in nodules in limestone rock, especially chalk. A hard igneous rock called diorite was used for making polished axe heads in Neolithic times.

quartz   *chert (a type of flint)*

AXES
Polished stone battle axes became the most important weapon in Scandinavia by the late Neolithic (New Stone Age) period. They date from about 1800BC.

TOOLMAKING LESSON
Stone Age people came to depend more and more on the quality of their tools. In this reconstruction, a father is passing on his skill in toolmaking to his son.

Prehistoric people used axes for chopping wood and cutting meat. They shaped a stone blade, then fitted it on to a wooden shaft.

4 Ask an adult to trim one end of a piece of thick dowelling using a craft knife. Paint the piece with wood stain and leave to dry.

5 To bind the axe head to the wooden shaft, first carefully cut a long strip of leather about 2.5cm wide from a chamois cloth.

6 Place the axe head on the trimmed end of the shaft. Wrap the strip of leather around the head and shaft in a criss-cross pattern.

7 Pull the leather strip tight and wrap the ends twice round the shaft below the head. Tie the ends together and trim them.

Tools for the Job

D URING THE STONE AGE, wood, bone, antler and ivory were as important as stone for making tools and other implements. These softer materials were easily carved and shaped by stone tools. They could also be used to make more specialized stone tools. Bone and antler hammers and punches, for example, could achieve sharper cutting edges and more delicate flakes of stone. Flint blades were fitted into handles and mounts of wood. Antlers were converted into picks to dig up roots and lever lumps of rock from the ground. The broad shoulder-blade bones of cattle were turned into shovels, while smaller bones served as awls to punch small holes. Antlers and bones were also carved into spear-throwers. Ivory, from the tusks of the woolly mammoth, and bone could be crafted into fine-pointed needles, fish hooks, harpoon heads and knives. Adzes were tools for shaping wood and for making bows and arrows. Sometimes, things were made just for fun. Whistles and little paint holders were carved from small bones. Some pieces of stone, wood and bone were beautifully carved with pictures of the animals that were hunted and fine decorative patterns.

SPEAR-THROWER
This carving of a reindeer's head is probably part of a spear-thrower. The hunter slotted his spear into a hook at one end of the thrower and took aim. As he threw, the spear detached from the thrower and travelled farther and faster than if the hunter had thrown it just by hand. Hunting became safer and more accurate. Prehistoric carvers often incorporated the natural form of wood or bone into a design to suggest an animal's outlines.

SHAPING
An adze was a bit like an axe, except that its blade was at right angles to the handle. The flint blade on this adze dates from about 4000BC to 2000BC. Its wooden handle and binding are modern replacements for the originals, which have rotted away. Adzes were swung in an up-and-down movement and were used for jobs such as hollowing out tree trunks and shaping them to make dugout canoes.

AXE
Early farmers needed axes to clear land for their crops. An experiment in Denmark using a 5,000-year-old axe showed that a man could clear one hectare of woodland in about five weeks. This axe head, dating from between 4000BC and 2000BC, has been given a modern wooden handle.

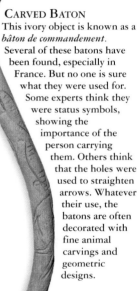

ANTLER PICK

Antlers were as useful to prehistoric humans as to the reindeer they came from! This tool comes from a Neolithic site near Avebury in England. Antler picks were used for digging and quarrying. Antler was a very hard material, but it could be carved into sharp spear points and barbed harpoons.

CRAFTSPEOPLE

A picture by an artist from the 1800s shows an imagined view of Stone Age. It shows tools being used and great care being taken over the work. Even everyday items were often finely carved and decorated by the craftspeople who made them.

CARVED BATON

This ivory object is known as a *bâton de commandement*. Several of these batons have been found, especially in France. But no one is sure what they were used for. Some experts think they were status symbols, showing the importance of the person carrying them. Others think that the holes were used to straighten arrows. Whatever their use, the batons are often decorated with fine animal carvings and geometric designs.

ANTLERS AT WORK

Two stags (male deer) fight. Male deer have large antlers, which they use to battle with each other to win territory and females. The stags shed and grow a new set of antlers each year, so prehistoric hunters and artists had a ready supply of material.

Useful Crafts

BASKET-MAKING WAS PROBABLY the very first handicraft. River reeds or twigs – whatever was found locally – were woven into shapes for carrying goods. Baskets were quick to make and easy to carry, but wore out easily and could not carry liquids. The discovery that clay turned into a hard, solid material when it was baked may have happened by accident, perhaps when a clay-lined basket was left in a bread oven. Although baked clay figures were made from about 24,000BC, it was thousands of years before pottery was used for cooking and storing food and drink. The first pots, shaped from coils or lumps of clay, were made in Japan around 10,500BC.

People learned how to spin thread from flax plants and animal hair. The loom, for weaving the thread into linen and wool cloth, was invented around 6000BC.

BAKED CLAY FIGURINE
This is one of the oldest fired-clay objects in the world. It is one of many similar figurines made around 24,000BC at Dolni Vestonice in the Czech Republic. Here, people hunted mammoths, woolly rhinoceroses and horses. They built homes with small, oval-shaped ovens, in which they fired their figurines.

CHINESE JAR
It is amazing to think that this elegant pot was for everyday use in 4500BC. It was made in Banpo, near Shanghai. The people of Banpo were some of China's earliest farmers. They grew millet and kept pigs and dogs for meat. The potters made a high quality black pottery for important occasions and this cheaper, grey pottery for everyday use.

MAKE A CLAY POT
You will need: terracotta modelling clay, wooden board, modelling tool, plastic flower pot, decorating tool, varnish, brush, sandpaper.

1 Roll out a long, thick sausage of clay on a wooden board. It should be at least 1cm in diameter.

2 Form the roll of clay into a coil to make the base of your pot. A fairly small base can be made into a pot, a larger one into a bowl.

3 Now make a fatter roll of clay. Carefully coil this around the base to make the sides of your pot.

HOUSEHOLD POTS

Many early pots were decorated with basket-like patterns. This one has a simple geometric design and was made in Thailand in about 3500BC. Clay pots like this were used for storing food, carrying water or cooking.

WOVEN THREADS

The earliest woven objects may have looked like this rope and cane mat from Nazca in Peru. It was made around AD1000. Prehistoric people used plant-fibre rope to weave baskets and bags. The oldest known fabric dates from about 6500BC and was found at Çatal Hüyük in Turkey. Few woven objects have survived, as they rot quickly.

EASY TO CARVE

Steatite, or soapstone, has been used to make this carving from the Cycladic Islands of Greece. Soapstone is very soft and easy to carve. Figurines like this one were often used in funeral ceremonies. They could also be used either as the object of worship itself or as a ritual offering to a god. This figure has a cross around its neck. Although the symbol certainly has no Christian significance, no one really knows what it means.

Fired-clay pots could only be made where there were natural deposits of clay. These areas seem to have specialized in baked-clay pottery and sculpture. The patterns used to decorate the pots vary from area to area.

4 With a modelling tool, smooth down the edges of the coil to make it flat and smooth. Make sure there are no air spaces.

5 Place your pot over a flower pot to support it. Keep adding more rolls of clay to build up the sides of your pot.

6 Smooth down the sides as you add more rolls. Then use a decorating tool with a serrated end to make different patterns.

7 Leave your pot to dry out. When the clay is dry, varnish the outside. Use sandpaper to smooth the inside of your pot.

Ceramic Skills in India

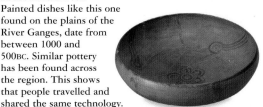

CLAY AND TERRACOTTA OBJECTS (known as ceramics) play an important part in the study of history. Because they were fired (baked), traces of carbon (burnt particles) are left on them. This enables archaeologists to date the objects quite accurately using a process called carbon-dating.

Making ceramics was one of the earliest crafts to be practised in India, for example. Many artefacts have been found at archaeological sites, dating as far back as 5000BC when a civilization began to develop in the Indus Valley. People made clay storage jars, terracotta seals and terracotta figurines of domestic animals. The animal figures may have been children's toys. Craftworkers also made terracotta figurines of gods and goddesses, though they gradually began to make stone and metal images as well. Clay containers continued to be used throughout India's history. They kept food and liquids cool in in the country's hot climate.

RECORD IN CLAY
This terracotta cart found at the ancient city of Mohenjo-Daro is about 4,000 years old. Figurines like this have been found throughout the Indus Valley. They may have been toys, but they give clues to how people lived. For example, we can see that wheeled carts drawn by animals were in use.

IDEA EXCHANGE
Painted dishes like this one found on the plains of the River Ganges, date from between 1000 and 500BC. Similar pottery has been found across the region. This shows that people travelled and shared the same technology.

SIMILAR STYLES
Black and red painted pottery has been found at sites dating from the Indus Valley civilization, and at later sites dating from around 500BC. It is found all over the Indian subcontinent.

MAKE A WATER POT

You will need: inflated balloon, large bowl, strips of newspaper, flour and water or wallpaper paste, scissors, fine sandpaper, strip of corrugated cardboard, sticky tape, terracotta and black paint, paintbrushes, pencil, PVA glue.

1 Cover the balloon with 4 layers of newspaper soaked in paste. When dry, cut a small slit and remove the balloon. Add more layers to give the pot a tapered top.

2 Roll the corrugated cardboard into a circle shape to fit on to the narrow end of the pot to form a base. Fix the base in place with sticky tape.

3 Cover the corrugated cardboard base with four layers of soaked newspaper. Leave to dry beween each layer. Smooth the edges with sandpaper.

TERRACOTTA GODDESS

A female terracotta figure found in Mathura, Uttar Pradesh may be an image of a mother goddess. Many terracotta images were made during the Mauryan period (400–200BC) and immediately afterwards. They were cheaper versions of the stone sculptures that were built at the imperial court.

bricks

BRICKS FOR BUILDING

In parts of India where there was no hard local stone – and throughout India for simple homes – clay was baked and made into bricks. Unlike buildings made of stone, structures made of brick have often not survived the ravages of time.

THROWING A POT

A village potter shapes a clay vessel as it spins on his potter's wheel. Pottery was an important part of the ancient urban and village economies and is still practised in India today. Clay used for making pottery is available in most parts of the land.

Clay water pots that are 4,000 years old have been found in the Indus Valley. People carried the pots on their heads.

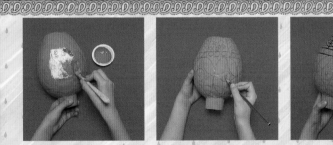

4 When it is dry, paint the water pot with two coats of terracotta paint, to make it look as though it is made of terracotta. Leave to dry between coats.

5 Draw some patterns on the water pot with a pencil. Copy the ancient Indian pattern shown here, or create your own individual design.

6 Carefully paint your designs using black paint and a fine paintbrush. Keep the edges of your lines neat and clean. Leave to dry.

7 Add final details, again using a fine paintbrush. When the paint is dry, seal the surface of the water pot with a coat of watered down PVA glue

Scientific Minds in Mesopotamia

T HE SUMERIAN PEOPLE in Mesopotamia developed the world's first system of arithmetic around 2500BC. It was useful for making records of goods bought and sold. One number system used 10 as a base and the other, 60. They also calculated time in hour-long units of 60 minutes. Sumerian astronomers worked out a calendar based on 12- and 28-day cycles and 7-day weeks from studying the moon and the

seasons. Later, the Babylonians made a detailed study of the heavens, and could predict events such as eclipses.

Mesopotamian doctors did not fully understand how the body worked, but they did make lists of symptoms. Their observations passed on to the Greeks centuries later and so became one of the foundations of modern medicine.

HEAVY COUGH CURE
Inscriptions on a clay tablet suggest mixing balsam (a herb) with strong beer, honey and oil to cure a cough. The mixture was taken hot, without food. Then the patient's throat was tickled with a feather to make him sick. Other prescriptions used mice, dogs' tails and urine.

BAD OMEN
Mesopotamians thought that eclipses were a bad sign – unless they were obscured by cloud. If an eclipse was covered by cloud in a particular city, the local king was told that it had nothing to do with him or his country.

MEDICINAL BREW
Servants are distilling essence of cedar, a vital ingredient for a Mesopotamian headache cure. Cedar twigs were heated to give off a vapour. This condensed against the cooler lid and trickled into the rim of the pot from where it was collected. The essence was mixed with honey, resin from pine, myrrh and spruce trees, and fat from a sheep's kidney.

MAKE A SET OF LION WEIGHTS

You will need: pebbles of various sizes, kitchen scales, modelling clay, cutting board, cocktail stick, paints and paintbrushes.

1 Weigh a pebble and add modelling clay to make it up to a weight of 225g. Once the clay has dried out, the final weight will be only about 200g.

2 Take a portion of the weighed modelling clay and shape it into a rectangle roughly 12cm by 7cm. This will be the base for your weight.

3 Wrap another piece of the weighed modelling clay around the weighed pebble to make the lion's body. Shape the body into a pear shape.

SKY MAP

The sky in this Mesopotamian astronomical map is divided into eight parts and the stars in each section are indicated. The heavens were seen as a source of information about the future, so the kings often consulted astronomers. One astronomer wrote to the king in the 600s BC: "I am always looking at the sky but nothing unusual has appeared above the horizon".

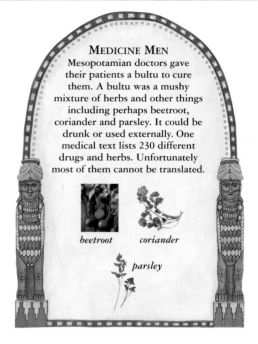

MEDICINE MEN

Mesopotamian doctors gave their patients a bultu to cure them. A bultu was a mushy mixture of herbs and other things including perhaps beetroot, coriander and parsley. It could be drunk or used externally. One medical text lists 230 different drugs and herbs. Unfortunately most of them cannot be translated.

beetroot   coriander

parsley

WEIGHTS AND MEASURES

Officials weigh metal objects that have been taken as booty after a victory. The duck-shaped object is a weight. The kings were responsible for seeing that weights and measures were exact and that nobody cheated customers. Prices were fixed by law and calculated in shekels (1 shekel was about 8g of silver).

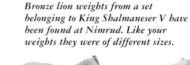

Bronze lion weights from a set belonging to King Shalmaneser V have been found at Nimrud. Like your weights they were of different sizes.

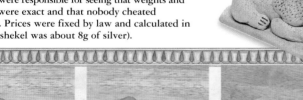

4 Position the pebble and clay on to its base. Add another piece of weighed clay to form the head and mane. Shape the face and jaw with your fingers.

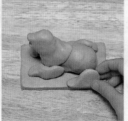

5 Model four pieces of weighed clay to make the lion's four legs and stick them on to the body. Flatten the clay slightly at each end for the paws.

6 Make a tail and ears using up the remaining weighed clay. Using the cocktail stick, add extra detail to the face, mane, paws and tail. Leave to dry.

7 Paint the lion and the base cream. Flick with brown paint for a mottled appearance. Add details to the face, mane and paws. Make more lions for a set.

Mesopotamian Technology

A WHOLE CULTURE OF SPECIALIST craftworkers grew up in Mesopotamia and quickened the pace of improvement and invention. The Sumerians learned to make pottery by shaping the wet clay on a potter's wheel by about 3500BC, and became experts at making cloth, leatherwork and making fine jewellery. They were among the first people in the world to use metal. A copper sculpture of a lion-headed eagle found near the ancient city of Ur, dates from around 2600BC. Mesopotamian armies used weapons and armour of bronze, an alloy of copper and tin, which is stronger than plain copper. The Mesopotamians were also experts at irrigation and flood control, building elaborate canals, water storage and drainage systems.

SUPPLYING THE CITY
Water wheels and aqueducts like these are still used in the Middle East today. The Assyrians built aqueducts to take water to the cities to meet the needs of their growing populations. The Assyrian king Sennacherib had 10km of canals cut. They led from the mountains to the city of Nineveh. He built dams and weirs to control the flow of water, and created an artificial marsh, where he bred wild animals and birds.

A WEIGHTY CHALLENGE
Workers in a quarry near the Assyrian city of Nineveh prepare to move an enormous block of stone roughly hewn in the shape of a lamassu (human-headed winged bull). The stone is on a sledge carried on wooden rollers. At the back of the sledge, some men have thrown ropes over a giant lever and pull hard. This raises the end of the sledge and other workers push a wedge underneath. More workers stand ready to haul on ropes at the front of the sledge. At a signal everyone pulls or pushes and the sledge moves forward.

MAKE A PAINTED PLATE
You will need: a plate, flour, water and newspaper to make papier mâché, scissors, pencil, fine sandpaper, ruler, paints and paintbrushes.

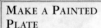

1 Tear strips of newspaper and dip them in the water. Cover the whole surface of the plate with the wet newspaper strips.

2 Mix up a paste of flour and water. Cover the newspaper strips with the paste. Allow to dry, then add two more layers, leaving it to dry each time.

3 When the papier mâché is dry, trim around the plate to make a neat edge. Remove the plate. Add more papier mâché to strengthen the plate.

336 SCIENCE, CRAFTS & TECHNOLOGY

MAKING CLOTH

Spinning and weaving were usually done by women in the home or in state or temple factories. Large herds of sheep and goats were kept to produce wool, to make clothing. Flax was grown for its fibres, which were used to make linen as early as 3000BC. Cotton was not introduced until the reign of the Assyrian king, Sennacherib, in the 700s BC.

sheep's wool

wool

sheep's fleece

METALWORKERS

Ceremonial daggers demonstrate the Sumerians' skill at working with gold as far back as 2600BC. Real weapons had bronze blades. The Sumerians made a wax model of the object required. They covered this with clay to make a mould. They heated the mould to harden the clay. The melted wax was poured out through a small hole, and molten metal poured in to replace it. When cool, the clay mould was broken, to reveal the metal object inside.

You have copied a plate from Tell Halaf, a small town where some of the finest pots in the ancient world were made. They were decorated with orange and brown paints made from oxides found in clay.

HAND-MADE VASES

Vases found in Samarra in the north of Mesopotamia were produced about 6,000 years ago. They were shaped by hand and fired in a kiln, then painted with geometric designs. Later, a wheel like a turntable was used to shape the clay, which speeded up the process.

 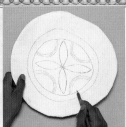  

4 When the papier mâché is completely dry, smooth it down with fine sandpaper. Then paint the plate on both sides with a white base coat.

5 When the paint is dry, use a pencil and ruler to mark a dot in the centre of the plate. Draw four large petals around this point and add details as shown above.

6 When you are happy with your design, paint in the patterns using three colours for the basic pattern. Allow each colour to dry before adding the next.

7 Add more detail to your plate, using more colours, including wavy lines around the edge. When you have finished painting, leave it to dry.

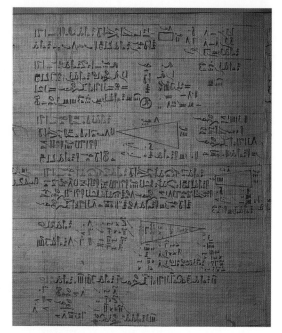

MATHEMATICAL PAPYRUS
This papyrus shows methods for working out the areas of squares, circles and triangles. It dates from around 850BC. These methods would have been used in calculations for land areas and pyramid heights on Egyptian building projects. Other surviving writings show mathematical calculations for working out how much grain might fit into a store. The Egyptians used a decimal system of numbering with separate symbols for one, ten, 100 and 1,000. Eight was shown by eight one symbols – 11111111.

Egyptian Calculations

THE ANCIENT EGYPTIANS had advanced systems of numbering and measuring. They put this knowledge to good use in building, engineering and surveying the land. However, their knowledge of science was often mixed up with superstitions and belief in magic. For example, doctors understood a lot about broken bones and surgery, but at the same time they used all kinds of spells, amulets (charms) and magic potions to ward off disease. Much of their knowledge about the human body came from their experience of preparing the dead for burial.

The priests studied the stars carefully. They thought that the planets must be gods. The Egyptians also worked out a calendar, which was very important for working out when the Nile floods were due and when to plant crops.

CUBIT MEASURE
Units of measurement included the royal cubit of about 52cm and the short cubit of 45cm. A cubit was the length of a man's forearm and was subdivided into palms and fingers.

MAKE A WATER CLOCK

You will need: self-drying clay, plastic flowerpot, modelling tool, skewer, pencil, ruler, masking tape, scissors, yellow acrylic paint, varnish, water pot and brush. Optional: rolling pin and board.

1 Begin by rolling out the clay. Take the plastic flowerpot and press its base firmly into the clay. This will be the bottom of your water clock.

2 Cut out an oblong of clay large enough to mould around the flowerpot. Add the base and use your modelling tool to make the joints smooth.

3 Make a small hole near the bottom of the pot with a skewer, as shown. Leave it in a warm place to dry. When the clay has dried, remove the flowerpot.

How Deep is the River?

A series of steps called a nilometer was used to measure the depth of water in the River Nile. The annual floods were desperately important for the farmers living alongside the Nile. A good flood measured about 7m. More than this and farm buildings and channels might be destroyed. Less, and the fields might go dry.

Star of the Nile

This astronomical painting is from the ceiling of the tomb of Seti I. The study of the stars, as in most of the ancient civilizations, was part religion, part science. The brightest star in the sky was Sirius, which we call the dog star. The Egyptians called it Sopdet, after a goddess. This star rose into view at the time when the Nile floods were due and was greeted with a special festival.

Medicine

Most Egyptian medicines were based on plants. One cure for headaches included juniper berries, coriander, wormwood and honey. The mixture was rubbed into the scalp. Other remedies included natron (a kind of salt), myrrh and even crocodile droppings. Some Egyptian medicines probably did heal the patients, but others did more harm than good.

coriander

garlic

4 Mark out lines at 3mm intervals inside the pot. Mask the ends with tape and paint the lines yellow. When dry, remove the tape. Ask an adult to varnish the pot inside.

5 Find or make another two pots and position them as shown. Ask a partner to put their finger over the hole in the clock while you pour water into it.

6 Now ask your partner to take their finger away. The length of time it takes for the level of the water to drop from mark to mark is the measure of time.

Time was calculated on water clocks by calculating how long it took for water to drop from level to level. The water level lowered as it dripped through the hole in the bottom of the pot.

Pyramid Construction

QUARRYING

The core of the pyramid was of rough stone, from local quarries. Better quality stone was shipped from Aswan, 966km away. Workers used wooden mallets to drive wedges and chisels into the stone to split it.

FOR MANY YEARS the Great Pyramid at Giza was the largest building in the world. Its base is about 230m square, and its original point was 147m high. It is made up of about 2,300,000 massive blocks of stone, each one weighing about 2.5 tonnes. The blocks were secured by rope on wooden rollers. Labourers hauled them up ramps of solid earth that were built up the side of the pyramid as it grew higher and higher. The ramps were destroyed when the pyramid was completed.

The Great Pyramid was amazingly accurate and symmetrical in shape. The land had to be absolutely flat for this to be possible. The Egyptians cut channels across the building site and filled them with water. They used the water line as a marker for making the site level. The four corners of the pyramid are aligned exactly to face north, south, east and west. This was worked out by astronomers, by observing the stars.

INSIDE WORK

Inside the pyramid were narrow passages, and tomb chambers. They were lined with good quality granite. Flickering light came from pottery lamps that consisted of a wick of twine or grass soaked in animal or fish oil. Bundles of papyrus (reeds) were dipped in resin or pitch and lit to use as torches.

MAKE A PYRAMID

You will need: card, pencil, ruler, scissors, pva glue and brush, masking tape, acrylic paint (yellow, white, gold), plaster paste, sandpaper, water pot and brush.

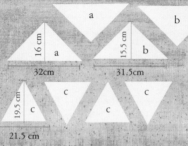

a
b
16 cm
a
32cm
15.5 cm
b
31.5cm
19.5 cm
c
c
21.5 cm
c
c

Make the pyramid in two halves. Cut out one triangle (a) for the base, one triangle (b) for the inside and two of triangle (c) for the sides of each half section.

1 Glue the half section of the pyramid together, binding the joints with pieces of masking tape, as shown. Now make the second half section in the same way.

INSIDE A PYRAMID

This cross-section shows the inside of the Great Pyramid. The design of the interior changed several times during its construction. An underground chamber may originally have been intended as the pharaoh Khufu's burial place. This was never finished. The Queen's Chamber was also found empty. The pharaoh was actually buried in the King's Chamber. Once the funeral was over, the tomb was sealed from the inside to prevent people breaking in. Blocks of stone were slid down the Grand Gallery. The workmen left through a shaft and along a corridor before the stones thudded into place.

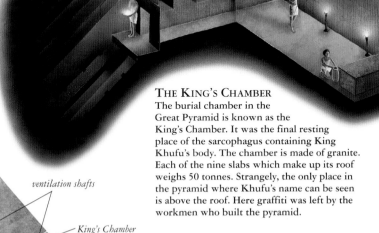

THE KING'S CHAMBER

The burial chamber in the Great Pyramid is known as the King's Chamber. It was the final resting place of the sarcophagus containing King Khufu's body. The chamber is made of granite. Each of the nine slabs which make up its roof weighs 50 tonnes. Strangely, the only place in the pyramid where Khufu's name can be seen is above the roof. Here graffiti was left by the workmen who built the pyramid.

ventilation shafts

King's Chamber

Grand Gallery

Queen's Chamber

escape shaft for workers

corridor

unfinished chamber

2 Mix up yellow and white paint with a little plaster paste to achieve a sandy texture. Then add a little glue so that it sticks to the card. Paint the pyramid sections.

3 Leave the painted pyramid sections to dry in a warm place. When they are completely dry, sand down the tips until they are smooth and mask them off with tape.

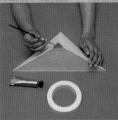

4 Now paint the tips of each half of the pyramid gold and leave to dry. Finally, glue the two halves together and place your pyramid on a bed of sand to display.

The building of the Great Pyramid probably took about 23 years. Originally the pyramids were cased in pale limestone, so they would have looked a brilliant white. The capstone at the very top of the pyramid was probably covered in gold.

The Thinking Greeks

THE ANCIENT GREEKS COULD AFFORD time for studying and thinking because their civilization was both wealthy and secure. They learned astrology from the Babylonians and mathematics from the Egyptians. They used their scientific knowledge to develop many practical inventions, including water clocks, cogwheels, gearing systems, slot machines and steam engines. However, these devices were not widely used as there were many slave workers to do the jobs.

The word 'philosophy' comes from the Greek word *philosophos*, meaning love of knowledge. The Greeks developed many different branches of philosophy. Three of these were politics (how best to govern), ethics (how to behave well) and cosmology (how the universe worked). Greek philosophers recognized the value of experimenting. But they could not always see their limitations. Aristotle discovered that distillation turned salt water into fresh water, and wrongly assumed wine would turn into water by the same process.

CLOCK TOWER
The Tower of the Winds in Athens contains a water clock. The original Egyptian invention was a bucket of water with a tiny hole in the bottom. As the water dripped out of it, the water level fell past scored marks on the inside of the bucket, measuring time. The Greeks improved on this design, using the flow of water to work a dial with a moving pointer.

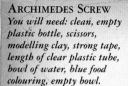

GREAT THINKER
The philosopher Aristotle (384–322BC) is often recognized as the founder of Western science. He pioneered a rational approach to the world, that was based on observing and recording evidence. For three years, he was the tutor of Alexander the Great.

ARCHIMEDES SCREW
You will need: clean, empty plastic bottle, scissors, modelling clay, strong tape, length of clear plastic tube, bowl of water, blue food colouring, empty bowl.

1 Cut off the bottle top. Place the modelling clay into the middle of the bottle, about 5cm from the end. Punch a hole here with the scissors.

2 Cut a strip of tape the same length as the bottle. Tape it to the middle of the bottle. This will give the tube extra grip later on.

3 Twist the length of tube around the bottle. Go from one end of the bottle to the other. Tape the tube into place over the first piece of tape.

WATER LIFTER

When an Archimedes screw is turned, it lifts water from one level to another. It is named after its inventor, the scientist Archimedes, who lived about 287–211BC, in Syracuse, Sicily. The device is still used today.

EUCLID

FATHER OF GEOMETRY

Euclid (about 330–260BC) was a mathematician. He lived in the Greek-Egyptian city of Alexandria. He is known as the father of geometry, which comes from the Greek word for 'measuring land'. Geometry is the study of points, lines, curves, surfaces and their measurements. His geometry textbook was called *Elements*. It was still widely used in the early part of the 1900s, over 2,000 years after Euclid's death. This picture shows the front page of an edition of the book that was printed in London in 1732.

4 Place a few drops of the blue food colouring into the bowl of water. Stir it in so that the colour mixes evenly throughout the water.

5 Place one end of the bottle into the bowl of blue water. Make sure that the tube at the opposite end is pointing towards the empty bowl.

6 Twist the bottle around in the blue water. As you do so, you will see the water start travelling up the tube and gradually filling the other bowl.

The invention of the Archimedes screw made it possible for farmers to water their fields with irrigation channels. It saved them from walking back and forth to the river with buckets.

Greek Medical Foundations

THE ANCIENT GREEKS LAID the foundations of modern medicine. Although they believed that only the gods had the power to heal wounds and cure sickness, they also developed a scientific approach to medicine. Greek doctors treated injuries and battle wounds by bandaging and bone-setting. They prescribed rest, diet and herbal drugs to cure diseases, although they were powerless against epidemics, such as plague. Doctors believed that good health was dependent on the balance between four main body fluids – blood, phlegm and yellow and black bile. If this balance was disturbed, they attempted to restore it by applying heated metal cups to the body to draw off harmful fluids. This mistaken practice continued in Europe until the 1600s.

FATHER OF MEDICINE
Hippocrates founded a medical school around 400BC. He taught that observation of symptoms was more important than theory. His students took an oath to use their skills to heal and never to harm. Doctors still take the Hippocratic oath today.

BODY BALANCE
Bleeding was a common procedure, intended to restore the body's internal balance. This carving shows surgical instruments and cups used for catching blood. Sometimes bleeding may have helped to drain off poisons, but more often it can only have weakened the patient.

HEALING GOD
The Greeks worshipped Asclepius, as the god of healing. He is shown here with a serpent, representing wisdom. Invalids seeking a cure made a visit to his shrine.

LEG OFFERING
You will need: self-drying modelling clay, rolling pin, board, ruler, modelling tool, paintbrush, cream acrylic paint.

1 Divide the clay into two pieces. With the rolling pin, roll out one piece to 15cm length, 10cm width and 2cm depth. This is the base for the leg.

2 Roll out the second piece of clay. With the modelling tool, carve out a leg and foot shape. It should be big enough to fit on one side of the base.

3 Gently place the leg on the right-hand side of the base. With the tool, draw a shallow outline around the leg into the base. Remove the leg.

THEORY AND PRACTICE

Patients would explain their dreams to doctors, who then prescribed treatment. In this relief, a healing spirit in the shape of a serpent visits a sleeping patient. In the foreground, the physician bandages the wounded arm.

NATURAL HEALING

The Greeks used a large variety of natural treatments to cure illnesses. Herbal remedies were particularly popular. Lentils, mustard and honey may have been combined in a poultice and applied to a wound.

lentils

mustard

honey

TOOL KIT

The Greeks used bronze surgical instruments, including forceps and probes. Surgery was usually a last resort. Even when it was successful, patients often died from the shock and pain, or from infection afterwards. Operations on limbs were more successful than those on body cavities such as the chest or stomach.

4 With the tool, score the outline with lines. Carve the ancient Greek message seen in the picture above next to the leg.

5 Mould the leg onto the scored area of the base. Use your fingers to press the sides of the leg in place. Carve toes and toenails into the foot.

6 Paint over the entire leg offering with a cream colour, to give it an aged look. Leave to dry overnight. Your leg offering is done.

This model is based on a real one that was left as a thanks offering to the god Asclepius by someone whose leg was affected by illness. This was a common practice in ancient Greece.

Roman Empire Builders

Tʜᴇ Rᴏᴍᴀɴꜱ ᴀᴅᴏᴘᴛᴇᴅ many of the ideas of the Greeks, such as the principles of architecture, and developed them further. They built magnificent domes, arched bridges and grand public buildings throughout the Empire, spreading their ideas and their expert skills.

They built long, straight roads to carry supplies, and messengers to the farthest corners of the Empire. The roads had a slight hump in the middle so that rainwater drained to the sides. Some were paved with stone and others were covered with gravel or stone chippings. Engineers designed aqueducts to carry water supplies to their cities. If possible, local stone and timber were used for building works. The Romans were the first to develop concrete, which was cheaper and stronger than stone. The rule of the Romans came to an end in western Europe over 1,500 years ago. Yet many of their techniques and principles of building are still in use today.

Rᴏᴍᴀɴ Rᴏᴀᴅꜱ
A typical Roman road stretches into the distance. It runs through the town of Ostia, in Italy. Roman road-building techniques remained unmatched in Europe until the 1800s.

Mᴜꜱᴄʟᴇ Pᴏᴡᴇʀ
Romans used big wooden cranes to lift heavy building materials. The crane is powered by a huge treadwheel. Slaves walk round and round in the wheel, making it turn. The turning wheel pulls on the rope, that is tied round the heavy block of stone, raising it off the ground.

Mᴀᴋᴇ ᴀ Gʀᴏᴍᴀ

You will need: large, strong piece of cardboard, scissors, ruler, pencil, square of card, PVA glue, masking tape, balsa wood pole, Plasticine, silver foil, string, large sewing needle, acrylic paints, paintbrush, water pot, broom handle.

1 Cut out three pieces of cardboard – two 20cm x 6cm, one 40cm x 6cm. Cut another piece, 15cm x 12cm, for the handle. Then cut them into shape, as shown above.

2 Measure to the centre of the long piece. Use a pencil to make a slot here, between the layers of cardboard. The slot is for the balsa wood pole.

3 Slide the balsa wood pole into the slot and tape the cardboard pieces in a cross. Use the card square to make sure the four arms of the groma are at right angles. Glue in place.

BUILDING MATERIALS

The Romans used a variety of stones for building, usually from local quarries. Limestone and a volcanic rock called tufa were used in the city of Pompeii. Slate was used for roofing in parts of Britain. Fine marble, used for temples and other public buildings, was available in the Carrara region of Italy, as it still is today. Marble was also imported from overseas.

marble

slate

ARCHING STRENGTH

The Roman bridge over the River Guadalquivir at Cordoba in Spain still stands today. The arch was a key element in many Roman buildings, including domed roofs. It gave stronger support than a simple beam.

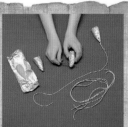  

WALLS OF ROME

The city of Rome's defences were built at many stages in its history. These sturdy walls were raised during the reign of the Emperor Marcus Aurelius, AD121–180. The Aurelian Walls were so well built that they are still in good condition.

Slot the arms on to the balsa wood pole. Use the plumb lines as a guide to make sure the pole is vertical. The arms can then be used to line up objects in the distance. Romans used a groma to measure right angles and to make sure roads were straight.

4 Roll the Plasticine into four small cones and cover them with foil. Thread string through the tops, as shown. These are the groma's plumb lines, or vertical guides.

5 Tie the plumb lines to each arm, as shown. They must all hang at the same length – 20cm will do. If the Plasticine is too heavy, use wet newspaper rolled up in the foil.

6 Split the top of the handle piece, and wrap it round the balsa wood pole. Glue it in place, as shown. Do the same on the other end with the broom handle. Paint the groma.

Roman Healing Powers

SOME ROMANS lived to old age, but most died before they reached the age of 50. Archaeologists have found out a lot about health and disease in Roman times by examining skeletons that have survived. They can tell, for example, how old a person was when he or she died and their general state of health during life. Ancient writings also provide information about Roman medical knowledge.

Roman doctors knew very little science. They healed the sick through a mixture of common sense, trust in the gods and magic. Most cures and treatments had come to Rome from the doctors of ancient Greece. The Greeks and Romans also shared the same god of healing, Aesculapius (the Greek Asclepius). There were doctors in most parts of the Empire, as well as midwives, dentists and eye specialists. Surgeons operated on wounds received in battle, on broken bones and even skulls. The only pain killers were made from poppy juice.

A CHEMIST'S SHOP
This pharmacy, or chemist's shop, is run by a woman. This was quite unusual for Roman times, as women were rarely given positions of responsibility. Roman pharmacists collected herbs and often mixed them for doctors.

GODDESS OF HEALTH
Greeks and Romans honoured the daughter of the god Aesculapius as a goddess of health. She was called Hygieia. The word hygienic, which comes from her name, is still used today to mean free of germs.

MEDICINE BOX
Boxes like this one would have been used by Roman doctors to store various drugs. Many of the treatments used by doctors were herbal, and not always pleasant to take!

MEDICAL INSTRUMENTS
The Romans used a variety of surgical and other instruments. These are made in bronze and include a scalpel, forceps and a spatula for mixing and applying various ointments.

TAKING THE CURE

These are the ruins of a medical clinic in Asia Minor (present-day Turkey). It was built around AD150, in honour of Aesculapius, the god of healing. Clinics like this one were known as therapy buildings. People would come to them seeking cures for all kinds of ailments.

BATHING THE BABY

This stone carving from Rome shows a newborn baby being bathed. The Romans were well aware of the importance of regular bathing in clean water. However, childbirth itself was dangerous for both mother and baby. Despite the dangers, the Romans liked to have large families, and many women died giving birth.

HERBAL MEDICINE

Doctors and travelling healers sold all kinds of potions and ointments. Many were made from herbs such as rosemary, sage and fennel. Other natural remedies included garlic, mustard and cabbage. Many of the remedies would have done little good, but some of them did have the power to heal.

garlic

sage

rosemary

Chinese Metalworkers

THE CHINESE MASTERED THE secrets of making alloys (mixtures of two or more metals) during the Shang dynasty (*c*.1600BC–1122BC). They made bronze by melting copper and tin to separate each metal from its ore, a process called smelting. Nine parts of copper were then mixed with one part of tin and heated in a charcoal furnace. When the metals melted, they were piped into clay moulds. Bronze was used to make objects such as ceremonial pots, statues, bells, mirrors, tools and weapons.

By about 600BC, the Chinese were smelting iron ore. They then became the first people to make cast iron – around 1500 years before the process was discovered in the West – by adding carbon to the molten metal. Cast iron is tougher than bronze and was soon being used to make weapons, tools and plough blades. By AD1000, the Chinese were mining and working a vast amount of iron. Coke (a type of coal) had replaced the charcoal used in furnaces, which were fired up by water-driven bellows.

SILVER SCISSORS
This pair of scissors is made of silver. They are proof of the foreign influences that entered China in the AD700s, during the boom years of the Tang dynasty. The metal is beaten, rather than cast in the Chinese way. It is decorated in the Persian style of the Silk Road, with engraving and punching.

BEWARE OF THE LION
This gilded lion is on guard at Beijing's imperial palace, the Forbidden City, built in the 1400s. The Chinese were expert at elaborately decorated metalwork, sometimes inlaying it with gold, silver and precious stones.

MAKE A NECKLACE

You will need: tape measure, thick wire, thin wire, masking tape, scissors, tin foil, measuring spoon, glue and brush, fuse wire.

1 Measure around your neck using a tape measure. Ask an adult to cut a piece of thick wire to 1½ times this length. Shape it into a rough circle.

2 Cut two 4cm pieces of thin wire. Coil loosely around sides of thick wire. Tape ends to thick wire. Slide thick wire through coils to adjust fit.

3 Cut out an oval-shaped piece of tin foil. Shape it into a pendant half, using a measuring spoon or teaspoon. Make 9 more halves.

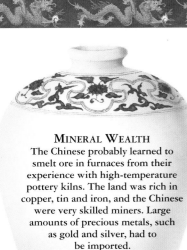

MINERAL WEALTH

The Chinese probably learned to smelt ore in furnaces from their experience with high-temperature pottery kilns. The land was rich in copper, tin and iron, and the Chinese were very skilled miners. Large amounts of precious metals, such as gold and silver, had to be imported.

gold nugget   *silver ore*

PEACE BE WITH YOU

The Hall of Supreme Harmony in Beijing's Forbidden City is guarded by this bronze statue of a turtle. Despite its rather fearsome appearance, the turtle was actually a symbol of peace.

DECORATIVE PROTECTION

A network of gold threads makes up these fingernail protectors of the 1800s. The blue decoration is enamel (glass) that was put into parts of the pattern in paste form, and then fired to melt and harden it.

GOLDEN FIREBIRDS

Chinese craftsmen fashioned these beautiful phoenix birds from thin sheets of delicate gold. The mythical Arabian phoenix was said to set fire to its nest and die, only to rise again from the ashes. During the Tang dynasty, the phoenix became a symbol of the Chinese empress Wu Zetian, who came to power in AD660. It later came to be a more general symbol for all empresses.

4 Glue the 2 pendant halves together, leaving one end open. Drop some rolled-up balls of foil into the opening. Seal the opening with glue.

5 Make 4 more pendants in the same way. Thread each pendant on to the neckband with pieces of thin fuse wire. Leave a gap between each one.

People of all classes wore decorative jewellery in imperial China. The design of this necklace is based on the metal bell bracelets worn by Chinese children.

Chinese Firsts

WHEN YOU WALK DOWN a shopping street in any modern city, it is very difficult to avoid seeing some object that was invented in China long ago. Printed words on paper, silk scarves, umbrellas or locks and keys are all Chinese innovations. Over the centuries, Chinese ingenuity and technical skill have changed the world in which we live.

A seismoscope is a very useful instrument in an earthquake-prone country such as China. It was invented in AD132 by a Chinese scientist called Zhang Heng. It could record the direction of even a distant earth tremor. Another key invention was the magnetic compass. Around AD1–100, the Chinese discovered that lodestone (a type of iron ore) could be made to point north. They realized that they could magnetize needles to do the same. By about AD1000, they worked out the difference between true north and magnetic north and began using compasses to keep ships on course.

Gunpowder is another Chinese invention, from about AD850. At first it was used to blast rocks apart and to make fireworks. Later, it was used in warfare.

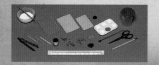

SHADE AND SHELTER
A Qing dynasty woman uses an umbrella as a sunshade to protect her skin. The Chinese invented umbrellas about 1,600 years ago and they soon spread throughout the rest of Asia. Umbrellas became fashionable with both women and men and were regarded as a symbol of high rank.

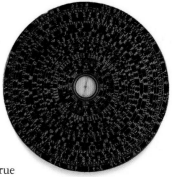

THE SAILOR'S FRIEND
The magnetic compass was invented in China around AD1–100. At first it was used as a planning aid to ensure new houses faced in a direction that was in harmony with nature. Later it was used to plot courses on long sea voyages.

MAKE A WHEELBARROW

You will need: thick card, ruler, pencil, scissors, compasses, 0.5cm diameter balsa strips, glue and brush, paintbrush, paint (black and brown), water pot, 3.5cm x 0.5cm dowel, 2cm diameter rubber washers (x4).

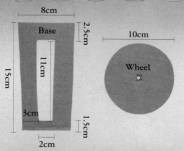

Base
8cm
2.5cm
11cm
15cm
3cm
1.5cm
2cm

10cm

Wheel

Using the measurements above, draw the pieces on to thick card. Draw the wheel with the compasses. Cut out pieces with scissors.

1 Cut 7cm, 8cm and 26cm (x2) balsa strips. Glue 7cm strip to short edge of base and 8cm strip to top edge. Glue 26cm strips to side of base.

SU SONG'S MASTERPIECE

This fantastic machine is a clock tower that can tell the time, chime the hours and follow the movement of the planets around the Sun. It was designed by an official called Su Song, in the city of Kaifeng in AD1092. The machine uses a mechanism called an escapement, which controls and regulates the timing of the clock. The escapement mechanism was invented in the AD700s by a Chinese inventor called Yi Xing.

EARTHQUAKE WARNING

The decorative object shown above is the scientist Zhang Heng's seismoscope. When there was an earthquake, a ball was released from one of the dragons and fell into a frog's mouth. This showed the direction of the vibrations. According to records, in AD138 the instrument detected a earth tremor some 500km away.

ONE-WHEELED TRANSPORT

In about AD100, the Chinese invented the wheelbarrow. They then designed a model with a large central wheel that could bear great weights. This became a form of transport, pushed along by muscle power.

The single wheelbarrow was used by farmers and gardeners. Traders wheeled their goods to market, then used the barrow as a stall. They sold a variety of goods, such as seeds, grain, plants and dried herbs.

2 Turn the base over. Cut two 2cm x 1cm pieces of thick card. Make a small hole in the middle of each, for the wheel axle. Glue pieces to base.

3 Use compasses and a pencil to draw 1 circle around centre of wheel and 1 close to the rim. Mark on spokes. Paint spaces between spokes black.

4 Paint the barrow, leave to dry. Cut two 7cm balsa strips with tapered ends to make legs, and paint them brown. When dry, glue to bottom of barrow.

5 Feed dowel axle between axle supports, via 2 washers, wheel, and 2 more washers. Dab glue on ends of axle to keep the wheel in place.

Extraordinary Chinese Engineering

THE ENGINEERING WONDER of ancient China was the Great Wall. It was known as *Wan Li Chang Cheng*, or the Wall of Ten Thousand *Li* (a unit of length). The Great Wall's main length was an incredible 6,400km. Work began on the wall in the 400s BC and lasted until the AD1500s. Its purpose was to protect China's borders from the fierce tribes who lived to the north. Despite this intention, Mongol invaders managed to breach its defences time after time. However, the Great Wall did serve as a useful communications route. It also extended the Chinese Empire's control over a very long distance.

The Grand Canal is another engineering project that amazes us today. It was started in the 400s BC, but was mostly built during the Sui Dynasty (AD581–618). Its aim was to link the north of China with the rice-growing regions in the south via the Chang Jiang (Yangzi River). It is still in use and runs northwards from Hangzhou to Beijing, a distance of 1,794 km. Other great engineering feats were made by Chinese mining engineers, who were already digging deep mine shafts with drainage and ventilation systems in about 160BC.

LIFE IN THE SALT MINES
Workers busily excavate and purify salt from an underground mine. Inside a tower *(shown bottom left)* you can see workers using a pulley to raise baskets of mined salt. The picture comes from a relief (raised carving) found inside a Han dynasty tomb in the province of Sichuan.

MINING ENGINEERING
A Qing Dynasty official tours an open-cast coalmine in the 1800s. China has rich natural resources and may have been the first country in the world to mine coal to burn as a fuel. Coal was probably discovered in about 200BC in what is now Jiangxi province. Other mines extracted metals and valuable minerals needed for the great empire. In the Han dynasty, engineers invented methods of drilling boreholes to extract brine (salty water) from the ground. They also used derricks (rigid frameworks) to support iron drills – over 1,800 years before engineers in other parts of the world.

HARD LABOUR

Chinese peasants use their spades to dig roads instead of fields. Imperial China produced its great building and engineering works without the machines we rely on today. For big projects, workforces could number hundreds of thousands. Dangerous working conditions and a harsh climate killed many labourers.

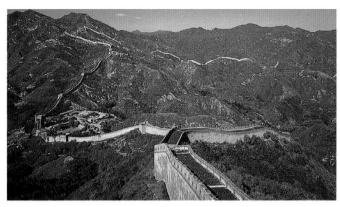

BUILDING THE WALL

The Great Wall snakes over mountain ridges at Badaling, to the northwest of Beijing. The Great Wall and Grand Canal were built by millions of workers. All men aged between 23 and 56 were called up to work on them for one month each year. Only noblemen and civil servants were exempt.

A GRAND OPENING

This painting from the 1700s imagines the Sui emperor Yangdi opening the first stage of the Grand Canal. Most of the work on this massive engineering project was carried out from AD605–609. A road was also built along the route. The transport network built up during the Sui dynasty (AD561–618) enabled food and other supplies to be moved easily from one part of the empire to another.

THE CITY OF SIX THOUSAND BRIDGES

The reports about China supposedly made by Marco Polo in the 1200s described 6,000 bridges in the city of Suzhou. The Baodai Bridge (*shown above*) is one of them. It has 53 arches and was built between AD618 and AD906 to run across the Grand Canal.

Chinese Science

Fʀᴏᴍ ᴛʜᴇ Cʜɪɴᴇꜱᴇ Eᴍᴘɪʀᴇ's earliest days, scholars published studies on medicine, astronomy and mathematics. The Chinese system of medicine had a similar aim to that of Daoist teachings, in that it attempted to make the body work harmoniously. The effects of all kinds of herbs, plants and animal parts were studied and then used to produce medicines. Acupuncture, which involves piercing the body with fine needles, was practised from about 2700ʙᴄ. It is believed to release blocked channels of energy and so relieve pain.

The Chinese were also excellent mathematicians, and from 300ʙᴄ they used a decimal system of counting based on tens. They may have invented the abacus, an early form of calculator, as well. In about 3000ʙᴄ, Chinese astronomers produced a detailed chart of the heavens carved in stone. Later, they were the first to record observations of sunspots and exploding stars.

NEW ILLS, OLD REMEDIES
A pharmacist weighs out a traditional medicine. Hundreds of medicines used in China today go back to ancient times. Many are herbal remedies later proved to work by scientists. Doctors are still researching their uses. Other traditional medicines are of less certain value, but are still popular purchases at street stalls.

PRICKING POINTS
Acupuncturists used charts to show exactly where to position their needles. The vital *qi* (energy) is thought to flow through the body along 12 lines called meridians. The health of the patient is judged by taking their pulse. Chinese acupuncture is practised all over the world today.

MAKE AN ABACUS
You will need: thick and thin card, ruler, pencil, scissors, wood glue and brush, masking tape, self-drying clay, cutting board, modelling tool, 30cm x 0.5cm dowel (x11), paintbrush, water pot, brown paint.

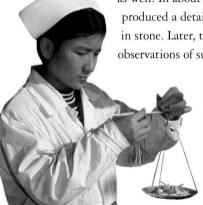

Side A (x2) — 32cm — 3cm
Edge A (x2) — 32cm — 0.5cm
Side B (x2) — 30cm / 16cm — 3cm
Edge B (x2) — 16cm / 15cm — 0.5cm — 32cm
Base — 32cm / 16cm
Divider — 30cm / Divider edge / 3cm / 0.5cm

Using the above measurements, cut out pieces from thick brown card and thin grey card. (pieces not shown to scale).

1 Glue sides A and B to the base. Hold the edges with masking tape until dry. Then glue edges A and B to the tops of the sides, as shown.

2 Roll the clay into a 2cm diameter sausage. Cut it into 77 small, flat beads. Make a hole through the centre of each bead with a dowel.

A STREET DOCTOR PEDDLES HIS WARES
This European view of Chinese medicine dates from 1843.
It shows snakes and all sorts of unusual potions being sold on
the streets. The doctor is telling the crowd of miraculous cures.

NATURAL HEALTH
Roots, seeds, leaves and flowers
have been used in Chinese medicine
for over 2,000 years. Today, nine out
of ten Chinese medicines are herbal
remedies. The Chinese yam is used
to treat exhaustion. Ginseng root is
used to help treat dizzy spells,
while mulberry wood is said to
lower blood pressure.

Chinese yam

ginseng root

BURNING CURES
A country doctor
treats a patient with
traditional techniques
during the Song
dynasty. Chinese
doctors relieved pain
by heating parts of the
body with the burning
leaves of a plant called
moxa (mugwort).
The process is
called moxibustion.

*The abacus is an ancient
counting frame that acts as
a simple but very effective
calculator. Using an abacus,
Chinese mathematicians
and merchants could carry
out very difficult
calculations quickly
and easily.*

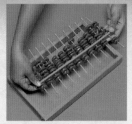

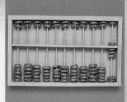

3 Make 11 evenly spaced holes
in the divider. Edge one side
with thin card. Thread a dowel
through each hole. Paint all of
the abacus parts. Leave to dry.

4 Thread 7 beads on to each
dowel rod – 2 on the upper
side of the divider, 5 on the
lower. Carefully fit the beads
and rods into the main frame.

5 Each upper bead on the
abacus equals 5 lower beads
in the same column. Each lower
bead is worth 10 of the lower
beads in the column to its right.

6 Here is a simple sum. To
calculate 5+3, first move
down one upper bead (worth 5).
Then move 3 lower beads in the
same column up (each worth 1).

Specialist Crafts in Japan

FROM ANCIENT TIMES, the finest quality craftsmanship was important in Japan. Although paper was invented in China, in 105AD, when the Japanese started papermaking 500 years later, they raised it to a craft of the highest level. Different papers were made into both luxury and everyday objects – from wall-screens and lanterns to clothes, windows and partitions in houses.

Working with wood was another Japanese speciality. Doorways, pillars and roofs on most large Japanese buildings, such as temples and palaces, were elaborately carved or painted, or even gilded. Inside, beams and pillars were made from strong tree trunks, floors were laid with polished wooden strips, and sliding screens had fine wooden frames. A display of woodworking skill in a building demonstrated the owner's wealth and power. However, some smaller wooden buildings were left deliberately plain, allowing the quality of the materials and craftsmanship, and the elegance of the design, to speak for themselves.

WOODEN STATUES
This statue of a Buddhist god was carved between AD800 and 900. Many powerful sculptures were inspired by religion at this time.

SCREENS WITH SCENES
Screens were movable works of art as well as providing privacy and protection from draughts. This screen of the 1700s shows Portuguese merchants and missionaries listening to Japanese musicians.

ORIGAMI BOX
You will need: a square of origami paper (15cm x 15cm), clean and even folding surface.

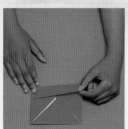

1 Place your paper on a flat surface. Fold it horizontally across the centre. Next fold it vertically across the centre and unfold.

2 Carefully fold each corner to the centre point as shown. Unfold each corner crease before starting to make the next one.

3 Using the creases, fold all the corners back into the centre. Now fold each side 2cm from the edge to make a crease and then unfold.

GRAND PILLARS

This row of red wooden pillars supports a heavy, ornate roof. It is part of the Meiji Shrine in Tokyo. Red (or cinnabar) was the traditional Japanese colour for shrines and royal palaces.

HOLY LIGHTS

Lamps of pleated paper were often hung outside Shinto shrines. They were painted with the names of people who had donated money to the shrines.

PAPER ART

Paper-making and calligraphy (beautiful writing) were two very important craft forms in Japan. These people have everything they need to decorate scrolls. Fine paper showed off a letter-writer's elegance and good taste.

PAPER RANGE

For artists such as the painter of this picture, Ando Hiroshige (1797-1858), the choice of paper was as important as the painting itself. The Japanese developed a great range of specialist papers.

Making boxes is a specialist craft in Japan. Boxes were used for storing all sorts of possessions.

4 Carefully unfold two opposite side panels. Your origami box should now look like the structure shown in the picture above.

5 Following the crease marks you have already made, turn in the side panels to make walls, as shown in the picture. Turn the origami round 90˚.

6 Use your fingers to push the corners of the third side in, as shown. Use the existing crease lines as a guide. Raise the box slightly and fold the wall over.

7 Next, carefully repeat step 6 to construct the final wall. You could try making another origami box to perfect your technique.

Fine Celtic Crafts

THE CELTS WERE A PROUD people to whom appearance was important. Beautiful objects carried important messages about their owner's wealth and power. From written descriptions of their clothes, we know that the Celts were skilled weavers and dyers. While the Roman invaders of their lands wore togas and tunics, the Celtic men were wearing trousers. Celtic craftworkers made finely worked jewellery, applying their expert glassmaking, enamelling and metalworking skills. They were also excellent potters. Some decorations have magic or religious meanings to protect people from harm or to inspire warriors setting off to war.

We do not know much about the craftworkers themselves. They may have been free and independent or the skilled slaves of wealthy families. However, towards the end of the Celtic period, around 60BC, many craftworkers worked in *oppida* (fortified towns) instead of in country villages.

SMOOTH AND SHAPELY

Tall, graceful vases with smoothly curving sides were a speciality of Celtic potters working in France. They date mostly from the La Tène era (450–50BC). Pots like these were produced on a potter's wheel. They were prestige goods, produced for wealthy or noble families.

ANGULAR ART

During the Hallstatt era (750–450BC), Celtic potters decorated their wares with spiky, angular designs like the patterns on this pottery dish. After about 500BC, when compasses were introduced into Celtic lands from countries near the Mediterranean Sea, designs based on curves and circles began to replace patterns made up of angles and straight lines.

MAKE A TORC

You will need: board, modelling clay, ruler, string, scissors, PVA glue and brush, gold or bronze paint, paintbrush.

1 On the board, roll out two lengths of modelling clay, as shown. Each length should be approximately 60cm long and about 1cm thick.

2 Keeping the two lengths of clay on the board, plait them together. Leave about 5cm of the clay unplaited at either end, as shown.

3 Make loops out of the free ends by joining them together. Dampen the ends with a little water to help join the clay if necessary.

PRECIOUS BOX

This gold and silver box was made in Scotland and was designed to hold Christian holy relics. It was associated with the Irish monk and Christian missionary St Columba. After the saint's death, it was kept as a lucky talisman (charm), and carried into battle by Scottish armies.

GLASS JEWELS

Glass was made from salt, crushed limestone and sand, and coloured by adding powdered minerals. Craftworkers melted and twisted different coloured strands together to make jewel-like beads. Glass paste was applied to metalwork and fired to bond it to the metal in a process called enamelling.

manganese   *glass*   *cobalt*   *lead*

MAKING WAVES

The sides of this pot are decorated with a moulded pattern of overlapping waves. The pot has survived unbroken from the La Tène era over 2,000 years ago. It was found in France and it is made from fired clay. Celtic potters built elaborate kilns to fire (bake) their pots at high temperatures.

ELEGANT ENAMEL

This bronze plaque is decorated with red and yellow enamel. It was made in southern Britain around 50BC and was designed to be worn on a horse's harness.

4 With the ruler, measure an opening between the two looped ends. The ends should be about 9cm apart so that the torc fits easily around your neck.

5 When the torc is semi-dry, cut two pieces of string about 8cm long. Use the string to decorate the torc's looped ends. Glue the string in place.

6 Allow the clay to dry completely. When it is hard, cover all the clay and string with gold or bronze paint. Leave to dry.

Torcs were status symbols for the Celtic people. They were made from precious metals such as iron, bronze and gold.

Celtic Metalworkers

Celtic metalworkers excelled in several different techniques. They were among the most important people in Celtic society because they made many of the items that Celtic people valued most, from bronze and iron swords to beautiful gold jewellery. Patterns and techniques invented in one part of the Celtic world were copied and quickly spread to other parts. Designs were sketched on to the back of the metal, then gently hammered from beneath to create raised patterns. The technique was called repoussé (pushed out).

It took several years to learn all the necessary skills, and metalworkers probably began their training very young. They extracted iron from raw nuggets or lumps of ore in a very hot fire, and then forged the red-hot metal into shape. The Celts were the first to shoe horses, and invented seamless iron rims for chariot wheels to strengthen them.

PUSHED OUT DESIGN
This bronze shieldboss was made between about 200BC and 10BC. A boss is the metal plate that was fixed to the centre of a shield to protect the hand of the person holding it. The raised pattern was created by pressing out the design in the thin covering sheet of metal from behind. The technique is called repoussé (pushed out).

TOOLS OF THE TRADE
Many bronze items, such as this horse's bit (below) and harness-ring (far left), were made by pouring molten metal into clay moulds, then leaving it to cool and become solid. You can also see fragments of the clay moulds, and the little crucible used for melting the bronze (top left).

MAKE A MIRROR

You will need: pair of compasses, pencil, ruler, stiff gold mirror card, scissors, tracing paper, pen, modelling clay, board, gold paint, paintbrush, PVA glue.

1 With the compasses, draw a circle 22 cm wide on to gold card. Cut out. Use this circle as a template to draw a second circle on to gold card.

2 Cut out the second gold circle. Draw another circle on tracing paper. Fold the piece of tracing paper in two and draw a Celtic pattern in pencil.

3 Lay the tracing paper on to one of the circles. Trace the pattern on to half of the gold circle, then turn the paper over and repeat. Go over the pattern with a pen.

From Earth and Sea

The most valuable materials for metalworking were difficult and sometimes dangerous to find. Silver ore was dug from mines underground, or from veins in rocks on the surface. Miners searched for nuggets of gold in gravel at the bottom of fast-flowing streams. Swimmers and divers hunted for coral that grew on little reefs in the Mediterranean Sea.

bronze ore

coral

gold nuggets

Bands of Gold

The Celts of the Hallstatt era (750–450BC) liked to wear bold, dramatic jewellery, such as the armband and ankle rings shown here. They were found in a tomb in central France. Both the armband and the ankle rings were made of sheets of pure gold and twisted gold wire which were carefully hammered and soldered together.

Delicate Design

This clothing toggle was created using the lost wax method of casting. The shape of the piece was modelled in beeswax, then the fine details were added. The wax model was covered with a thick layer of clay. Then the clay-covered model was heated, and the wax ran out. Finally, molten gold was poured into the space where the wax had been.

Tools of the Trade

These little bone spatulas (knives for scooping and spreading) were used by metalworkers to add fine details to the surface of wax models when casting bronze objects using the lost wax process.

The bronze on a Celtic mirror would have polished up so that the owner could see his or her reflection in it.

4 Roll out several snakes of modelling clay and sculpt them into a handle, as shown here. The handle should be about 15 cm long and 9 cm wide.

5 Leave the modelling clay to dry. Then paint one side of the handle with gold paint. Leave to dry, then turn over and paint the other side.

6 Stick the two pieces of mirror card together, white side to white side. Glue the handle on to one side of the mirror.

Viking Crafts

SNARL OF THE DRAGON
This masterpiece of wood carving and metalwork is a dragon-head post. It is from the Oseberg ship burial in Norway and dates from about 850. Its patterns include monsters known as 'gripping beasts'.

IN EVERY VIKING HOME, people turned their hand to craft work. The men made and repaired tools and weapons. They carved walrus ivory and wood during long winter evenings.

The women made woollen cloth. They washed and combed the wool and then placed it on a long stick called a distaff. The wool was pulled out and spun into yarn on a whirling stick called a spindle. The yarn was woven on a loom, a large upright frame.

Blacksmiths' furnaces roared and hammers clanged against anvils as the metal was shaped and re-shaped. Professional craftworkers worked gold, silver, bronze and pewter – a mixture of tin and lead. They made fine jewellery from amber and from a glassy black stone called jet. Beautiful objects were carved from antlers and ivory from the tusks of walruses. Homes, and later churches, had beautiful wood carvings. Patterns included swirling loops and knots, and birds and animals interlaced with writhing snakes and strange monsters.

SILVER SWIRLS
Can you see a snake and a beast in the design of this silver brooch? The Vikings were very fond of silver and collected hoardes of coins, ornaments, silver ingots and jewellery from their raids.

MAKE A SILVER BRACELET

You will need: tape measure, self-drying clay, board, scissors, white cord or string, modelling tool, silver acrylic paint, paintbrush, water pot.

1 Measure your wrist with the tape measure to see how big your bracelet should be. Allow room for it to pass over your hand, but not fall off.

2 Roll the clay between the palms of your hand. Make three snakes that are just longer than your wrist measurement. Try to make them of equal thickness.

3 Lay out the three snakes on the board in a fan shape. Cut two lengths of white cord, a bit longer than the snakes, and place them in between.

COLOURS FOR CLOTH

Woollen cloth was dyed in bold colours from leaves, roots, bark and flowers. A wildflower called weld, or dyer's rocket, was used for its yellow dye. The root of the madder gave a red dye. Bright blue came from the leaves of woad plants.

woad   *madder*

THE SMITH AT WORK

This fine wood carving comes from a church in Urnes, Norway. It shows Regin the blacksmith forging a sword on an anvil, for the legendary hero Sigurd. The smith is using bellows to heat up the furnace. The skills of metal working were so important in ancient times that smiths were often seen as magical figures or gods.

TOOLS FROM THE FORGE

Viking blacksmiths used hammers for beating and shaping metal. Tongs were used for handling red-hot iron. Shears were for cutting metal sheets. The blacksmith made everything from nails and knives to farm tools.

Vikings liked to show off their wealth and rank by wearing expensive gold and silver jewellery.

4 While the clay is still soft, plait the snakes of clay and the two cords together. Ask an adult to help if you are not sure how to make a plait.

5 Trim each end of the plait with a modelling tool. At each end, press the strands firmly together and secure with a small clay snake, as shown above.

6 Carefully curl the bracelet round so that it will fit neatly over your wrist, without joining the ends. Leave it in a safe place to harden and dry.

7 When the bracelet is completely dry, paint it silver. Cover the work surface if necessary. Leave the bracelet to dry again – then try it on!

Mesoamerican Time

DIFFERENT CULTURES and civilizations devised different ways of splitting the year into seasons. The Egyptian calendar, based on a 365-day year, was linked to the annual flooding of the River Nile. The Maya and Aztec peoples in Mesoamerica had three different calendars. One, based on a 260-day year, was probably based on the time a baby spends in the womb. It was divided into 13 cycles of 20 days each. The calendar followed by Mesoamerican farmers was based on the movements of the Sun, because the seasons made their crops grow. Its 360-day year was divided into 18 months of 20 days, with five extra days that were considered unlucky. Every 52 years, measured in modern time, the two calendars ended on the same day. For five days before the end of the 52 years, people feared the world might end. There was a third calendar, of 584 days, used for calculating festival days.

SUN STONE
This massive carving was made to display the Aztec view of creation. The Aztecs believed that the world had already been created and destroyed four times and that their Fifth World was also doomed.

STUDYING THE STARS
The Caracol was constructed as an observatory to study the sky. From there, Maya astronomers could observe the planet Venus, which was important in the Mesoamericans' measurement of time.

MAKE A SUN STONE
You will need: pencil, scissors, thick card, self-drying clay, modelling tool, board, rolling pin, masking tape, PVA glue, glue brush, water bowl, pencil, thin card, water-based paints, paintbrush, water pot.

1 Cut a circle about 25cm in diameter from thick card. Roll out the clay and cut out a circle, using the card as a guide. Place the clay circle on the card one.

2 With a modelling tool, mark a small circle in the centre of the clay circle. Use a roll of masking tape as a guide. Do not cut through the clay.

3 Carve the Sun-god's eyes, mouth, teeth and earrings. You can use the real Aztec Sun stone, shown at the top left of this page, as a guide.

alligator

wind

house

lizard

serpent

death's head

deer

rabbit

water

dog

monkey

grass

reed

jaguar

eagle

vulture

motion

flint knife

rain

flower

NAMES OF DAYS

These pictures from an Aztec codex show the 20 names for days from the farmers' calendar. These symbols were combined with a number from one to 13 to give the date, such as Three Vulture. The days were named after familiar creatures or everyday things, such as the lizard or water. Each day also had its own god. Children were often named after the day on which they were born, a custom that still continues in some parts of Mexico up to the present day.

Your finished Sun stone will not be as big as the original Aztec one. That measures 4m across and is the largest Aztec sculpture discovered so far.

4 Roll out more clay and cut out some Sun's rays, a tongue and eyebrows. Glue them to the clay circle. Smooth the edges with water and leave to dry.

5 Copy the 20 Aztec symbols (*above*) for days on to squares of thin card. The card squares should be no more than 2cm x 2cm. Cut out. Paint brown.

6 Cover the clay circle with a thin coat of dark brown paint. Leave it to dry. Then add a thin coat of white paint to make the circle look like stone.

7 Glue the card symbols evenly around the edge of the clay circle, as shown. Paint the Sun stone with a thin layer of PVA glue to seal and varnish it.

Practical Incas

T HOUGH THE INCAS were known for their fine work in precious metals, they also found practical solutions to more everyday needs. They built 24,000km of roads through the mountains of their empire. Their main buildings constructed from giant, many-sided blocks of stone all perfectly interlocking, were earthquake-proof.

Although there was no iron in the mountains, the Incas used many other materials for everyday items. Reeds were woven into baskets and mats from early prehistoric times. Bone, stone and wood were carved into small items such as bowls, pins, spoons and figures. Pottery was made in Peru from about 2000BC, rather later than in the lands to the north and east, and revolutionized the production, storage, transportation and cooking of food. South American potters did not use a wheel to shape their pots, but built them up in layers from coils of clay. The coils were smoothed out by hand or with tools, marked or painted, dried in the sun and then baked hard.

Many of the pre-Incan civilizations of the Andes produced beautifully patterned pottery.

POLISHED WOOD

This fine black *kero* (drinking vessel) was made by an Inca craftsman. It is of carved and polished wood. Timber was always scarce in the Inca Empire, but wood was widely used to make plates and cups. Rearing up over the rim of the beaker is a fierce-looking big cat, perhaps a puma or a jaguar.

MODELLED FROM CLAY

A fierce puma bares his teeth. He was made from pottery between AD500 and 800. The hole in his back was used to waft clouds of incense during religious ceremonies in the city of Tiwanaku, near Lake Titicaca.

A TIWANAKU POTTERY JAGUAR

You will need: chicken wire, wire-cutters, ruler, newspaper, scissors, pva glue, masking tape, flour, water, card, paint, water pot, paintbrush.

1 Cut a rectangle of chicken wire about 14cm long and 20cm wide. Carefully wrap it around to form a sausage shape. Close one end neatly.

2 Squeeze the other end of the sausage to form the jaguar's neck and head. Fold over the wire at the end to make a neat, round shape for his nose.

3 Make rolls of newspaper about 2.5cm long to form the jaguar's legs. Use strips of paper and glue to join them securely to the jaguar's body as shown.

PRETTY POLLY

This pottery jar, like many from Peru, comes with a handle and a spout. It is shaped and painted to look like a parrot and was made, perhaps 1,000 years before the Incas, by the Nazca potters of southern Peru.

IN THE POTTER'S WORKSHOP

The potter needed a good supply of sticky clay and plenty of water. He also needed large supplies of firewood or dung for fuel. The potter would knead the clay until it was soft and workable. Sometimes he would mix in sand or crushed shells from the coast to help strengthen the clay. Colours for painting the pottery were made from plants and minerals.

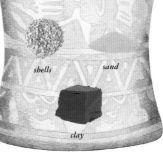

shells   sand

clay

WATER OF LIFE

This Inca bottle is carved with a figure inside a tower collecting water. No community could survive very long without a good supply of fresh water. Many pots, bottles and beakers from the South American civilizations are decorated with light-hearted scenes of everyday activities. They give us a vivid idea of how people used to live.

The handle and spout design of your Tiwanaku jaguar is known as a stirrup pot, because the arrangement looks rather like the stirrup of a horse.

4 Mix the flour and water to a paste. Use it to glue a layer of newspaper strips all over the jaguar's body. Allow this layer to dry. You will need 3 layers.

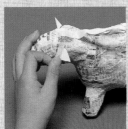

5 Cut ears from card. Fix on with masking tape. Tape on rolls of newspaper to make the handle, spout and tail as in the finished pot above.

6 Leave the model in a warm and airy place to dry. Then paint it all over with reddish brown paint. Allow the paint to dry completely.

7 Use black paint and a fine brush to decorate the jaguar as shown in the picture. When the paint is dry, varnish with pva glue if you wish.

Inca Mining and Metalwork

THERE WERE RESOURCES OF gold and silver in the Andes mountains and the Inca peoples became expert at working these precious metals into fabulous vessels, jewellery and life-sized figures of animals. Copper was mined for weapons. Metalworkers were highly respected members of Inca communities. A stone bowl that was discovered in the Andahuaylas Valley was nearly 3,500 years old. It contained metalworking equipment and finely beaten gold foil.

The Incas often referred to gold as 'sweat of the Sun' and to silver as 'tears of the Moon'. These metals were sacred to the gods and also to the Inca emperor and empress. At the Temple of the Sun in the city of Cuzco, there was a whole garden made of gold and silver, with golden soil, golden stalks of maize and golden llamas. Copper was used by ordinary people. It was made into cheap jewellery, weapons and everyday tools. The Incas' love of gold and silver eventually led to their downfall, for it was rumours of their fabulous wealth that lured the Spanish to invade the region.

A SICAN LORD

This ceremonial knife with its crescent-shaped blade is called a *tumi*. Its gold handle is made in the shape of a nobleman or ruler. He wears an elaborate headdress and large discs in his ears. It was made between 1100 and 1300. The knife is in the style of the Sican civilization, which grew up after the decline of the Moche civilization in the AD700s.

A CHIMÚ DOVE

Chimú goldsmiths, the best in the Empire, made this plump dove. When the Incas conquered Chimor in 1470, they forced many thousands of skilled craftsmen from the city of Chan Chan to resettle in the Cuzco area and continue their work.

A TUMI KNIFE

You will need: card, ruler, pencil, scissors, self-drying clay, cutting board, rolling pin, modelling and cutting tools, PVA glue, gold paint, paintbrush, water pot, blue metallic paper.

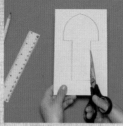

1 On card, draw a knife shape as shown and cut it out. The rectangular part should be 9cm x 3.5cm. The rounded part is 7cm across and 4.5cm high.

2 Roll out a slab of clay about 1cm thick. Draw a *tumi* shape on it as shown. It should be 12.5cm long and measure 9cm across the widest part at the top.

3 Use the cutting tool to cut around the shape you have drawn. Carefully take away the leftover clay. Make sure the edges are clean and smooth.

MINERAL WEALTH

To this day, the Andes are very rich in minerals. The Incas worked with gold, silver, platinum and copper. They knew how to make alloys, which are mixtures of different metals. Bronze was made by mixing copper and tin. However, unlike their Spanish conquerors, the Incas knew nothing of iron and steel. This put them at a disadvantage when fighting the Europeans.

copper *silver*

gold

PANNING FOR GOLD

A boy labourer in modern Colombia pans for gold. Some Inca gold was mined, but large amounts also came from panning mountain rivers and streams in the Andes. The river bed was loosened with sticks, and then the water was sifted through shallow trays in search of any flecks of the precious metal that had been washed downstream.

INCA FIGURES

Small ritual figures of women and men from about 6cm high were often made in the Inca period. They were hammered from sheets of silver and gold and were dressed in miniature versions of adult clothing. They have been found on mountain-top shrine sites in the south-central Andes, in carved stone boxes in Lake Titicaca and at important temples.

The Chimú gold and turquoise tumi was used by priests at religious ceremonies. It may have been used to kill sacrifices.

4 Cut a slot into the bottom edge of the clay shape. Lifting it carefully, slide the knife blade into the slot. Use glue to make the joint secure.

5 Use a modelling tool to mark the details of the god on to the clay. Look at the finished knife above to see how to do this. Leave everything to dry.

6 When the clay has hardened, paint the whole knife with gold paint. Leave it to dry completely before painting the other side as well.

7 The original knife was decorated with turquoise. Glue small pieces of blue metallic paper on to the handle as shown in the picture above.

Inca Medicine and Magic

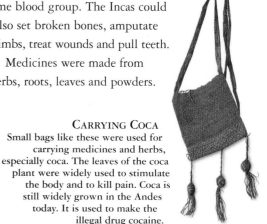

LIKE MOST PEOPLES in the world five hundred years ago, the Incas and their neighbours had some idea of science or medicine. However, curing people was believed to be chiefly a matter of religious rituals and magical spells. No doubt some of these did help people to feel better. Curing sick people was the job either of priests, or of the local healer or medicine man.

As in Europe at that time, Inca healers used fasting and blood-letting (allowing blood to flow from a cut) for many cures. They also tried blood transfusion (putting new blood into someone's body). They succeeded in this far earlier than doctors in other parts of the world, because peoples of the Andes shared the same blood group. The Incas could also set broken bones, amputate limbs, treat wounds and pull teeth. Medicines were made from herbs, roots, leaves and powders.

THE MEDICINE MAN
This Moche healer or priest, from about AD500, seems to be going into a trance and listening to the voices of spirits or gods. He may be trying to cure a sick patient, or he may be praying over the patient's dead body.

MAGIC DOLLS
Model figures like this one, made from cotton and reed, are often found in ancient graves in the Chancay River region. They are often called dolls, but it seems unlikely that they were ever used as toys. They were probably believed to have magical qualities. The Chancay people may have believed that the dolls helped the dead person in another world.

CARRYING COCA
Small bags like these were used for carrying medicines and herbs, especially coca. The leaves of the coca plant were widely used to stimulate the body and to kill pain. Coca is still widely grown in the Andes today. It is used to make the illegal drug cocaine.

MEDICINE BAG

You will need: scissors, cream calico fabric, pencil, ruler, paintbrush, water pot, acrylic or fabric paints, black, yellow, green and red wool, PVA glue, needle and thread, masking tape.

1 Cut two 20cm squares of fabric. Draw a pattern of stripes and diamonds on the fabric and use acrylic or fabric paints to colour them.

2 For the tassels, cut about 10 pieces of wool 8cm long. Fold a piece of wool 15cm long in half. Loop it around each tassel as shown above.

3 Wind a matching piece of wool, 50cm long, around the end of the tassel. When you have finished, knot the wool and tuck the ends inside.

HERBAL REMEDIES

Drugs widely used in ancient Peru included the leaves of tobacco and coca plants. A yellow-flowered plant called calceolaria was used to cure infections. Cinchona bark produced quinine, a medicine we use today to treat malaria. That illness only arrived in South America after the Spanish conquest. However, quinine was used earlier to treat fevers. Suppliers of herbal medicines were known as *hampi kamayuq*.

cinchona tree *tobacco plant*

SKULL SURGERY

Nazca surgeons were able to carry out an operation called trepanation. This involved drilling a hole in the patient's skull in an attempt to relieve pressure on the brain. The Incas believed this released evil spirits. A small silver plate was sometimes fitted over the hole as a protection.

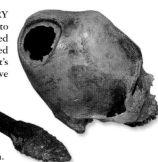

Doctor on call! An Inca medicine chest took the form of a woven bag, carried on the shoulder.

A BAD OMEN

A comet shoots across the night sky. The Incas believed such sights would bring plague or disease in their wake. Other common causes of illness were believed to include witchcraft, evil spirits and a failure to please the gods. People tried to make themselves better by making offerings to the gods at *waq'as (*local shrines). Healers used charms or spells to keep their patients free from evil spirits.

4 Make nine tassels in all. Place them in groups of three along the bottom of the unpainted side of one of the pieces of fabric. Use glue to fix them in place.

5 Allow the glue to dry. Place the unpainted sides of the fabric pieces together. Sew around the edges as shown. Leave the top edge open.

6 Make a strap by plaiting together strands of wool as shown. Cross each outer strand in turn over the middle strand. Tape will help keep the work steady.

7 Knot the ends of the strap firmly. Attach them to both sides of the top of the bag with glue. Make sure the glue is dry before you pick the bag up.

Calculations Inca-style

INCA MATHEMATICIANS used a decimal system, counting in tens. To help with their arithmetic, people placed pebbles or grains of maize in counting frames. These had up to twenty sections. *Quipu* strings were also used to record numbers. Strings were knotted to represent units, tens, hundreds, thousands or even tens of thousands.

The Incas worked out calendars of twelve months by observing the Sun, Moon and stars as they moved across the sky. They knew that these movements marked regular changes in the seasons. They used the calendar to tell them when to plant crops. Inca priests set up stone pillars outside the city of Cuzco to measure the movements of the Sun.

As in Europe at that time, astronomy, the study of the stars, was confused with astrology, which is the belief that the stars and planets influence human lives. Incas saw the night sky as being lit up by gods and mythical characters.

FORTUNES FROM THE STARS AND PLANETS
An Inca astrologer observes the position of the Sun. The Incas believed that careful watching of the stars and planets revealed their influence on our lives. For example, the star pattern or constellation that we call the Lyre was known to the Incas as the Llama. It was believed that it influenced llamas and those who herded them.

THE SUN STONE
A stone pillar called *Inti Watana* (Tethering Post of the Sun) stood at the eastern edge of the great square in Machu Picchu. It was like a giant sundial and the shadows it cast confirmed the movements of the Sun across the sky – a matter of great practical and religious importance.

A QUIPU

You will need: scissors, rope and string of various thicknesses, a 90cm length of thick rope, paints, paintbrush, water pot.

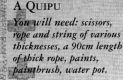

1 Cut the rope and string into about 15 lengths measuring from 20cm to 80cm. Paint them in various bright colours. Leave them to dry completely.

2 To make the top part of the *quipu*, take a piece of thick rope, about 90cm long. Tie a knot in each end as shown in the picture above.

3 Next, take pieces of thinner rope or string of various lengths and colours. Tie them along the thicker rope, so that they all hang on the same side.

THE MILKY WAY

On dark nights, Inca priests looked for the band of stars that we call the Milky Way. They called it *Mayu* (Heavenly River) and used it to make calculations about seasons and weather conditions. In its darker spaces they saw the shadow of the Rain god Apu Illapu. The shape of the Milky Way was believed to mirror that of the Inca Empire.

SUN WATCH

The *Inti Watana* (Tethering Post of the Sun) at Machu Picchu was one of many Sun stones across the Empire. *Sukana* (stone pillars) near Cuzco showed midsummer and midwinter sun positions. The Sun god, Inti, was believed to live in the north and go south each summer.

KEEPERS OF THE QUIPU

Vast amounts of information could be stored on a *quipu*. A large one might have up to 2,000 cords. The *quipu* was rather like an Inca version of the computer, only the memory had to be provided by the operator's brain rather than a silicon chip. Learning the *quipu* code of colours, knots, and major and minor strings took many years. Expert operators were called *quipu-kamayuq*.

You have now designed a simple quipu. *Can you imagine designing a system that would record the entire population of a town, their ages, the taxes they have paid and the taxes they owe? The Incas did just that!*

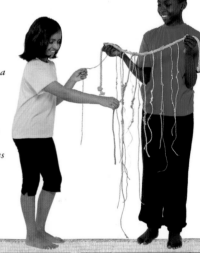

4 Tie knots in the thinner ropes or strings. One knot you might like to try begins by making a loop of rope as shown in the picture above.

5 Pass one end of the rope through the loop. Pull the rope taut but don't let go of the loop. Repeat this step until you have a long knot. Pull it tight.

6 Make different sizes of knots on all the ropes or strings. Each knot could represent a family member, school lesson or other important detail.

7 Add some more strings to the knotted strings. Your *quipu* may be seen by lots of people. Only you will know what the ropes, strings and knots mean!

Tribal Crafts in North America

NORTH AMERICAN INDIANS were expert craftsmen and women. Beautiful pots have been found dating back to around 1000BC. The people of the Southwest were renowned for their pottery. Black and white Mimbres bowls were known as burial pots because they were broken when their owner died and buried along with the body. Baskets and blankets were the other most important crafts. The ancient Anasazis were known as the basket-making culture because of the

range of baskets they produced. Some were coiled so tightly they could hold water. The Apaches coiled large, flat baskets from willow and plant fibre, and the Paiutes made cone baskets, which were hung on their backs for collecting food. All North American Indians made use of the materials they had to hand such as wood, bark, shells, porcupine quills, feathers, bones, metals, hide and clay.

BASKET WEAVER
A native Arizona woman is creating a traditional coiled basket. It might be used for holding food or to wear on someone's head. Tlingit and Nootka tribes from the Northwest Coast were among those who wore cone-shaped basket hats.

POTTERY
Zuni people in the Southwest created beautiful pots such as this one. They used baskets as moulds for the clay or coiled thin rolls of clay around in a spiral. Afterwards, they smoothed out the surface with water. Birds and animals were favourite decorations.

DRILLING WALRUS TUSKS
An Inuit craftsman is working on a piece of ivory. He is using a drill to etch a pattern. The drill bit is kept firmly in place by his chin. This way, his hands are free to move the bow in a sawing action, pushing the drill point into the ivory.

MAKE A TANKARD
You will need: air-drying modelling clay, board, water in pot, pencil, ruler, cream or white and black poster paints or acrylic paints, fine and ordinary paintbrushes, non-toxic varnish.

1 Roll out a round slab of clay and press it into a flat circle with a diameter of about 10cm. Now, roll out two long sausage shapes of clay.

2 Slightly dampen the edges of the clay circle. Place one end of the clay sausage on the edge of the circle and coil it around. Carry on spiralling around.

3 Continue coiling with the other clay sausage. Then, use your dampened fingers to smooth the coils into a good tankard shape and smooth the outside.

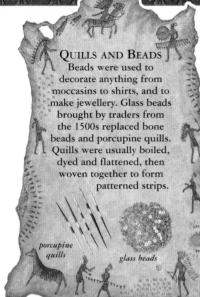

QUILLS AND BEADS

Beads were used to decorate anything from moccasins to shirts, and to make jewellery. Glass beads brought by traders from the 1500s replaced bone beads and porcupine quills. Quills were usually boiled, dyed and flattened, then woven together to form patterned strips.

porcupine quills

glass beads

TALKING BLANKET

It could take half a year for a Tlingit woman to make one of the famous Chilkat blankets. She wove cedar bark fibre and mountain goat wool with her fingers. The Tlingits said that if you knew how to listen, the blankets could talk.

FRUITS OF THE LOOM

Striped blankets were the speciality of Indians in the Southwest. This Hopi woman is using an upright loom made from poles. Pueblo people were the first North American Indians to weave like this.

Each tribe had its own pottery designs and colours. These geometric patterns were common in the Southwest.

4 Roll out another, small sausage shape of clay to make a handle. Dampen the ends and press it on to the clay pot in a handle shape. Leave to dry out.

5 Using a sharp pencil, mark out the design you want on your jug. You can follow the traditional indian pattern or make up your own.

6 Using poster paints or acrylic paints, colour in the pattern on the mug. Use a fine-tipped brush to create the tiny checked patterns and thin lines.

7 When the paint is dry, coat your mug in one or two layers of non-toxic varnish using an ordinary paintbrush. This will protect it.

TRIBAL CRAFTS IN NORTH AMERICA 377

Home, Family & Everyday Life

Here is an inside view of what home and school, family, food and everyday life were like in the past for young and old, rich and poor. Discover how people of the first civilizations built their homes and organized their daily lives. From earliest times, children worked with their parents, learning the skills they would need as adults. Compare the necessities of life around the world and throughout history.

From Shelters to Homes

Everyone needs somewhere to live. All over the world, people from different civilizations have built many kinds of homes. Whether simple, prehistoric cave-shelters or splendid palaces in Mughal India, a home serves many purposes that are common in all cultures. It provides protection from cold and damp, shade from the hot sun, and a comfortable refuge for sleeping, preparing food, raising a family and entertaining guests.

The layout and construction of houses varied widely. Homes were designed to provide maximum comfort in the local climate, and to withstand local environmental hazards, such as storms, floods, earthquakes or heavy snow. In northern Europe, the Vikings built houses with thick thatched roofs for insulation from the cold. In Japan, an earthquake zone, lightweight paper screens were used as inner walls in the construction of houses. If these collapsed, they

Round, early farming huts, such as this one, whose remains were found in Banpo in China, date from 6000BC. They had stout wooden frames, plastered walls and a central hole to let out smoke.

Longhouses were alternatives to the round house. They were often found in Europe and north and south America. Thatch made from reeds from a nearby river lasted longer than straw.

TIMELINE 10,000–200BC

10,000BC People around the world live as nomads, moving from place to place, hunting animals and gathering wild foods. They shelter in strong, solid houses, made of wood, stone or snow in winter but travel around, living in tents, in summer. Semi-nomadic lifestyle continued until the 1900s in places such as arctic Russia.

Inside an igloo home of the Arctic Inuit people

10,000BC People living in north and south America build homes that are shaped by the local environment. Some are simple shelters of branches and leaves; others include huts, longhouses made of woven tree saplings, buffalo-skin tepees and mud-brick pueblo apartments.

8000–7000BC The world's first settled farming villages are built in the Middle East.

4500BC European farmers build villages of longhouses.

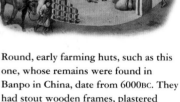

3100–30BC Peak of ancient Egyptian civilization. Egyptian families live in houses of sun-dried mud brick.

European longhouse village

800BC–AD100 The Celts in central and north-western Europe live as farmers,

10,000BC   4500BC   3000BC

would not harm people or cause much damage.

The materials used to construct a house also shaped its design. Most homes were built using local resources that were easily available. In many countries, including Aztec Mexico and ancient Egypt, mud and clay were shaped into bricks and dried in the sun. Elsewhere, homes were made from wood, stone or dried grass. Fine stone and timber were rare, and it was difficult to carry them long distances, so they were expensive. The materials used and the size of homes therefore depended on the wealth of the owner. Houses of the wealthy were large and luxurious, with many spacious rooms. Among the poor, all family members might share a simple room that combined as sleeping and living space.

Houses were built on stilts in the marshy regions of Japan. Rice was cultivated in wet paddy fields.

Tipis made of animal skins were held up with wooden poles and served as a short-term shelter for native North American tribes.

Most homes were built as permanent shelters, but in some environments, they were designed to fulfil temporary needs. Nomads were people who moved from place to place, hunting animals and gathering wild plants for foods. They built homes that were designed to be easily packed away and moved several times a year. Native American hunters on the Great Plains of North America made tepees of buffalo skin. Inuit hunters in the Arctic built shelters from blocks of snow, called igloos,

building large roundhouses of wattle-and-daub, thatched with straw. They also build fortified towns, as centres of trade.

600BC Wealthy families in India build houses of brick and stone. The houses are painted different colours, according to caste (social status).

600–200BC Ancient Greek families live in houses made of stone or mud brick. They have separate, private quarters for women, and a dining room for entertaining, that is used only by men of the family.

c.300BC–AD300 Wealthy Roman families build splendid houses. Town houses were often built around a small enclosed garden, or a courtyard called an atrium. Country houses had elegant rooms for entertaining, plus barracks where slaves and farmworkers could sleep.

300BC In central America, the Maya people build new cities surrounded by fields and farms. Maya families live in simple homes, with wood or mud walls and thatched roofs.

A wealthy Roman family home

800BC   400BC   300BC   200BC

Backstrap looms started to be used as early as 2500BC by the people who lived in the Andes mountains of Peru.

to live in during the winter.

For many people, homes were also places of work. From the time when humans first began to live together in families, women worked at home, caring for babies and young children. In most cultures, women did the cooking and produced household textiles, such as blankets and clothes for their families. Archaeologists have found childrens' toys, cooking pots and the remains of weaving looms in family homes from places as far apart as India and Inca Peru. Men, who made their living as farmers and craftworkers, also worked at home, with other family members helping them. Teamwork was essential for survival. Children worked alongside their parents, learning the skills they would need in adult life. Schooling was only provided for children from wealthy families, as in China and imperial Rome.

All these family and working needs were reflected in house design. Craft workshops, rooms to display finished goods and shelters for farm animals often formed part of the family home. Cultural values also influenced housing. In ancient Greece, homes had private rooms where women lived, out of sight of

Home life in early Middle Eastern farming villages was a cluster of activity. People often shared their house with the animals. Everyone in the family had a role to play.

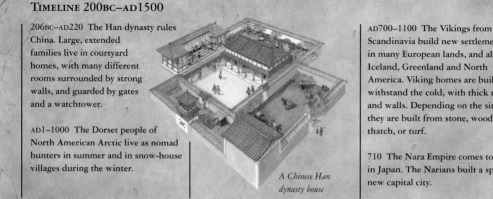

Timeline 200BC–AD1500

206BC–AD220 The Han dynasty rules China. Large, extended families live in courtyard homes, with many different rooms surrounded by strong walls, and guarded by gates and a watchtower.

AD1–1000 The Dorset people of North American Arctic live as nomad hunters in summer and in snow-house villages during the winter.

A Chinese Han dynasty house

AD700–1100 The Vikings from Scandinavia build new settlements in many European lands, and also in Iceland, Greenland and North America. Viking homes are built to withstand the cold, with thick roofs and walls. Depending on the site, they are built from stone, wood and thatch, or turf.

710 The Nara Empire comes to power in Japan. The Narians built a splendid new capital city.

200BC   AD100   700   800

non-family men. Almost everywhere, people liked to decorate their houses, sometimes in bright colours and patterns, and to furnish them with comfortable bedding, seating and floor-coverings. Some of these decorations had a meaning, with the aim of protecting a house or watching over those

In every Chinese kitchen, a new paper picture of the kitchen god and his wife was put up on New Year's Day.

who lived there. Chinese families often displayed a picture of the Kitchen God, who oversaw their behaviour. Some Native Americans put up tall totem poles outside their homes, carved with images of ancestor spirits to guard the families.

This section charts the development of domestic history in various cultures in turn. It focuses on aspects of everyday life that are common to major civilizations, such as family, childhood, education, housing and food. You will be able to see how these themes evolved and compare how people's lives varied with local environments around the world.

A well-off Aztec couple sit by the fire, while their meal is being cooked. Their colourful clothes and braided hair indicate that they are people of rank.

Wooden totem poles outside Native American homes kept a record of the family histories of the people living inside.

1000–1325 The Aztec people of central America leave their homeland in the north of Mexico, and travel south in search of a better place to live. They settle in the central valley of Mexico, and build a new capital city there. It soon grows into one of the largest cities in the world.

1000–1600 The Thule people of the North American Arctic live in huts made of stone and turf.

Inca man and woman gather straw for thatch

c.1300–1536 The Inca Empire is powerful in Peru. The Incas are expert builders of stone temples, palaces and city walls, without using metal tools. Ordinary families live in small stone houses, thatched with straw.

1500 In Japan, samurai (noble warriors) build splendid castles where their servants, soldiers and families live.

An Inca home

1000   1300   1500

Stone Age Villages

PRIMITIVE HUMANS hunted wild animals, caught fish and gathered berries and plants to eat. When people took up farming as a way of life, it meant that they had to stay in the same place for a long time. Some farmers practised slash and burn. This means they cleared land, but moved on after a few years, when their crops had exhausted the soil. Elsewhere, early farming settlements grew into villages five to ten times bigger than earlier hunter-gatherer camps. At first, the farmers still hunted animals, but soon their herds and crops supplied most of their needs. They lived in villages of rectangular or circular one-storey houses of stone, mud brick, or timber and thatch. Houses were joined by narrow lanes or courtyards. Most villages lay near well-watered, easily worked land. By using irrigation and crop rotation, later farmers were able to stay in one place for a long time.

INSIDE A LONG HOUSE
The inside of a long house was a place of work as well as providing shelter for the family and their animals. Around the hearth of this reconstructed house are baskets woven from reeds and skins laid out on the floor. Around the walls, tools are stored.

A LONG HOUSE
This is a reconstruction of a typical long house in an early farming village in Europe. The village dates from around 4500BC.

A TOWN HOUSE

This picture shows how a house at Çatal Hüyük in Turkey may have looked. The walls were made of mud brick, with poles covered with reeds and mud as the roof. All the houses were joined together, with no streets in between. People went about by climbing over the rooftops, entering their homes by a ladder through the roof.

The main room of each house had raised areas for sitting and sleeping on. More than a thousand houses were packed together like this at Çatal Hüyük.

STONE WALLS

These are the remains of the walls of a house in an early farming village in Jordan. It was built around 7000BC. The walls are made of stone collected from the local area.

The first farming towns and villages appeared in the Near East. Most were built of mud brick and, over hundreds of years, such settlements were often rebuilt many times on the same site.

THE OVEN

Many houses contained ovens or kilns, used for baking bread and firing pottery. A kiln allowed higher temperatures to be reached than an open hearth, and therefore produced better pottery. Each village probably made its own pottery.

Family Life in Mesopotamia

LIFE WAS HARD for ordinary families in Mesopotamia. Many babies and young children died from disease or because of poor maternity care. Boys from poorer families did not go to school but worked with their fathers, who taught them their trades. Girls stayed at home with their mothers and learned how to keep house and helped to look after the younger children. Some of the details of family life are described in ancient clay tablets. In one tablet, a boy is rudely tells his mother to hurry up and make his lunch. In another one, a boy is scared of what his father will say when he sees his bad school report.

In some ways, Mesopotamian society was quite modern. The law said that women could own property and get a divorce. However, if a woman was unable to have a baby she had to agree to her husband taking a second wife. The second wife and her children had rights too. They remained part of the household even if the first wife had a child after all.

MOTHERHOOD
Having lots of healthy children, especially sons, was very important because families needed children to grow up and work for them. Most women stayed at home to look after their families. Women did not usually go out to work although some had jobs as priestesses. Some priestesses were single but others were married women.

HOUSEHOLD GOODS
Pottery was used in Mesopotamian homes from the time of the first villages. At first it was handmade, but later a potter's wheel was used. This clay jug may have been based on one made of metal. Tools and utensils were made of stone or metal. There was not much furniture in a Mesopotamian house, just mud brick benches for sitting or sleeping on. There may have been rugs and cushions to make the homes more comfortable, but none have survived.

MODEL HOUSE
From models such as this one, we know that homes in Mesopotamia were similar to village houses in modern Iraq. They were built of mud brick and were usually rectangular, with rooms around a central courtyard. Doors and windows were small to keep the house warm in the cold winters, and cool during the hot summers. Flat roofs, reached by stairs from the central court could be used as an extra room in summer.

Mesopotamian Fashions

A statue of a worshipper found in a temple shows the dress of a Sumerian woman. Dresses were of sheepskin, sometimes with a sheepskin shawl as well, or of woollen cloth. One shoulder was left bare. Some women, who may have been priestesses, wore tall, elaborate hats like this one. Later fashions included long, fringed garments. Sumerian men wore sheepskin kilts, but men in the Assyrian and Babylonian Empires wore long, woollen tunics. Both men and women wore jewellery.

Earning a Living

Most families in ancient Mesopotamia depended on agriculture for a living, just as many people in the Middle East do today. Farmers rented their land from bigger landowners, such as important officials, kings or temples, and had to give part of what they produced in taxes. Many townspeople had jobs in local government or worked in the textile and metalwork industries.

Build It Up

Homes in Mesopotamia were often made from mud brick. Mud bricks are made from a mixture of mud and straw mixed with water. The straw stops the bricks from cracking. The mixture is put in square or oblong moulds and left to dry in the sun for several weeks. The bricks are usually made in the summer after the harvest when there is plenty of straw available, and it is less likely to rain (which would damage the bricks).

straw

clay

Gone Fishing

There were lots of fish in the rivers and fishponds of ancient Iraq, and fish seem to have been an important part of people's diet. Fishbones were found at Eridu, in the south of Sumer, in the oldest level of the temple. Perhaps fish were offered to the water god Enki as an offering. (He is the god with streams of water containing fish springing out of his shoulders.) Some of the carved reliefs from the Assyrian palaces give us rare glimpses into everyday life and include little scenes of men going fishing.

Egyptian Houses and Gardens

THE GREAT CITIES of ancient Egypt, such as Memphis and Thebes, were built along the banks of the River Nile. Small towns grew up haphazardly around them. Special workmen's towns such as Deir el-Medina were also set up around major burial sites and temples to help with building work.

Egyptian towns were defended by thick walls and the streets were planned on a grid pattern. The straight dirt roads had a stone drainage channel, or gutter, running down the middle. Parts of the town housed important officials, while other parts were home to craft workers and poor labourers.

Only temples were built to last. They were made of stone. Mud brick was used to construct all other buildings from royal palaces to workers' dwellings. Most Egyptian homes had roofs supported with palm logs and floors made of packed earth. In the homes of wealthier Egyptians, walls were sometimes plastered and painted. The rooms of their houses included bedrooms, living rooms, kitchens in thatched courtyards and workshops. Homes were furnished with beds, chairs, stools and benches. In the cool of the evenings people would sit on the flat roofs or walk and talk in shady gardens.

THE GARDEN OF NAKHT

The royal scribe Nakht and his wife Tjiui take an evening stroll through their garden. Trees and shrubs surround a peaceful pool. Egyptian gardens included date palms, pomegranates, grape vines, scarlet poppies and blue and pink lotus flowers. Artists in ancient Egypt showed objects in the same picture from different angles, so the trees around Nakht's pool are flattened out.

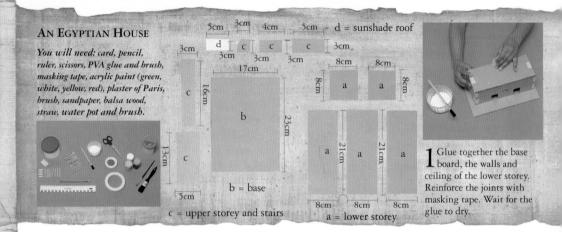

AN EGYPTIAN HOUSE

You will need: card, pencil, ruler, scissors, PVA glue and brush, masking tape, acrylic paint (green, white, yellow, red), plaster of Paris, brush, sandpaper, balsa wood, straw, water pot and brush.

d = sunshade roof

b = base

c = upper storey and stairs

a = lower storey

1 Glue together the base board, the walls and ceiling of the lower storey. Reinforce the joints with masking tape. Wait for the glue to dry.

ABOVE THE FLOODS

The homes of wealthy people were often built on platforms to stop damp passing through the mud brick walls. This also raised it above the level of any possible flood damage.

SOUL HOUSES

Pottery models give us a good idea of how the homes of poorer Egyptians looked. During the Middle Kingdom (2050–1786BC), these soul houses were left as tomb offerings. The Egyptians placed food in the courtyard of the house to feed the person's soul after death.

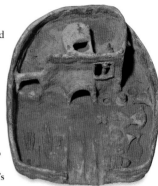

NILE SOILS

The Egyptians built their homes from mud bricks that were made from the thick clay soil left behind by the Nile floods. The clay was taken to the brickyard and mixed with water, pebbles and chopped straw. Mud brick is still used for building houses in Egypt today and is made in the same way.

straw

mud

BRICK MAKING

A group of labourers make bricks. First mud was collected in leather buckets and taken to the building site. There, it was mixed with straw and pebbles. Finally the mixture was put into a mould. At this stage, bricks were sometimes stamped with the name of the pharaoh or the building for which they were made. They were then left to dry in the hot sunshine for several days, before being carried away in a sling.

Egyptian houses had a large main room that opened directly onto the street. In many homes, stairs led up to the roof. People would often sleep there during very hot weather.

2 Now glue together the top storey and stairs. Again, use masking tape to reinforce the joints. When the top storey is dry, glue it to the lower storey.

3 Glue the balsa pillars into the front of the top storey. When the house is dry, cover it in wet paste of plaster of Paris. Paint the pillars red or a colour of your choice.

4 Paint the whole building a dried mud colour. Next paint a green strip along the side. Use masking tape to ensure straight edges. Sand any rough edges.

5 Now make a shelter for the rooftop. Use four balsa struts as supports. The roof can be made of card glued with straw. Glue the shelter into place.

Egyptian Food

LABOURERS IN ANCIENT Egypt were often paid in food. They ate bread, onions and salted fish, washed down with a sweet, grainy beer. Flour was often gritty and the teeth of many mummified bodies show signs of severe wear and tear. Dough was kneaded with the feet or by hand, and pastry cooks produced all kinds of cakes and loaves.

BEAUTIFUL BOWLS
Dishes and bowls were often made of faience, a glassy pottery. The usual colour for this attractive tableware was blue-green or turquoise.

A big banquet for a pharaoh was a grand affair, with guests dressed in their finest clothes. A royal menu might include roast goose or stewed beef, kidneys, wild duck or tender gazelle. Lamb was not eaten for religious reasons, and in some regions certain types of fish were also forbidden. Vegetables such as leeks were stewed with milk and cheese. Egyptian cooks were experts at stewing, roasting and baking.

Red and white wines were served at banquets. They were stored in pottery jars marked with their year and their vineyard, just like the labels on modern wine bottles.

A FEAST FIT FOR A KING
New Kingdom (1550–1070BC) noblewomen exchange gossip at a dinner party. They show off their jewellery and best clothes. The Egyptians loved wining and dining. They would be entertained by musicians, dancers and acrobats during the feast.

MAKE A CAKE

You will need: 200g stoneground flour, $^1/_2$tsp salt, 1tsp baking powder, 75g butter, 60g honey, 3tbsp milk, caraway seeds, bowl, wooden spoon, floured surface, baking tray.

1 Begin by mixing together the flour, salt and baking powder in the bowl. Next, chop up the butter and add it to the mixture.

2 Using your fingers, rub the butter into the mixture, as shown. Your mixture should look like fine breadcrumbs when you have finished.

3 Now add 40g of your honey. Combine it with your mixture. This will sweeten your cakes. The ancient Egyptians did not have sugar.

WOMAN MAKING BEER

This wooden tomb model of a woman making beer dates back to 2400BC. Beer was made by mashing barley bread in water. When the mixture fermented, becoming alcoholic, the liquid was strained off into a wooden tub. There were various types of beer, but all were very popular. It was said that the god Osiris had brought beer to the land of Egypt.

DRINKING VESSEL

Beautiful faience cups such as this one could have been used to drink wine, water or beer. It is decorated with a pattern of lotus flowers.

DESERT DESSERTS

A meal in ancient Egypt was often finished off with nuts, such as almonds, or sweet fruits, juicy figs, dates, grapes, pomegranates or melons. Sugar was still unknown so honey was used to sweeten cakes and pastries.

pomegranates

dates

PALACE BAKERY

Whole teams of model cooks and bakers were left in some tombs. This was so that a pharaoh could order them to put on a good banquet to entertain his guests in the other world. Models are shown sifting, mixing and kneading flour, and making pastries. Most of our knowledge about Egyptian food and cooking comes from the food boxes and offerings left in tombs.

Egyptian pastries were often shaped in spirals like these. Other popular shapes were rings, like doughnuts, and pyramids. Some were shaped like crocodiles!

4 Add the milk and stir the mixture until it forms a dough. Make your dough into a ball and place it on a floured board or surface. Divide the dough into three.

5 Roll the dough into long strips, as shown. Take the strips and coil them into a spiral to make one cake. Make the other cakes in the same way.

6 Now sprinkle each cake with caraway seeds and place them on a greased baking tray. Finish off by glazing the cakes carefully with a little extra honey.

7 Ask an adult to bake them in an oven at 180°C/Gas Mark 4 for 20 minutes. When they are ready, take them out and leave on a baking rack to cool.

Rich and Poor in India

HOUSES IN INDIA differed according to social class. Poor people made their homes out of mud, clay and thatch. Materials such as these do not last long, so few of these houses have survived. By about 600BC, wealthier people were building homes made of brick and stone. It is thought that people's caste (class) determined not only the part of a town or city that they lived in, but also what colour they painted their homes. The Brahmins (priests caste) of Jodhpur in Rajasthan, for example, painted their houses blue.

A wealthy man's house of about AD400 had a courtyard and an outer room where guests were entertained. Behind this were the inner rooms where the women of the house stayed and where food was cooked. Beyond the house itself there were often gardens and fountains surrounded by an outside wall. Homes like this stayed much the same in design over many centuries.

Royal palaces were more elaborate. They had many courtyards and enclosures surrounded by numerous walls. These were to protect the king from beggars and servants who might make a nuisance of themselves. Unlike ordinary homes, palaces changed in design with each new wave of rulers.

DECORATED DOORSTEP
Pictures in chalk and rice powder were drawn on the doorsteps of houses. Over time, they came to signify prosperity and good luck. Making such drawings was one of 64 forms of art that a cultured person was expected to be able to do.

birdcage

mango leaves hung for good luck

water trough

courtyard

MOUNTAIN HOMES
These modern mountain homes made from mud and thatch continue a tradition that is thousands of years old. Unlike valley homes, they have to be well insulated for protection against the colder climate.

THE GOOD LIFE
Life in a rich man's household was divided between the inner area, where he slept and ate, and the outer regions, dominated by a courtyard where he entertained friends, read, listened to music and strolled in the garden. Here, salons (groups) of men would meet to discuss life and politics.

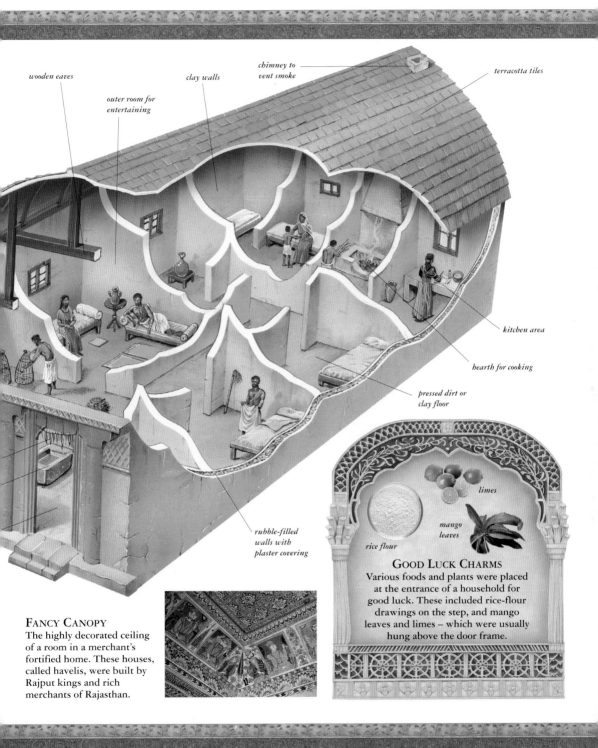

wooden eaves

outer room for entertaining

clay walls

chimney to vent smoke

terracotta tiles

kitchen area

hearth for cooking

pressed dirt or clay floor

rubble-filled walls with plaster covering

FANCY CANOPY
The highly decorated ceiling of a room in a merchant's fortified home. These houses, called havelis, were built by Rajput kings and rich merchants of Rajasthan.

limes

mango leaves

rice flour

GOOD LUCK CHARMS
Various foods and plants were placed at the entrance of a household for good luck. These included rice-flour drawings on the step, and mango leaves and limes – which were usually hung above the door frame.

Eating in India

PEOPLE'S STAPLE (BASIC) FOOD in the ancient world depended on what they could grow. In the wetter areas of eastern, western, southern and central India, rice was the staple diet. In the drier areas of the north and north-west, people grew wheat and made it into different kinds of breads.

Apart from these staple foods, people's diets depended on their religion. Buddhists thought that killing animals was wrong, so they were vegetarians. Most Hindus, particularly the upper castes, became vegetarian too. Because they believed the cow was holy, eating beef became taboo (forbidden). When Islam arrived, it brought with it a new set of rules. Muslims are forbidden to eat pork, although they do eat other meat.

The Indians used a lot of spices in cooking, in order to add flavour and to disguise the taste of rotten meat. Ginger, garlic, turmeric, cinnamon and cumin were used from early times. Chillis were only introduced from the Americas after the 1500s.

CELESTIAL FRUITS
A heavenly damsel offers fruits in this stucco painting from Sri Lanka. From earliest times, Indians ate with their hands rather than with implements. Even so, there were rules to be followed. Generally, they could only eat with the right hand, taking care only to use their fingers.

EVENING DELIGHTS
A princess enjoys an evening party in the garden. She listens to music by candlelight, and is served drinks, sweets and other foods.

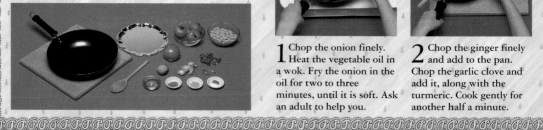

MAKE A CHICKPEA CURRY

You will need: knife, small onion, 30ml vegetable oil, wok or frying pan, wooden spoon, 4cm piece fresh ginger root, 2 cloves garlic, ¼tsp turmeric, 450g tomatoes, 225g cooked chickpeas, salt and pepper, 2tbsp finely chopped fresh coriander, plus coriander leaves to garnish, 2tsp garam masala, a lime.

1 Chop the onion finely. Heat the vegetable oil in a wok. Fry the onion in the oil for two to three minutes, until it is soft. Ask an adult to help you.

2 Chop the ginger finely and add to the pan. Chop the garlic clove and add it, along with the turmeric. Cook gently for another half a minute.

A RICH BANQUET

Babur, the founder of the Mughal Empire in India in AD1526, enjoys a banquet of roast duck in Herat, Persia. Under the Mughals, a cuisine known as Mughlai developed. It became famous for its rich and sophisticated flavours.

turmeric

black mustard seeds

cardamom

THREE ESSENTIAL SPICES

Many spices are used in Indian dishes. Turmeric is ground from a root to give food an earthy flavour and yellow colour. Black mustard seed has a smoky, bitter taste. Cardamom – a favourite in northern India – gives a musky, sugary flavour suitable for both sweet and savoury dishes.

LEAF PLATE

In south India, banana leaves were (and are still) used as plates for serving and eating food. South Indian food uses more coconut than the north, and rice-flour is used in several dishes.

DAILY BREAD

Indians eat a variety of baked, griddled or fried breads, such as these parathas. In much of northern and western India, the staple food is wheat, served in the form of unleavened (flat) breads.

Chickpeas are a popular ingredient in Indian cooking. They have been grown in India for thousands of years.

3 Peel the tomatoes, cut them in half and remove the seeds. Then chop them roughly and add them to the onion, garlic and spice mixture.

4 Add the chickpeas. Bring the mixture to the boil, then simmer gently for 10-15 minutes, until the tomatoes have reduced to a thick paste.

5 Taste the curry and then add salt and pepper as seasoning, if it is needed. The curry should taste spicy, but not so hot that it burns your mouth.

6 Add the chopped fresh coriander to the curry, along with the garam masala. Garnish with fresh coriander leaves and serve with slices of lime.

Chinese Homes in Harmony

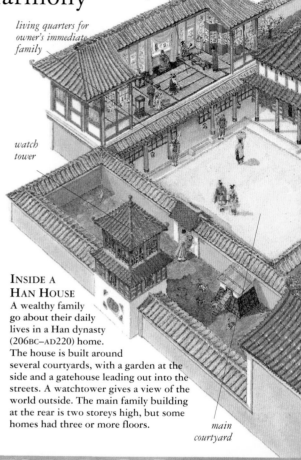

reception

living quarters for owner's immediate family

watch tower

main courtyard

I N CHINESE CITIES, all buildings were designed to be in harmony with each other and with nature. The direction they faced, their layout and their proportions were all matters of great spiritual importance. Even the number of steps leading up to the entrance of the house was considered to be significant. House design in imperial China, before it became a republic in 1912, varied over time and between regions. In the hot and rainy south, courtyards tended to be covered for shade and shelter. In the drier north, courtyards were mostly open to the elements. Poor people in the countryside lived in simple, thatched huts. These were made from timber frames covered in mud plaster. They were often noisy, draughty and overcrowded. In contrast, wealthy people had large, peaceful and well-constructed homes. Many had beautiful gardens, filled with peonies, bamboo and wisteria. Some gardens also contained orchards, ponds and pavilions.

INSIDE A HAN HOUSE

A wealthy family go about their daily lives in a Han dynasty (206BC–AD220) home. The house is built around several courtyards, with a garden at the side and a gatehouse leading out into the streets. A watchtower gives a view of the world outside. The main family building at the rear is two storeys high, but some homes had three or more floors.

MAKE A HOUSE

You will need: thick card, corrugated card, ruler, felt tip pen, scissors, glue and brush, 2.5cm x 0.5cm dowel (x2), masking tape, paint (white, grey, pink), thick and thin paintbrushes, water pot.

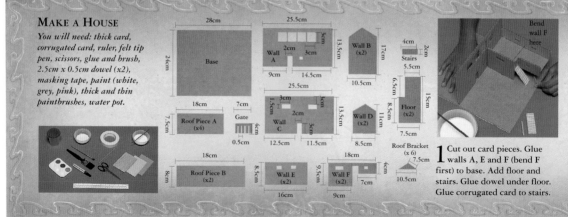

1 Cut out card pieces. Glue walls A, E and F (bend F first) to base. Add floor and stairs. Glue dowel under floor. Glue corrugated card to stairs.

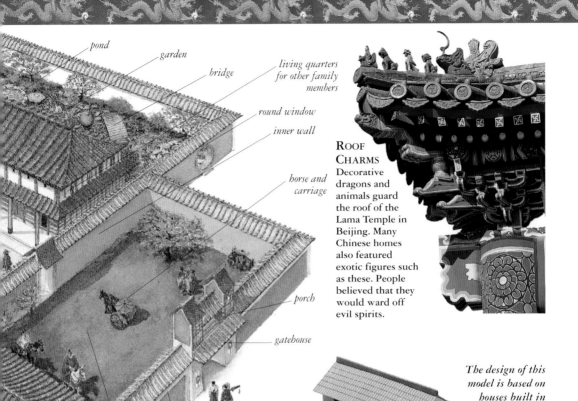

pond
garden
bridge
living quarters for other family members
round window
inner wall
horse and carriage
porch
gatehouse
outer wall
outer courtyard

ROOF CHARMS Decorative dragons and animals guard the roof of the Lama Temple in Beijing. Many Chinese homes also featured exotic figures such as these. People believed that they would ward off evil spirits.

The design of this model is based on houses built in southern China. The overhanging roofs cover the courtyard. This helps to keep out rain and to provide shelter from the sun.

2 To assemble second side, repeat method described in step 1. If necessary, hold pieces together with masking tape while the glue dries.

3 Glue B walls to the sides of the base, C wall to the back and D walls to the front. Hold with tape while glue dries. Glue gate between D walls.

4 Assemble A roofs (x2) and B roof (x1). Fix brackets underneath. Glue corrugated card (cut to same size as roof pieces) to top side of roofs.

5 Fix a small piece of card over the gate to make a porch. Paint house, as shown. Use a thin brush to create a tile effect on the removable roofs.

Traditional Life in China

THE THINKER, KONG FUZI (Confucius), lived from 551BC to 479BC. He taught that just as the emperor was head of the state, the oldest man was head of the household and should be obeyed by his family. In reality, his wife often controlled the daily lives of everyone in the household.

During the Han dynasty (206BC–AD220) noblewomen were kept apart from the outside world. They could only gaze at the streets from the watchtowers of their homes. It was not until the Song dynasty (AD960–1279) that they gained more freedom. In poor households women worked all day, spending long, tiring hours farming, cooking, sweeping and washing.

For children of poor families, education meant learning to do the work their parents did. This involved carrying goods to market, or helping with the threshing or planting. Wealthier children had private tutors at home. Boys hoping to become scholars or civil servants learned to read and write Chinese characters. They also studied maths and the works of Kong Fuzi.

LESSONS FOR THE BOYS
A group of Chinese boys take their school lessons. In imperial China, boys generally received a more academic education than girls. Girls were mainly taught music, handicrafts, painting and social skills. Some girls were taught academic subjects, but they were not allowed to sit the civil service examinations.

CHINESE MARRIAGE
A wedding ceremony takes place in the late 1800s. In imperial China, weddings were arranged by the parents of the bride and groom, rather than by the couples themselves. It was expected that the couple would respect their parents' wishes, even if they didn't like each other!

FOOT BINDING
This foot looks elegant in its beautiful slipper, but it's a different story when the slipper is removed. Just when life was improving for Chinese women, the cruel new custom of footbinding was introduced. Dancers had bound their feet for some years in the belief that it made them look dainty. In the Song dynasty the custom spread to wealthy and noble families. Little girls of five or so had their feet bound up so tightly that they became terribly deformed.

TAKING IT EASY

A noblewoman living during the Qing dynasty relaxes on a garden terrace with her children (c.1840). She is very fortunate as she has little else to do but enjoy the pleasant surroundings of her home. In rich families like hers, servants did most of the hard work, such as cooking, cleaning and washing. Wealthy Chinese families kept many servants, who usually lived in quarters inside their employer's home. Servants accounted for a large number of the workforce in imperial China. During the Ming dynasty (1368–1644), some 9,000 maidservants were employed at the imperial palace in Beijing alone!

RESPECT AND HONOUR

Children in the 1100s bow respectfully to their parents. Confucius taught that people should value and honour their families, including their ancestors. He believed that this helped to create a more orderly and virtuous society.

THE EMPEROR AND HIS MANY WIVES

Sui dynasty emperor Yangdi (AD581–618) rides out with his many womenfolk. Like many emperors, Yangdi was surrounded by women. An emperor married one woman, who would then become his empress, but he would still enjoy the company of concubines (secondary wives).

Food and Diet in China

TODAY, CHINESE FOOD is among the most popular in the world. Rice was the basis of most meals in ancient China, especially in the south, where it was grown. Northerners used wheat flour to make noodles and buns. Food varied greatly between the regions. The north was famous for pancakes, dumplings, lamb and duck dishes. In the west, Sichuan was renowned for its hot chilli peppers. Mushrooms and bamboo shoots were popular along the lower Chang Jiang (Yangzi River).

For many people, meat was a rare treat. It included chicken, pork and many kinds of fish, and was often spiced with garlic and ginger. Dishes featured meat that people from other parts of the world might find strange, such as turtle, dog, monkey and bear. Food was stewed, steamed or fried. The use of chopsticks and bowls dates back to the Shang dynasty (*c*.1600–1122BC).

THE KITCHEN GOD
In every kitchen hung a paper picture of the kitchen god and his wife. Each year, on the 24th day of the 12th month, sweets were put out as offerings. Then the picture was taken down and burned. A new one was put in its place on New Year's Day.

A TANG BANQUET
In this picture, elegant ladies of the Tang court are sitting down to a feast. They are accompanied by music and singing, but there are no men present – women and men usually ate separately. This painting dates from the AD900s, when raised tables came into fashion in China. Guests at banquets would wear their finest clothes. The most honoured guest would sit to the east of the host, who sat facing the south. The greatest honour of all was to be invited to dine with the emperor.

MAKE RED BEAN SOUP
You will need: measuring jug, scales, measuring spoon, 225g aduki beans, 3 tsp ground nuts, 4 tsp short-grain rice, cold water, tangerine, saucepan and lid, wooden spoon, 175g sugar, liquidizer, sieve, bowls.

1 Use the scales to weigh out the aduki beans. Add the ground nuts and the short-grain rice. Measure out 1 litre of cold water in the jug.

2 Wash and drain the beans and rice. Put them in a bowl. Add the cold water. Leave overnight to soak. Do not drain off the water.

3 Wash and dry the tangerine. Then carefully take off the peel in a continuous strip. Leave the peel overnight, until it is hard and dry.

THAT SPECIAL TASTE

The Chinese flavour their food with a variety of herbs and spices. Garlic has been used in Chinese dishes and sauces for thousands of years. It may be chopped, crushed, pickled or served whole. Root ginger is another crucial Chinese taste. Fresh chilli peppers are used to make fiery dishes, while sesame provides flavouring in the form of paste, oil and seeds.

sesame   *root ginger*

SHANG BRONZEWARE FIT FOR A FEAST

This three-legged bronze cooking pot dates from the Shang dynasty (*c.*1600BC–1122BC). Its green appearance is caused by the reaction of the metal to air over the 3,500 years since it was made. During Shang rule, metalworkers made many vessels out of bronze, including cooking pots and wine jars. They were used in all sorts of ceremonies, and at feasts people held in honour of their dead ancestors.

BUTCHERS AT WORK

The stone carving (*shown right*) shows farmers butchering cattle in about AD50. In early China, cooks would cut up meat with square-shaped cleavers. It was then flavoured with wines and spices, and simmered in big pots over open fires until tender.

Most peasant farmers lived on a simple diet. Red bean soup with rice was a typical daily meal. Herbs and spices were often added to make the food taste more interesting.

4 Put the soaked beans and rice (plus the soaking liquid) into a large saucepan. Add the dried tangerine peel and 500ml of cold water.

5 Bring the mixture to the boil. Reduce the heat, cover the saucepan and simmer for 2 hours. Stir occasionally. If the liquid boils off, add more water.

6 Weigh out the sugar. When the beans are just covered by water, add the sugar. Simmer until the sugar has completely dissolved.

7 Remove and discard the tangerine peel. Leave soup to cool, uncovered. Liquidize the mixture. Strain any lumps with a sieve. Pour into bowls.

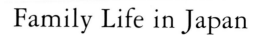

Family Life in Japan

FAMILIES IN EARLY JAPAN survived by working together in the family business or on the family land. Japanese people believed that the family group was more important than any one individual. Family members were supposed to consider the wellbeing of the whole family first, before thinking about their own needs and plans. Sometimes, this led to quarrels or disappointments. For example, younger brothers in poor families were often not allowed to marry so that the family land could be handed on, undivided, to the eldest son.

Daughters would leave home to marry if a suitable husband could be found. If not, they also remained single and stayed in their parents' house.

Family responsibility passed down the generations, from father to eldest son. Japanese families respected age and experience because they believed it brought wisdom.

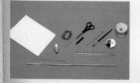

LOOKING AFTER BABY
It was women's work to care for young children. This painting shows an elegant young mother from a rich family dressing her son in a *kimono* (a robe with wide sleeves). The family maid holds the belt for the boy's *kimono*, while a pet cat watches nearby.

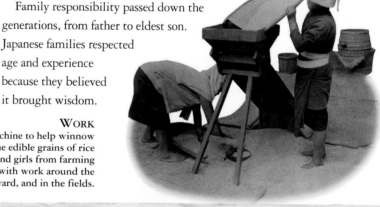

WORK
A little boy uses a simple machine to help winnow rice. (Winnowing separates the edible grains of rice from the outer husks.) Boys and girls from farming families were expected to help with work around the house and farmyard, and in the fields.

CARP STREAMER
You will need: pencil, 2 sheets of A1 paper, felt-tip pen, scissors, paints, paintbrush, water pot, glue, wire, masking tape, string, cane.

1 Take the pencil and one piece of paper. Draw a large carp fish shape on to the paper. When you are happy with the shape, go over it in felt-tip pen.

2 Put the second piece of paper over the first. Draw around the fish shape. Next, draw a border around the second fish and add tabs, as shown.

3 Add scales, eyes, fins and other details to both of the fishes, as shown above. Cut them both out, remembering to snip into the tabs. Paint both fishes.

PLAYTIME

These young boys have started two tops spinning close to one another. They are waiting to see what will happen when the tops touch. Japanese children had many different toys with which to play. As well as the spinning top, another great favourite was the kite.

TRADITIONAL MEDICINE

Kuzu (Japanese arrowroot) and ginger are ingredients that have been used for centuries as treatments in traditional Japanese medicine. Most traditional drugs are made from vegetables. The *kuzu* and ginger are mixed together in different ways depending on the symptoms of the patient. For example, there are 20 different mixtures for treating colds. Ginger is generally used when there is no fever.

kuzu   *ginger*

HONOURING ANCESTORS

A mother, father and child make offerings and say their prayers at a small family altar in their house. The lighted candle and paper lantern help guide the spirits to their home. Families honoured their dead ancestors at special festivals. At the festival of Obon, in summer, they greeted family spirits who had returned to earth.

4 Put the two fish shapes together, with the painted sides out. Turn the tabs in and glue the edges of the fish together, except for the tail and the mouth.

5 Use picture or garden wire to make a ring the size of the mouth. Twist the ends together, as shown Then bend them back. Bind the ends with masking tape.

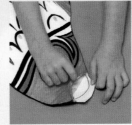

6 Place the ring in the fish's mouth. Glue the ends of the mouth over the ring. Tie one end of some string on to the mouth ring and the other end to a garden cane.

Families fly carp streamers on Boy's Day (the fifth day of the fifth month) every year. One carp is flown for each son. Carp are symbols of perseverence and strength.

Growing Up in Greece

BRINGING UP BABY
This baby is waving a rattle while sitting in a high chair. The chair also served as a potty. It might have wheels on it to help the baby learn how to walk.

Children in early times faced many obstacles while growing up. In ancient Greece, when a baby was born, its father would decide whether to keep or abandon it. A sick or handicapped baby might be left outdoors at birth. Whoever rescued the child could raise it as their slave. Girls were more likely to be rejected because they could not provide for their parents in adulthood. Many children died in infancy through lack of healthcare.

Education was considered to be important for boys. Even so, it was usually only sons of rich families who received a complete schooling. They were taught a variety of subjects, including reading, music and gymnastics. Boys from poor families often learned their father's trade. Education in domestic skills was essential for most girls. A notable exception was in Sparta, where girls joined boys in hard physical training.

BULLY OFF
These two boys are playing a game similar to hockey. On the whole, team sports were ignored in favour of sporting activities where an individual could excel. Wrestling and athletics are two such examples. They were encouraged as training for war.

YOU ARE IT
Two girls play a kind of tag game in which the loser has to carry the winner. Girls had less free time than boys did. They were supposed to stay close to home and help their mothers with housework, cooking and looking after the younger children.

MAKE A SCROLL
You will need: 2 x 30cm rods of balsa wood, 5cm in diameter, 4 doorknobs, double-sided sticky tape, sheet of paper 30cm x 30cm, 1 x 7cm rod of balsa wood, 2cm in diameter, craft knife, paintbrush, PVA glue, ink powder.

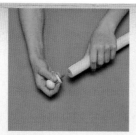

1 Carefully screw a door knob into either end of each 30cm rod of balsa wood, or ask an adult to do it for you. These are the end pieces of the scroll.

2 Cut two pieces of double-sided sticky tape 30cm long. Stick one piece of tape along the top of the paper and another along the bottom.

3 Wrap the top of the paper once around one of the pieces of balsa wood. Repeat this step again for the second piece at the bottom of the paper.

ACTION DOLL

The arms and legs on this terracotta figure are attached with cord so that the shoulders and knees can be moved. A doll such as this was a luxury item, which only a wealthy family could afford to buy for its children. Other popular toys were rattles and hoops.

THE ALPHABET

The first two of the Greek alphabet's 24 letters are called alpha and beta – these names give us the English word "alphabet".

ΑΒΓΔΕΖΗΘΙ
A BG DEZ e THI
ΚΛΜΝΞΟΠΡΣ
K L M N X O P R S
ΤΥΦΧΨΩ
T U PH KH PS o

LIGHT OF LEARNING

This lamp takes the form of a teacher holding a scroll. Education involved learning poems and famous speeches from scrolls by heart. This was thought to help boys make effective speeches in court or public meetings. Good orators were always well thought of and could wield much influence.

Scrolls in ancient Greece were usually made from animal skin.

A SECOND MOTHER

Greeks often hired wet nurses (on the left) to breastfeed their babies. Some nurses were forbidden to drink wine in case it affected their milk or made them so drunk that they might harm the baby.

ΑΧΙΛΛΕΥΣ

4 Ask an adult to help you with this step. Take the 7cm piece of balsa wood, and use your craft knife to sharpen the end of it into a point.

5 Paint the nib of your pen with glue. This will stop the wood from soaking up the ink. Add water to the ink powder to make ink.

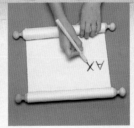

6 Write some letters or a word on your scroll with your pen. We've translated the Greek alphabet above in the fact box. Use this as a guide.

7 We have copied out some letters in ancient Greek. You could also write a word. Ask a friend to translate what you have written, using the alphabet.

Roman Houses

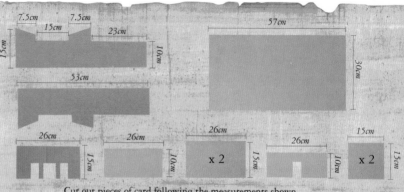

garden

bedroom

tablinium
(living room
and office)

DURING THE ROMAN ERA, wealthy
citizens could afford to live in their
own private house. A typical town house was
designed to look inwards, with the rooms
arranged round a central courtyard and a
walled garden. Outside walls had few windows
and these were small and shuttered. The front door
opened on to a short passage leading into an airy courtyard
called an *atrium*. Front rooms on either side of the passage
were usually used as bedrooms. Sometimes they were used as
workshops or shops, having shutters that opened out to the street.

The centre of the atrium was open to the sky. Below this opening
was a pool, set into the floor, to collect rainwater. Around
the atrium were more bedrooms and the kitchen. If
you were a guest or had important business
you would be shown into the *tablinium*.

The dining room, or *triclinium*, was often
the grandest room of all. The very rich
sometimes also had a summer dining
room, which looked on to the garden.

Houses were made of locally available
building materials. These might include
stone, mud bricks, cement and timber.
Roofs were made of clay tiles.

LOCKS AND KEYS
This was the key to
the door of a Roman house.
Pushed in through a
keyhole, the prongs at the
end of the key fitted into
holes in the bolt in the
lock. The key could then
be used to slide the bolt
along and unlock the door.

INSIDE A ROMAN HOME
The outside of a wealthy Roman's
town house was usually quite plain,
but inside it was highly decorated
with elaborate wall paintings and
intricate mosaics. The rooms were
sparsely furnished, with couches or
beds, small side tables, benches and
folding stools. There were few
windows, but high ceilings and wide
doors made the most of the light from
the open atrium and the garden.

MAKE A ROMAN HOME
*You will need: pencil, ruler,
thick card, scissors, PVA glue,
paintbrushes, masking tape,
corrugated cardboard, thin
card, water pot, acrylic paints.*

7.5cm   7.5cm
15cm   23cm
15cm   10cm
57cm
30cm
53cm
26cm   26cm   26cm   26cm   15cm
15cm   10cm   x 2   15cm   10cm   x 2   15cm

Cut out pieces of card following the measurements shown.

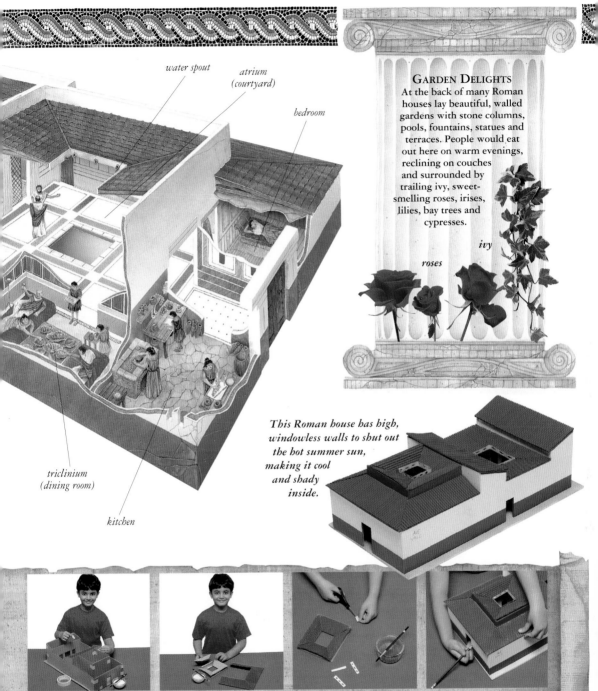

water spout

atrium
(courtyard)

bedroom

triclinium
(dining room)

kitchen

GARDEN DELIGHTS
At the back of many Roman houses lay beautiful, walled gardens with stone columns, pools, fountains, statues and terraces. People would eat out here on warm evenings, reclining on couches and surrounded by trailing ivy, sweet-smelling roses, irises, lilies, bay trees and cypresses.

ivy

roses

This Roman house has high, windowless walls to shut out the hot summer sun, making it cool and shady inside.

1 Cut out the pieces of thick card. Edge each piece with glue. Press the pieces together and reinforce with masking tape, as shown. You have now made the walls of your house.

2 Measure your model and cut out pieces of corrugated cardboard for the roofs. Stick them together with glue, as shown above. Paint the roofs red.

3 Rainwater running down the sloped atrium roof was directed into a pool below by gutters and water spouts. Make gutters from strips of thin card, with holes as spouts.

4 Paint the house walls as shown, using masking tape to get a straight line. Glue on the roofs. Why not finish off your Roman house with some authentic graffiti!

Family Occasions in Rome

THE FAMILY was very important to Romans. The father was the all-powerful head of the family, which included everyone in the household – wife, children, slaves and even close relatives. In the early days of Rome, a father had the power of life and death over his children! However, Roman fathers were rarely harsh and children were much loved by both parents.

Childhood was fairly short. Parents would arrange for a girl to be betrothed at the age of 12, and a boy at 14. Marriages took place a few years later. Brides usually wore a white dress and a yellow cloak, with an orange veil and a wreath of sweetly scented flowers. A sacrifice would be made to the gods, and everyone would wish the couple well. That evening, a procession with flaming torches and flute music would lead the newly weds to their home.

Funerals were also marked with music and processions. By Roman law, burials and cremations had to take place outside the city walls.

HAPPY FAMILIES
This Roman tombstone from Germany shows a family gathered together for a meal. From the Latin inscription on it, we know that it was put up by a soldier of the legions, in memory of his dead wife. He lovingly describes her as the "sweetest and purest" of women.

MOTHER AND BABY
A mother tends to her baby in the cradle. When children were born, they were laid at the feet of their father. If he accepted the child into the family, he would pick it up. In wealthy families, a birth was a great joy, but for poorer families it just meant another mouth to feed. Romans named a girl on the 8th day after the birth, and a boy on the 9th day. The child was given a *bulla*, a charm to ward off evil spirits.

TOGETHERNESS
When a couple were engaged, they would exchange gifts as a symbol of their devotion to each other. A ring like this one might have been given by a man to his future bride. The clasped hands symbolize marriage. Gold pendants with similar patterns were also popular.

MOURNING THE DEAD

A wealthy Roman has died and his family have gone into mourning. Laments are played on flutes as they prepare his body for the funeral procession. The Romans believed that the dead went to Hades, the Underworld, which lay beyond the river of the dead. A coin was placed in the corpse's mouth, to pay the ferryman. Food and drink for the journey was buried with the body.

TILL DEATH US DO PART

A Roman marriage ceremony was rather like a present-day Christian wedding. The couple would exchange vows and clasp hands to symbolize their union. Here, the groom is holding the marriage contract, which would have been drawn up before the ceremony. Not everyone found happiness, however, and divorce was quite common.

WEDDING FLOWERS

Roman brides wore a veil on their wedding day. This was often crowned with a wreath of flowers. In the early days of the Empire, verbena and sweet marjoram were a popular combination. Later fashions included orange blossom and myrtle, whose fragrant flowers were sacred to Venus, the goddess of love.

orange blossom

verbena

Roman Education

MOST CHILDREN in the Roman Empire never went to school. They learned a trade from their parents or found out about sums by trading on a market stall. Boys might be trained to fight with swords or to ride horses, in preparation for joining the army. Girls would be taught how to run the home, in preparation for marriage.

Wealthy families did provide an education for their sons and sometimes for their daughters, too. They were usually taught at home by a private tutor, but there were also small schools. Tutors and schoolmasters would teach children arithmetic, and how to read and write in both Latin and Greek. Clever pupils might also learn public speaking skills, poetry and history. Girls often had music lessons at home, on a harp-like instrument called a lyre.

INKPOTS AND PENS
Pen and ink were used to write on scrolls made from papyrus (a kind of reed) or thin sheets of wood. Ink was often made from soot or lamp-black, mixed with water. It was kept in inkpots such as these. Inkpots were made from glass, pottery or metal. Pens were made from bone, reeds or bronze.

WRITING IN WAX
This painting shows a couple from Pompeii. The man holds a parchment scroll. His wife is probably going through their household accounts. She holds a wax-covered writing tablet and a stylus to scratch words into the wax. A stylus had a pointed end for writing and a flat end for rubbing out.

A WRITING TABLET
You will need: sheets and sticks of balsa wood, craft knife, ruler, PVA glue, paintbrush, brown acrylic paint, water pot, modelling clay, work board, rolling pin, modelling tool, skewer, purple thread, pencil (to be used as a stylus), gold paint.

1 Use the craft knife to cut the balsa sheet into two rectangles 10cm x 22cm. The sticks of balsa should be cut into four lengths 22cm long and four lengths 10cm long.

2 Glue the sticks around the edges of each sheet as shown. These form a shallow hollow into which you can press the 'wax'. Paint the two frames a rich brown colour.

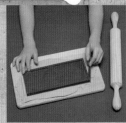

3 Roll out the modelling clay on a board and place a balsa frame on top. Use the modelling tool to cut around the outside of the frame. Repeat this step.

WRITING IT DOWN

Various materials were used for writing. Melted beeswax was poured into wooden trays to make writing tablets. Letters were scratched into the wax, which could be used again and again. Powdered soot was mixed with water and other ingredients to make ink for writing on papyrus, parchment or wood.

soot

melted beeswax

Roman numerals on papyrus

I II III IV V
1 2 3 4 5
VI VII VIII IX X
6 7 8 9 10

TEACHER AND PUPILS

A stone sculpture from Roman Germany shows a teacher seated between two of his pupils. They are reading their lessons from papyrus scrolls. Children had to learn poetry and other writings by heart. Any bad behaviour or mistakes were punished with a beating.

LETTERS IN STONE

Temples, monuments and public buildings were covered in Latin inscriptions, such as this one. Each letter was beautifully chiselled by a stonemason. These words are carved in marble. The inscription marked the 14th birthday of Lucius Caesar, the grandson of the Emperor Augustus.

4 Cut off about 1cm all around the edge of each modelling clay rectangle. This helps to make sure that the modelling clay will fit inside the balsa wood frame.

5 Carefully press the clay into each side – this represents the wax. Use the skewer to poke two holes through the inside edge of each frame, as shown.

6 Join the two frames together by threading purple thread through each pair of holes and tying it securely together. You have now made your tablet.

Paint the pencil gold to make it look as if it is made of metal. Use it like a stylus to scratch words on your tablet. Why not try writing in Latin? You could write CIVIS ROMANVS SVM, which means "I am a Roman citizen".

Life on a Celtic Farm

MEN, WOMEN AND CHILDREN were all expected to play their parts in running a Celtic farm. It seems likely that both men and women worked in the fields. Men usually did the ploughing, but the women probably carried out tasks such as weeding the crops. Everyone helped at harvest time because it was vital to gather the grain as soon as it was ripe. There were countless other jobs that needed doing to keep the farm running smoothly, such as combing sheep, caring for sick animals, milking cows, collecting eggs, repairing thatched roofs and fetching water. Along with all the other tasks around the farm, parents had to teach their children the skills they would need in adult life. Many Celtic parents sent their sons and daughters to live in other households until they were grown up. This was a way of making close bonds of friendship between families and tribes and also taught the children extra skills.

WRAPPED AND WARM
This carved stone statue of a baby wrapped in a blanket was made in Celtic France. Compared with today, it must have been difficult for mothers and grandmothers to keep young children clean, warm, dry and out of danger on a busy farm.

LOCKED UP
Keys like these were used to lock wooden chests containing valuable goods, such as the family's marriage wealth. This was the bride's dowry (money or treasure given by her father) plus an equal amount given by the husband on their wedding day. In some Celtic lands, wives had the right to inherit this if they outlived their husbands.

MAKE A POT

You will need: paper, bowl, PVA glue, water, balloon, petroleum jelly, card, pair of compasses, pencil, ruler, scissors, masking tape, cardboard core from roll of adhesive tape, pin, red and black paint, paintbrushes.

1 To make papier-mâché, tear paper or newspaper up into small strips. Fill a bowl with 1 part PVA glue to 3 parts water. Add the paper pieces and soak.

2 Blow up the balloon and cover in petroleum jelly. Cover the balloon in a layer of papier-mâché mixture. Leave to dry, then slowly build up more layers.

3 On the card draw a circle 20 cm in diameter. Draw a second circle inside it 9 cm in diameter. Mark off a quarter of both circles. Cut the large circle out.

DYED IN THE WOOL

The Romans reported that the Celts liked patterned, brightly coloured clothes. Sheep's wool was often dyed before being woven into cloth. Dyes were made from flowers, bark, berries, leaves or lichen boiled together with salt, crushed rock or stale urine. The wool was soaked in this mixture then boiled again, or left to soak for several hours.

sheep's wool   *lichen*

HAND-WOVEN

Many Celtic women made clothes and blankets from sheep's wool from their own farms. First, they cleaned and sorted the wool, then they spun it into thread. The thread was woven on an upright loom. Heavy weights kept the warp (vertical) threads straight while the weft (horizontal) thread was passed in-between.

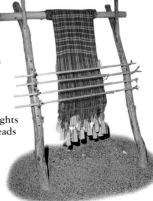

PEDESTAL POTS

Celtic women made simple pottery bowls and dishes for use at home. Wealthy Celtic people could also afford elegant vases and jugs like these pedestal pots (pots with feet), made by expert craftworkers in towns.

BUTTER BUCKET

Wooden buckets such as this were used on many Celtic farms, but few have survived. This one was found buried in a bog in northern Scotland. It contained butter. The damp, airless conditions in the bog had stopped the wood rotting.

Decorate your pedestal pot with a swirling pattern in typical Celtic style. The Celts liked bright colours – the pot that inspired this model was originally bright red.

4 Cut out a quarter of the outer circle and all of the inner circle, as shown. The outer circle will be the pot base. Stick the ends together with tape.

5 Use the cardboard inner from a roll of adhesive tape to make the stem of the pot. Attach it to the card base with masking tape.

6 Burst the balloon with a pin. Cut the top end of the pot off evenly. Attach the base and stem to the bottom of the pot with masking tape.

7 Paint the whole pot with red paint, including the stem and neck. Then add the Celtic pattern, as shown above, in black paint.

Celtic Food and Drink

FOOD WAS VERY IMPORTANT TO THE CELTS. They enjoyed eating and drinking, and were not ashamed of getting drunk, or of rowdy behaviour. They did not, however, approve of people getting too fat. Roman writers reported that Celtic warriors were ordered not to let out their belts, but to lose weight, when clothes around their waists became too tight! The Celts produced most of their own food on their farms. They needed to buy only items such as salt (used to preserve meat and fish), and luxury goods such as wine. They also hunted and fished for many wild creatures, and gathered wild fruits, nuts, herbs and mushrooms from meadows and forests. Celtic families were famous throughout Europe for their hospitality to strangers. It was their custom to offer food and drink to any visitor, and not to ask who they were or where they were from until the end of the meal.

HANGING CAULDRON

Meals for large numbers of people were cooked in a big cauldron. This bronze cauldron, iron chain and hook were made around 300BC in Switzerland. A cauldron could also be used for boiling water, heating milk to make cheese, or brewing mead.

CELTIC CASSEROLE

Meat, beans, grains and herbs were stewed in a covered clay pot. The pot could be placed directly on glowing embers or (as shown here) balanced on a hearthstone. This stone hearth, with a hollow pit for the fire, was found at an oppidum (Celtic town) in France.

MAKE SOME OATCAKES

You will need: 225 g oatmeal, 75 g plain flour, salt, baking soda, 50 g butter, water, bowl, sieve, wooden spoon, small saucepan, heat-resistant glass, board, rolling pin, baking tray, wire tray.

1 Preheat the oven to 220°C/425°F/Gas 7. Put 225 g of oatmeal into a large bowl. Add 75 g of plain flour. Sieve the flour into the bowl.

2 Next add 1 teaspoon of salt to the oatmeal and flour mixture. Mix all the ingredients in the bowl together well using a wooden spoon.

3 Add a quarter teaspoon of bicarbonate of soda (baking soda) to the oatmeal and flour mixture. Mix it in well and then put the bowl to one side.

GRINDING GRAIN

All kinds of grain were ground into flour using hand-powered querns (mills) like this one. The grains were poured through a hole in the top stone. This stone was then turned round and round. The grains became trapped and were crushed between the top and bottom stones, spilling out of the quern sides as flour.

FRUITS FROM THE FOREST

The Celts liked eating many of the same fruits and nuts that we enjoy today. However, they had to go and find them growing on bushes and trees. We know that the Celts ate fruit because archaeologists have found many seeds and pips on rubbish heaps and in lavatory pits at Celtic sites.

wild cherries

apples

hazelnuts

blackberries

OUT HUNTING

Celtic men went hunting and fishing for sport, and also as a way of finding food. This stone carving, showing a huntsman and his dogs chasing deer, was made around AD800 in Scotland. By then, Celtic power had declined, but many Celtic traditions persisted.

Enjoy your oatcakes plain, like the Celts did, or eat them with butter, cheese or honey. All these were favourite Celtic foods. Today, some people put jam on their oatcakes, but sugar (used to make jam) was unknown in Europe in Celtic times.

4 Next, melt the butter in a small saucepan over a low heat. Make sure that it does not burn. Add the melted fat to the oat and flour mixture.

5 Boil some water. Place a little of the water in a mug or heat-resistant glass. Gradually add the boiled water to the mixture until you have a firm dough.

6 Turn the dough out on to a board sprinkled with a little oatmeal and flour. Roll the dough until it is about 1 cm thick. Cut the dough into 24 circles.

7 Place the circles of dough on a greased baking tray. Bake in the oven for 15 minutes. Allow the oatcakes to cool on a wire tray before serving.

Viking Family Life

IN EARLY TIMES, everybody in the family knew who was related to whom and where they lived. For the Vikings, even distant relatives played an important role in the family, including grandparents, aunts and uncles. They were all very aware of family links, and loyalty was fierce. If one member of a family was harmed, then the other members of the family would seek revenge. This led to feuds – quarrels between one family and another that simmered on from one generation to the next. Feuds led to fights, theft and sometimes even as far as murder.

The father of the household had great power over other members of the family. If he thought a newborn baby was a weakling, he could leave it to die. When a Viking farmer died, his eldest son inherited the farm. The rest of the family would have to move away, and the younger sons had to find new land of their own to farm. Mothers were often strong, determined women who had great influence in the family. There was little schooling. Learning how to fight with a sword or use an axe was more important than reading and writing. As children grew up, they were expected to work hard and to help around the house. They were sometimes fostered out to families on other farms and had to work in return for their keep.

HELPING OUT
This reconstruction of a market stall in Jorvik shows a young lad helping his parents during a day's trading. Children often followed in the same trade as their parents. This boy would have learnt how to haggle over prices. He would also know how to weigh silver.

FAMILY MEMORIALS
The Vikings often put up memorial stones to honour relatives and friends when they died. This stone from Sweden was put up by Tjagan and Gunnar in loving memory of their brother Vader.

LIVING IN FEAR

Old tales tell how Vikings fought each other mercilessly during long, bitter feuds between families. Murderous bands might turn up at a longhouse by night, threatening to burn down the roof and kill everybody inside. Viking households also risked attack from local peoples or other raiders wherever they settled.

WANTING CHILDREN

A woman who wanted to make a good marriage and have children would pray to Frey, the god of love and fertility. On these gold foil charms from Sweden, Frey is shown with his beautiful wife Gerda. She was the daughter of a giant called Gymir.

GROWING UP

Children were expected to work hard in Viking times. Boys were taught farming, rowing and sailing. Girls were taught how to spin and weave, milk cows and prepare food. When all the daily tasks had been done, boys probably played games or went fishing. Viking girls may have spent some of their free time gathering berries and mushrooms.

BURIAL GRAVE

This skeleton belongs to a Viking woman from Iceland. Archaeologists have been able to tell how women lived in the Viking age by examining the goods placed in their graves. These were possessions for them to use in the next world.

Viking Women

Viking women could not speak in public assemblies, where laws and judgements were passed, yet they had more independence than many European women at the time. They could choose their own husband, own property and be granted a divorce. At a wedding, both the bride and groom had to make their marriage vows before witnesses. Memorial stones show that many husbands loved their wives and treated them with respect.

It was the women who usually managed the farm while their men were off raiding or trading. They never knew if their husbands, brothers and sons would return from their travels or be lost in a storm at sea. Women certainly needed to be tough in the harsh landscapes and cold climates of countries such as Iceland or Greenland. It was their job to make woollen or linen clothes for the family, to prepare and cook food and to clean the home.

WELCOME HOME
A woman in typical Viking dress welcomes a warrior returning from the wars. She has long hair tied back by a scarf and is wearing a pleated dress. The woman is a valkyrie, one of Odin's maidens in Valholl. This charm comes from Öland in Sweden.

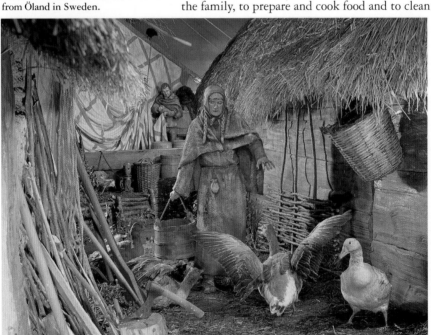

A DAY'S WORK
In this reconstruction from Jorvik (York), a Viking woman goes out to fetch water from the well. Hissing geese beat their wings and scatter in her path. Women's work lasted from dawn till nightfall, with clothes to darn, poultry to look after, meals to cook and children to scold! Most women also spent several hours a day spinning and weaving wool into cloth to make clothes.

PRACTICAL BUT PRETTY

Viking women wore long tunics fastened by a pair of brooches. This Viking brooch was found in Denmark. It is over 1,000 years old and is made of gold. Women wore clothing that was both practical and comfortable.

GETTING READY

Before a wedding or a visit to the fair, a Viking woman may have smoothed or pleated her dress on a board like this one. A glass ball would have been used instead of an iron. This whalebone board comes from Norway.

WEAVING AT HOME

Viking looms were like this one. The warps, or upright threads, hang from a crossbar. The weft, or cross threads, pass between them to make cloth. Weaving was done by women in every Viking home.

THE NEW QUEEN

In this picture, Queen Aelfgyfu is shown alongside her husband King Cnut, in England. Aelfgyfu was Cnut's second wife. They are placing a cross on an altar. Queens were the most powerful women in Scandinavian society.

BELOVED WIFE

This stone was put up by King Gorm as a monument to his wife. The inscription reads 'King Gorm made this memorial to his wife Thyri, adornment of Denmark'. The messages written on such stones show the qualities that Vikings admired most in women.

North American Homes

NATIVE AMERICAN INDIANS built houses that were cleverly adapted to their surroundings. During the winter months, the Inuit of the far north built dome-shaped homes out of blocks of ice or with hard soil, wood and whale bones. Where wood was plentiful such as in the eastern part of the United States, Indians built a variety of homes. The wikiup, or wigwam, was dome shaped and made out of thatch, bark or hide, tightly woven across an arch of bent branches. Basic, rectangular thatched houses were built from a construction of chopped twigs covered with a mixture of clay and straw, or mud. Near the east coast, massive longhouses, up to 45m long, with barrel-shaped roofs, were made from local trees. Some tribes lived in different kinds of shelters depending on the season. The Plains Indians mostly lived in tipis (tents made of hide) or sometimes in earth lodges. The nearest to modern buildings were the homes of the Pueblos in the Southwest. These were terraced mud brick villages. Pueblo Indians also built round underground ceremonial chambers with hidden entrances in the roof.

AT HOME
A Mandan chief relaxes with his family and dogs inside his lodge. Notice how a hole is cut in the roof to let out smoke from the fire and let fresh air in. Earth lodges were popular with Mandan and Hidatsa people on the Upper Missouri. The layout followed strict customs. The family would sleep on the south side, guests slept on the north. Stores and weapons were stored at the back. The owner of this home has his horse inside to prevent it from being stolen while the family is asleep.

HOMES ON THE PLAINS
The hides of around 12 buffaloes were used to cover a family tipi belonging to a Plains Indian. Tipi comes from a Siouan word meaning to dwell. Hides were sewn together and stretched over wooden poles about 8m high. When it became too hot inside, the tipi sides were rolled up. In winter, a fire was lit in the centre.

TOTEM POLE
Totem poles were usually found in the far northwest of the United States. They were carved out of wood, often from the mighty thuja (red cedar) trees. Tall totem poles were erected outside the long plank houses of the Haida people. These homes were shared by several families. The poles were carved and painted to keep a record of the family histories of the people inside. They were also sometimes made to honour a great chief.

EARTH LODGES

Mandan Indians perform the Buffalo Dance in front of their lodges. These were built by using logs to create a dome frame, which was then covered over with tightly packed earth.

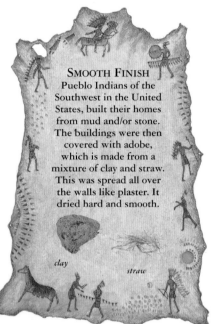

SMOOTH FINISH

Pueblo Indians of the Southwest in the United States, built their homes from mud and/or stone. The buildings were then covered with adobe, which is made from a mixture of clay and straw. This was spread all over the walls like plaster. It dried hard and smooth.

clay

straw

LAYERS OF BRICK

This ruin was once part of a complex of buildings belonging to Pueblo Indians. Pueblo homes were often multi-storeyed with flat roofs. The floors were reached by ladders. Circular brick chambers were built underground. These were the kivas used for religious and ceremonial rites.

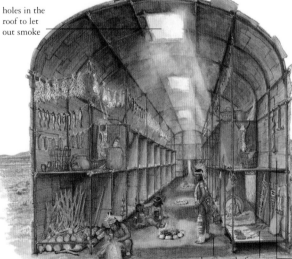

holes in the roof to let out smoke

sleeping platform

THE LONGHOUSE

Iroquois people of the Woodlands built long wooden houses. The frame was made of poles hewn from tree trunks with cladding made from sheets of thick bark. Homes were communal. Many families lived in one longhouse, each with their own section built around an open fire.

higher platform for storing food

Groups of longhouses were built together, sometimes inside a protective fence.

Tribal Family Roles

R OLES WITHIN THE TRIBAL INDIAN FAMILY were well defined. The men were the hunters, protectors and leaders. Women tended crops, made clothes, cared for the home and the sick, and prepared the food. The children's early days were carefree, but they quickly learned to respect their elders. From an early age, young girls were taught the skills of craftwork and homemaking by their mothers, while the boys learned to use weapons and hunt from the men. Girls as young as 12 years old could be married. Boys had to exchange presents with their future in-laws before the marriage was allowed to take place. At birth, most children were named by a grandparent. Later, as adults, they could choose another name of their own.

BONES FOR DINNER
This spoon was carved from animal bone. For the early family there were no metal utensils. Many items were made from bone, tusks, antlers or horns. Bone was also used to make bowls.

A DAY'S HUNTING
Blackfoot tribe girls look on as men leave camp on a hunting trip. They are in search of bison. If the hunt is successful, the women will help skin the animals then stretch out the hide to dry. Buffalo skins were used to make tipi covers. Softer buckskin, from deer, was used for clothing.

HOLDING THE BABY
A woman holds her baby strapped to a cradleboard. Domestic scenes were often the focus of Indian crafts, reflecting the importance of family life.

MAKE A KATCHINA DOLL
You will need: cardboard roll, ruler, scissors, compasses, pencil, thick card, PVA glue, brush for glue, masking tape, paints in cream/yellow, green/blue red and black, paintbrush, water pot, red paper.

1 Take the cardboard roll and cut a section of about 4cm (or a third) off the top. This will form the head piece. The larger end will form the body.

2 Use the compass (or end of the cardboard roll) to draw four circles of 2cm radius on card. Then draw a smaller circle 1.5cm radius. Cut them all out.

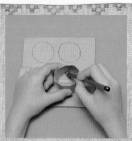

3 Glue the larger circles to either end of both of the cardboard roll tubes. Leave to dry. Glue the smaller circle of card on top of one end of the longer roll.

ROLE PLAY

Children love to copy their elders, and this little Sioux girl is wearing an adult's large headdress. She is holding a favourite doll to pose for the picture. Playing with dolls taught girls about their future role as a carer. Boys enjoyed learning how to ride, shoot arrows and hunt.

FAMILY GATHERING

A family from the Cree tribe in Canada enjoys a quiet evening around the fire. American Indian families were usually small as no more than two or three children survived the harsh life. However, a lodge was often home to an extended family. There could be two or three sisters, their families and grandparents under one roof.

Katchina dolls were made by the Hopi people to represent different spirits. This is the Corn katchina. Some parents gave the dolls to their children to help them learn about tribal customs.

BABY CARRIER

For the first year of its life, a baby would spend its time strapped to a cradleboard, such as this one influenced by the eastern Woodland tribes. It was also used by eastern Sioux, Iowa, Pawnee and Osage parents. A baby could sleep or be carried in safety while laced in its cradle, leaving the mother free to work. The board was strapped to the mother's back.

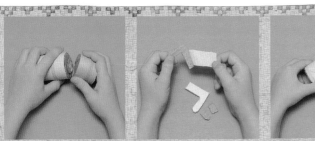

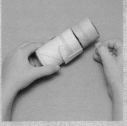

4 The smaller cardboard circle forms the doll's neck. Fix the small cardboard roll (the head) on top of the larger cardboard roll (the body) with glue.

5 Cut two small L-shapes from card to form the arms. Then cut two small ear shapes from the card. Cover these shapes with masking tape.

6 Glue the arms on to the body and the ears on to the sides of the head, so that they stick out at right angles. Paint the doll the colours shown above.

7 While the paint is drying, cut two small feather shapes from red paper. Glue these on to the top of the doll's head, so that they stick into the air.

Cold-climate Homes

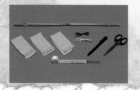

MOST ANCIENT ARCTIC GROUPS lived in small villages containing a few families at most. The villages were spread out over a wide area, so each group had a large territory in which to hunt. In winter, the Inuit, Saami and other Arctic tribes lived in sturdy houses built partly underground to protect them from the freezing conditions above. In summer, or when travelling from place to place, they lived in tents or temporary shelters.

In Siberia and parts of Scandinavia, groups such as the Nenets did not settle in one place. Their homes were lightweight tents, called chums in Siberia, made up of a framework of wooden poles and covered with animal skins. These chums could withstand severe Arctic blizzards and kept everyone warm inside when temperatures were icy.

TENT LIFE
A Nenet herder loads up a sledge outside his family's chum in preparation for another day's travel across Siberia. Chums were convenient, light and easy to assemble and dismantle. Some Nenets still live in chums, as their ancestors have done for generations.

BUILDING MATERIALS
A deserted building made from stone and whale bone stands on a cliff in Siberia. Building materials were scarce in the Arctic. In coastal regions, people built houses with whale bones and driftwood gathered from the beach. Inland, houses were mainly built with rocks and turf.

ARCTIC DWELLING
This illustration shows a house in the Alaskan subarctic with a portion cut away to show how it is made. Houses such as this one were buried under the ground. People entered by ladder through the roof.

MAKE A NENET TENT

You will need: 3 blankets (two at 2 x 1.5m and one at 1.2 x 1.2m), tape measure, string, scissors, 10 bamboo sticks (nine 180cm long and one 30cm long), black marker, black thread, a log or stone.

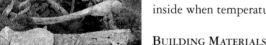

1 Cut small holes 10cm apart along the shorter sides of the two large blankets. Thread a piece of string through the holes and tie the string together.

2 Cut a 60cm length of string. Tie the 30cm-long stick and a black marker 55cm apart. Use the marker to draw a circle on the smaller blanket.

3 Tie four bamboo sticks together at one end. Open out the sticks onto the base blanket. Place the sticks on the edge of the circle so they stand up.

BONY BUNKER

Whale bone rafters arch over the remains of a home in Siberia. Part of the house was often built underground. First, the builders dug a pit to make the floor. Then they built low walls of rocks and turf. Long bones or driftwood laid on top of the walls formed sturdy rafters that supported a roof made from turf and stones.

MAKING WINDOWS

An old stone and turf house stands in Arctic Greenland. Ancient peoples made windows by stretching a dried seal bladder over a hole in the wall. The bladder was thin enough to allow light through.

A tent covered with several layers of animal skins made an extremely warm Arctic home, even in the bitterly cold winter. The wooden poles were lashed together with rope.

4 Lean the five extra bamboo sticks against the main frame, placing the ends around the base circle. Leave a gap at the front for the entrance.

5 Tie the middle of the edge of the two larger blankets to the back of the frame, at the top. Make two tight knots to secure the blankets.

6 Bring each blanket round to the entrance. Tie them at the top with string. Roll the blankets down to the base so they lie flat on the frame.

7 Tie five one-metre lengths of thread along the front edge of the blanket. Pull these tight and tie to a log or stone to weigh down the base of the tent.

Arctic Seasonal Camps

CHEERFUL GLOW
An igloo near Thule in Greenland is lit up by the glow of a primus stove. The light inside reveals the spiralling shape of the blocks of ice used to make the igloo. Snow crystals in the walls scatter the light so the whole room is bathed in the glow. In the Inuit language, *iglu* was actually a word to describe any type of house. A shelter such as this one was called an *igluigaq*.

SUMMER IS A BUSY TIME for Arctic animals and plants. The lives of Arctic peoples changed with the seasons too. The rising temperature melts the sea ice, and the oceans teem with tiny organisms called plankton. On land, the tundra bursts into flower. Insects hatch out and burrowing creatures, such as lemmings, leave their tunnels in search of food. Wild reindeer, whales and many types of birds migrate to the Arctic to feast on the plentiful supply of food.

In Canada, Alaska and Greenland, the Inuit left their winter villages and travelled to the summer hunting grounds. They hunted fish and sea mammals and gathered fruits and berries, taking advantage of the long, bright summer days.

During winter hunting trips, the Inuit built temporary shelters made of snow blocks, commonly called igloos. The basic igloo design was developed hundreds of years ago. It kept the hunters warm even in the harshest Arctic storm.

BUILDING AN IGLOO
An Inuk (a man of the Inuit tribe) builds an igloo, using a long ice knife to cut large blocks of tightly packed snow. First, he lays a ring of ice blocks to make a circle up to 3 metres in diameter. Then, some of the blocks are cut to make them slope. As new blocks are added, the walls of the igloo begin to lean inwards, forming a dome-shaped igloo. This method is exactly the same as the one used by his ancestors centuries ago.

MAKE A MODEL IGLOO
You will need: self-drying clay, rolling pin, cutting board, ruler, modelling tool, scissors, thick card (20 x 20cm), pencil, water bowl, white paint, paint brush.

1 Roll out the self-drying clay. It should be around 8mm thick. Cut out 30 blocks of clay; 24 must be 2 x 4cm and the other 6 blocks must be 1 x 2cm.

2 Cut out some card to make an irregular shape. Roll out more clay (8mm thick). Put the template on the clay and cut around it to make the base of the igloo.

3 Mark out a circle with a diameter of 12cm. Cut out a small rectangle on the edge of the circle (2 x 4cm) to make the entrance to the igloo.

IGLOO VILLAGE
This engraving, made in 1871, shows a large Inuit village in the Canadian Arctic. Most Inuit igloos were simple, dome-like structures. The Inuit built these temporary shelters during the winter hunting trips.

THE FINAL BLOCK
An Inuit hunter carefully places the final block of ice onto the roof of his igloo. Ancient hunters used sharp ice knives to shape the blocks so that they fitted together exactly. Any gaps were sealed with snow to prevent the icy winds from entering the shelter.

A SNUG HOME
An Inuit hunter shelters inside his igloo. A small entrance tunnel prevents cold winds from entering the shelter and traps warm air inside. Outside, the temperature may be as low as -70°C. Inside, heat from the stove, candles and the warmth of the hunter's body keeps the air at around 5°C.

Inuit hunters built temporary shelters by fitting ice blocks together to form a spiralling dome structure called an igloo. Only firmly packed snow was used to make the building blocks.

4 Stick nine large blocks around the edge of the circle. Use water to make the clay stick to the base. Cut across two rectangular blocks as shown above.

5 Using your modelling tool, carefully cut a small piece of clay from the corner of each of the remaining blocks as shown above.

6 Starting from the two blocks cut earlier, build up the walls, slanting each block in as you go. Use the six small blocks at the top. Leave a hole at the top.

7 Use the modelling tool to form a small entrance to the igloo behind the rectangle already cut into the base. When the clay has dried, paint the igloo white.

Arctic Children

MODEL IGLOO

An Inuit toddler plays with a model igloo at a nursery in the Canadian Arctic. The blocks of wood spiral upwards in the same way as the blocks of ice do in a real igloo, so the toy helps modern children to learn the ancient art of building igloos.

CHILDREN WERE AT THE CENTRE of most Arctic societies. Inuit babies and younger children spent most of their time riding on their mother's back, nestled in a snug pouch called an *amaut*. The babies of many Arctic groups were named for a respected member of the community and their birth was celebrated with a huge feast. As children grew older, other members of the family helped the mother to bring up her child.

Today, most Arctic children go to school when they are young. However, the children of past generations travelled with their parents as the group moved to fresh reindeer pastures or new hunting grounds. Very young boys and girls were treated equally. As they grew up, however, children helped with different tasks and learned the skills that they would need later on in life. Boys learned how to hunt and look after animals. Girls learned to sew and cook and to work with animal skins.

BIRTHDAY FEAST

Traditional food is prepared at the birthday celebration of the young boy sitting at the table. Parents often named their newborn babies after people who had been respected in the community, such as a great hunter. The baby was thought to inherit that person's skills and personality.

FEEDING BIRDS TOY

You will need: self-drying clay, rolling pin, ruler, modelling tool, board, two toothpicks, white and brown paint, water pot, paint brush.

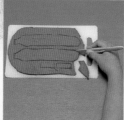

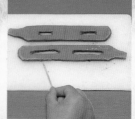

1 Roll out some of the clay into a 22 x 14cm rectangle with a thickness of around 1cm. Cut out two large paddles (18 x 3cm) and two stalks (4 x 2cm).

2 Cut two slots on paddle 1 (5cm x 8mm) and two on paddle 2 (2.5cm x 8mm). Use a toothpick to pierce a hole in the side of paddle 1 through these slots.

3 Roll out two egg shapes, each about 5 x 3.5cm, in the palm of your hands. Make two bird heads and stick them to the egg-shaped bodies.

Lending a Hand

A Nenet boy and his younger brother help to feed a reindeer calf that has lost its mother. Fathers taught their sons to handle animals from a very early age. Children were encouraged to look after the family's tame deer and dogs.

Riding High

One of the children in this old illustration is being carried in a special hood, called an *amaut,* high on the back of his mother's jacket. The second child is tucked inside her mother's sealskin boots. However, it was less common for a child to be carried in this way.

Playing with Dolls

A doll dressed in a soft fleecy coat rests on a Nenet sledge in Arctic Russia. Many Arctic girls like to play with dolls, as children do around the world. Traditionally, the dolls' heads were carved from ivory. The doll in the picture, however, is made of modern plastic.

Some Arctic children had toys with moving parts, such as this model of two birds. Traditionally, the animals would have been carved from bone or ivory. The child pulled the paddles to make the birds bob up and down.

4 Stick the stalks you made earlier to the base of each bird's body. Using the toothpick, pierce a small hole through the stalk, close to the body.

5 Leave the clay bird to dry on its side. You will need to support the stalk with a small piece of clay to hold the bird upright as it dries.

6 Place the stalk of each bird in the slots in the paddles. Push a toothpick into the holes in the edge of paddle 1, through the stalks and out the other side.

7 Add two small pieces of clay to the bottom of each stalk to keep the birds in place. You can paint the toy once the clay has dried.

Aztec and Maya Homes

AZTEC AND MAYA PEOPLE LIVING in Mesoamerica (known today as Central America) used local materials for building. They had no wheeled transport, so carrying building materials long distances was quite difficult. Stone was the most expensive and longest-lasting building material. It was used for religious buildings, rulers' palaces and tombs. The homes of ordinary people were built more quickly of cheaper materials, such as sun-dried mud bricks, called adobe, or mud smeared over a framework of wooden poles.

All Mesoamerican homes were very simply furnished. There were no chairs or tables, curtains or carpets – just some jars and baskets for storage and a few reed mats. Everyone, from rulers to slaves, sat and slept on mats on the floor. Most ordinary Aztec homes were L-shaped or built around a courtyard, with a separate bathroom for washing and a small shrine to the gods in the main room.

FAMILY HOME
This present-day Maya family home is built in traditional style, with red-painted mud-and-timber walls. It has one door and no windows. The floor is made of pounded earth. The roof, thatched with dried grass, is steeply sloped so the rain runs off it.

BURIED UNDERGROUND
Archaeologists have discovered these remains of houses at the Maya city of Copan. The roofs, walls and doors have rotted away, but we can still see the stone foundations, used to strengthen the walls. The houses are small and tightly packed together.

MAKE A MAYA HOUSE

You will need: thick card, pencil, ruler, scissors, glue, masking tape, terracotta plaster paste (or thin plaster coloured with paint), balsa wood strips, water pot, wide gummed paper tape, brush, short lengths of straw.

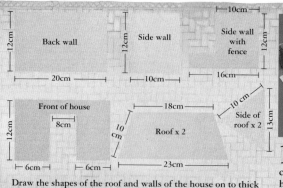

Back wall — 12cm / 20cm

Side wall — 12cm / 10cm

Side wall with fence — 10cm / 12cm / 16cm

Front of house — 12cm / 8cm / 6cm / 6cm

Roof x 2 — 18cm / 10cm / 23cm

Side of roof x 2 — 10 cm / 13cm

Draw the shapes of the roof and walls of the house on to thick card, using the measurements shown. (Please note that the templates are not shown to scale.) Cut the pieces out.

1 Cut out a rectangle 25cm x 15cm from thick card for the base. Stick the house walls and base together with glue. Use masking tape for support.

Stonemasons at Work

Mesoamerican masons constructed massive buildings using very simple equipment. Their wedges were made from wood, and their mallets and hammers were shaped from hard volcanic stone. Until around AD900 metal tools were unknown. Fine details were added by polishing stonework with wet sand.

Plaster

Big stone buildings, such as temples, were often covered with a kind of plaster called stucco. This was then painted with ornate designs. Plaster was made by burning limestone and mixing it with water and coloured earth. By the 1400s, there was so much new building in Tenochtitlan that the surrounding lake became polluted with chemicals from the plaster making.

plaster   *limestone*

Skilful Stonework

This carved stone panel from the Maya city of Chichen-Itza is decorated with a pattern of crosses. It was used to provide a fine facing to thick walls made of rubble and rough stone. This wall decorates a palace building.

A Maya house provided a cool shelter from the very hot Mexican sun, as well as keeping out rain.

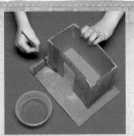

2 Paint the walls and base with plaster paste. This will make them look like Sun-dried mud. You could also decorate the doorway with balsa wood strips.

3 Put the house on one side to dry. Take your roof pieces and stick them together with glue. Use masking tape to support the roof, as shown.

4 Moisten the wide paper tape and use it to cover the joins between the roof pieces. There should be no gaps. Then cover the whole roof with glue.

5 Press lengths of straw into the glue on the roof. Work in layers, starting at the bottom. Overlap the layers. Fix the roof to the house using glue.

Mesoamerican Families

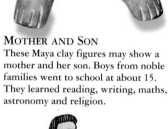

Families were very important in Maya and Aztec times. By working together, family members provided themselves with food, jobs, companionship and a home. Each member of a family had special responsibilities. Men produced food or earned money to buy it. Women cared for babies and the home. From the age of about five or six, children were expected to do their share of the family's work by helping their parents. Because family life was so important, marriages were often arranged by a young couple's parents, or by a matchmaker. The role of matchmaker would be played by an old woman who knew both families well. Boys and girls got married when they were between 16 and 20 years old. The young couple usually lived in the boy's parents' home.

Aztec families belonged to local clan-groups, known as *calpulli*. Each *calpulli* chose its own leader, collected its own taxes and built its own temple. It offered help to needy families, but also kept a close eye on how members behaved. If someone broke the law, the whole clan might be punished for that person's actions.

MOTHER AND SON
These Maya clay figures may show a mother and her son. Boys from noble families went to school at about 15. They learned reading, writing, maths, astronomy and religion.

PAINFUL PUNISHMENT
This codex painting shows a father holding his son over a fire of burning chillies as a punishment. Aztec parents used severe punishments in an attempt to make their children honest and obedient members of society.

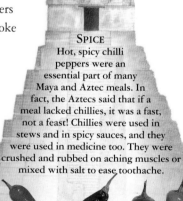

SPICE
Hot, spicy chilli peppers were an essential part of many Maya and Aztec meals. In fact, the Aztecs said that if a meal lacked chillies, it was a fast, not a feast! Chillies were used in stews and in spicy sauces, and they were used in medicine too. They were crushed and rubbed on aching muscles or mixed with salt to ease toothache.

red chillies

dried chillies, preserved for winter use

green chillies

IXTILTON

This Aztec mask is made of a black volcanic stone called obsidian. It shows the god Ixtilton, helper of Huitzilopochtli, the Aztecs' special tribal god. Aztec legends told how Ixtilton could bring darkness and peaceful sleep to tired children.

HUSBAND AND WIFE

The bride and groom in this codex picture of an Aztec wedding have their clothes tied together. This shows that their lives are now joined. Aztec weddings were celebrated with presents and feasting. Guests carried bunches of flowers, and the bride wore special make-up with her cheeks painted yellow or red. During the ceremony, the bride and groom sat side by side on a mat in front of the fire.

GUARDIAN GODDESS

The goddess Tlazolteotl is shown in this codex picture. She was the goddess of lust and sin. Tlazolteotl was also said to watch over mothers and young children. Childbirth was the most dangerous time in a woman's life, and women who died in childbirth were honoured like brave soldiers.

LEARNING FOR LIFE

A mother teaches her young daughter to cook in this picture from an Aztec codex. The girl is making tortillas, which are flat maize pancakes. You can see her grinding the corn in a *metate* (grinding stone) using a *mano* (stone used with the metate). Aztec mothers and fathers trained their children in all the skills they would need to survive in adult life. Children from the families of expert craftworkers learned their parents' special skills.

An Inca House

THE INCAS BEGAN AS A SMALL TRIBE living in the Andes mountains of Peru in South America. Like the Aztec and Maya people, the Incas preferred to build their homes from stone. White granite was the best, as it is very hard. The roof of each house was pitched at quite a steep angle, so that heavy mountain rains could drain off quickly. Timber roof beams were lashed to stone pegs on the gables, and supported a wooden frame. This was thatched with a tough grass called *ichu*.

Most houses had just one storey, but a few had two or three, joined by rope ladders inside the house or by stone blocks set into the outside wall. Most had a single doorway hung with cloth or hide.

Each building was home to a single family and formed part of a compound. As many as half a dozen houses would be grouped around a shared courtyard. All the buildings belonged to families who were members of the same *ayllu*, or clan.

MUD AND THATCH

Various types of houses were to be seen in different parts of the Inca Empire. Many were built in old-fashioned or in regional styles. These round and rectangular houses in Bolivia are made of mud bricks (adobe). The houses are thatched with *ichu* grass.

upper storey

inside hearth

courtyard

FLOATING HOMES

These houses are built by the Uru people, who fish in Lake Titicaca, in the southern part of Peru, and hunt in the surrounding marshes. They live on the lake shore and also on floating islands made of matted *totora* reeds. Their houses are made of *totora* and *ichu* grass. Both these materials would have been used in the Titicaca area in Inca times. The reeds are collected from the shallows and piled on to the floor of the lake. New reeds are constantly added.

PICTURES AND POTTERY

Houses with pitched roofs and windows appear as part of the decoration on this pottery from Pacheco, Nazca, in Peru. To find out about houses in ancient Peru, historians look at surviving towns and ruins, at housing styles still in use today and at old pictures and designs on objects.

SQUARE STONE, ROUND PEG

Squared-off blocks of stone are called ashlars. These white granite ashlars make up a wall in the Inca town of Pisaq. They are topped by a round stone peg. Pegs like these were probably used to support roof beams or other structures, such as ladders from one storey to another.

gable

roofbeam

roof peg

wall niche

BUILDING MATERIALS

The materials used to build an Inca house depended on local supplies. Rock was the favourite material. White granite, dark basalt and limestone were used when possible. Away from the mountains, clay was made into bricks and dried hard in the sun to make adobe. Roof beams were formed from timber poles. Thatch was made of grass or reed.

clay *white granite*

thatch *timber*

BUILDING TO LAST

The Incas built simple, but solid, dwellings in the mountains. The massive boulders used for temples and fortresses are here replaced by smaller, neatly cut stones. See how the roof beams are lashed to the gables to support the thatch. Stone roofs were very rare, even on the grandest houses. Timber joists provide an upper storey. The courtyard is used just as much as the inside of the house for everyday living.

Married Life in Inca Times

WEDDINGS WERE SOME of the happiest occasions in an Inca village. They offered a chance for the whole community to take time off work. The day was celebrated with dancing, music and feasting. The groom would probably be 25 years of age, at which point he was regarded as an adult citizen, and his bride would be a little younger – about 20.

For the first year of the marriage, a couple did not have to pay any tax either in goods or labour. However, most of their lives would be spent working hard. When they were elderly, they would still be expected to help with household chores. Later still, when they became too old or sick to look after themselves, they received free food and clothes from the State warehouse. They would then be cared for by their clan or family group.

Not everyone was expected to get married. The *mamakuna* (virgins of the sun) lived rather like nuns, in a special convent in the Inca town of Cuzco. They wove fine cloth and carried out religious duties. No men were allowed to enter the *mamakuna*'s building.

WEDDING CLOTHES
An Inca nobleman would get married in a very fine tunic. This one is from the southern coast of Peru. Commoners had to wear simpler clothes, but couples were presented with free new clothes from the State warehouses when they married.

REAL PEOPLE
This jar is over 1,300 years old. Unlike the portraits on many jars, it seems to show a real person sitting down and thinking about life. It reminds us that ancient cultures and civilizations were made up of individuals who fell in love, raised children and grew old, just as people do today.

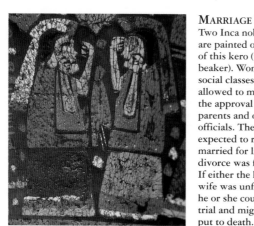

MARRIAGE PROSPECTS
Two Inca noble women are painted on the side of this kero (wooden beaker). Women of all social classes were only allowed to marry with the approval of their parents and of State officials. They were expected to remain married for life and divorce was forbidden. If either the husband or wife was unfaithful, he or she could face trial and might even be put to death.

A ROYAL MARRIAGE

A prince of the emperor's family marries in Cuzco. The scene is imagined by an artist of the 1800s. An emperor had many secondary wives in addition to his sister-empress. Between them they produced very many princes and princesses. Inca royal families were divided by jealousy and by complicated relations, which often broke out in open warfare. The emperor ordered his officials to keep tight control over who married whom. His own security on the throne depended on it.

A HOME OF THEIR OWN

When a couple married, they left their parents' houses and moved into their own home, like this one at Machu Picchu, in the Andes. The couple now took official control of the fields they would work. These had been allocated to the husband when he was born. Most couples stayed in the area occupied by their own clan, so their relatives would remain nearby.

HIS AND HERS

The everyday lives of most married couples in the Inca Empire were taken up by hard work. Men and women were expected to do different jobs. Women made the chicha beer and did the cooking, weaving and some field work. Men did field work and fulfilled the mit'a labour tax in service to the Inca State. They might build irrigation channels or repair roads.

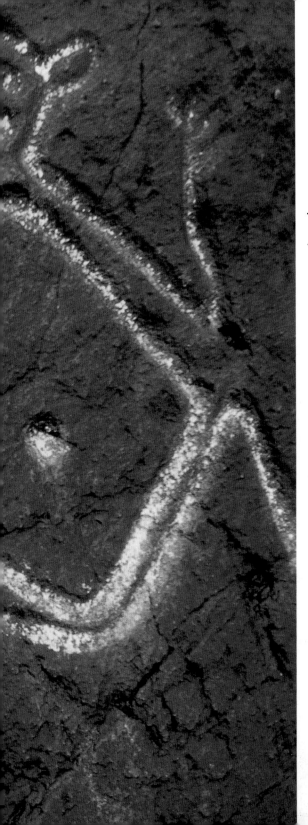

Art, Culture & Entertainment

Learn about the development of
art and music, sport and entertainment,
and story-telling and writing in this
exciting cultural history of pleasure and
leisure in many different civilizations.
Compare fashions around the ancient
world from the silks of China and Japan,
and the fabulous jewellery of Egypt to
the body piercings, paint and tattoos of
native Americans, Celts and Vikings.

Life, Leisure and Enjoyment

Daily life is more than just working, eating and sleeping. From the time of the earliest organized human societies, over 50,000 years ago, men and women have enjoyed telling stories, listening to music, dancing and playing games. Early humans decorated their clothes, tools, weapons and shelters with patterns and magic symbols. They even created lifelike images of the world around them. The earliest-known paintings of people and animals – discovered in caves in Europe – date from almost 30,000 years ago. The artwork is skilled, which suggests a long tradition of artists working for hundreds of years before, slowly perfecting their techniques. It seems clear that, even though early peoples' lives were often a struggle for survival in a harsh environment, there was time to draw and paint.

Animals were often depicted in cave paintings. They are believed to represent the creatures that Stone Age people hunted for food.

Music has always been a popular form of entertainment in Japan. This woman is playing a *shamisen* – a three-stringed instrument.

Sculpture, ornaments and painting have always been important for many reasons. Most simply, people like things to look

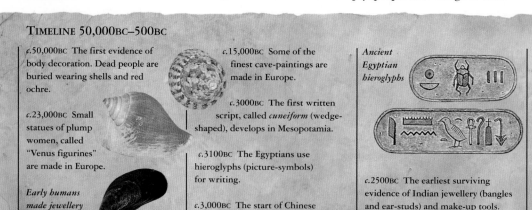

TIMELINE 50,000BC–500BC

*c.*50,000BC The first evidence of body decoration. Dead people are buried wearing shells and red ochre.

*c.*23,000BC Small statues of plump women, called "Venus figurines" are made in Europe.

Early humans made jewellery from shells

*c.*15,000BC Some of the finest cave-paintings are made in Europe.

*c.*3000BC The first written script, called *cuneiform* (wedge-shaped), develops in Mesopotamia.

*c.*3100BC The Egyptians use hieroglyphs (picture-symbols) for writing.

*c.*3,000BC The start of Chinese pottery-making.

Ancient Egyptian hieroglyphs

*c.*2500BC The earliest surviving evidence of Indian jewellery (bangles and ear-studs) and make-up tools.

50,000BC   15,000BC   2500BC   1500BC

An Aztec woman is shown wearing bangles, a chunky necklace and earrings. She obviously took a lot of pride in her appearance.

Tribal peoples valued the skills that went into creating patterned pots.

good. All around the world, craftworkers made everyday items, such as blankets or food-baskets, as attractive as possible. The type and style of decoration used varied from culture to culture, and over the centuries. The available materials were also important, such as clay for pottery, or coloured pigments for paints and dyes. Wealthy people could afford items made from valuable substances, such as silk or porcelain (both from China), or employ skilled artists to create fine statues, carvings, pottery and mosaics, such as those surviving from ancient Greece and Rome.

People have also always liked to look good. Men and women in ancient Egypt wore make-up and had elaborate hairstyles. In India, traditional clothing was simple, but people wore fancy accessories and jewels. In many civilizations, people have also liked decorating their own bodies, with piercing, body-paint and tattoos.

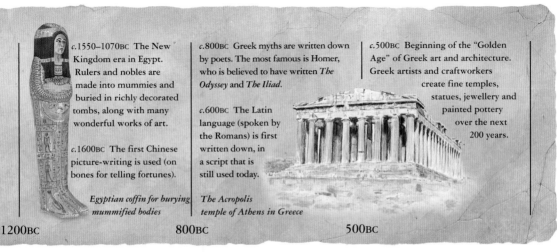

*c.*1550–1070BC The New Kingdom era in Egypt. Rulers and nobles are made into mummies and buried in richly decorated tombs, along with many wonderful works of art.

*c.*1600BC The first Chinese picture-writing is used (on bones for telling fortunes).

Egyptian coffin for burying mummified bodies

*c.*800BC Greek myths are written down by poets. The most famous is Homer, who is believed to have written *The Odyssey* and *The Iliad*.

*c.*600BC The Latin language (spoken by the Romans) is first written down, in a script that is still used today.

The Acropolis temple of Athens in Greece

*c.*500BC Beginning of the "Golden Age" of Greek art and architecture. Greek artists and craftworkers create fine temples, statues, jewellery and painted pottery over the next 200 years.

1200BC

800BC

500BC

Patterns, pictures, stories, myths, legends, dancing and music added an extra layer of meaning to people's lives. They helped people to express their beliefs, manage their fears and sometimes (they thought), to make contact with the invisible world of gods, spirits, ghosts and dead ancestors. Some art forms offered magical protection to hunters and children. Others, such as costumes and jewellery were used in ceremonies that marked important stages in peoples' lives, such as birth, marriage or death.

Chinese letters are called characters. They are read down, from right to left.

The arts often provided excellent entertainment. Watching skilled performances – from simple tunes played on prehistoric deer-bone flutes to elegant Japanese court theatre – gave people pleasure. Sometimes, they helped them to understand their feelings, hopes and fears, and the world around them. Singers, poets and storytellers retold ancient myths in words and music. This often became a way of preserving the history of families and tribes. Around 5,000 years ago,

The decorations of North American Indian tribes, such as this rattle, often had spiritual significance.

This Mesopotamian board game may have been played like Ludo. It is made from wood and decorated with a mosaic of shell and coloured stone.

Ancient civilizations in the Near East, such as those of Egypt and Mesopotamia, put great effort into creating visually stunning interiors. This is the internal hall of a Mesopotamian palace.

in the Middle East, artists and craftworkers also began to use picture symbols to record useful information or important events. Picture-writing was also developed in China before 1500BC. From that time on, many people around the world used writing as a new art form. It was another way of passing on traditions, telling ancient stories, myths and legends, or expressing important beliefs and ideas.

In a thematic history such as this, you can follow developments in different aspects of art and culture in turn. You will be able to see how dress, accessories, sport, entertainmnent, ornamental and decorative arts, writing and storytelling evolved through time and varied from culture to culture.

Greek girls were expected to spend their time helping in the home but many still had time to enjoy a game of tag.

Costumes at the Inca August Festival

feathers, many of which they wear to seasonal festivals.

1500 A new garment, a long, loose robe called a *kimono,* becomes fashionable in Japan.

1500s to 1700s Musicians and dancers entertain Mughal rulers at royal courts in India. The Mughals also collect beautiful books, paintings and jewels.

1600 Start of Japanese Kabuki popular drama and bunraku puppet plays.

Kabuki actor

1500   1600   1700

Stone Age Jewellery

CEREMONIAL DRESS
The amazing headdress, face painting and jewellery still seen at ceremonies in Papua New Guinea may echo the richness of decoration in Stone Age times.

Mᴇɴ ᴀɴᴅ ᴡᴏᴍᴇɴ ᴡᴏʀᴇ ᴊᴇᴡᴇʟʟᴇʀʏ from as early as the Stone Age. Necklaces and pendants were made from all sorts of natural objects. Brightly coloured pebbles, snail shells, fishbones, animal teeth, seashells, eggshells, nuts and seeds were all used. Later, semi-precious amber and jade, fossilized jet and handmade clay beads were also used. The beads were threaded on to thin strips of leather or twine made from plant fibres.

Other jewellery included bracelets made of slices of elephant or mammoth tusk. Strings of shells and teeth were made into beautiful headbands. Women plaited their hair and put it up with combs and pins. People probably decorated their bodies and outlined their eyes with pigments such as red ochre. They may have tattooed and pierced their bodies too.

BODY PAINT
These Australian Aboriginal children have painted their bodies with clay. They have used patterns that are thousands of years old.

BONES AND TEETH
Necklaces were often made from the bones and teeth of a walrus. This one comes from Skara Brae in the Orkney Islands. A hole was made in each bead with a stone tool, or with a wooden stick spun by a bow drill. The beads were then strung on to a strip of leather or twine.

MAKE A NECKLACE
You will need: self-drying clay, rolling pin and board, modelling tool, sandpaper, ivory and black acrylic paint, paintbrush, water pot, ruler, scissors, chamois leather, card, double-sided sticky tape, PVA glue, leather laces.

1 Roll out the clay on a board and cut out four crescent shapes with the modelling tool. Leave them on the board to dry.

2 Rub the crescents lightly with sandpaper and paint them an ivory colour. You could varnish them later to make them shiny.

3 Cut four strips of leather about 9cm x 3cm. Use the edge of a piece of card to make a black criss-cross pattern on the strips.

NATURAL DECORATION

We know about the wide variety of materials used in Stone Age jewellery from cave paintings and ornaments discovered in graves. Shells were highly prized and some were traded over long distances. Other materials included deers' teeth, mammoth and walrus ivory, fish bones and birds' feathers.

a selection of sea shells

BANGLES AND EAR STUDS

Jewellery found at Harappa in Pakistan included these items. They date from between 2300BC and 1750BC and are made from shells and coloured pottery. Archaeologists in Harappa have found remains of the shops that sold jewellery.

A WARRIOR'S HEADDRESS

The headdress of this Yali warrior from Indonesia is made of wild boars' teeth. The necklace is made of shells and bone. Headdresses and necklaces made of animals' teeth may have had a spiritual meaning for Stone Age people. The wearer may have believed that the teeth brought the strength or courage of the animal from which they came.

Stone Age people believed that wearing a leopard claw necklace brought them magical powers.

4 When they are dry, fold back the edges of each strip and hold in place with double-sided sticky tape.

5 Brush the middle of each crescent with glue and wrap the leather around, forming a loop at the top, as shown.

6 Plait together three leather laces to make a thong. Make the thong long enough to go around your neck and be tied.

7 Thread the leopard's claws on to the middle of the thong, arranging them so that there are small spaces between them.

STONE AGE JEWELLERY   445

Egyptian Vanity

THE ANCIENT EGYPTIANS were very fond of jewellery. The rich wore pieces finely crafted from precious stones and metals. Cheaper adornments were made from glass and polished stones. Make-up was also important for both men and women. They wore green eyeshadow made from a mineral called malachite and black eyeliner made from galena, a type of lead. Lipsticks and blusher were made from red ochre. The Egyptians liked to tattoo their skin, and they also used perfumes. Most men were clean shaven. Wigs were worn by men and women, even by those who had plenty of hair of their own. Grey hair was dyed and there were various remedies for baldness.

A TIMELESS BEAUTY
This limestone head is of Queen Nefertiti, the wife of the Sun-worshipping pharaoh Akhenaten. She seems to be the ideal of Egyptian beauty. She wears a headdress and a necklace. The stone is painted and so we can see that she is also wearing make-up and lipstick.

LOOKING GOOD
Mirrors were made of polished copper or bronze, with handles of wood or ivory. This bronze mirror is from 1900BC. Mirrors were used by the wealthy for checking hairstyles, applying make-up, or simply for admiring one's own good looks! The poor had to make do with seeing their reflection in water.

MAKE A MIRROR
You will need: mirror card, pencil, scissors, self-drying clay, modelling tool, rolling pin and board, small piece of card or sandpaper, gold paint, PVA glue and brush, waterpot and brush.

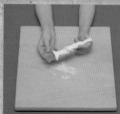

1 Begin by drawing a mirror shape on the white side of a piece of mirror card, as shown. Carefully cut the mirror shape out. Put the card to one side.

2 Take your clay and roll it into a tube. Then mould it into a handle shape, as shown. Decorate the handle with a lotus or papyrus flower, or other design.

3 Now make a slot in the handle with a square piece of card or sandpaper, as shown. This is where the mirror card will slot into the handle.

BIG WIGS AND WAXY CONES

Many pictures show nobles at banquets wearing cones of perfumed grease on their heads. The scent may have been released as the cones melted in the heat. However, some experts believe that the cones were drawn in by artists to show that the person was wearing a scented wig. False hairpieces and wigs were very popular in Egypt. It was common for people to cut their hair short, but some did have long hair that they dressed in elaborate styles.

COSMETICS

During the early years of the Egyptian Empire, black eye kohl was made from galena, a type of poisonous lead! Later soot was used. Henna was painted on the nails and the soles of the feet to make them red. Popular beauty treatments included pumice stone to smooth rough skin and ash face packs.

face pack   *pumice stone*   *kohl*   *henna*

COSMETICS BOWL

Make-up, oils and lotions were prepared and stored in jars and bowls, as well as in hollow reeds or tubes. These containers were made of stone, pottery and glass. Minerals were ground into a powder and then mixed with water in cosmetics bowls to make a paste. Make-up was applied with the fingers or with a special wooden applicator. Two colours of eye make-up were commonly used – green and black. Green was used in the early period, but later the distinctive black eye paint became more popular.

The shape of mirrors and their shining surface reminded Egyptians of the Sun disc, so they became religious symbols. By the New Kingdom, many were decorated with the goddess Hathor or lotus flowers.

4 Place the handle on a wire baking tray and leave it in a warm place to dry. Turn it over after two hours. When it is completely dry, try your mirror for size.

5 It is now time to paint the handle. Paint one side carefully with gold paint and leave it to dry. When it has dried, turn the handle over and paint the other side.

6 Finally, you can assemble your mirror. Cover the base of the mirror card in glue and insert it into the handle slot. Leave it in a warm place to dry.

Clothing and Jewellery in India

BOTH RICH AND POOR PEOPLE IN INDIA have always tended to wear simple clothes dressed up with lots of jewellery, such as earrings, armbands, breastplates, noserings and anklets. They also had elaborate hairstyles decorated with flowers and ornaments.

Religious beliefs influenced how people dressed. Hindu men and women dressed simply in a single piece of fabric that was draped around the hips, drawn up between the legs, then fastened securely again at the waist. For men this was called a *dhoti*. Women wore bodices above the waist but men were often barechested. The female style of dress evolved into the *sari*.

When Islam arrived in India, tailored garments became widespread in the north of the country. People wore sewn cotton trousers called *paijama* or *shalwar*, with a long tunic called a *kamiz* or *kurta*. For men, turbans became popular. Muslim women were expected to dress modestly, so they began to wear veils, a practice that Hindu women also adopted.

SETTING THE TREND
Bangles and ear studs from the Indus Valley are among the earliest ornaments found in India. They are more than 4,000 years old. The styles of these pieces of jewellery, and the designs on them, were used again in later forms of decoration.

BEAUTY AIDS
This mirror, collyrium applicator and hair pin are over 4,000 years old. Large dark eyes were considered a sign of beauty, so women drew attention to their eyes by outlining them with collyrium, a black substance.

ANCIENT DRESS
A painted fragment of a pillar shows a woman wearing a long red skirt and jewellery. The pillar is about 2,000 years old.

MAKE A FLOWER BRACELET

You will need: A5 sheets of thin white card, pencil, scissors, gold paint, paintbrush, A5 sheets of white paper, PVA glue, foil sweet papers, gardening wire, pliers.

1 Draw some simple flower shapes on the white card. They should be about 2 cm in diameter. Give each flower six rounded petals.

2 Carefully cut out each of the flower shapes. Then paint both sides of each flower with gold paint. Leave the flowers to dry.

3 Draw 10 to 12 wedge shapes on the white paper sheets. They should be wider at the bottom than at the top. Cut out the wedge shapes.

HINDU DRESS
In this detail from a painted panel, a Hindu man and woman wear typical dress – a *dhoti* for the man and for the woman, a *sari*. Both men and women liked to wear brightly coloured clothes.

JEWELS FOR ALL
A Rajasthani woman wears traditional jewellery and dress. Nowadays in India, jewellery is still so valued that even the poorer peasants own pieces for special occasions.

COLOURFUL SILK
Silk is a fine, soft thread produced by the larva (grubs) of the silkworm moth when it makes its cocoon. The thread is woven into cloth and dyed. Silk was first brought to India from China along the Silk Road. Indian silk is mostly dyed in bright colours.

silk

Floral designs are common patterns used throughout Indian art.

CLOTHING FOR THE COURT
Courtiers from the Mughal Empire (1526-1857) wore a side-fastening coat called a *jama*. It has a tight body, high waist and flared skirt reaching to below the knees. It is worn over tight-fitting trousers, or *paijama*, gathered at the ankle. A sash, called a *patuka*, is tied to the waist. Courtiers also wore a small turban as a mark of respect.

4 Apply glue to the wedge shapes and roll them up to make beads, leaving a hole through the middle. Paint the beads gold and leave to dry.

5 Carefully cut out tiny circles from the coloured foil paper. Make sure you have enough to stick on to the centre of each flower.

6 Measure gardening wire long enough to go around your wrist. Add 4 cm for a loop. Tape the flowers to the wire and thread on the beads.

7 To finish the flower bracelet, use a pair of pliers to bend back one end of the wire to form a loop and the other end to form a hook.

Greek Garments

PHYSICAL BEAUTY AND AN ATTRACTIVE appearance were admired in ancient Greece in both men and women. Clothes were simple and practical, and made of wool and linen, which were spun at home. The rich, however, could afford more luxurious garments made from imported cotton or silk. Fabrics were coloured with dyes made from plants, insects and shellfish.

Men and women wore long tunics, draped loosely for comfort in the warm climate, and held in place with decorative pins or brooches. A heavy cloak was added for travelling or in bad weather. The tunics of soldiers and labourers were cut short, so they could move easily. Sandals were usually worn outdoors, though men sometimes wore boots. In hot weather, hats made of straw or wool kept off the sun. A tan was not admired in ancient Greece, because it signified outdoor work as a labourer or a slave. Men cut their hair short, while women coiled long hair in elaborate styles, sometimes with ribbons.

SEE FOR YOURSELF
Glass mirrors were not known to the Greeks. Instead, they used highly polished bronze to see their reflection in. This mirror has a handle in the shape of a woman. Winged sphinxes sit on her shoulders.

GOLDEN LION
This heavy bracelet dates from around the 4th century BC. It is made of solid gold and decorated with two lion heads. Gold was valuable because there was little of it found in Greece. Most of it was imported from Asia Minor or Egypt.

KEEP IT SIMPLE
The figurine above is wearing a peplos. This was a simple, sleeveless dress worn by Greek women. The only adornment was a belt tied underneath the bust. This statue comes from a Greek colony in southern Italy.

CHITON
You will need: tape measure, rectangle of cloth, scissors, pins, chalk, needle, thread, 12 metal buttons (with loops), cord.

1 Ask a friend to measure your width from wrist to wrist, double this figure. Measure your length from shoulder to ankle. Cut your cloth to these figures.

2 Fold the fabric in half widthways. Pin the two sides together. Draw a chalk line along the fabric, 2cm away from the edge of the fabric.

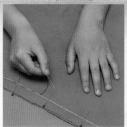

3 Sew along the chalk line. Then turn the material inside out, so the seam is on the inside. Refold the fabric so the seam is at the back.

TEXTILE TRADE

Clothes in ancient Greece were usually made from wool and linen. The Greeks exported their wool, which was admired for its superior quality. Cotton and silk were imported to make clothes. But only wealthy Greeks could afford clothes made from these materials.

cotton

raw wool

linen

POWDER POT

Greek women used face powder and other cosmetics and kept them in a ceramic pot called a pyxis. This one was was made in Athens in about 450BC. The painted decoration shows women spinning and weaving.

Clothes were handmade in ancient Greece. Enough material would be woven to fit the person they were being made for exactly, to avoid waste.

spiral band

BURIAL JEWELLERY

Some pieces of jewellery, like the ones pictured here, were made especially for burial. Very thin sheet gold was beaten into belts and wreaths. Important people like the Kings and Queens of Macedonia were buried in crowns of gold leaves.

wreath

belt

4 Make a gap big enough for your head to fit in, at one of the open ends of the fabric. Mark where the gap is going to be and pin the fabric together there.

5 From the head gap mark a point every 5cm to the end of the fabric. Pin together the front and back along these points. Your arms will fit through here.

6 At each pin, sew on a button to hold the two sides of material together. To secure the button, sew through the loop several times and knot it.

7 Cut a length of cord, to fit around your waist with a little bit spare to tie. Tie this cord around your waist and bunch the material up, over the cord.

Palace Fashions in Japan

Clothing in early times often depended on how rich you were. In Japan, from around AD600 to 1500, wealthy noble men and women at the emperor's court wore very different clothes from ordinary peasant farmers. Fashions were based on traditional Chinese styles. Both men and women wore long, flowing robes made of many layers of fine, glossy silk, held in place by a sash and cords. Men also wore wide trousers underneath. Women kept their hair loose and long, while men tied their hair into a topknot and wore a tall black hat. Elegance and refinement were the aims of this style.

After about 1500, wealthy samurai families began to wear *kimono* – long, loose robes. *Kimono* also became popular among wealthy artists, actors and craftworkers. The shoguns passed laws to try to stop ordinary people from wearing elaborate *kimono*, but they proved impossible to enforce.

PARASOL
Women protected their delicate complexions with sunshades made of oiled paper. The fashion was for pale skin, often heavily powdered, with dark, soft eyebrows.

GOOD TASTE OR GAUDY?
This woman's outfit dates from the 1700s. Though striking, it would probably have been considered too bold to be in the most refined taste. Men and women took great care in choosing garments that blended well together.

MAKE A FAN

You will need: thick card (38cm x 26cm), pencil, ruler, compasses, protractor, felt tip pen (blue), paper (red), scissors, paints, paintbrush, water pot, glue stick.

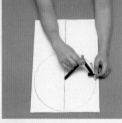

1 Draw a line down the centre of the piece of card. Place your compasses two-thirds of the way up the line. Draw a circle 23cm in diameter.

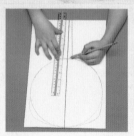

2 Add squared-off edges at the top of the circle, as shown. Now draw your handle (15cm long). The handle should be directly over the vertical line.

3 Place a protractor at the top of the handle and draw a semicircle around it. Now mark lines every 2.5 degrees. Draw pencil lines through these marks.

FEET OFF THE GROUND

To catch insects in a garden by lamplight these women are wearing *geta* (clogs). *Geta* were designed to protect the wearer's feet from mud and rain by raising them about 5–7cm above the ground. They were worn outdoors.

SILK *KIMONO*

This beautiful silk *kimono* was made in about 1600. Women wore a wide silk sash called an *obi* on top of their *kimono*. Men fastened their *kimono* with a narrow sash.

PAPER FAN

Folding fans, made of pleated paper, were a Japanese invention. They were carried by both men and women. This one is painted with gold leaf and chrysanthemum flowers.

BEAUTIFUL HAIR

Traditional palace fashions for men and women are shown in this scene from the imperial palace. The women have long, flowing hair that reaches to their waists – a sign of great beauty in early Japan.

It was the custom for Japanese noblewomen to hide their faces in court. They used decorated fans such as this one as a screen. Fans were also used to help people keep cool on hot, humid summer days.

4 Draw a blue line 1cm to the left of each line you have drawn. Then draw a blue line 2mm to the right of this line. Add a squiggle between sections.

5 Cut out your card fan. Now use this as a template. Draw around the fan top (not handle) on to your red paper. Cut out the red paper.

6 Now cut out the in-between sections on your card fan (those marked with a squiggle). Paint the card fan brown on both sides. Leave to dry.

7 Paint the red paper with white flowers and leave to dry. Paste glue on to one side of the card fan. Stick the undecorated side of the red paper to the fan.

Cold-climate Dress

I**N THE FREEZING A**RCTIC, clothes needed to be warm as well as beautiful. Strips or patches of different furs were used to form designs and geometric patterns on outer clothes. Fur trimmings, toggles and other decorative fastenings added the final touches to many clothes. Jewellery included pendants, bracelets, necklaces and brooches. These ornaments were traditionally made of natural materials, such as bone and walrus ivory.

In North America, Inuit women often decorated clothes with birds' beaks, tiny feathers or even porcupine quills. In Greenland, lace and glass beads were popular decorations. Saami clothes were the most colourful in the Arctic. Saami men, women and children wore blue outfits with a bright red and yellow trim. Mens' costumes included a tall hat and a short flared tunic. Womens' clothes included flared skirts with embroidered hems and colourful hats, shawls and scarves.

SAAMI COSTUME
A Saami man wears the traditional costume of his region, including a flared tunic trimmed with bright woven ribbon at the neck, shoulders, cuffs and hem. Outfits such as the one above were worn all year round. In winter, Saami people wore thick fur parkas, called *peskes,* over the bright tunics.

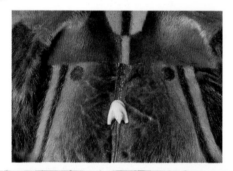

BEAR TOGGLE
An ivory toggle carved into the shape of a polar bear completes this traditional sealskin jacket. Arctic people took great pride in their appearance and loved to decorate their clothes in this way. In ancient times, the Inuit, for example, decorated their garments with hundreds of tiny feathers or the claws of mammals, such as foxes or hares. Women often decorated all the family's clothes.

MAKE A SAAMI HAT
You will need: red felt (58 x 30 cm), PVA glue, glue brush, black ribbon (58 x 2 cm), coloured ribbon, white felt, ruler, pencil, compass, red card, scissors, red, green and white ribbon (3 at 44 x 4 cm), red ribbon (58 x 4 cm).

1 Mark out the centre of the red felt along its length. Carefully glue the length of black ribbon along the centre line, as shown above.

2 Continue to decorate the felt with different kinds of coloured ribbon and white felt, making a series of strips along the red felt, as shown above.

3 Cut out a circle of red card with a diameter of 18 cm. Draw a circle inside with a diameter of 15 cm. Cut into the larger circle to the 15 cm line.

CURVING BOOT

This picture shows a curved boot worn by the Saami people from Arctic Scandinavia. These boots are designed for use with skis and are decorated with traditional woollen pompoms. The curved boot tips stop the skier from slipping out of the skis when travelling uphill.

WEDDING FINERY

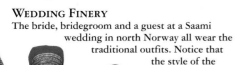

The bride, bridegroom and a guest at a Saami wedding in north Norway all wear the traditional outfits. Notice that the style of the man's wedding hat differs from the one shown in the picture on the opposite page. Both men and women wear brooches encrusted with metal disks. Saami women's wedding outfits include tall hats, tasselled shawls and ribbons.

BEADS AND LACE

A woman from western Greenland wears the traditional beaded costume of her nation, which includes a top with a wide black collar and cuffs and high sealskin boots. After European settlers arrived in Greenland, glass beads and lace became traditional decorations on clothing. Hundreds of beads were sewn onto jackets to make intricate patterns.

The style of Saami hats varied from region to region. In southern Norway, men's hats were tall and rounded. Further north, their hats had four points.

4 Glue the ends of the decorated red felt together, as shown above. You will need to find the right size to fit around your head.

5 Fold down the tabs cut into the red card circle. Glue the tabs, then stick the card circle to the felt inside one end of the hat.

6 While the hat is drying, glue the coloured ribbon strips together. Glue these strips 15 cm from the end of the 58 cm long red ribbon band.

7 Glue the 58 cm band of red ribbon onto the base of the hat, making sure the shorter strips of red, green and white ribbons go over the top of the band.

Bold Designs in South America

Festival costumes in the Andes today are in dazzling pinks, reds and blues. In the Inca period it was no different. People loved to wear brightly coloured braids, threads and ribbons. Sequins, beads, feathers and gold were sewn into fabric, while precious stones, red shells, silver and gold were made into beautiful earplugs, necklaces, pendants, nostril-rings and discs. However, it was only the nobles who were allowed to show off by wearing feathers, jewels and precious metals. Some of the most prized ornaments were gifts from the emperor for high-ranking service in the army.

Much of the finest craft work went into making small statues and objects for religious ceremonies, temples and shrines. During the Inca period, craft workers were employed by the State. They produced many beautiful treasures, but some of the best of these were the work of non-Inca peoples, particularly the Chimú. Treasures shipped to Spain after the Conquest astounded the Europeans by their fine craftsmanship.

PLUMES OF THE CHIEF
An impressive headdress like this would have belonged to a high-ranking Inca official or general in northern Chile over 500 years ago. The hat is made from coils of dyed llama wool. It is decorated with bold designs, and topped by a spray of feathers.

A SACRED PUMA
This gold pouch in the shape of a puma, a sacred animal, was made by the Moche people between 1,300 and 1,700 years ago. It may have been used to carry *coca* leaves. These were used as a drug during religious ceremonies. The pattern on the body is made up of two-headed snakes.

A GOLD AND SILVER NECKLACE
You will need: self-drying clay, cutting board, ruler, large blunt needle, gold and silver paint, paintbrush, water pot, card, pencil, scissors, strong thread.

1 Form pieces of clay into beads in the shape of monkey nuts. You will need 10 large beads (about 3.5cm x 2cm) and 10 smaller beads (about 2.5cm x 1.5cm).

2 Use the needle to mark patterns on the beads, so that they look like nut shells. Then carefully make a hole through the middle of each bead. Leave to dry.

3 Paint half the shells of each size gold and half of them silver. You should have 5 small and 5 large gold beads, and 5 small and 5 large silver beads.

PRECIOUS AND PRETTY

The most valued stone in the Andes was blue-green turquoise. It was cut and polished into beads and discs for necklaces, and inlaid in gold statues and masks. Blue lapis lazuli, black jet and other stones also found their way along trading routes. Colombia, on the northern edge of the Inca Empire, mined many precious stones and metals. Seashells were cut and polished into beautiful beads.

emerald turquoise

lapis lazuli

BIRDS OF A FEATHER

Birds and fish decorate this feather cape. It was made by the Chancay people of the central Peruvian coast between the 1300s and 1500s. It would have been worn for religious ceremonies. Feather work was a skilled craft in both Central and South America. In Inca times, the brilliantly coloured feathers of birds called macaws were sent to the emperor as tribute from the tribes of the Amazon forests.

Necklaces made of gold, silver and jewels would only have been worn by Inca royalty, such as the Quya (Inca empress).

TREASURE LOST AND FOUND

A beautifully made gold pendant created in the Moche period before the Incas rose to power. After the Spanish conquest of Peru, countless treasures were looted from temples or palaces by Spanish soldiers. Gold was melted down or shipped back to Europe. A few items escaped by being buried in graves. Some have been discovered by archaeologists.

4 Paint some card gold on both sides. On it draw 11 rectangles (3cm x 1cm) with rounded ends. Cut them out and carefully prick a hole in each end.

5 Thread the needle and make a knot 10cm from the end of the thread. Then thread the card strips and large beads alternately, using the gold beads first.

6 Be sure to start and end with card strips. When you have finished, knot the thread tightly next to the last card strip. Cut the thread 10cm from the knot.

7 Repeat steps 5 and 6 using more thread and the small beads, so that the beads are joined as shown. Finally, knot the ends of the two threads together.

Interior Design in Assyria

ASSYRIAN KINGS IN NORTH MESOPOTAMIA (present-day Iraq) loved the luxury of ivory furniture. They filled their palaces with ivory beds, arm chairs, foot stools and tables. No complete pieces of ivory furniture have survived to modern times, but archaeologists found part of an ivory throne during their excavations at the city of Nimrud in the 1840s. They also found some elephant tusks and many small, carved ivory plaques that were once attached to the wooden framework of pieces of furniture. Today, it is considered cruel to kill elephants for their ivory, and the animals have become an endangered species.

No textiles have survived but Assyrian palaces would probably have been made comfortable with cushions and woollen rugs. Stone entrances to the palace rooms carved in the form of floral-patterned carpets give us an idea of what the rugs may have looked like.

WOMAN IN A WINDOW
A piece of carved ivory from Phoenicia. The Phoenicians probably supplied the Assyrians with most of their ivory. They were great traders from the eastern Mediterranean shores.

INSIDE THE PALACE
Palaces were built from mud brick, but the lower interior walls were decorated with carved and painted slabs of stone. Teams of sculptors and artists produced scenes showing the king's military campaigns and wild bull and lion hunts. The upper walls were plastered and painted with similar scenes to glorify the king and impress foreign visitors. Paints were ground from minerals. Red and brown paints were made from ochres, blues and greens from copper ores, azurite and malachite.

MAKE A BRONZE AND IVORY MIRROR
You will need: pencil, strong white and reflective card, ruler, scissors, thick dowel, masking tape, flour, water and newspaper to make papier mâché, paints, brushes, sandpaper, glue.

1 Draw around a saucer to mark a circle 12 cm across on to the strong white card. Add a handle about 6cm long and 2.5cm wide as shown. Cut out.

2 Take a length of dowel measuring about 20cm long. Fix the dowel to the handle using masking tape. Bend the card round the dowel as shown.

3 Scrunch up a piece of newspaper into a ball. Attach the newspaper ball to the top of the handle with masking tape as shown.

LUXURY IN THE GARDEN

King Ashurbanipal and his wife even had luxurious ivory furniture in the palace gardens at Nineveh. In this picture, the king is reclining on an elaborate ivory couch decorated with tiny carved and gilded lions. The queen is sitting on an ivory chair with a high back and resting her feet on a footstool. Cushions make the furniture more comfortable. Ivory workers used drills and chisels similar to those used by carpenters. The ivory plaques had signs on them to show how they should be slotted together.

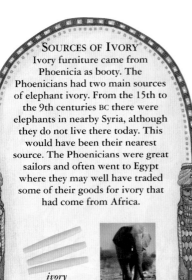

SOURCES OF IVORY

Ivory furniture came from Phoenicia as booty. The Phoenicians had two main sources of elephant ivory. From the 15th to the 9th centuries BC there were elephants in nearby Syria, although they do not live there today. This would have been their nearest source. The Phoenicians were great sailors and often went to Egypt where they may well have traded some of their goods for ivory that had come from Africa.

ivory

African elephant

Polished bronze was used for mirrors in ancient times. A mirror with a handle of carved ivory like this would have belonged to a wealthy woman.

BOY-EATER

This furniture plaque shows a boy being eaten by a lioness. Sometimes ivory was stained or inlaid with paste to imitate jewels. The boy's kilt is covered with gold leaf, and his curly hair is made of tiny gold pins. There are lotus flowers and papyrus plants in the background, inlaid with real lapis lazuli and carnelian.

4 Make a paste with flour and water. Tear the newspaper into strips and dip them into the paste. Cover the handle in the papier mâché strips.

5 Use newspaper to make the nose and ears. Add a strip of papier mâché at the top of the head for the crown. Leave to dry, then sandpaper until smooth.

6 Paint a base coat of grey paint on the face and bronze on the handle. Then add the details of the face and crown in black using a fine paintbrush.

7 Cut out a circle of reflective card to match the mirror shape. Glue the reflective card carefully on to the white card. This is your bronze mirror.

Egyptian Crafts

THE ANCIENT EGYPTIANS loved beautiful objects, and the craft items that have survived still amaze us today. There are shining gold rings and pendants, necklaces inlaid with glass and a dazzling blue glazed pottery called faience. Jars made of a smooth white stone called alabaster have been preserved in almost perfect condition, along with chairs and chests made of cedar wood imported from the Near East.

Egyptians made beautiful baskets and storage pots. Some pottery was made from river clay, but the finest pots were made from a chalky clay found at Quena. Pots were shaped by hand or, later, on a potter's wheel. Some were polished with a smooth pebble until their surface shone. We know so much about Egyptian craft work because many beautiful items were placed in tombs, so that the dead person could use them in the next world.

ALABASTER ART
Jars such as this would have held oils and perfumes. This elaborate jar was among the treasures in the tomb of King Tutankhamun (1334–1325BC).

GLASS FISH
This beautiful stripy fish looks as if it should be swimming in the reefs of the Red Sea. In fact, it is a glass jar used to store oils. Glass-making became popular in Egypt after 1500BC. The glass was made from sand and salty crystals. It would then have been coloured with metals and shaped while still hot.

MAKE A LOTUS TILE

You will need: card (2 sheets), pencil, ruler, scissors, self-drying clay, modelling tool, sandpaper acrylic paint (blue, gold, green, yellow ochre), water pot and brush. Optional; rolling pin & board.

1 Using the final picture as reference, draw both tile shapes onto card. Cut them out. Draw the whole pattern of tiles onto the sheet of card and cut around the border.

2 Roll out the clay on a board with a rolling pin or bottle. Place the overall outline over the clay and carefully trim off the edges. Discard the extra clay.

3 Mark the individual tile patterns into the clay, following the outlines carefully. Cut through the lines, but do not separate them out yet.

DESERT RICHES

The dwellers of the green Nile valley feared and disliked the desert. They called it the Red Land. However, the deserts did provide them with great mineral wealth, including blue-green turquoise, purple amethyst and blue agate.

blue agate   *turquoise*   *amethyst*

ROYAL TILES

Many beautiful Egyptian tiles have been discovered by archaeologists. It is thought that they were used to decorate furniture and floors in the palaces of the pharaohs.

TUTANKHAMUN'S WAR CHEST

Tutankhamun is in battle against the Syrians and the Nubians on this painted chest. On the lid, the young king is seen hunting in the desert. The incredible detail of the painting shows that this was the work of a very skilled artist. When Tutankhamun's tomb was opened, the chest was found to contain children's clothes. The desert air was so dry that neither the wood, leather nor fabric had rotted.

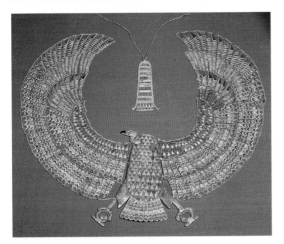

NEKHBET COLLAR

In this splendid collar, the spectacular wings of the vulture goddess Nekhbet include 250 feather sections made of coloured glass set in gold. The vulture's beak and eye are made from a black, volcanic glass called obsidian. It was one of 17 collars found in Tutankhamun's tomb. As one of many amazing objects found in the young king's tomb, it shows us the incredible skill of Egyptian craftsmen.

4 Now use the tool to score patterns of leaves and flowers into the surface of the soft clay, as shown. Separate the pieces and allow them to dry.

5 When one side of each tile has dried, turn it over. Leave the other side to dry. Then sand down the edges of the tiles until they are smooth.

6 The tiles are now ready for painting. Carefully paint the patterns in green, yellow ochre, gold and blue. Leave them in a warm place to dry.

These tiles are similar to those found at a royal palace in Thebes. The design looks rather like a lotus, the sacred waterlily of ancient Egypt.

Chinese Pottery

POTTERY MAKING developed in the Far East long before it was mastered in north-west Europe. Over 5,000 years ago, Chinese potters had worked out how to shape clay, and bake it in kilns (ovens) at temperatures of about 900°C to make it hard. Gradually, they discovered how to bake better clays at much higher temperatures to make more hardwearing and water-resistant pottery, and to coat it with shiny, waterproof glazes. The toughest, most waterproof and most delicate ceramic of all was porcelain. This was invented by the Chinese about 800 years before it was produced in Europe. Porcelain was one of China's most important exports to Asia and Europe.

The Chinese were also the first to use lacquer, a smooth, hard varnish made from the sap of a tree. From about 1300BC, lacquer was used for coating wooden surfaces, such as house timbers, bowls or furniture. It could also be applied to leather and metal. Natural lacquer is grey, but in China pigment was added to make it black or bright red. It was applied in many layers until thick enough to be carved or inlaid with mother-of-pearl.

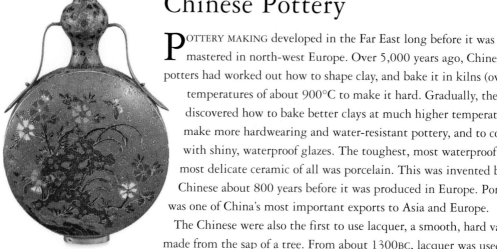

ENAMEL WARE
Ming dynasty craft workers created this ornate flask. They made a design with thin metal wire, then filled the wire compartments with drops of coloured, melted glass. The technique is called cloisonné.

CHINA'S HISTORY TOLD ON THE BIG SCREEN
A beautifully detailed, glossy lacquer screen shows a group of Portuguese merchants on a visit to China. It was made in the 1600s. Chinese crafts first became popular in Europe at this time, as European traders began doing business in southern China's ports.

FLORAL BOTTLE
This attractive Ming dynasty bottle is decorated with a coating of bright red lacquer. The lacquer is coloured with a mineral called cinnabar. It would have taken many long hours to apply and dry the many layers of lacquer. The bottle is carved with a design of peonies, which were a very popular flower in China.

FISH ON A PLATE

Pictures of fish decorate the border of this precious porcelain plate. It was made during the reign of the Qing emperor Yongzheng (1722–1736), a period famous for its elegant designs. It is coloured with enamel. Porcelain is made from a fine white clay called kaolin (china clay) and a mineral called feldspar. They are fired (baked) to a very high temperature.

A JUG OF WINE

An unknown Chinese potter made this beautiful wine jug about 1,000 years ago. It has been fired to such a high temperature that it has become strong and water-resistant. It was then coated with a grey-green glaze called celadon and fired again.

LIFE-LIKE FIGURES

A Ming dynasty entertainer smiles at his audience. All sorts of pottery figures have been found in Ming dynasty tombs. Potters made lively figures of merchants, musicians, court ladies and animals. Some are comic, while others are beautiful.

DEEP BLUE, PURE WHITE

Blue-and-white vases are typical of the late Ming dynasty (1368–1644). In the 1600s, large numbers were exported to Europe. Many were produced at the imperial potteries at Jingdezhen, in northern Jiangxi province. The workshops were set up in 1369, as the region had plentiful supplies of the very best clay. Some of the finest pottery ever made was produced there in the 1400s and 1500s.

Fine Crafts in Japan

THERE IS A LONG TRADITION among Japanese craftworkers of making everyday things as beautiful as possible. Craftworkers created exquisite items for the wealthiest and most knowledgeable collectors. They used a wide variety of materials – pottery, metal, lacquer, cloth, paper and bamboo. Pottery ranged from plain, simple earthenware to delicate porcelain painted with brilliantly coloured glazes. Japanese metalworkers produced alloys (mixtures of metals) before they were known elsewhere in the world. Cloth was woven from fibres in elaborate designs. Bamboo and other plants from the grass family were woven into elegant *tatami* mats (floor mats) and containers of all different shapes and sizes. Japanese craftworkers also made beautifully decorated *inro* (little boxes, used like purses) which dangled from men's *kimono* sashes.

SHINY LACQUER

This samurai helmet was made for ceremonial use. It is covered in lacquer (varnish) and decorated with a diving dolphin. Producing shiny lacquerware was a slow process. An object was covered with many thin layers of lacquer. Each layer was allowed to dry, then polished, before more lacquer was applied. The lacquer could then be carved.

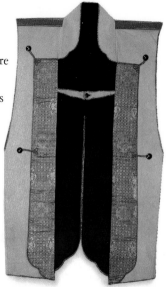

SAMURAI SURCOAT

Even the simplest garments were beautifully crafted. This surcoat (loose, sleeveless tunic) was made for a member of the noble Mori family, probably around 1800. Surcoats were worn by samurai on top of their armour.

MAKE A NETSUKE FOX

You will need: paper, pencil, ruler, self-drying clay, balsa wood, modelling tool, fine sandpaper, acrylic paint, paintbrush, water pot, darning needle, cord, small box (for an inro*), scissors, toggle, wide belt.*

1 Draw a square 5cm by 5cm on a piece of paper. Roll out a ball of clay to the size of the square. Shape the clay so that it comes to a point at one end.

2 Turn your clay over. Lay a stick of balsa approximately 6cm long, along the back. Stick a thin sausage of clay over the stick. Press to secure.

3 Turn the clay over. Cut out two triangles of clay. Join them to the head using the tool. Make indentations to shape them into a fox's ears.

METALWORK

Craftworkers polish the sharp swords and knives they have made. It took many years of training to become a metalworker. Japanese craftsmen were famous for their fine skills at smelting and handling metals.

BOXES FOR BELTS

Inro were originally designed for storing medicines. The first *inro* were plain and simple, but after about 1700 they were often decorated with exquisite designs. These *inro* have been lacquered (coated with a shiny substance made from the sap of the lacquer tree). Inside, they contain several compartments stacked on top of each other.

MASTERWORK

This beautiful jar is decorated with a design of white flowers, painted over a shiny red and black glaze. It was painted by the master-craftsman Ogata Kenzan, who lived from 1663 to 1743.

Wear your inro *dangling from your belt. In early Japan,* inro *were usually worn by men. They were held in place with carved toggles called* netsuke.

4 Use the handle of your modelling tool to make your fox's mouth. Carve eyes, nostrils, teeth and a frown line. Use the top of a pencil to make eye holes.

5 Leave to dry. Gently sand the *netsuke* and remove the balsa wood stick. Paint it with several layers of acrylic paint. Leave in a warm place to dry.

6 Thread cord through the four corners of a small box with a darning needle. Then thread the cord through a toggle and the *netsuke,* as shown.

7 Put a wide belt round your waist. Thread the *netsuke* under the belt. It should rest on the top of it. The *inro* (box) should hang down, as shown.

Roman Decoration

URING THE ROMAN ERA, houses and public places were decorated with paintings and statues. Mosaics were pictures made using *tesserae,* squares of stone, pottery or glass, which were pressed into soft cement. Mosaic pictures might show hunting scenes, the harvest or Roman gods. Geometric patterns were often used as borders.

Wall paintings, or murals, often showed garden scenes, birds and animals or heroes and goddesses. They were painted on to wooden panels or directly on to the wall. Roman artists loved to trick the eye by painting false columns, archways and shelves. The Romans were skilled sculptors, using stone, marble and bronze. They imitated the ancient Greeks in putting up marble statues in public places and gardens. These might be of gods and goddesses or emperors and generals.

A COUNTRY SCENE
This man and wild boar are part of a mosaic made in Roman North Africa. Making a mosaic was quite tricky – rather like doing a jigsaw puzzle. Even so, skilled artists could create lifelike scenes from cubes of coloured glass, pottery and stone.

SCULPTURE
Statues of metal or stone were often placed in gardens. This bronze figure is in the remains of a house in Pompeii. It is of a faun, a god of the countryside.

FLOOR MOSAICS
Birds, animals, plants and country scenes were popular subjects for mosaics. These parrots are part of a much larger, and quite elaborate, floor mosaic from a Roman house.

MAKE A MOSAIC

You will need: rough paper, pencil, ruler, scissors, large sheet of card, self-drying clay, rolling pin, wooden board, modelling knife, acrylic paints, paintbrush, water pot, clear varnish and brush (optional), plaster paste, spreader, muslin rag.

1 Sketch out your mosaic design on rough paper. A simple design like this one is a good start. Cut the card so it measures 25cm x 10cm. Copy the design on to it.

2 Roll out the clay on the board. Measure out small squares on the clay. Cut them out with the modelling knife. Leave to dry. These will be your tesserae.

3 Paint the pieces in batches of different colours. When the paint is dry, coat them with clear varnish for extra strength and shine. Leave to dry.

MOSAIC MATERIALS

Mosaics were often made inside frames, in workshops, and then transported to where they were to be used. Sometimes, the tesserae were brought to the site and fitted on the spot by the workers. The floor of an average room in a Roman town house might need over 100,000 pieces.

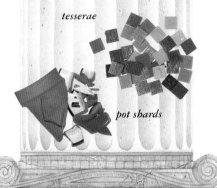

tesserae

pot shards

MUSICIANS AND DANCERS

This dramatic painting is on the walls of an excavated villa in Pompeii. It is one in a series of paintings that show the secret rites, or mysteries, honouring the Greek god of wine, Dionysus, who was called Bacchus in Rome.

REAL OR FAKE?

Roman artists liked to make painted objects appear real enough to touch. This bowl of fruit on a shelf is typical of this style of painting. It was found on the wall of a villa that belonged to a wealthy Roman landowner.

4 Spread the plaster paste on to the card, a small part at a time. While it is still wet, press in your tesserae following the design, as shown above.

5 When the mosaic is dry, use the muslin rag to polish up the surface. Any other soft, dry cloth would also be suitable. Now your mosaic is ready for display.

The Romans liked to have mosaics in their homes. Wealthy people often had elaborate mosaics in their courtyards and dining rooms, as these were rooms that visitors would see.

Viking Picture Stories

THE VIKINGS WERE SKILLED ARTISTS and metalworkers as well as fierce warriors, although they rarely painted pictures. Instead, they embroidered tapestries, and carved pictures on wooden panels or stones.

Viking art often recorded events. Pieces of tapestry found in a Viking ship burial site in Oseberg, in Norway, show a procession of horses and wagons. The tradition of making tapestries to tell stories and events was continued by the Normans, descendants of the Vikings who settled in Normandy, in France, in the 8th century AD. Over 150 years later, the Bayeux Tapestry was made there. In 79 embroidered scenes, the Bayeux Tapestry told the story of the Norman conquest of England in 1066.

Many Viking artworks often describe the doom of the gods and destruction of the world in tales of great feuds and battles between gods, mythical monsters and giants. These often show bold, powerful figures, intricate, swirling patterns and graceful animals. They demonstrate the Viking artists' love of movement and line.

After the Viking Age, their style of art disappeared as Europeans brought different styles to the area.

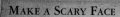

TWILIGHT OF THE GODS
This stone carving from the Isle of Man shows the final battle of the gods. Odin, the father of the gods, is shown here armed with a spear and a raven on his shoulder. He is killed by Fenrir, the grey wolf.

ART FROM URNES
At Urnes, in Norway, there is a stave church that has old wood panels. They date from the final years of the Viking Age. This one shows a deer eating Yggdrasil, the tree that holds up the world. Urnes has given its name to the last and most graceful period of Viking art and design.

MAKE A SCARY FACE

You will need: pencil, paper, scissors, self-drying clay, rolling pin, board, modelling tool, sandpaper, thick brush, acrylic paints, fine brush, water pot.

1 Draw a scary monster face on paper. Copy this one or one from a book, or make up your own. Make your drawing big and bold. Then cut it out.

2 Roll out a large piece of modelling clay into a slab. Use a modelling tool to trim off the edges to look like the uneven shape of a rune stone.

3 Lay your design on top of the clay slab. Use a modelling tool to go over the lines of your drawing, pushing through the paper into the clay.

WOLF BITES GOD

In the picture below, Tyr, god of the assemblies and law-makers. His hand is being bitten off by Fenrir, the grey wolf. Fenrir is straining against a magic chain forged by the dwarfs. The chain is made from all sorts of impossible things, such as fish's breath and a mountain's roots. Tyr's name survives in the English word 'Tuesday'.

WHISTLE

This tiny whistle was made from a bird's leg bone. It may have been used to scare birds away from the crops.

WALL HANGING

The bold design on this tapestry shows the gods Odin, Thor and Frey. It comes from a church in Sweden and dates from the 1100s, just after the Viking Age. It is probably similar to the wall hangings woven for royal halls in the earlier Viking times.

4 Go over all the lines in the picture. Make sure the lines show up on the clay below. Remove the paper to see the monster's outline in clay.

5 Leave the clay to dry, turning it over to make sure it is well aired. When it is hard, smooth it down with fine sandpaper, then brush with a paintbrush.

6 Now paint the face as shown, using yellow ochre, black, red and blue. Let each colour dry completely before starting the next. Leave to dry.

Here's a face to scare off evil spirits on a dark night! Faces like this, with interlacing beard and moustache, appeared on stone memorials in the Viking Age.

Sport and Games in China

FROM EARLY IN CHINA's history, kings and nobles loved to go hunting for pleasure. Horses and chariots were used to hunt deer and wild boar. Dogs and even cheetahs were trained to chase the prey. Spears, bows and arrows were then used to kill it. Falconry (using birds of prey to hunt animals) was commonplace by about 2000BC.

In the Ming and Qing dynasties ancient spiritual disciplines used by Daoist monks were brought together with the battle training used by warriors. These martial arts (*wu shu*) were intended to train both mind and body. They came to include the body movements known as tai chi (*taijiquan*), sword play (*jianwu*) and the extreme combat known as kung fu (*gongfu*).

Archery was a popular sport in imperial China. The Chinese also loved gambling, and may have invented the first card games over 2,000 years ago.

PEACE THROUGH MOVEMENT
A student of tai chi practises his art. The Chinese first developed the system of exercises known as tai chi more than 2,000 years ago. The techniques of tai chi were designed to help relax the human body and concentrate the mind.

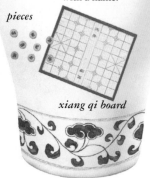

CHINESE CHESS
The traditional Chinese game of xiang qi is similar to western chess. One army battles against another, with round discs used as playing pieces. To tell the discs apart, each is marked with a name.

pieces

xiang qi board

MAKE A KITE

You will need: 30cm barbecue sticks (x12), ruler, scissors, glue and brush, plastic insulating tape, A1-size paper, pencil, paint (blue, red, yellow, black and pink), paintbrush, water pot, string, piece of wooden dowel, small metal ring.

1 Make a 40cm x 30cm rectangle by joining some of the sticks. Overlap the sticks for strength, then glue and tape together. Add a centre rod.

2 Make another rectangle 15cm x 40cm long. Overlay the second rectangle on top of the first one. Tape rectangles together, as shown above.

3 Place frame on to a sheet of white A1-size paper. Draw a 2.5cm border around outside of frame. Add curves around the end of the centre rod.

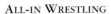

BAMBOO BETTING

Gamblers place bets in a game of *liu po.* Bamboo sticks were thrown like dice to decide how far the counters on the board should move. Gambling was a widespread pastime during the Han dynasty. People would bet large sums of money on the outcome of card games, horse races and cock fights.

ALL-IN WRESTLING

This bronze figure of two wrestling muscle men was made in about 300BC. Wrestling was a very popular entertainment and sport in imperial China. It continues to be an attraction at country fairs and festivals.

POLO PONIES

These women from the Tang dynasty are playing a fast and furious game of polo. They are probably noblewomen from the Emperor's royal court. The sport of polo was originally played in India and central Asia. It was invented as a training game to improve the riding skills of soldiers in cavalry units.

Chinese children today still play with home-made paper kites. Kites were invented in China in about 400BC.

4 Cut out the kite shape from the paper. Using a pencil, draw the details of your dragon design on the paper. Paint in your design and leave to dry.

5 Cut a triangular piece of paper to hang from the end of your kite as a tail. Fold tail over rod at bottom of kite, as shown. Tape tail into position.

6 Carefully tape and glue your design on to the frame. Fold over border that you allowed for when cutting out the paper. Tape to back of paper, as shown.

7 Wrap 10m of string around dowel. Tie other end to ring. Pass 2 pieces of string through kite from the back. Tie to centre rod. Tie other ends to ring.

Popular Music in Ancient Greece

MUSIC AND DANCE WERE important parts of Greek life. People sang, played and danced at religious ceremonies. Music was enjoyed for pleasure and entertainment at family celebrations, dramatic performances, feasts and drinking parties. Few written records remain of the notes played, but examples of the instruments do. The most popular instruments were the pipes. They were wind instruments similar to the oboe or clarinet. One pipe on its own was called the *aulos*, two played together were known as *auloi*. The stringed lyre and flute were other popular instruments. The stringed lyre produced solemn and dignified music. It was often played by men of noble birth to accompany a poetry recital. The flute was more usually played by slaves or dancing girls.

BREATH CONTROL
The leather strap tied around the auloi-player's cheeks helped to focus the power of his breath. One tube of the auloi supplied the melody, while the other produced an accompanying drone to give more depth to the sound. The aulos had as few as three or as many as 24 fingerholes for making the different notes.

Greek soldiers complained that lack of music was a hardship of war. Spartan soldiers resolved this problem by blowing tunes on pipes as they marched. Music was believed to have magical powers. Greek legend tells of Orpheus soothing savage beasts by playing his lyre. Another myth tells how Amphion (a son of Zeus) made stones move on their own and built a wall around the city of Thebes, by playing his lyre.

BANG! CRASH!
The bronze figurine above is playing the cymbals. They made a sound similar to castanets. The Greeks used the cymbals to accompany dancing. Other percussion instruments included wooden clappers and hand-held drums, like tambourines.

TIMPANON
You will need: scissors, corrugated card, tape measure, plate, white card, pair of compasses, pencil, PVA glue, tape, strips of newspaper, cream paper, red and purple felt-tip pens, ochre card, red and yellow ribbons.

1 Cut out a strip of corrugated card 5cm wide. Wrap it around a dinner plate. Add 6cm on to the length of this card and cut it off.

2 Put the plate upside down on the white card. Draw around it. Draw another circle 3cm inside the first. Cut this out to make a ring.

3 Glue the cardboard strip that you made in step 1 to the edge of the cardboard ring you made in step 2. Then tape them together for extra hold.

DIVINE MUSIC

Terpsichore was one of the Nine Muses, or spirits of the arts. She was the spirit of dance and music. Here Terpsichore plays a harp while her attendants hold the lyre and auloi. Other Muses included Polyhymnia, the spirit of hymns, and Euterpe, the spirit of flute-playing.

PERCUSSION

The timpanon was a tambourine made of animal skin, stretched over a frame. It was tapped to provide rhythmic accompaniment at dances or recitals. Stringed and wind instruments were thought superior because they made fitting music for solemn or exclusive occasions. Drums, cymbals and clappers were associated with buskers.

ENTERTAINING

In this plate painting a young man plays the auloi while his female companion dances. Professional musicians were often hired to entertain guests at dinner parties. Sometimes the musicians were household slaves.

To play the timpanon tap on it with your fingers, as the ancient Greeks would have done.

4 Make up some papier mâché solution with 1 part glue to 2 parts water. Soak strips of newspaper in it and cover the card ring with the wet strips.

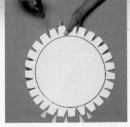

5 Draw around the plate on to cream paper. Draw another circle 5cm outside this. To make tabs, cut out about 28 small triangles around the edge.

6 Draw the design shown above on to the paper. Place the paper over the top of the card ring. Dab glue on each tab and stick on to the corrugated card.

7 Cut a strip of ochre card big enough to fit around the timpanon. Decorate it as above and glue on. Make 4 bows with the ribbons and glue around the edge.

POPULAR MUSIC IN ANCIENT GREECE   473

Mythical Tales of Greece

GREEK MYTHOLOGY IS RICH in stories of victorious heroes and heroines, quarrelling gods and goddesses, and mysterious and unusual creatures. While keeping people entertained, the stories also tried to answer questions about how the world and humans came into existence. These powerful tales provided inspiration for ancient Greek art and material for their plays, which were performed to audiences of over 10,000. In addition, they were a valuable historical record and encouraged the Greeks to take pride in their cultural past.

Traditionally, mythical stories were passed down generations by word of mouth. Sometimes travelling bards were paid to recite poems, which they had learnt by heart. Eventually, these tales came to be written down. The earliest of these that survive are thought to be the work of the poet Homer (*c.*800BC). Two poems that we know about are *The Odyssey* and *The Iliad*. Both tell tales of heroes battling against supernatural forces.

MONSTER KILLER
According to Greek legend the Minotaur was half-bull and half-man. It lived in a maze called the labyrinth on the island of Crete. Many people had entered the maze but never come out. Each year the people of Athens were forced to send human sacrifices to feed the bull. The hero Theseus made it his mission to kill the Minotaur. A princess presented Theseus with a sword and a ball of string to help him. Theseus unwound the string as he walked through the maze. After killing the Minotaur he followed the string back to the entrance of the cave.

SNAKE STRANGLER
The super-strong Heracles was the only human being to become a Greek god. This Roman fresco shows him as a baby strangling serpents sent by the jealous goddess Hera to kill him.

HEAD OF MEDUSA
You will need: board, self-drying modelling clay, rolling pin, ruler, modelling tool, pencil, sandpaper, acrylic paints, one small and one large paintbrush, varnish (1 part water to 1 part PVA glue).

1 With a rolling pin, roll out a slab of clay 20cm by 20cm and 2cm thick. With the modelling tool, cut out a head in the shape shown in the picture.

2 Shape a small piece of clay into a nose. Mould it on to the head with your fingers. Use the modelling tool to smooth the edges into the face.

3 Carve a mouth with lots of teeth and two eyes and etch a gruesome design into the head. Press the end of a pencil into the eyes to make eyeballs.

STONY STARE

Medusa was a winged monster with hair of snakes. She was one of three such female gorgons. Medusa had a face so horrific that any human who looked directly at it was turned to stone. The only way to kill her was to cut off her head. Medusa, whose name means 'cunning', outwitted several would-be killers. The hero Perseus finally killed her with help from Athena and Hermes. They lent Perseus a magic cap to make him invisible, a sickle to cut off Medusa's head and a shield in which to see her reflection. Even dead, Medusa remained powerful. Perseus killed his enemy Polydectes by forcing him to look at her face.

FLYING HORSE

The winged horse Pegasus appeared on the coins of Corinth as the city's symbol. Pegasus helped Bellerophon, a Corinthian hero, in his battles. First against the Chimaera which was a monster with a lion's head, a goat's middle and a snake's tail and then against the Amazons, a race of female warriors.

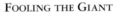

FOOLING THE GIANT

King Odysseus was a mythical hero who had many adventures. One escapade found him captured in a cave by a one-eyed giant. To escape, Odysseus stabbed out the giant's eye and rode out of the cave clinging to the underside of a ram.

The word gorgon in Greek suggests the monster's glaring eyes.

4 Between the palms of your hands, roll out four thin strips of clay to represent the snakes on Medusa's head. Press them into place as shown above.

5 Press a finger down on the end of each roll to make a snake's head. Use the modelling tool and pencil to carve in scales on the snakes' bodies.

6 The head needs to dry completely before you can paint the face. To dry it, let it sit for a few hours on either side. Be careful when you turn it over.

7 When the head is completely dry, sand with fine sandpaper. Paint the face in black, red, white and gold as shown here. Leave to dry and varnish.

Roman Sport and Combat

MOST ROMANS preferred watching sport to taking part. There were some, however, who enjoyed athletics and keeping fit. They took their exercise at the public baths and at the sports ground or *palaestra*. Men competed at wrestling, the long jump and swimming. Women also exercised by working out with weights.

Boxing matches and chariot races were always well attended. The races took place on a long, oval racetrack, called a circus. The crowds watched with such excitement that violent riots often followed. Charioteers and their teams became big stars. Roman crowds also enjoyed watching displays of violence. Bloody battles between gladiators and fights among wild animals took place in a special oval arena, called an amphitheatre. Roman entertainments became more spectacular and bloodthirsty with time. The arenas of amphitheatres were sometimes flooded for mock sea battles.

A COLOSSEUM
This is the colosseum in the Roman city of El Djem, in Tunisia. A colosseum was a kind of amphitheatre. Arenas such as this were built all over the Empire. The largest and most famous is the Colosseum in Rome.

DEATH OR MERCY?
Gladiators usually fought to the death, but a wounded gladiator could appeal for mercy. The excited crowd would look for the emperor's signal. A thumbs-up meant his life was spared. A thumbs-down meant he must die.

COME ON YOU REDS!

Charioteers belonged to teams and wore their team's colours when they raced. Some also wore protective leather helmets, like the one in this mosaic. In Rome, there were four teams – the Reds, Blues, Whites and Greens. Each team had faithful fans and charioteers were every bit as popular as football stars today.

A DAY AT THE RACES

This terracotta carving records an exciting moment at the races. Chariot racing was a passion for most Romans. Chariots were usually pulled by four horses, though just two or as many as six could be used. Accidents and foul play were common as the chariots thundered round the track.

THE CHAMP

Boxing was a deadly sport. Fighters, like this boxer, wore studded thongs instead of padded boxing gloves. Severe injuries, and even brain damage, were probably quite common.

THE GREEK IDEAL

The Romans admired all things Greek, including their love of athletics. This painted Greek vase dates from about 333BC and shows long-distance runners. However, Roman crowds were not interested in athletic contests in the Greek style, such as the Olympic Games.

American Indian Storytelling

ORTH AMERICAN INDIANS LOVED storytelling. Many stories taught the children to respect nature and animals or described social behaviour. Stories were also a way of passing on tribal customs, rituals and religious beliefs. Some tribes considered it unlucky to tell tales of mythological events during the summer months. They looked forward to the long winter nights when they would gather in their tipis or lodges and huddle around the fire. Then, they listened to the storyteller who was often one of the elders. A story might recall past hunts and battles, or it could be complete fiction, although the listener could never be sure as the tales were always embellished. This was especially true if the storyteller was from the Yuma tribe. The Great Dreams of the Yuma people were fantastical tales, usually performed as plays and often based on tribal rituals and folklore.

SCROLL RECORDS

This is a fine example of a birchbark scroll. It is a Midewiwin (Grand Medicine Society) record of the Ojibwa. Most ceremonies were so long and complicated that a chart had to be made to remember all the songs and prayers in the right order. A document such as this was used to record the history and initiation rites of a tribe. Without it, knowledge of them might be lost forever.

STORY BEHIND THE PICTURES

A proud Mandan chief and his wife pose for a picture to be painted. It is not just the chief's headdress that reveals great prowess in battle. The painted skin displayed by the woman tells stories of the tribe's history. The war scenes show that the tribe has been involved in many victorious battles in the past. This group picture was painted between 1833 and 1835 by George Catlin. He was an artist whose paintings of North American Indians are themselves a form of storytelling. They are an important source of information about tribal lives, customs and dress, particularly as the Indians at that time did not write any books about themselves.

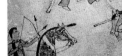

COLOURED SAND

Although many tribes made sandpaintings *(shown above)* it was the Navajo who developed the art. The painter trickled powders of yellow, white and red ochre and sandstone into patterns on the sand. Each picture described humans and spirits connected with creation stories and was usually used as part of a healing ceremony.

HEROIC TALES

The Sioux chief, seen at the bottom of this picture, must have been exceptionally brave as his headdress is very long. Painting warrior shields was an ancient art used to pass on tales of battle heroics. This shield may have been painted by one of the warriors involved. Shields were kept in the lodge and brought out when the warrior retold how brave he was. It would be given to his children to keep his memory alive.

WRITTEN IN STONE

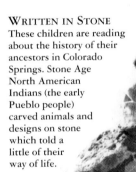

These children are reading about the history of their ancestors in Colorado Springs. Stone Age North American Indians (the early Pueblo people) carved animals and designs on stone which told a little of their way of life.

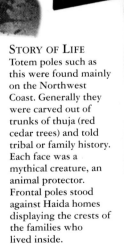

THE HISTORIAN

A young boy looks on as his father records tribal stories on dried animal hide. He is already learning the importance of recording the family history. Even in 1903, when this picture was painted, many tribes used picture writing, not the printed word of the white man.

STORY OF LIFE

Totem poles such as this were found mainly on the Northwest Coast. Generally they were carved out of trunks of thuja (red cedar trees) and told tribal or family history. Each face was a mythical creature, an animal protector. Frontal poles stood against Haida homes displaying the crests of the families who lived inside.

Celtic Bards and Musicians

THE CELTS ENJOYED MUSIC, poems and songs as entertainment, and for more serious purposes. Music accompanied Celtic warriors into battle and made them feel brave. Poems praised the achievements of a great chieftain or the adventures of bold raiders, and recorded the history of a tribe. Dead chieftains and heroes, and possibly even ordinary people, too, were mourned with sad laments. On special occasions, and in the homes of high-ranking Celts, poems and songs were performed by people called bards.

Roman writers described the many years of training to become a bard. Bards learned how to compose using all the different styles of poetry, and memorized hundreds of legends and songs. They also learned how to play an instrument, and to read and write, although most Celtic music and poetry was never written down. Becoming a bard was the first step towards being a druid (priest).

HOLY MUSIC
We do not know what part music played in Celtic religious ceremonies, but it was probably important. This stone statue shows a Celtic god playing a lyre. The Celts believed that religious knowledge, and music, was too holy to be written down. Sadly, this means that many Celtic poems and songs have been lost for ever.

GRACEFUL DANCER
Naked dancing girls may have entertained guests at important feasts. This little bronze statue, just 13cm high, dates from around 50BC. The Celts enjoyed dancing, and from the evidence of this statue it seems likely that their dances were quite wild in their movements.

MAKE A HARP
You will need: card 39 cm x 49 cm, pencil, ruler, scissors, cardboard 39 cm x 49 cm , felt-tip pen, paints, paintbrushes, bradawl, coloured string, paper fasteners.

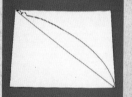

1 On the piece of card, draw a diagonal line from corner to corner. Draw a second, gently curving line, shaped at one end, as shown.

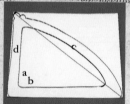

2 Draw two lines (a and b), 4.5 cm in from the edge of the paper. Join them with a curved line c. Finally add a curved line d parallel to a, as shown.

3 Cut out the harp shape. Place it on cardboard. Carefully draw round it with a felt-tip pen both inside and out. Cut the cardboard harp out.

HARPIST

This harpist is pictured on the Dupplin Cross, from Scotland. The harp itself is large and triangular in shape. It was placed on the ground and held between the harpist's knees. Such harps were popular at the end of the Celtic period.

MUSICAL GROUP

Musicians are shown playing at a religious ceremony on this stone carving from Scotland, dating from around AD900. The bottom panel shows a harpist plucking the strings of his harp, while a fellow musician plays a pipe. In the foreground is a drum, possibly made from a barrel with a skin stretched over it.

INSPIRED BY A DREAM

While a Celtic bard sleeps, he dreams of a beautiful woman from the world of the spirits. She will be the subject of his next song. Dreams and visions were a common theme in many ancient Celtic poems and legends. For example, Oisin, son of the great hero Finn MacCool, ran away with Niamh of the Golden Hair. Niamh was a spirit who appeared to Finn in a dream and invited him to come to a magic land across the waves.

Most Celtic poetry was not spoken, but sung or chanted to the music of a harp or a lyre. Bards used the music to create the right atmosphere to accompany their words, and to add extra dramatic effects, such as shivery sounds during a scary ghost tale.

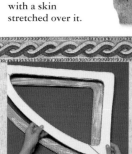

4 Glue the one side of the card and and one side of the cardboard. Stick them together. Paint the harp brown and leave it in a warm place to dry.

5 Use a bradawl to make holes approximately 5 cm apart along the two straight sides of the harp. These will be the holes for the strings.

6 Cut a length of string 40 cm long. Cut 7 more pieces of string each 5 cm shorter than the last. Tie a paper fastener to both ends of each string.

7 Push the paper fasteners in to the harp frame so that the strings lie diagonally across the harp. Adjust the strings so that they are stretched tightly.

Games in Mesoamerica

MESOAMERICAN PEOPLE of Central America enjoyed sports and games after work and on festival days. Two favourite games were *tlachtli* or *ulama*, the famous Mesoamerican ball game, and *patolli*, a board game. The ball game was played in front of huge crowds, while *patolli* was a quieter game. Mesoamerican games were not just for fun. Both the ball game and *patolli* had religious meanings. In the first, the court symbolized the world, and the rubber ball stood for the Sun as it made its daily journey across the sky. Players were meant to keep the ball moving in order to give energy to the Sun. Losing teams were sometimes sacrificed as offerings to the Sun god. In *patolli*, the movement of counters on the board represented the passing years.

PATOLLI
A group of Aztecs are shown here playing the game of *patolli*. It was played by moving dried beans or clay counters along a cross-shaped board with 52 squares. It could be very exciting. Players often bet on the result.

THE ACROBAT
This Olmec statue shows a very supple acrobat. Mesoamericans admired youth, fitness and beauty. Sports were fun, but they could also be good training for the demands of war. Being fit was considered attractive.

FLYING MEN
Volador was a ceremony performed on religious festival days. Four men, dressed as birds and attached to ropes, jumped off a high pole. As they spun round, falling towards the ground, they circled the pole 13 times each. That made 52 circuits – the length of the Mesoamerican holy calendar cycle.

PLAY PATOLLI
You will need: thick card, pencil, ruler, black marker pen, paints, small paintbrush, water pot, coloured papers, scissors, PVA glue and glue brush, dried broad or butter beans, self-drying clay.

1 Measure a square of thick card about 50cm x 50cm. Using a marker pen and a ruler, draw three lines from corner to corner to make a cross-shape.

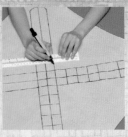

2 Draw seven pairs of spaces along each arm. The third space in from the end should be a double space. Paint triangles in it.

3 Draw eight jaguar heads and eight marigolds on differently coloured paper. Cut them out. Paint the face of the Sun god into the centre.

TARGET RING

This stone ring comes from Chichen-Itza. Ball-game players used only their hips and knees to hit a solid rubber ball through rings like this fixed high on the ball-court walls.

ALL DRESSED UP

A man dressed to play the Mesoamerican ball-game is shown in this terracotta statue. The figure was made around AD800 on the Maya island of Jaina, off the western coast of the Yucatan peninsula. He wears a protective belt of leather and wood, padded wrist-guards and knee-guards, a pointed cap and big earrings. Being a ball-game player was risky but could bring rich rewards. Winners were sometimes allowed to claim the spectators' clothes and jewels as prizes.

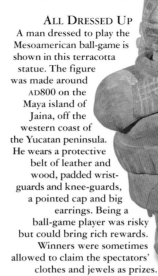

PLAY BALL

The ruins of a huge ball-court can still be seen in the Maya city of Uxmal. The biggest courts were up to 60m long and were built next to temples, in the centre of cities. People crowded inside the court to watch. Play was fast, furious and dangerous. Many players were injured as they clashed with opponents.

4 Stick the jaguars and marigolds randomly on the board. Paint a blue circle at the end of one arm, and a crown at the opposite end. Repeat in green on the other arms.

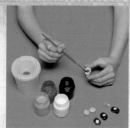

5 Paint five dried beans black with a white dot on one side. The beans will be thrown as dice. Make two counters from clay. Paint one green and one blue.

Most of the original rules for patolli have been lost. In this version, start each counter on the circle of the same colour. The aim is to move your counter to the crown of the same colour and back. Lose a turn if you land on a jaguar and get an extra turn if you land on a marigold.

At the Theatre in Japan

GOING TO THE THEATRE and listening to music were popular in Japan among the wealthy. There were several kinds of Japanese drama. They developed from religious dances at temples and shrines, or from slow, stately dances performed at the emperor's court.

Noh is the oldest form of Japanese drama. It developed in the 1300s from rituals and dances that had been performed for centuries before. Noh plays were serious and dignified. The actors performed on a bare stage, with only a backdrop. They chanted or sang their words, accompanied by drums and a flute. Noh performances were traditionally held in the open air, often at a shrine.

Kabuki plays were first seen around 1600. In 1629, the shoguns banned women performers and so male actors took their places. Kabuki plays became very popular in the new, fast-growing towns.

GRACEFUL PLAYER
This woman entertainer is holding a *shamisen* – a three-stringed instrument, played by plucking the strings. The *shamisen* often formed part of a group, together with a *koto* (zither) and flute.

POPULAR PUPPETS
Bunraku (puppet plays) originated about 400 years ago, when *shamisen* music, dramatic chanting and hand-held puppets were combined. The puppets were so large and complex that it took three men to move them about on stage.

NOH THEATRE MASK
You will need: tape measure, balloon, newspaper, bowl, glue, petroleum jelly, pin, scissors, felt-tip pen, modelling clay, bradawl, paints (red, yellow, black, and white), paintbrush, water pot, cord.

1 Ask a friend to measure around your head above the ears. Blow up a balloon to fit this measurement. This will be the base for the papier-mâché.

2 Rip up strips of newspaper. Soak in a water and glue mixture (1 part glue to 2 parts water). Cover the balloon with a layer of petroleum jelly.

3 Cover the front and sides of your balloon with a layer of papier-mâché. Leave to dry. Repeat 2 or 3 times. When dry, pop the balloon.

TRAGIC THEATRE

An audience watches a scene from an outdoor performance of a Noh play. Noh drama was always about important and serious topics. Favourite subjects were death and the afterlife, and the plays were often very tragic.

LOUD AND FAST

Kabuki plays were a complete contrast to Noh. They were fast-moving, loud, flashy and very dramatic. Audiences admired the skills of the actors as much as the cleverness or thoughtfulness of the plots.

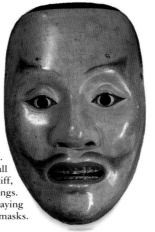

BEHIND THE MASK

This Noh mask represents a warrior's face. Noh drama did not try to be lifelike. The actors all wore masks and moved very slowly using stiff, stylized gestures to express their feelings. Noh plays were all performed by men. Actors playing women's parts wore female clothes and masks.

Put on your mask and feel like an actor in an ancient Noh play. Imagine that you are wearing his long, swirling robes, too.

4 Trim the papier-mâché so that it forms a mask shape. Ask a friend to mark where your eyes, nose and mouth are when you hold it to your face.

5 Cut out the face holes with scissors. Put clay beneath the side of the mask at eye level. Use a bradawl to make two holes on each side.

6 Paint the face of a calm young lady from Noh theatre on your mask. Use this picture as your guide. The mask would have been worn by a man.

7 Fit the cord through the holes at each side. Tie one end. Once you have adjusted the mask so that it fits, tie the other end.

Entertaining Royal India

USIC AND DANCE have long entertained noble people in the royal courts. In Mughal India (1526–1857), courtiers listened to poetry and music every day. They loved riddles and word games, and in contests, poets were given half a verse and asked to complete it. Different art forms were connected to one another. For example, the *Natyashastra*, an ancient text on dance and drama, includes a long section on music. Dancers were also storytellers, using hand gestures to show meaning. North and south India developed their own musical traditions – Hindustani in the north and Karnatak in the south. Islam introduced new instruments, such as the sitar (a stringed instrument) and the tabla (a drum). Outside the courts, religion played a part in the development of singing. Muslim mystics sang and played musical pieces called *qawwali*, while Hindus sang songs to the god, Krishna.

JOYFUL OCCASION
Drummers and trumpeters at the Mughal court joyfully proclaim the birth of Akbar's son, Prince Salim. Music was often used to announce celebrations. Though they enjoyed royal patronage and were often renowned for their talent, musicians, dancers and actors were generally considered to be of low social standing.

INSTRUMENTAL BIRD
An instrument called a *sarongi* has been finely carved in the shape of a peacock. The *sarongi* was played with a bow and usually accompanied the dance performances of courtesans during late Mughal times.

MAKE A PAIR OF ANKLETS

You will need: measuring tape, gardening wire, pliers, strips of red felt fabric, scissors, glue or adhesive tape, darning needle, strong thread, silver bells.

1 Measure the diameter of your ankle. Multiply this figure by three, then add 4 cm for a loop. Use the pliers to cut two pieces of wire to this length.

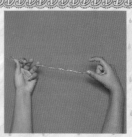

2 Loop the first cut piece of wire around itself about three times. Twist it tightly as you go. Then twist the second piece of wire in the same way.

3 Using the pliers, bend one end of each strip of twisted wire to form a loop. Bend the other end to form a hook. These act as a fastener.

FOLK DANCING

This tapestry shows a folk dance in the Punjab. Folk dances were common in the villages, among ordinary people. Each dance usually involved lots of performers. People danced to celebrate births, weddings and many other special occasions.

ON A STRING

A woman from Rajasthan plays with a yo-yo. Games with balls and strings were not expensive, so they could be enjoyed by both rich and poor people. Many other kinds of games were afforded only by the wealthy.

ENTERTAINING AT COURT

Dancers perform the style of dance known as a Kathak for the great Mughal emperor Akbar. Dance was a popular form of entertainment at court. Many of the complicated dance styles known in India today originated at the courts of kings in ancient times. The dances performed at court often told a story.

Anklets were worn by dancers who performed at ceremonies in the royal courts of the Mughals.

4 Cut out two strips of felt fabric that are slightly longer than your strips of wire. Glue or tape a felt strip on to the end of the twisted wire.

5 Wrap the felt around the wire, overlapping the edges of the felt. Glue the end of the felt to the place where you began. Wrap the second wire strip.

6 Thread a darning needle with sewing thread. Sew lots of tiny silver bells to the felt fabric covering your wire loops.

7 Repeat your stitches several times to make sure that the bells stay firmly in place. Add more bells, so that you cover both anklets completely.

Picture-writing in Mesopotamia

W RITING, AS A MEANS of recording information, first developed in the ancient worlds of Mesopotamia (present-day Iraq), Egypt and China. The earliest examples are about 5,000 years old and come from the Sumerian city-state of Uruk. At first, writing was in the form of pictures and numbers. It was used to make lists of produce such as barley, wine and cheese, or numbers of cattle and donkeys. Gradually, this picture-writing was replaced by groups of wedge-shaped strokes formed by a reed pen as it was pressed into the clay. This type of writing is called cuneiform, which means 'wedge-shaped'. To begin with, cuneiform was only used to write Sumerian, but later it was adapted to write several other languages, including Assyrian and Babylonian.

CLAY TABLET

Writing was done on clay tablets with a stylus (pen) made from a reed. The writer pressed the stylus into a slab of damp clay. This was left to dry and harden. The clay tablet in the picture, from around 3000BC, has symbols on it. One symbol looks like a hand and others resemble trees or plants. It is not clear which language they represent, although it is likely to be Sumerian.

TWO SCRIBES

The scribe on the right is writing on a clay tablet with a stylus. He is making a list of all the booty and prisoners that his king has captured in battle. He is writing in Akkadian, one of the languages used by the Assyrians. The other scribe is writing on a leather roll, possibly in Aramaic, another language the Assyrians used. Aramaic was an easier language to write because it used an alphabet unlike Akkadian, which used about 600 different signs.

SHAPES AND SIZES

Differently shaped clay tablets, including prisms and cylinders, were used for writing. Many tablets were flat but some were three-dimensional and hollow like vases. One like this, that narrows at each end, is called a prism. It is about 30cm long and records the military campaigns of King Sargon of Assyria.

A CLAY TABLET

You will need: pen, stiff card, ruler, scissors, modelling clay, cutting board, rolling pin, blunt knife, paper, paint and paintbrush, cloth.

1 Draw a pointed stylus 20cm by 1.5cm on to the stiff card with the pen. Use the shape in the picture as a guide. Cut the shape out with the scissors.

2 Roll out the clay on the cutting board with the rolling pin until it measures about 30cm by 15cm. Use the knife to cut out the clay as shown.

3 Take your card stylus and start writing cuneiform script on your clay tablet. Use the wedge shape of your stylus to make the strokes.

COMMUNICATING IDEAS

Cuneiform signs gradually came to be used for ideas as well as objects. At first, a drawing of a head meant simply 'head', but later came to mean 'front' and 'first'. The symbols also came to represent spoken sounds and could be used to make new words. For example, in English, you could make the word 'belief' by drawing the symbols for a bee and a leaf. The chart shows how cuneiform writing developed. On the top row are simple drawings. In the middle row the pictures have been replaced by groups of wedges, and in the bottom row are the even more simplified versions of the signs.

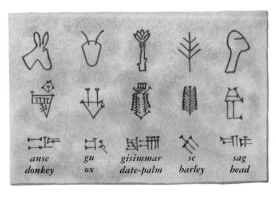

anse	gu	gisimmar	se	sag
donkey	ox	date-palm	barley	head

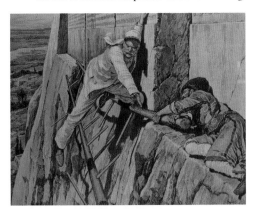

The tablet you have made is about half the size of the original. Flat tablets were used for everything from scholarly works on medicine and mathematics to dictionaries and stories. The Epic of Gilgamesh took up 12 large tablets. Letters were written on tiny tablets.

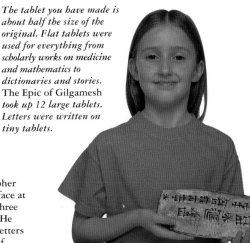

WRITING ON THE ROCK FACE

Henry Rawlinson, a British army officer who helped decipher cuneiform in the mid-1800s, risks his life climbing a cliff face at Behistun to copy the writing there. The inscription was in three languages, Old Persian, Elamite and Babylonian (Akkadian). He guessed that the cuneiform signs in Old Persian represented letters of the alphabet and found the name of Darius, the King of Persia. This helped scholars work out all three languages.

4 Copy the wedge-shapes of the cuneiform script shown here. See how each group of strokes combines to make a particular letter or word.

5 Move your tablet on to a piece of clean paper. Take the paintbrush and paint and cover the clay, working the paint well into the cuneiform script.

6 When the painting is finished, wipe across the clay with the cloth. Most of the paint should come off, leaving the lettering a darker colour.

7 Leave the clay and the paint to dry. The lettering on your finished tablet reads: Nebuchadnezzar King of Babylon.

Decoding Egyptian Script

MOST OF WHAT WE KNOW about the people of the past comes from the written language they left behind. Inscriptions providing information about the ancient Egyptians can be found on everything from obelisks to tombs. From 3100BC the Egyptians used pictures called hieroglyphs. Each picture stood for an object, an idea or a sound. There were around 1,000 hieroglyphic symbols. The term hiero means sacred. This is because it was initially used by the Egyptians for religious texts.

By 1780BC, hieroglyphs had evolved into hieratic, a more flowing text. In the latter days of ancient Egypt, an even simpler script called demotic (popular) was used. However, by AD600, long after the last of the pharaohs, no one understood hieroglyphs. The secrets of ancient Egypt were lost for 1,200 years, until the discovery of the Rosetta Stone.

THE ROSETTA STONE

The discovery of the Rosetta Stone was a lucky accident. In 1799, a French soldier discovered a piece of stone at an Egyptian village called el-Rashid or Rosetta. On the stone, the same words were written in three scripts representing two languages. Hieroglyphic text is at the top, demotic text is in the centre, and Greek is at the bottom.

EGYPTIAN CODE CRACKED

French scholar Jean-François Champollion cracked the Rosetta Stone code in 1822. The stone contains a royal decree written in 196BC when the Greek king Ptolemy V was in power in Egypt. The Greek on the stone enabled Champollion to translate the hieroglyphs. This one discovery is central to our understanding of the way the ancient Egyptians used to live.

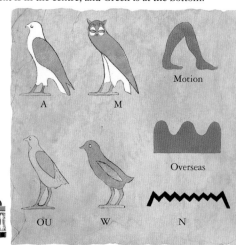

A

M

Motion

OU

W

N

Overseas

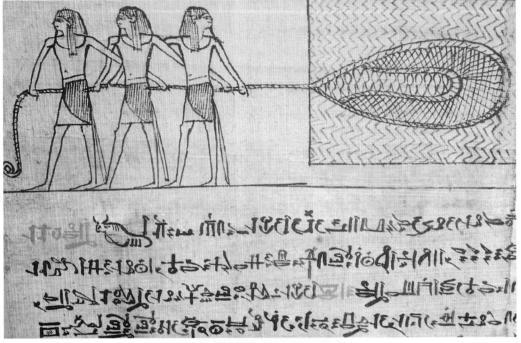

HIERATIC SCRIPT

The picture symbols of hieroglyphs, developed into hieratic script (above), which had signs that were more like letters. This script was more flowing and could be written quickly. It was used for stories, letters and business contracts. It was always read from right to left.

DEMOTIC SCRIPT

A new script, demotic (*left*), was introduced towards the end of the New Kingdom (1550–1070BC). This could be written even more quickly than hieratic script. Initially it was used for business, but soon it was also being used for religious and scientific writings. It disappeared when Egypt came under Roman rule in 30BC.

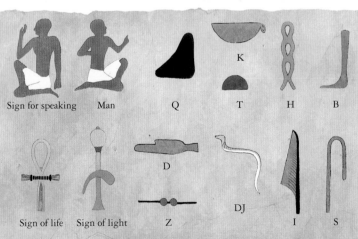

Sign for speaking   Man   Q   K   T   H   B

Sign of life   Sign of light   Z   D   DJ   I   S

HIEROGLYPHS

Made up of small pictures, hieroglyphs were based on simplified sketches of birds and snakes, plants, parts of the body, boats and houses. Some hieroglyphs represented complete ideas such as light, travel or life. Others stood for letters or sounds that could be combined to make words.

Chinese Word Symbols

THE CHINESE LANGUAGE is written with symbols (characters) that stand for sounds and words. The first-known Chinese writing dates to more than 1000 years after the invention of writing in Egypt and Mesopotamia. With few outside influences, these early symbols changed little over the ages, making modern Chinese the oldest writing in use today. A dictionary from 1716 lists over 40,000 characters. Each character was written with a brush, using 11 basic strokes. The painting of these beautiful characters is called calligraphy, and was always seen as a form of art.

Before the Chinese began using woodblocks for printing in 1600BC, books were often handwritten on bamboo strips. Movable type was invented in the AD1040s. The Chinese also invented paper, nearly 2,000 years ago. Cloth or bark was shredded, pulped and dried on frames. Ancient writings included poetry, practical handbooks and encyclopedias. During the 1500s, popular folk tales such as *The Water Margin* were published, and about 200 years later, the writer Cao Xuequin produced the novel, *A Dream of Red Mansions.*

MAGICAL MESSAGES
The earliest surviving Chinese script appears on animal bones. They were used for telling fortunes in about 1200BC. The script was made up of small pictures representing objects or ideas. Modern Chinese script is made up of patterns of lines.

ART OF CALLIGRAPHY
This text was handwritten during the Tang dynasty (AD618–906). Traditional Chinese writing reads down from right to left, starting in the top right-hand corner.

MAKE PRINTING BLOCKS

You will need: plain white paper, pencil, paint, soft Chinese brush or thin paintbrush, water pot, tracing paper, board, self-drying clay (15cm x 20cm, 2.5cm thick), modelling tool, wood glue, block printing ink, damp rag.

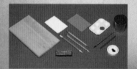

1 Copy or trace the characters from the reversed image block (see opposite). Start off with a pencil outline, then fill in with paint. Leave to dry.

2 Copy design on to tracing paper. Turn the paper over. Place it on the clay. Scribble on the clean side of the paper to leave a mirror image in the clay.

3 Use a modelling tool to carve out characters. Cut away clay all around characters to make a relief (raised pattern). Smooth clay base with your fingertips.

THE BEST WAY TO WRITE

A calligrapher of the 1840s begins to write, surrounded by his assistants. The brush must be held upright for the writing of Chinese characters. The wrist is never rested on the table. Many years of practice and study are necessary to become a good calligrapher.

INKS AND COLOURS

The watercolours and inks used for Chinese calligraphy were based on plant and mineral pigments in reds, blues, greens and yellows. Black ink was made from carbon, obtained from soot. This was mixed with glue to form a solid block. The ink block was wetted during use. Brushes were made from animal hair fitted into bamboo handles.

Chinese brushes

THE PRINTED PAGE

The Buddhist scripture called the *Diamond Sutra (shown right)* is probably the oldest surviving printed book in the world. It includes both text and pictures. The book was printed from a wood block on 11 May AD868 and was intended to be distributed to the public free of charge.

reversed image   *actual image*

Moon   Ruler

Mouth Sun

Block rubbings of characters were an early form of printing.

4 When the relief has dried, paint the clay block with wood glue. Leave it to dry thoroughly. When dry, the glue seals and protects the pattern.

5 Now paint the design. Apply a thick layer of printing ink to the raised parts of the clay with a Chinese brush or a soft paintbrush.

6 Lay a thin piece of plain white paper over the inked block. Use a dry brush to press the paper into the ink, so that the paper takes up the design.

7 Lift up the paper to reveal your design. Look after your printing block by cleaning it with a damp rag. You can then use it again and again.

Celtic Messages in Stone

IN EUROPE, the Celts had several different languages, but no single Celtic alphabet. To write something down, the Celts had to borrow other peoples' scripts. Sometimes they used Greek letters, sometimes Latin (the Romans' language). In the British Isles, a script known as Ogham was based on the Latin alphabet, but used straight lines instead of letters. Celtic craftworkers used all these different ways of writing to carve messages in stone. Their inscriptions might commemorate an important event, or a person who had died, or be a proud symbol of a leader's power. Craftworkers also decorated stones with beautiful patterns, sometimes copied from jewellery and metalworking designs. In some parts of Celtic Europe, standing stones and lumps of rock were carved with special symbols. Historians believe that these picture-carvings were designed to increase respect for powerful leaders, and for the gods.

STANDING STONE
Tall, carved standing stones were a special feature of Celtic lands in north-west France and Ireland. Archaeologists are not sure why they were put up or decorated, but they probably marked boundaries or holy sites. This stone comes from Turoe, in Ireland.

PRACTICE MAKES PERFECT
Before using precious metals such as gold, or starting to chip away at hard, valuable materials such as stone, craftworkers made sketches and worked out patterns on little pieces of bone. These bone fragments, marked with compass designs, were found in Ireland. They belonged to craftworkers from around AD50.

MAKE AN OGHAM STONE

You will need: modelling clay, board, rolling pin, ruler, modelling tool, sandpaper, white paint, paintbrush, green card, scissors, PVA glue.

1 Roll out the modelling clay to make a strip roughly 33 cm long, 5 cm wide and 3 cm thick. Carefully shape the top as shown.

2 Take the modelling tool and make a hole in the top end of the strip. This tall "holed" Ogham stone is based on one in southern Ireland from AD400.

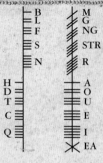

3 These are some of the Ogham letters.

ON LIVING ROCK

This rough slab of stone is decorated with a carving of a wild boar. It was found in Dunadd, Scotland. Archaeologists have many theories as to why it was carved. It may have been a memorial to a dead leader or a notice announcing an alliance between friendly clans. An alternative view is that it was a tribal symbol, put up as a proud boast of the local peoples' power or a sign of a local chieftain's land.

THE CELTS LIVE ON

The Picts were a mysterious people who lived in Scotland from about AD300 to 900. They were descended from Celtic people and they continued many of the Celts' customs and traditions. In particular, they carved picture-symbols and Ogham letters on stone slabs, in caves and on lumps of rock. This stone monument, from Orkney, Scotland, shows three warriors and various other common Pictish symbols.

ALL CHANGE

Many tall, carved stones had religious power for the Celts. When Christian missionaries arrived in Celtic lands, they sometimes decided to make old carved stones into Christian monuments. They hoped this might help people understand that the Christian God was more important than the old Celtic ones. This stone is at Oronsay in the Orkney Islands off the north-east coast of Scotland.

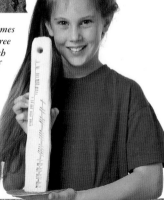

Ogham is sometimes referred to as the "tree alphabet" because each letter takes the name of a tree. In many cases the Ogham inscription on a stone is read from the bottom up and contains the name of the person being commemorated and that of the carver.

4 Ogham writing is done as a series of lines or notches scored across a long stem. Use the alphabet in step 3 to help you write something on your stone.

5 Ogham inscriptions are often found on memorials featuring a person's name. You could try writing your name on your model Ogham stone.

6 Sand the modelling clay gently to remove any rough edges. Then paint one side of your stone. Leave to dry, turn over and paint the other side.

7 Cut a circular base out of green card, roughly 14 cm wide. Glue the bottom of your stone on to the base, as shown. Now leave the stone to dry.

Mesoamerican Writing

THE MAYA OF CENTRAL AMERICA were the first – and only – Mesoamerican people to invent a complete writing system. By AD250, Maya picture-symbols and sound-symbols were written in books, carved on buildings, painted on pottery and inscribed on precious stones. Maya scribes also developed an advanced number system, including a sign for zero, which Europeans at the time did not have.

Maya writing used glyphs (pictures standing for words) and also picture-signs that stood for sounds. The sound-signs could be joined together, like the letters of the Roman alphabet, to make words and complete sentences. The Aztecs used picture-writing too, but theirs was much simpler and less flexible. Maya and Aztec picture-symbols were difficult to learn. Only specially trained scribes could write them, and only priests or rich people could read them. They could spare time for study and afford to pay a good teacher.

MAYA READER
A Maya statue showing a wealthy woman seated cross-legged with a codex (folding book) on her lap. A Maya or Aztec codex was made of long strips of fig-bark paper, folded like a concertina. The writing was read from top to bottom and left to right.

CITY EMBLEM
Four separate images make up this emblem-glyph for the Maya city-state of Copan. Together they give a message meaning 'the home of the rulers of the royal blood of Copan'. At the bottom, you can see a bat, the special picture-sign for the city.

MAKE A CODEX
You will need: thin card, ruler, pencil, scissors, white acrylic paint, eraser, large and small paintbrushes, water pot, paints in red, yellow, blue and black, palette, tracing paper.

1 Draw a rectangle about 100cm x 25cm on to thin card. Cut the rectangle out. Cover it evenly with white acrylic paint. Leave it to dry.

2 Using a pencil and ruler, lightly draw in four fold-lines 20cm apart. This will divide the painted card into five equal sections.

3 Carefully fold along the pencil lines to make a zig-zag book, as shown. Unfold the card and rub out the pencil lines with an eraser.

MAYA CODEX

Maya scribes wrote thousands of codices (folding, hand-painted books), but only four survive. All the rest were destroyed by Spanish missionaries. These pages from a Maya codex show the activities of several different gods. The figure at the top, painted black with a long nose, is Ek Chuah, the god of merchants.

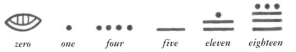

| zero | one | four | five | eleven | eighteen |

AZTEC ENCYCLOPEDIA

These pictures of Aztec gods come from a book known as the Florentine Codex. This encyclopedia was compiled between 1547 and 1569 by Father Bernardino de Sahagun, a Spanish friar. He was fascinated by Aztec civilization and wanted to record it before it disappeared. This codex is the most complete written record of Aztec life we have.

MAYA NUMBERS

The Maya number system used only three signs – a dot for one, a bar for five, and the shell-symbol for zero. Other numbers were made by using a combination of those signs. When writing down large numbers, Maya scribes put the different symbols on top of one another, rather than side by side as we do today.

If you went to school in Aztec or Maya times, you would find out how to recognize hundreds of different picture-symbols. You would also be taught to link them together in your mind, like a series of clues, to find out what they meant.

4 Trace or copy Aztec or Maya codex drawings from this book. Alternatively, make up your own, based on Mesoamerican examples.

5 Paint your tracings or drawings, using light, bright colours. Using the Maya numbers on this page as a guide, add some numbers to your codex.

Glossary

A

abacus A wooden frame with beads on rods, used for calculating.

acupuncture The treatment of the body with fine needles to relieve pain or cure illness.

adobe Plaster, made from clay and straw, used in buildings.

agriculture Farming – the activity of growing crops and breeding animals.

alabaster A gleaming white stone, used for making ornaments.

alloy A mixture of metals melted together to create a new metal that may be stronger or easier to work.

Althing An assembly of free men that passed laws in Iceland at the time of the Vikings.

amaut Black pouch used by Inuit tribes of the north American Arctic to carry babies and young children.

amethyst A purple crystal, a type of quartz.

amphitheatre An oval open-air arena used for public shows such as gladiator fights.

ancestor A member of the same family who died long ago.

Anno Domini (AD) A system used to calculate dates after the supposed year of Christ's birth. Anno Domini dates in this book are prefixed AD up to the year 1000 (e.g. AD521). After 1000 no prefixes are used (e.g. 1929).

anvil A heavy iron block on which metal objects can be hammered into shape.

aqueduct A channel for carrying water over long distances.

archaeologist Someone who studies ancient ruins and artefacts to learn about the past.

archaeology The scientific study of the past looking at the things people left behind, such as tools.

Arctic The region in the far north of our planet, surrounding the North Pole.

aristocracy A ruling class of wealthy, privileged people, or government by such people.

artefact An object that has been preserved from the past.

astrology The belief that stars, planets and other heavenly bodies shape our lives.

astronomy The scientific study of stars, planets and other heavenly bodies. In ancient times it was often mixed up with astrology.

atrium The hallway or courtyard of a Roman house. The centre of the atrium was open to the sky.

auloi A pair of musical pipes used in ancient Greece.

auxiliaries Soldiers recruited from non-Roman citizens.

Aztecs Mesoamerican people who lived in northern and central Mexico. They were at their most powerful between AD1350 and AD1520.

B

banquet A rich, elaborate feast served with great ceremony.

barbarians Wild, rough and uncivilized people. The word was invented in ancient Greece to describe foreign people, whose lifestyle was different to their own.

bard A poet, or someone who recites poetry. Becoming a bard was the first stage in the training of a druid (a Celtic priest).

barter The exchange of goods, one for another.

Before Christ (BC) The system used to calculate dates before the supposed year of Christ's birth. Dates are calculated in reverse (e.g. 2000BC is longer ago than 200BC). After 1000 no prefixes are used (e.g. 1929).

bellows A mechanism for pumping air into a fire or furnace.

booty Valuable things taken away by a victorious army.

brahmins The priests, members of the first caste (social class) in India.

brazier A metal stand for holding burning coals.

bronze A metal alloy, made by mixing copper with tin.

Buddha An Indian prince who left his family to seek enlightenment. Founder of the Buddhist way of life.

Buddhism World religion founded in ancient India by the Buddha in the 6th century BC.

burial ship Finely decorated ships in which Vikings were sometimes buried or cremated.

burin A chisel-like flint tool.

C

calpulli An Aztec family or neighbourhood group. The calpulli enforced law and order.

campaign A series of battles fought by a ruler.

cartouche The oval border used in Egyptian hieroglyphs to show that the name it contains is a pharaoh or a god.

caste One of four social classes into which Hindus in India were divided.

catapult A large wooden structure used during a siege to fire stones and iron bolts at the enemy.

causeway A raised walkway.

cavalry Soldiers on horseback.

century A unit of the Roman army, numbering from 80 to 100 soldiers.

chainmail Small rings of metal linked together to form a fine mesh, which is used to protect the body during battle.

chalcedony A reddish, semi-precious stone.

chinampa An Aztec garden built on the fertile, reclaimed land on the lake shore.

chullpa A burial chamber in the form of a tower.

circa (c.) Meaning approximately. The symbol *c.* is used when the exact date of something is not known by the writer.

citizen A free person with the right to vote.

city-state A city and the area surrounding it which is controlled by one leader or government.

civil servant Official who carries out government administration.

civilization A society that has made advances in arts, science and technology, law and government.

clan A group of people related to each other by ancestry or marriage.

codex An early form of book; the Aztec codex was a folding book.

cohort A division of the Roman army, at times numbering about 500 soldiers.

collyrium A black paste used as an eyeliner.

colonies Communities or groups of people who settle in another land, but still keep links with their own country.

Confucianism The western name for the teachings of the Chinese philosopher Kong Fuzi (Confucius), which call for social respect for one's ancestors.

conscript Someone who is called up by the government to serve in the army for a period of time.

conscription A term of service to the State, in which people have to work as labourers or soldiers.

consul One of two leaders of the Roman Republic elected each year.

coracle A small boat made of leather stretched over a wooden frame.

courtier A person attending at royal court.

cremation The burning of dead bodies.

crossbow A mechanical bow that fires small arrows called bolts.

cubit A unit of measurement, the length of a forearm.

cuirass Armour that protects the upper part of the body.

cuneiform The first system of writing. It was invented by the Sumerians of Mesopotamia.

currency Form of exchange for goods such as money.

cylinder seal A stone with a raised or sunken pattern. It could be rolled over soft clay to leave an impression.

D

daikon A white radish vegetable grown in Japan.

daimyo A Japanese noble or warlord.

Danegeld Money paid to Vikings by English or French rulers to prevent their lands being attacked.

Daoism Chinese philosophy based on contemplation of the natural world. It later became a religion with a belief in magic.

deity A god or goddess.

delta A coastal region where the river slips into coastal waterways before flowing into the sea.

democracy Government by the many, in which every citizen has the right to vote and hold public office.

descendant Person who is descended from an individual or group of people who lived earlier.

dhoti Traditional Indian dress worn by Hindu men.

dictator A ruler with complete and unrestricted power.

die A tool for punching a design.

distil The process of heating liquid to boiling point and collecting the steam to make a purer liquid. Alcoholic spirits are made in this way.

dowry Money that is given to a newly married couple, usually by the bride's father.

drought A long period of time without rainfall.

druid Celtic priest.

dugout canoe A canoe made by hollowing out a tree trunk.

dynasty A period of rule by the same royal family.

E

edict An order from a ruler or a government.

electrum A mixture of gold and silver, used for making coins.

embalm To preserve a dead body.

emperor The ruler of an empire.

empire A group of lands ruled or governed by a single country.

enamel A hard, coloured glass-like substance, applied as a decorative or protective covering to metal or glass.

estate A large amount of land, houses and farms, usually owned by a single person or group.

evolution The changes that take place in a human, animal or plant species over millions of years, as it becomes more complex.

excavate To dig in the ground to discover ancient ruins and remains.

F

faience A type of opaque glaze that is often blue or green. It is made from quartz or sand, lime, ash and natron.

federal Central government of a federation (a group).

festival A special day set aside to honour a god or goddess.

feud A long-standing quarrel, especially between two families.

firing The process of baking clay or glass paste in a kiln to harden it and make it waterproof.

flax A plant that yields fibres, which are woven into a fabric called linen.

flint A hard stone that flakes easily, creating sharp edges. It is used to make tools and weapons.

frontier A boundary between two countries.

G

galley A warship powered by oars.

garrison A band of soldiers living in a particular place.

geometric pattern A pattern made by lines, circles and triangles.

geometry A branch of mathematics concerning the measurements of lines, angles and surfaces.

gilding The process of applying a thin layer of gold, to metal or pottery.

gladiator A professional fighter in Roman times.

gorgon A Greek female monster of such horrific appearance that anyone who looked at her died.

government The way in which a country or state is ruled.

greaves Armour for the legs.

groma An instrument used by Roman surveyors to measure right angles and straight lines.

guilds Groups of skilled workers.

gypsum A type of limestone used for sculpture.

H

haft The handle of an axe.

harpoon A spear-like weapon with a detachable head that is tied to a line.

hemp A fibrous plant used to make coarse clothes or textiles.

henna A reddish dye, made from the leaves of a shrub.

herbalism A method of healing people by using medicines made from plants.

hieroglyph A picture symbol used in writing.

hilt The handle of a sword.

Hinduism Religion that includes the worship of several gods and belief in reincarnation.

Homo sapiens (wise man) The species to which all modern humans belong.

human sacrifice Killing humans as an offering to a god.

hunter-gatherer A person whose way of life involves hunting wild animals and gathering plant foods.

I

igloo An Inuit word meaning house, often used to refer to Inuit shelters built of ice or snow blocks.

immigrants People who come to live in a land from other countries.

immortal An idea or person that can live forever.

imperial Relating to the rule of an emperor or empress.

indigenous Native or originating from a country.

inlay To set or embed pieces of wood or metal in another material so that the surfaces are flat.

inro A small, decorated box, worn hanging from the belt in Japan.

inscribed Lettering, pictures or patterns carved into stone or wood.

inua An Inuit word for spirit.

Inuit The native people of the Arctic regions of North America, Canada and Greenland as distinguished from those of Asia and the Aleutian Islands.

iron ore The rock that contains iron in its raw, natural form.

irrigation Bringing water to dry lands so that crops can grow.

Islam The religion of the Muslim people.

ivory The hard, smooth, cream-coloured part of the tusks of elephants or walruses.

J

jade A smooth, green stone.

javelin A throwing spear.

junk A traditional Chinese sailing ship with square sails.

K

kabuki Popular plays, performed in Japan from about AD1600.

kami Japanese holy spirits.

kaolin A fine white clay used in porcelain and paper making.

keel The long beam that supports the frame of a wooden ship, running along the base of the hull.

kero An Inca drinking vessel.

kiln Industrial oven.

Koran Sacred book of Islam.

L

lacquer A thick, coloured varnish, used to coat wood, metal or leather.

lapis lazuli A dark blue, semi-precious stone used for jewellery.

latitude Imaginary lines that run parallel to the Equator of the Earth. Navigators calculate latitude to know how far north or south they are.

legion A section of the Roman army made up only of Roman citizens.

legislation Making laws.

limestone A type of rock.

litter A portable bed or chair.

llama A camel-like creature of south America. It is shorn for its wool.

longhouse The chief building of a Viking and Native American homestead.

longitude A series of imaginary circles that pass around the Earth through the North and South poles. These are measured in degrees east and west of the Greenwich meridian.

loom A frame or machine used for weaving cloth.

lyre A harp-like instruments.

M

magistrate An imperial officer of justice, similar to a local judge.

mammals A type of warm-blooded animal such as human beings, whales, bats and cats.

marl Natural lime, dug from under the ground.

martial arts Physical exercises that are often based on combat, such as sword play and kung fu.

Maya People who lived in south-western Mexico, Guatemala and Belize.

mercenary A soldier who fights in an army for money.

merchant A person who buys and sells goods for a profit.

Mesoamerica Central America.

Mesopotamia The ancient name for the fertile region between the Tigris and Euphrates rivers.

metic A foreign resident in Athens, in ancient Greece.

midden A rubbish tip or dunghill.

midwife Someone who provides care and advice for women, before and after childbirth.

migration The movement of people, to other regions either permanently or at specific times of the year.

millet A grass type of grain plant that produces edible seeds.

minotaur A mythical beast, half man, half bull, that lived in a maze under a palace in Crete.

missionary A member of a religious organization who carries out charitable work and religious teaching.

mit'a Conscripted labour, owed to the Inca state as a form of tax.

monarchy Government by a king or queen.

monsoon Seasonal winds that blow in south Asia, bringing heavy rain.

mosaic A picture or decorated object made up of many small squares or cubes of glass, stone or pottery, set in soft concrete.

mother-of-pearl A hard, shiny substance found in shells.

mummification Preserving a human or animal body, by drying.

myth An ancient story about gods and heroes.

N

nation Group of people who live in one territory and usually share the same language or history.

Neanderthals A group of *Homo sapiens* who were the first people to bury their dead.

Near East The countries of the eastern Mediterranean, known today as the Middle East.

Nenet A reindeer herding people of southern Siberia.

Neolithic (New Stone Age) A period that began about 2 million years ago when the first stone tools were made.

netsuke Small toggles, carved from ivory and used to attach items to belts in Japan.

New Kingdom The period of Egyptian history between 1550–1070bc.

nobles People who are high in social rank.

Noh A serious, dignified drama that originated in Japan in around 1300.

nomad A member of a group that roams from place to place to find food or better land or to follow herds.

Normans Descendants of the Vikings who settled in northern France.

O

obelisk A pointed pillar, erected as a monument.

obi A wide sash, worn only by women in Japan.

ochre A yellow- or red-coloured earth used as pigment in paint.

Odin The most powerful Viking god. He was god of war, magic and poetry.

oligarchy Government by a group of rich and powerful people.

Olmec A Mesoamerican people who lived in southern central Mexico, from 1200bc and 400bc.

Olympic Games A sports competition held every year at Olympia in ancient Greece in honour of the god Zeus. The first games were held in 776bc.

omen A sign of good or bad fortune in the future.

oppida The Roman name for fortified Celtic towns.

P

pack ice Floating sea ice.

Panathenaic festival A yearly procession with sacrifices in honour of the goddess Athena, which took place at the Parthenon in Athens.

papyrus A tall reed that grows in the river Nile, used to make a kind of paper by the ancient Egyptians.

paratha A fried wheat bread eaten in northern India.

Parthenon A temple in Greece on the Acropolis in Athens dedicated to the city's goddess, Athena.

peasant A farm worker or a poor country dweller.

peske Thick fur parka worn by Saami people in the Arctic over their tunics.

pewter An alloy or mixture of metals, made from tin and lead.

phalanx A solid block of Greek hoplites (foot soldiers) in battle.

pharaoh Ruler of ancient Egypt.

philosophy A Greek word meaning love of knowledge. Philosophy is the discipline of thinking about the meaning of life.

pigment Any material used to provide colour for paint or ink.

pilgrim A person who makes a journey to a holy place.

plate-armour Protective clothing made of overlapping plates of metal.

plateau High, flat land, usually among mountains.

plebeian A member of the (free) common people of ancient Rome.

plumbline A weighted cord, held up to see if a wall or other construction is vertical.

plunder Stolen goods.

politics The art and science of government (from *polis*, city state).

porcelain The finest quality of pottery. It was made from kaolin and baked at a high temperature.

potcheca Aztec merchants.

prehistoric Belonging to the time before written records were made.

priest An official who offered prayers and performed sacrifices and other religious rituals on behalf of worshippers at a temple.

propylaea The momumental gateways to the temple complex on top of the Acropolis in Athens in Greece.

prospector A person who searches for valuable minerals such as gold.

prow The front end of a ship. Longship prows were often carved with dragon heads.

Pueblo People from the southwestern USA and Mexico who lived in villages built of mud and stone.

pyramid A large pointed monument with a square base and triangular sides.

pyxis A box that was used for storing face powder or other cosmetics in Greece.

Q

quern A simple machine, made from two stones, that is used to grind corn.

R

rampart A defensive mound of earth.

regent Someone who rules a country on behalf of another person.

relic Part of the body of a saint or martyr, or some object connected with them, preserved as an object of respect.

relief A sculpture in which a design is carved from a flat surface such as a wall.

repoussé A metalworking technique that is used to create decorative raised patterns on a metal object.

republic A country that is not ruled by a king, queen or emperor but by representatives elected by citizens.

rigging The ropes used to support a ship's mast and sails.

rites Solemn procedures carried out for a religious purpose or ceremony.

ritual A procedure or series of actions that is often religious.

S

sacrifice The killing of a living thing in honour of the gods.

samurai Brave and highly trained Japanese warriors.

sanctuary The most holy place in a temple.

sari Traditional dress for women in India.

scabbard The container for a sword-blade. It is usually fixed to a belt.

scribe A professional writer, a clerk or civil servant.

seismoscope An instrument that reacts to earthquakes and tremors.

Senate The law-making assembly of the Roman Empire.

serfs People who are not free to move from the land they farm without the permission of their landlord.

shaduf A bucket on a weighted pole, used by the Egyptians to move water from the river Nile into the fields on the banks.

shamans Medicine men or women in tribal cultures. These people were healers, doctors, spiritual and ceremonial leaders.

shamisen A traditional Japanese three-stringed musical instrument.

shield boss The metal plate that is fixed to the centre of a shield in order to protect the hand of the person holding the shield.

Shinto An ancient Japanese religion, known as 'the way of the gods', based on honouring holy spirits.

shogun A Japanese army commander. From 1185–1868, shoguns ruled Japan.

shrine A container of holy relics or a place for worship.

sickle A tool with a curved blade used to harvest crops.

Silk Road The overland trading route that stretched from northern China through Asia to Europe.

silt Fine grains of soil found at the bottom of rivers and lakes.

slaves People who were owned by their masters as opposed to being free.

smelt To extract a metal from its ore by heating it in a furnace.

society All the classes of people living in a particular community or country.

soldered Something that is joined together with pieces of melted metal.

spear-thrower A tool that acted as an extension of the arm, to give an extra leverage for throwing spears.

sphinx A creature with a human's head and a lion's body.

spindle A whirling tool used to make fibre, such as wool, into yarn for weaving.

standard A banner used by armies to rally troops in battle or carry in parades.

stela A tall stone pillar on which important records in words or pictures were inscribed.

stern The rear end of a ship.

stylus A pointed tool, such as the one used to scratch words on to a wax tablet.

sultan A Muslim ruler.

surcoat A long, loose tunic worn over armour.

survey To measure land or buildings. Land is surveyed before the construction of a building or road or any other sructure.

symbol A mark in a painting or on a stone that has a special meaning.

T

tabla A drum played in north Indian classical music.

tablet A flat piece of clay of varying shape and size used for writing.

taboo A rule or custom linked with a religious belief that shows respect to the spirit.

tachi The long sword that was carried by a samurai.

tanbo Flooded fields where rice was grown in Asia.

tapestry A cloth with a picture or design woven by hand on its threads.

tax Goods, money or services paid to the government.

temple A special building where a god or goddess is worshipped.

terracotta Baked, unglazed, orange-red clay.

textile Any cloth that has been woven, such as silk or cotton.

Thing An assembly of free men that passed laws in Viking lands.

Thor The Viking god of thunder.

timpanon A tambourine made with animal skin.

threshing To beat or thrash out grain from corn.

tipi Conical tent with a frame of poles, covered with animal skins, used by Plains Indians.

Torii The traditional gateway to a Shinto shrine.

totem pole A tall post carved with good luck charms.

trading post General store where people from a wide area traded or swapped goods.

travois A platform for baggage formed by poles roped together. It was dragged by a person or tied to the back of a dog or horse.

treadwheel A wooden wheel turned by the feet of people, that was used to power mills or some other form of machinery.

treaty Peace agreement.

tribe A group of families who owe loyalty to a chief and who share a common language and way of life.

tribute Goods given by a country to its conquerors, as a mark of submission.

turban Headdress worn by Muslim, Sikh and some Hindu men.

tyranny Government by a cruel ruler.

U

uictli A Mesoamerican digging stick used like a spade.

umiak An Arctic rowing boat made from whalebone, covered with walrus hide and waterproofed with seal oil.

Underworld This was the place to which the spirits of the dead were supposed to travel in ancient Greece.

V

Vaishnavism Hindu belief in Vishnu as lord of the Universe.

vallus The Roman name for a Celtic farm machine, used for reaping (cutting) grain crops.

Veda Ancient Aryan texts.

Venus figurine A statue of a woman, usually shown with large hips, breasts and buttocks and a full stomach.

vicuña A llama-like animal whose wool was used to make cloth.

Viking One of the Scandinavian peoples in northern Europe who lived by sea-raiding in the Middle Ages.

Vishnu A chief Hindu god.

vizier The treasurer or the highest ranking official in the Egyptian court.

W

walrus A sea mammal with long tusks.

wampum Shells strung together and used by Native Americans as currency or to record a historical event.

warlord A man with a private army who controls a large region or territory by force.

warrior A man, or less commonly woman, who fights in wars.

wigwam A Native American house that is made of bark, rushes or skins that are spread over arched poles lashed together.

winnowing The process of separating grains of wheat and rice from their papery outer layer, called chaff.

woad A blue dye extracted from a plant that ancient Britons used to decorate their bodies to make them look fierce in battle.

X

xiang qi A traditional Chinese board game, similar to chess.

Y

yoke A long piece of wood or bamboo, used to help carry heavy loads. The yoke was placed across the shoulders and a load was hung from each end to balance it.

Z

zakat Alms that must be given to the poor in Islam.

ziggurat A large temple with a broad, square base and stepped sides.

Index

A

abacus 356, 357
Abraham 86
accessories 440, 448–9
acupuncture 356
administration 138, 140
afterlife 90–1, 112
alabaster 460
alcohol 313
alphabet 405
amber 308
amphitheatres 52
amphorae (pottery jars)
    206, 207, 301
Amun-Ra 89, 92

ancestor worship 80, 83, 106
ancestors 403
animals 22, 30, 36, 72,
    89, 198, 199, 202,
    208, 218, 264, 270–1,
    278, 286, 296, 297
anklets 486–7
antlers 328–9, 364
Aphrodite 109
aqueducts 53, 318, 336,
    346
archaeologists 22, 28, 34, 40,
    41, 47, 53, 58, 62, 64, 70
archery 470
arches, 347, 355
architecture 39, 46, 346
Arctic 273, 312–1,
    424–9, 454–5

art 266–7, 300–1, 450–1
aristocrats 168, 175
armies 222–30, 249
armour 221–5, 232, 236–7
Artemis 108
arts 38, 39, 43, 54
Ashur 85
assemblies 180, 181
astrology 338, 342, 374
astronomy 323–5, 334–6,
    339–40, 356, 366, 374
athletics 476–7
Aztecs 130–3, 314–17,
    482, 496–7

B

Babylonians 189, 488
ball games 130, 482
banking 274
banquets 390–1, 395, 400
bards 474, 480–1
barges 204, 206
barley 268, 269, 278,
    279, 304, 305
            bartering 266,
        272–3, 282,
        292, 316
        basket-making
    330, 368, 376
    battle art 468–9
    battles 220, 221, 236,
    246, 247, 254, 255
Bayeux tapestry 468
beads 454, 455
beer 390, 391
Bible 86, 87
blacksmiths 362, 364–5
boatbuilding 324, 325
boats 198, 202–7, 210,
    213, 217
body paint 441, 444
bodyguards 148, 173, 184
bone 16–17, 53, 58
bows and arrows 220–3,
    225–6, 228, 236
boxes 464, 465
boxing 476–7
bread 390, 391, 395
bricks 384–5, 387–9,
    421, 430, 434
bridges 203, 208, 212

bronze 229, 236–7,
    323, 336, 345,
    348, 350–1,
    358–9, 362–3,
    371, 401
Buddhism 34–5,
    38–9, 42–3, 286,
    294–5
Buddhists 394
building 265, 266, 318–19
    materials 380, 384–5,
    387–9, 396, 406, 420,
    424, 430, 434, 435
burials 78, 82, 90, 112, 117
business 266, 274–5
butchers 401

C

calendars 42, 66, 323,
    334, 338, 366–7, 374
calligraphy 492, 493
camels 208, 209
canals 210, 324, 336,
    354, 355
cannibals 245
canoes 198, 216, 217
canopic jars 90, 91
captives 234, 235
caravans 274, 293
carbon-dating 332
cargo-boats 206, 213, 214
carpenters 281
carpets 295
carving 468
casting 323, 337, 351, 362–3
castles 165
cats 89
cattle 264, 270–1, 287,
    297, 304
cavalry 199, 222, 228,
    230, 234
Celts 116–17, 304–7,
    412–15, 480–1
ceramics 332–3
ceremonies 100, 119,
    127, 143, 159,
    191, 194
chariots 198–200,
    208–9, 220–2,
    229, 234–5,
    476–7

chieftains 138–40, 143,
    176–7, 178
childbirth 433
children 142, 170, 178,
    191, 349, 381, 386,
    398–9, 402–4, 408,
    412, 416, 422–3, 428–1
China 102–5, 265,
    284–91, 396–7, 462–3,
    470–1, 488, 492–3
Christianity 33, 57–8, 61–2,
    73, 102, 122–3, 135
cities 22, 23, 24, 27, 29,
    34, 36, 38, 40, 47, 52,
    64, 66, 138, 140, 144,
    145, 160, 166
citizens 170, 172
citizenship 54, 56, 75
city-states 22, 24, 46, 48,
    49, 66, 168, 170, 182,
    184
civil service 42, 304, 305
civil war 43, 54–5, 62, 68
clans 139, 142–3, 160, 164,
    176, 188, 432, 434
clay 323, 326, 330–1,
    332–3, 337, 368
    tablets 23, 26–7, 488–9
clocks 325, 339, 342, 353
cloth 288, 294–5, 322,
    330, 336–7, 364–5
clothes 402, 413, 418,
    419, 436
Cnut, King 419
cocoa 315
codex 65, 68, 496–7
coins 54, 57, 61, 62,
    136, 265, 266, 290,
    292–3, 298, 300,
    302, 306, 308

Acknowledgements

b=bottom, t=top, c=centre, l=left, r=right

TRIBES, EMPIRES & CIVILIZATIONS

AKG: 22tl,26tl, 27cr, 39tr, 75r; Lesley and Roy Adkins: 53cr; Ancient Art and Architecture Collection: 28b, 33tc, 35cl, 46tr, 50cr, 51bl, 56b, 56l, 57tl, 57tc, 58cl, 63tr, 63cr; E.T Archive: 39c, 44l, 45tl, 45tr, 45bl, 69br; Bildarchiv Preussischer Kulturbesitz: 27tr; Bridgeman Art Library: 34tr, 35tl, 47cr, 69tl; British Museum: 62tr; Macquitty Collection: 41c; Corbis: 34cl, 70, 71br; James Davis: 41tr, 68br; C.M Dixon: 32tr, 32b, 33b, 46c, 50c, 51tr, 51cl, 71tl, 71tc, 71tr; Mary Evans Picture Library: 50tl, 51tl, 57bl, 57br; Robert Harding: 23t; Michael Holford: 23cr, 26tr, 27tl, 40tl, 53tr, 65c; Griffin Institute, Ashmolean Museum: 28t; Link Photo Library: 35c; South American Picture Library: 64br, 65tl, 68tl, 69tl; Pierpont Morgan Library/Art source, New York: 19r; Peter Newark: 74tl, 74tr, 75tl, 75tc; University of Oslo: 62cr; Ann and Bury Peerless: 39tl; Tony Stone: 52–3; Visual Arts Library: 44r, 45br; Zefa: 32tl, 33tl, 33tr, 40c, 56r

GODS, BELIEFS & CEREMONIES

AKG: 84tl, 87tr & 94cl, 116tl, 119bl; B & C Alexander: 128br, 129tl & 129tr; The Ancient Art & Architecture Collection Ltd: 79cr, 81tl, 83tr, 86t, 88t & 88b, 89bc & 89tr, 92t, 93tl, 108cr, 112tl, 114bl, 116c, 117c, 118br; Andes Press Agency: 135bl; Bildarchiv Preussischer Kulturbesitz: 85bl & 85t, 86b; The Bridgeman Art Library: 95tl, 95tr & 95c, 96tr, 100cr, 101tl & 101c, 108cl, 108tr & 108c, 113r, 120br, 121l, 123bl; The British Museum: 109cl; Peter Clayton: 82bl, 83tl, 83bl & 83br; Copyright British Museum: 90l & 90r; Corbis: 126tl & 126b, 127tl, 127c, 127bl & 127br, 129c; James Davis: 131br, 132tl; C M Dixon: 78tr, 82br & 82t, 102tl, 110tl, 114tl & 114br, 115tl, 117tr & 117tl, 120tr, 122l & 122br, 123tr, 124tl, 125tr, 125c & 125bl; E T Archive: 87bl, 102bl, 105t, 106tl & 106c, 107bl & 107tr, 120tr, 130tl, 132bl, 133bl; Mary Evans Picture Library: 92l, 99bl, 103br, 113bl; Werner Forman Archives: 103tr, 107tl, 118tl, 123cl; Robert Harding: 98b, 99tr; Michael Holford: 79tl, 84bl, 91bl, 109tr, 110cr, 113tl, 115tr & 115bl, 122tr; The Hutchinson Library: 97tr, 99tl, 101tr, 104c, 105c; Images of India: 96b; Link Picture Library: 97br; Manchester Museum: 91tl; Peter Newark: 124br; Michael Nicholson: 111tl, 111cl & 111bl; Roman Baths Museum: 117bl; Scott Polar Research Institute Ltd: 129l; Mick Sharp: 119tl, 123br, 133tl; South American Photo Library: 130br, 134tl & 134br, 135tl & 135br; Statens Historic Museum, Stockholm: 120tr; Tony Stone Images: 97tl; TRIP: 104tr; V & A Picture Library: 97bl, 98t, 131tl & 131tr; ZEFA: 89tl, 91tl, 93tr & 93cr, 103tl & 103b

POLITICS, SOCIETY & LEADERSHIP

AKG:144tl, 147tr, 148tr, 149c, 164tl, 187tl, 188tl, 193br; Lesley and Roy Adkins: 175t; The Ancient Art and Architecture Collection Ltd:150r, 150–1, 152br, 169tl, 173tl, 178t, 186cl, 187cl, 191tr; Japan Archive: 161tr, 161cr, 163tr, 164br, 165tl, 165tr, 166bl, 167tr; The Bodleian Library: 185cl; The Bridgeman Art Library: 142bl, 143tr, 143br, 154cl, 155tr, 157c, 163tl, 170bl, 175b; The British Museum: 151tl, 181b; Bildarchiv Preussischer Kulturbesitz: 145bl, 146tl, 149tl; Bulloz: 145br; C M Dixon: 142tl, 152c, 160tl, 170br, 171tr, 171cl, 171br, 172l, 174bl, 176tl, 181t, 181cl, 182tl, 183bl, 183tr, 193bl; Musee Calvet, Avignon: 176br; Christies: 163bl; Peter Clayton: 153c, 153b, 169bl; Corbis-Bettman: 192tr; Corbis: 154tl, 157tl, 161tl, 194tl, 194br, 195tr, 195cl, 195cr, 195b; Sylvia Corday: 143tl; E.T Archive (Art Archive): 136–7, 155tl, 156tl, 159t, 159bl, 162br, 162bl, 182bl, 185tl; Mary Evans Picture Library: 156c, 159br, 168tl, 172r; Werner Forman Archive: 149bl, 158bl, 160bl, 163cr, 177bl, 186tr, 189br, 190cl, 190tr; Robert Harding: 143bl, 146cr, 147cl; David Hawkins: 145t; Michael Holford: 152bl, 161br, 174tr, 174br, 178cl, 183br, 184br; The Hutchison Library: 162tl, 167bl, 167tr; Michael Nicholson: 168c, 169tr; National Museum of Wales: 177br; Peter Newark's Pictures: 192l, 193tl, 193tr; Andes Press Agency: 191tl; Mick Sharp: 178b, 179t, 181cl; South American Photo Library: 184tl, 185tr, 187tr, 189tl, 189tr, 191cl; Still Pictures:188b; Tony Stone: 157tr; TRIP: 158br; University of Oslo: 180t; Visual Arts Library: 182br; Victoria and Albert Museum: 155c; York University Trust: 179l; Zefa: 150l, 151b, 158tr, 180b

TRAVEL, CONQUEST & WARFARE

AKG: 210br, 221c, 236tl, 238tr, 243t, 250b, 252bl, 253tl, 245b, 254tl, 255tr; Lesley and Roy Adkins: 231tl; B and C Alexander: 203tl, 217tl, 217cr; The Ancient Art and Architecture Collection Ltd: 204l, 205r, 208tl, 210br, 225b, 227tl, 228tr, 230tr, 232tl, 235tr, 239tl; Japan Archive: 225tr, 226tl; Bildarchiv Preussischer Kulturbesitz: 220tl, 220cl; The Bridgeman Art Library: 211tr, 211bl, 211br, 223br, 240b, 241tr, 241cl, 249bl; The British Museum: 233b; Bruce Coleman: 219bl; Bulloz: 220cr; Christies: 224bl, 224br, 225tl, 227bl; Corbis: 212bl, 217bl, 243b, 252tl; Corbis-Bettman: 242b, 242tl, 243bl, 252br, 254bl, 255bl; Sue Cunningham Photographic: 248tr, 250cr; James Davis: 215c; C.M Dixon: 202tl, 209cl, 228cl, 229cr, 231tr, 231b, 232l, 233tr, 237tl, 237tr, 238br, 240tr, 245c, 255tl; E.T Archive (Art Archive): 206bl, 209cl, 211tr, 222tl, 222cr, 223t, 219r, 222tl, 222br, 223tr, 239tr, 239bl, 246br, 248tl, 250tl; Planet Earth pictures: 216bl; Mary Evans Picture Library: 196–7, 215t, 217tr, 219tl, 229cl, 230br, 232r, 246tl, 251b; Fine Art Photographic Library: 234c; Werner Forman Archive: 203c, 207tr, 213cl, 237bl, 237c, 241tl, 249cl; Fortean Picture Library: 202r; Idemitsu Museum of Arts: 227cl; Images Colour Library: 213tr; Robert Harding: 213tr, 214tl, 215t; Michael Holford: 212tl, 213t, 221t, 224tl, 226br, 230bl, 239br, 247; Radio Times Hulton Picture Library: 204r, 205r; Jenny Laing: 235tl, 235bl; MacQuitty Collection: 206tl, 207cl, 207br; Peter Newark's Pictures: 253tr; Oxford Scientific Films: 216tl; Mick Sharp: 1234tl, 241br; Skyscan: 235br; South American Picture Library: 244t, 247, 248c, 249t, 250tl, 251tr; Visual Arts Library: 207tl, 208cl, 218c, 245t, 246bl; Zefa: 204r, 205l

WORK, TRADE & FARMING

Lesley & Roy Adkins Picture Library: 303b; AKG: 274t, 275tr, 304bl; B & C Alexander: 273tl, 312tr, 313tr; The Ancient Art & Architecture Collection Ltd: 278c, 279t, 280l & 280r, 281l, 285tl & 285br, 292bl, 296cr, 297br, 298bl, 299cl, 300c, 300tr; E T Archives: 286br, 287tr, 289tr, 291bl & 291tr, 293tl, 314tl & 314bl, 315br; The Bridgeman Art Library: 285tl, 287bl, 294tl, 295tl; The British Museum: 269t, 277bc, 278bl, 281bl; Peter Clayton: 277bl & 277br, 278br, 281bl, 282t, 296tl, 302tl; Bruce Coleman: 268br, 269ct, 287br, 319cl; Corbis: 292br, 293b, 310c; Sue Cunningham Photographic: 318cl, 319tl & 319tr; C M Dixon: 268tl, 272tl, 276c, 277t, 283tl, 283bl, 286tl, 287bl, 289tl, 292tl, 297tl, 305tr, 298tr & 298br, 299bl, 302tr & 302b, 303t & 303c, 306tl, 307bl, 310tl; Ecoscene: 272tl; Mary Evans Picture Library: 288br, 291tl, 298cl, 312b, 313tl; FLPA: 269br, 289cr & 289bl; Fortean Picture Library: 273tl; Werner Forman Archives: 291cl & 291tr, 304tl & 304bl, 306bl & 306br, 308tl, 316tl; Robert Harding: 274b; Michael Holford: 283bl, 288tl, 299tr; The Hutchinson Library: 294cr; MacQuitty Collection: 287tl, 289bl; Museum of London: 268bl; National Museum of Copenhagen: 308cl; Peter Newark: 310tr, 311br; NHPA: 272bl; John Oakes: 275bl; Bob Partridge & the Ancient Egypt Picture Library: 281tr; Ann & Bury Peerless: 293c; Planet Earth Pictures: 315cr; Ann Ronan: 313cl; Royal Asiatic Society: 295c; Science & Society: 388cr; Scotland in Focus: 305tl; Skyscan: 305br; South American Photo Library: 314r, 316tl, 318tr; V & A Picture Library: 295cl; Visual Arts Library: 283tl & 283c, 290cl; Wilderness Photo Library: 273bl; York Archaeological Trust: 308cl, 309bc

SCIENCE, CRAFTS & TECHNOLOGY

AKG: 360tl, 361bl, 361br, 363tr, 373bl, 377tl; The Ancient Art and Architecture Collection Ltd: 329tr, 331tl, 344cl, 347bl, 349t, 358tl, 364cr, 373, 375tr; Ancient Egypt Picture library: 339t, 339br; Japan Archive: 359tl; The Bridgeman Art Library: 332cl, 332cr, 333tr, 355bl, 357tl, 357tl, 372cl; Peter Clayton: 329cr, 343tr, 345tl, 345cl; Bruce Coleman: 329bl, 351tl; Corbis-Bettman: 376br; Corbis: 332tl, 333tl; C M Dixon: 327tr, 327c, 328t, 328bl, 328br, 330l, 338l, 338r, 342cl, 342tr, 346l, 346r, 348cl, 348tr, 349bl, 358bl, 360c, 361tl, 362tl, 376l, 377tr; Sue

HOME, FAMILY & EVERYDAY LIFE

AKG: 386b, 387tl, 394c, 395tl, 420bl; B & C Alexander: 424cl, 425cl & 425tr, 426cl, 427c, 428cl & 428cr, 429tr & 429cl; The Ancient Art & Architecture Collection Ltd: 388, 389bl, 390b, 391bc, 399br, 408tr, 408tr & 408bl, 411bl, 419tr; Andes Press Agency: 437bl; Lesley & Roy Adkins Picture Library: 411bl; GDR Barnett Images: 430tl; The Bodleian Library: 432bl, 433bl; A–Z Botanical Collection Ltd: 409r; Bildarchiv Preussischer Kulturbesitz: 386t, 387br; The Bridgeman Art Library: 419l; The British Museum: 389tr, 390t, 391tl, 408br, 410l; Bulloz: 386m; Jean-Loup Charmet: 437t & 437br; Peter Clayton: 404cl, 405tr, 406l; Corbis: 390tr, 392tr, 394tl, 395cl, 420br, 421cl, 422c, 427tl; Sue Cunningham Photographic: 435tl & 435br; C M Dixon: 384tl & 384b, 385bl & 385br, 389cl, 391tl, 403cl, 410r, 412tl & 412c, 413tr & 413c, 414cr, 415tl & 415cl, 417tr, 419tl, 422cl & 423tr, 423cl, 432tl; E T Archive: 378, 383tc, 398tr & 398bl, 399bl, 400tr, 401tr, 402tl, 403tr, 416bl, 419br, 430tr; Mary Evans Picture Library: 398br, 429tl, 433br; Werner Forman Archive: 400cr, 409t, 417tl, 433tr, 436t & 436br; Robert Harding: 387tr, 390b, 391bl, 392b, 393bl, 417bl, 419c; MacQuitty Collections: 401cl; Michael Holford: 404tl, 405tl, 409bl; National Museum of Scotland: 413cl; Peter Newark: 420tr, 421tl, 423tl & 423tr; NHPA: 403c; Planet Earth: 424tl, 426tl, 434b; South American Photo Library: 402bl, 430cl, 434t, 436bl; Statens Historic Museum: 418tr; Tony Stone: 427t; Visual Arts Library: 399tr, 402tl; Keith Welch: 413tl; York University Trust: 416tr, 417br, 418b; ZEFA: 397tr

ART, CULTURE & ENTERTAINMENT

Leslie and Roy Adkins Picture Library: 466l, 467br; AKG: 448cr, 449cr, 449tr & 449cl, 483c, 485tl, 487tl; B and C Alexander: 445tr, 454tl & 454c, 455tl, 455cl & 455tr; The Ancient Art and Architecture Collections Ltd: 443tl, 446r, 447r, 450tl & 450cl, 451c, 450t, 451cl & 451br, 472tr, 473tcr, 475cl, 490tl, 491t; Charles Tait/AAA Collection: 495bl; Corbis-Bettman: 479tl, 479cl & 479br; The Bridgeman Art Library Ltd: 445c, 448tl & 448cl, 450tr, Standing Courtesan by Kaigetsudo 452br, Collecting Insects by Harunobu 453tl, 463bl, 469l & 469r, Courtesan with Musical Instrument by Kuniyoshi 440tl & 484tl, Urban Life 485tr, 487c; Celebrated Beauties by Utamaro 452tl reproduced by kind permission of the Fitzwilliam Museum Cambridge through Bridgeman Art Library; The British Museum: 447l, 475tl; Bulloz: 488tl; Rennes Cedex: 480tl; Christies Images: 453tr; Bruce Coleman: 444tl; Corbis: 442tl; C M Dixon: 444c, 461tr, 466br, 473cl, 474tl, 475tl, 476t, 477tl, 477cl & 477bl, 478tr, 479tr & 479bl, 491b; E T Archive: 459c, 462br, 464tl, 465tr & 465bl, 482cl, 493cl, 497tl; Mary Evans Picture Library: 476b; Werner Forman Archive: 456cl, 457tr, 462bl, 468l & 468r, 485bc, 492c & 492tr, 494bl; Sonia Halliday Photographs: 466tr; Historic Scotland: 481tl; Michael Holford: 456tr, 472cl, 473tr, 477br; The Hutchinson Library: 470cl; The Idemitsu Museum of Art: 453cl; Japan Archive: 484br; Peter Newark's Pictures: 479bl; NHPA: 444cl; MacQuitty Collections: 463br, 471tl, 471tr & 471cl, 492tr; Muriel and Giovanni Dagli Orti: 458t, 488cr; Radiotimes Hulton Picture Library: 490b; Stuart Rae: 495tr; Sacamoto Photo Research Laboratory/Corbis: 453bl; Scotland in Focus: 495tl; Mick Sharp: 494tl; South American Photo Library: 483tl & 483c, 496c; V & A Picture Library: 495tl & 495cl; Visual Arts Library: 441tl, 462t, 463tl & 463tr, 464tl & 464c, 466tr, 493tl, 496tl & 496tr; ZEFA: 446l

Cunningham Photographic: 374l; E.T Archive (Art Archive): 320–1, 354bl, 356tr, 365tr, 369tl, 369cl, 371cl; Mary Evans Picture Library: 329tl, 343cl, 344tl, 344cr; Werner Forman Archive: 351bl, 351br, 362bl, 368cr, 370l, 375bl; Geoscience Features Picture library: 347tr; Michael Holford: 347tl, 348bl, 348br, 370cr; The Hutchison Library: 359tl; Images of India: 332cl; Jenny Laing: 363bl; Macquitty Collection: 374tr; Peter Newark's Pictures: 376br; Andes Press Agency: 372tr; Science Photo Library: 371cl; South American Photo Library: 366c, 368c, 373tl, 373tr, 374t; Statens Historik Museum: 365c; Still Pictures: 371tr, 372tr, 367tl. Zefa: 350tl, 351tr, 355tr, 355br

This edition is published by Armadillo, an imprint of Anness Publishing Ltd,
Hermes House, 88–89 Blackfriars Road, London SE1 8HA;
tel. 020 7401 2077; fax 020 7633 9499

www.annesspublishing.com

Anness Publishing has a new picture agency outlet for images for publishing,
promotions or advertising. Please visit our website www.practicalpictures.com for more information.

UK distributor: Book Trade Services; tel. 0116 2759086; fax 0116 2759090; uksales@booktradeservices.com; exportsales@booktradeservices.com
Australian distributor: Pan Macmillan Australia; tel. 1300 135 113; fax 1300 135 103; customer.service@macmillan.com.au
New Zealand distributor: David Bateman Ltd; tel. (09) 415 7664; fax (09) 415 8892

PUBLISHER: Joanna Lorenz
EDITORIAL DIRECTOR: Helen Sudell
EDITOR: Joy Wotton
AUTHORS: Daud Ali, Jen Green, Charlotte Hurdman, Fiona Macdonald,
Lorna Oakes, Philip Steele, Michael Stotter, Richard Tames
CONSULTANTS: Cherry Alexander, Nick Allen, Clara Bezanilla, Felicity Cobbing,
Dr Penny Dransart, Jenny Hall, Dr John Haywood, Dr Robin Holgate, Michael Johnson,
Lloyd Laing, Jessie Lim, Heidi Potter, Louise Schofield, Leslie Webster
DESIGNERS: Simon Borrough, Matthew Cook, Joyce Mason, Adelle Morris, Caroline Reeves,
Margaret Sadler, Alison Walker, Stuart Watkinson at Ideas Into Print, Sarah Williams, Alix Wood
SPECIAL PHOTOGRAPHY: John Freeman
STYLISTS: Konika Shakar, Thomasina Smith, Melanie Williams

ETHICAL TRADING POLICY

Because of our ongoing ecological investment programme, you, as our customer, can have the pleasure and reassurance of knowing that a tree is being
cultivated on your behalf to naturally replace the materials used to make the book you are holding. For further information
about this scheme, go to www.annesspublishing.com/trees

Previously published as two volumes: *Everyday Life in the Ancient World* and *Great Empires & Discoveries*
Page 1: The Parthenon, Athens. Page 2: The Great Pyramid of Cheops. Page 3: The lion hunt of the Assyrian kings.

PUBLISHER'S NOTE

KEY

Look out for the patterns used throughout this book, there is one for each culture

The Stone Age   Japan   North American

Mesopotamia   Ancient Greece   Indians

Ancient Egypt   Roman Empire   The Arctic

India   The Celts   Aztec & Maya

China   The Vikings   Inca Empire